58

EDINBURGH UNIVERSITY PUBLICATIONS

HISTORY, PHILOSOPHY AND ECONOMICS No. 4

The illuminated initial M of the charter granted to Kelso Abbey by Malcolm IV in 1159 containing miniature portraits of the young Malcolm IV and his grandfather David I. Reproduced by permission of His Grace the Duke of Roxburghe and the Trustees of the National Library of Scotland

THE NORMANS
IN SCOTLAND

BY

R. L. GRÆME RITCHIE

EDINBURGH
AT THE UNIVERSITY PRESS
1954

THE EDINBURGH UNIVERSITY PRESS

Agents

THOMAS NELSON AND SONS LTD
Parkside Works Edinburgh 9
36 Park Street London W1
312 Flinders Street Melbourne C1
218 Grand Parade Centre Cape Town

THOMAS NELSON AND SONS (CANADA) LTD
91-93 Wellington Street West Toronto 1

THOMAS NELSON AND SONS
19 East 47th Street New York 17

SOCIÉTÉ FRANÇAISE D'ÉDITIONS NELSON
25 rue Henri Barbusse Paris Ve

PRINTED IN GREAT BRITAIN
BY R. & R. CLARK, LTD, EDINBURGH

PREFACE

THE Normans in England have called forth general works, specialist studies, monographs, without number; comparatively, the Normans in Scotland have been neglected. As Normans are recorded in Scotland from 1052, the appearance in 1954 of the first full and connected account of their arrival and settlement can hardly be regarded as premature. Yet the neglect cannot have been due to any feeling that the subject is lacking in interest or importance.

It is interesting to see strangers settling permanently in a strange land, to watch the impact of French civilization upon Scotland, to observe the historic Norman qualities coming into operation north of Tweed: qualities like military ardour—as when a troop of Norman cavalry died to the last man, fighting for Macbeth at Dunsinane; skill in horsecraft, horsemanship and cavalry warfare—which fascinated Malcolm Canmore and the more soldierly of his reigning sons; zeal for religious and social reform, strict regard for legality, a genius for organization, a feeling for ceremony and symbol—which appealed to Malcolm Canmore's saintly spouse Queen Margaret no less strongly than to David, the youngest and most gifted of their sons; a sturdy belief in the superiority of French civilization— so completely shared by David that he filled all Scotland with Normans and with their help fashioned his ancient Kingdom into the likeness of a Norman state.

There is further interest, at times sardonic, in the reflection that the Normans had the defects of their qualities and that these were probably more apparent to the Scottish people than to the Scottish Kings or their nobles. Hence the haunting problem: Why is there no

Preface

clear evidence of any fierce or sustained native resistance to alien domination ? What degree of compulsion was there ? Can it be that the incomers, welcomed by the Kings and having round their brows the aureole of a Conquest that had been spiritual as well as military, laid as firm a hold on the imagination of the Scots as on the more valuable of their lands ?

As to the importance of the subject, few chapters of Scottish history can have more. On Scotland, as on England, the Norman stamp is indelible, but it is deeper, fresher, less worn by time. The Norman-feudal system and the imported institutions, such as the Castle, the Sheriffdom and the Burgh, have entered more fully into the national consciousness. The great Norman families flourished as never in England and to-day their names are borne by many Scotsmen, perhaps most. The lines on which Scotland has developed as a civilized country were laid down once and for all before the death of King David in 1153, and these lines were Norman.

For many such reasons, and also because of the arresting personalities, the picturesque incidents and the stirring scenes, the story of the Normans in Scotland is often stranger than fiction and often more readable.

The way in which I have dealt with the subject has been largely determined by the nature of the extant materials. A description of these is given in the Introduction, together with some discussion of the original sources. The numerous works which I have consulted, most assiduously and gratefully, are described in the footnotes or in the list at the end of the volume. The bibliography thus constituted is as complete as I could make it, till 1949. I have indeed consulted some works with more profit than others, some very sparingly, some very fully, but from all I have freely taken what seemed sound and relevant, while abstaining from criticism of their writers and eschewing controversy.

Preface

I am grateful for help and counsel to numerous friends and well-wishers, chiefly in the Universities of Edinburgh and Birmingham and the University College of Exeter. I am most deeply indebted to Professor W. Croft Dickinson, without whose initial help and criticism this book might not have been published, and to Miss E. A. Francis and Miss J. J. Milne, without whom it might not even have been written. In the various stages of writing and re-writing, re-casting, shortening and writing all over again Miss Francis has kept me well posted in the very latest research, particularly on Old French (language and literature) and on Norman family history, while Miss Milne has provided much French and Scottish lore and greatly furthered my efforts towards clarity of treatment and expression.

R. L. G. R.

CONTENTS

ix

Contents

MAPS

between pages 84 and 85

INTRODUCTION

Dynasty and Conquest

THERE was a " Norman Conquest " of Scotland. It was not a Conquest in the military sense. It was not exclusively Norman. Nor did it begin in 1066. In a sense it began before. It flowed imperceptibly from the Norman Conquest of England which began in 1002.

The entire process, the Normanization of Britain, was primarily dynastic. That is certainly not its main interest. Of much greater moment are the incoming ideas and institutions which spread northwards in a tide eventually submerging the whole Island and making profound and permanent changes in almost every department of life. The vast movement none the less proceeded along dynastic lines. Its landmarks are Royal marriages.

In the spring of 1002 an alliance between England and Normandy was sealed by a Royal marriage, Æthelred II (Unræd) taking as his second wife Emma, daughter of Richard I, late Duke of the Normans. When Æthelred died Cnut married Emma. For nearly forty years this strong-minded and, in her later days, formidable Norman lady lived at the centre of affairs, exercising some authority in a distracted land, " placing " fellow-countrymen, spreading French influence—and unwittingly preparing the way for the coming of William, grandson of her brother Duke Richard II. During all those troubled years Emma and her Norman entourage formed the one element of continuity in English Court life. In the Church and in the Anglo-Danish and Anglo-Saxon aristocracy Normans acquired a certain prestige. In Southern England there was

Introduction

infiltration and settlement—probably extensive, as we have endeavoured to show elsewhere.[1] Yet, decisive though Emma's dynastic importance proved to be, it cannot have been foreseen, for both her first and her second husbands had already sons who might succeed them on the throne and who in fact did.[2]

But in 1042, as the result of varied happenings, unpredictable inasmuch as they depended on births and deaths in a particular family, a son of Æthelred and Emma became King. The son, Edward—known, though not till long after his death, as Edward the Confessor—was a middle-aged bachelor with pronounced monastic tendencies who had lived in Normandy most of his life. In the twenty-three and a half years of his reign he lost no opportunity of giving practical expression to his abiding love and admiration for the Church in France, for the civilization and the language of the French, for the French way of life. Not only from Normandy but from other parts of the French-speaking world he gathered round him men of culture, and from them he chose his counsellors, his lieutenants and his friends. He made Frenchmen sheriffs, earls, bishops, one even Archbishop of Canterbury. Recent historians belittle the French influence on England before 1066. It was not of the sort to be assessed in terms of home or foreign policy. It was cultural and social, strongest in the Church, in Court circles, among the aristocracy, of birth or of intellect. After sixty years and more the cumulative effect was considerable. Many people were familiarized with French ideas and institutions. A French fashion was set.

Not long after the Coronation Earl Godwine had bestowed, perhaps thrust, his daughter Edith on the new King. The marriage was said to have remained formal;

---

[1] *The Normans in England before Edward the Confessor*, Publications of University College, Exeter, 1948.
[2] Edmund (Ironside) and Harthacnut.

xii

it was childless : hence the ever-present problem of the Succession and, subsequently, the widespread belief in the Sainthood of Edward. Edith's brother Harold made himself King and reigned nine months. Then Duke William established by the sword a claim based on kinship with Edward through Emma and for nearly seventy years, till 1135, England was governed by a Norman and two of his sons.

For nearly a century, from 1058 to 1153, Scotland was governed by one man and four of his sons. He was Malcolm III (Malcolm Canmore) ; they were : Duncan II (son of his first marriage, with Ingibiorg, daughter of Thorfinn the Mighty) ; Edgar, Alexander I and David I (sons of his second marriage, with Margaret, grand-niece of Edward). Under Edward's protection, in an England permeated by French influence, Malcolm and Margaret, and no doubt several of their counsellors and friends, spent all their formative years, and when the Normans invaded Scotland in 1072 they found a king and queen in some degree familiar with their language and their ways. In 1100, seven years after the death of Malcolm and Margaret, William's reigning son Henry married their daughter Edith. The Scottish, the Norman and the Old English Houses were then linked together, permanently. For dynastic purposes much stress was laid on the bride's relationship to Edward the Holy King. Her brothers, who already had spent several years among the Normans in England, came into close contact with the Norman Court. Edgar, who had reached the throne with the help of Rufus, could rely on continued Norman support. Alexander married a granddaughter of the Conqueror. David married a grand-niece. He was in right of his wife Earl of Northampton and Huntingdon. Normans in these shires migrating to Scotland formed under him a ruling class which, naturally, ruled in the Norman way.

History after all is the history of persons. Any account of the dealings of the Normans with Scotland must be in great part the history of Royal persons, Scottish and Norman, and their Norman friends, counsellors, servants, dependants, beneficiaries. Not that Royal persons were actuated solely by a desire for each other's welfare. But mediaeval man did not reason much about principles of government, and the most conscientious of monarchs had real difficulty in distinguishing between their duty towards the peoples committed to their charge and their duty towards their own children, their own sons-in-law or brothers-in-law. In like manner the distinction between personal servant and public servant or between counsellor and beneficiary was apt to be obscure. In the Normanization of Scotland the central fact is that the Conqueror's son married Malcolm Canmore's daughter. The important dates are of marriages : 1069, Margaret, grand-niece of half-Norman Edward, son of Norman Emma, to Malcolm III ; 1072, Judith, niece of Norman William, to Earl Waltheof ; 1100, Edith (Maud), elder daughter of Malcolm and Margaret, to Henry I, youngest son of William ; *c.* 1107, Sibylla, natural daughter of Henry, to Alexander, son of Malcolm and Margaret, from 1107 to 1124 King of Scots ; 1113, Maud, daughter of Waltheof and Judith, to David, from 1107 ruler in South Scotland, from 1124 to 1153 King of Scots.

There was no Scottish Hastings. There were Norman invasions, but there was little fighting and they ended in negotiations. Till 1093 there are no known " casualties ". In that year Malcolm Canmore perished in a Norman ambush, an event deplored by many Normans and by none more bitterly than their King. The war in Scotland which followed was a civil war, a dynastic struggle fought and won with Norman assistance. From the accession of Edgar in 1097, for nearly forty years peace reigned between Scots and Normans.

Scotland was Normanized by or under her own Kings : Malcolm Canmore and his sons, chiefly David.

Introduction

David's Normans came to Scotland as Edward's Normans had come to England—as advisers, clerical and lay, as administrators, as invited guests, as individuals judged on their merits by a native ruler of Norman outlook and training. David reigned even longer than Edward, was a much more forceful ruler and rewarded Normans on a much greater scale. It might almost be said that like an Old Testament king he gave them half his kingdom. But he gave it of his own free will and if his subjects ever made any protest no record of it has remained. Before, probably long before, his death in 1153 Scotland was Normanized beyond recall. Normans held the chief offices in church and state. Land and power had largely passed into Norman hands. The old feudal system had been changed to Norman-feudal. A French aristocracy had been established, a French civilization implanted.

By 1153 our tale is told. It is only to mak' siccar, only to note final consolidation and the settlement of the last incomers who can properly be called Normans, that we continue twelve years more, till the death of David's grandson and successor Malcolm IV (the Maiden) in 1165. It marks the end of an epoch. In the forty-nine years' reign of his brother William (the Lion) the history of the Normans in Scotland becomes indistinguishable from that of the Scottish people.

" The Normans in Scotland "

From the dim beginnings till the death of Malcolm the Maiden the dealings of the Normans with Scotland form a strange and complicated story. Our aim is to relate it as clearly as may be, to set forth the circumstances of their approach, their arrival, their reception and their settlement, to consider what manner of men they were, what sets of ideas, what institutions they brought with them, what contribution they made to Scottish life. The general facts are known, but much detail has to be filled in. Artistically the subject is like a battle-scene : it requires a large canvas and the interest is in the detail. Historically it must be entitled " The Normans in Scotland ", but its nature is such that neither " Normans " nor " in " nor " Scotland " can always be taken quite literally.

" In " cannot always mean " inside ". Events in Scotland were often determined by events outside. The apparent ease and rapidity with which Normans settled in the country, built castles, took root, established themselves and their families, made themselves at home, occupied the best land and became as it were part of the scenery, must always be a source of wonder. But perhaps an even greater wonder is how they came to be there at all. None of them, as far as is known, came straight from Normandy. They arrived from England and the extent to which they, and the institutions they brought with them, were already Anglicized needs some discussion. Once arrived, they did not all stay. Many returned whence they came, yet their sojourn, however brief, may have had its importance. On that autumn day in 1072 when Malcolm Canmore met the Conqueror face to face at Abernethy, William was in Perthshire between two visits to Rouen. Others made their mark without even a flying visit. David's lifelong friend Walter Espec had properties on the south bank of the Tweed. There is no evidence that he ever set foot on the north bank, yet few men took so decisive a part in the development of David's Normanizing policy. If our narrative too often strays from Scottish shores and the scene shifts too abruptly, it may be because the most marked characteristic of the chief *personae dramatis* is their extreme mobility. For a certain time, probably till the accession of Edgar in 1097, " Normans in Scotland " must be taken to mean mostly emissaries, visitors, invaders friendly and hostile, birds of passage or birds of prey. That period is dealt with in a preliminary chapter. After 1097 the phrase means mostly immigrants, settlers, residents. But they too are furth of Scotland for long periods—like Edgar and like David.

Conquest, military or matrimonial, cultural or social, in England or in Scotland, was not exclusively Norman. The " Normans " brought to England by Emma and by Edward—often ecclesiastics, but they were accompanied by lay relatives who settled in the country—included, besides natives of Normandy, men born in the rest of France, Lotharingia and Flanders. Duke William's enterprise was based chiefly on the resources of landowners in the neighbourhood of Rouen, but, judging his task to be beyond the powers of his small Duchy, he issued a general appeal for volunteers in a war to be waged in the name of justice, righteousness and religion against a forsworn usurper. The war also opened prospects of earthly reward. In all parts of France, in Brittany, in over-populated Flanders and beyond, there was a quick response from men actuated by varied motives : vindication of the outraged Norman Saints, religious enthusiasm, martial ardour, horror of perjury, love of adventure, need of pay, confidence in William's leadership, faith in his promises of land or office beyond the Channel. The host which fought in the field seven miles from Hastings under a banner consecrated by the Pope included Breton and Flemish contingents, and numerous Lotharingians, Picards, men of Artois, Maine, Anjou, Central France and Aquitaine. There was even a decorative sprinkling of Sicilians and Apulians from the Norman colonies. In the subsequent large-scale immigration the non-Norman element was very strong. How many of the incomers whose sons went on to Scotland were natives of Normandy no man can tell.

It is customary to class all " Conquerors ", civil and military, and their immediate descendants, under the generic term " Norman ", which must, however, be understood as only conventional. All Normans were French, but all Frenchmen in England were not Normans. Nor were they generally so called. The Royal scribes studiously avoid the word *Normanni* : the approved official term is *Francigenae* or *Franci*. The Bayeux Tapestry has " Hic Franci pugnant "—at Hastings. The *Anglo-Saxon Chronicle* speaks of " Frenchmen ". " French " is correct : it has always been an elastic term referring more to culture than to geography, and it can be safely stretched to cover many Lotharingians, Flemings and Bretons.

The eleventh century already distinguished perfectly well between " French " and " Germans ", and settled border-line cases on their merits. " French " was applicable, strictly to the exiguous domain of the Capets, loosely to all Gaul, to what we now call France, Flanders and the Rhineland. In an indeterminate borderland on the north and north-east of the present France men of rank or of education could be very " French ". " Lotharingia " had various senses, and in its widest sense included Flanders and many districts which were " Germanic " or " French " or bilingual to an extent seldom possible to determine as regards individuals because it varied with social conditions.[1] Thus there is a distinction to be drawn not only between *la Flandre flamingante*, which was Germanic, and *la Flandre gallicante*, which was Latin, but also in both these regions between the common folk and the aristocracy, which was French-speaking and to all intents and purposes French.[2] There were Lotharingians who were born far from Normandy, but not far from Reims, the religious centre of Northern France, to which the Archdiocese of Rouen was very closely attached, and the geographical centre, from which the roads spread fan-

[1] " Lotharingia " meant, strictly, the old province of Trèves (Metz, Toul and Verdun) ; less strictly, the district of Liège as well, and sometimes even Flanders. The *County* of Flanders included the vassal County of Boulogne, as well as Artois and Saint-Omer.
[2] Pirenne, p. 90.

wise, as they were afterwards to spread from Paris. There were Flemings who could see from their own doors the smiling fields of Normandy or the white cliffs across the Channel. The inhabitants of Boulogne were Flemings, for a short time in their history they had been Lotharingians. Numerous Bretons lived in full view of the Mont-Saint-Michel. While retaining its own language and customs, their country had long been in close contact, military and other, with Normandy and in many parts there were " French " settlements. Landowners on both sides of the Breton border had intermingled and there can have been little apparent difference between their representatives at Hastings and after.

In England most of the immigrants could be justly classed as Normans, were it only as land-holders or place-holders under the Norman King or as his nominees for ecclesiastical preferment. " The First Norman Archbishop of Canterbury ", Lanfranc, was an Italian, a Lombard. Anselm his successor was a Lombard, but not an Italian : he was a Burgundian of Aosta, in the Duchy held by the younger branch of the Capets. But Lanfranc, Prior of Bec, and Anselm, Abbot of Bec, had for long lived in Normandy, where many of the prelates were incomers, and at Canterbury both must have seemed as Norman as Archbishop Robert Champart in King Edward's time actually was. " The First Norman Bishop of Durham " was a Lotharingian, a secular clerk of Liège. He was none the less a Norman, in the sense of having laboured in the Duchy, of being an old friend of Duke William's and sharing his views on Church matters, as no doubt on most others. His name, which is found in two forms, the outlandish Walcher and the too familiar Walker,[1] was merely a Northern French form of Gaucher (left-handed), and his mother-tongue was certainly French. " The First

---

[1] " Gualcherus, Gualgerus "—*Liber Vitae*, pp. 44 and 140 ; " Walkerus " —*Chron. Melrose, s.a.* 1071.

Introduction

Norman Earl of the Northumbrians ", Robert Cumin, was perhaps a Fleming,[1] but he was a Norman official and presumably as French in language and outlook as the Bishop. It would be unjust to deny either of them the title of "Norman" which both paid for at Durham with their lives.

Local differences were ironed out by the conditions of occupation. The centrifugal methods of land-distribution in vogue from before the Conquest separated Normans, Bretons, Flemings and the other Continentals from men of their own native districts. Had the extensive lands held by the Breton Count Alain all been in the North Riding of Yorkshire, the Bretons settled round his castlery of Richmond would have come to form a separate community instead of being quickly absorbed into the French section of the population. " Conquerors " were or had become French before they moved to Scotland. Her first Bruce was a Norman of Normandy and so no doubt were most of the immigrants. But her first Balliol was a Picard, her first Stewart a Breton. The Riddells were Gascons. The earliest known " Norman " landlord in Fife was a Burgundian; the earliest known provost of a burgh was a Fleming with a French name. In Upper Clydesdale and in Moray Normanization was carried on with the help of Flemings, and it may be doubted if the local population made much distinction between them and Normans. Differences in Continental origin are of small consequence. What is important is that the " Conquerors " represented a clearly marked type—a French type—and that they implanted in England and afterwards in Scotland a civilization which was not specifically Norman but general French. Henceforward we shall call them all Normans, but specify their Continental home when it can be ascertained.

[1] Simeon of Durham calls him " Robertus cognomento Cumin ", which suggests a nickname of the ordinary Norman type, meaning the condiment cumin. Orderic alone calls him " de Cuminis ", *i.e.* Commines, Latin *Cuminae,* in Flanders. See Round, *The Ancestor,* X, July 1904.

Introduction

Norman Personal Names

In the matter of personal names no such simplification is possible. Nor is consistency in form and spelling; the names have been handed down in too many languages—Latin, French and English—with too great a multiplicity of variants, dialectal or scribal, and have been treated by different historians too differently. In English writing on the Conquest it has become impossible to avoid an unhappy mixture of Latin, French and English, sometimes even in the same sentence.

Everywhere except in pre-Conquest England official documents were written in Latin, and the Normans continued in the Kingdom the practice they had followed in the Duchy. The vast majority, from the Conqueror and Rufus downwards, could not read or write. The few who could, wrote and read Latin. Illustrious memorials of Norman practice are Domesday Book, compiled in Latin by an army of French clerks, and the Bayeux Tapestry, provided with captions in Latin for the further enlightenment of anyone who could read. The vast majority of Normans went down to the grave without being personally mentioned in a charter. Those who did appear in one appeared with their names Latinized, a Guillaume as " Gulielmus " or " Willelmus ", a Gautier or Walter (both forms occur in early French) as " Gualterus " or " Walterus ". Le Blond was " Blundus " or " Flavus ", according to the scribe's notions of style or the extent of his Latinity. The fact that a man happened to have been mentioned in an official document, or to have witnessed one, does not mean that the Latin form of his name pursued him into private life. The regular use of Latin as the written language is a pleasing illustration of the care which the French have always had for universalism, and it had obvious practical advantages in France and England so long as these countries had no standard language, but only a variety of local dialects.

From the reign of Henry I the French vernacular came to be used for literary and for historical purposes. In a *chanson de geste* or the works of a Gaimar or a Jourdain Fantosme Guillaume was plain Guillaume, while in a *Historia Regum Anglorum* or in a charter he was " Gulielmus " as before. Meantime the few writers of English were making what they could of the French names, and neither then nor for long after did any writers in any language much concern themselves with consistency in the form and spelling of personal names.

The historians have thus from the beginning been confronted with an infinite variety of perfectly authentic names and it is not surprising that they have failed to arrive at consistency or at fixed conventional forms. French historians can choose from three main types: for instance, Mathilda or Matildis (Latin), Mathilde (learned French), Mahaut (popular Northern French); in the same gradation Adelisa, Adelise, Aaliz or Alice; Drogo, Drogon, Dreux; Hugo, Hugon, Hugue; Odo, Odon, Eude. English historians can select from these three types and also from a certain number of English forms which have become conventional but are seldom correct. They can adopt the Latin or French forms used in the original document which they have before them, or can Anglicize them, as Macaulay did with " Lewis the Fourteenth ". In manipulating this highly miscellaneous material they must preserve the " atmosphere " of the Conquest, retain the local colour, safeguard historical truth and keep the well of English undefiled by Gallic admixture.

The task may have been feasible at one time, but not now. For instance, the historical truth is that in the family circle and in the ordinary circumstances of life, save only when witnessing a legal document or being mentioned in one, the wives of the Conqueror, Henry I, David and Stephen, and the ex-Empress Maud or Matilda, and the innumerable other Mauds or Matildas who graced the English or the Scottish scene till the year 1165, went by the name Mahaut. This is also the textual truth,[1] and it is the phonetic truth; " the good Queen Mold " owed her name to the fact that in English *Mahaut* (*Mahalde*, etc.) contracts into Maud (Mold, etc.), which *Matilda* could never have done. It is too late to give all Mahauts their real name; some have been indelibly inscribed Maud, others Matilda. Even so the unhappy mixture of French and English still remains, for if David's wife has to be distinguished from other Queen Mauds and Queen Matildas, what can she be called but Queen Maud (or Matilda) de Saint-Liz ? It is dangerous to meddle with the French preposition; too often *de* means " from " or is only part of a French surname.[2] This Maud or Matilda had no surname and her second husband David had none. Her first husband was Simon de Saint-Liz, a fanciful variant of Senlis. In the town and district of Senlis, so far as is known, he had no seigneurial rights and possessed no property. He only " came from " there, which perhaps is why " Saint-Liz " seemed a suitable form to his own contemporaries—and why *de* seems better left untranslated.

Convention in the matter of Norman names has varied. Until recently English historians regularly described a twelfth-century Archbishop of York as Roger of Bishopsbridge, which seems to suggest that Roger was of English birth and that Bishopsbridge is in Yorkshire, whereas it is Pont-l'Évêque. At the present moment the practice is for " William Rufus ", returning from Scotland in 1091, to be met at Durham by " Robert of Mowbray " and " Bishops William de St. Calais and Remigius ", which is strictly unhistorical. In " William Rufus " the odd combination

---

[1] In Gaimar, l. 5740, the Conqueror's " Good Queen Matilda " is " Mahald [= Mahaut] ki menat bone vie ". *A-S.C.* MS. E, *s.a.* 1100, has : " se Kyng genam Mahalde him to wif ". Henry II was known as fitz Mahaut, *e.g.* in Jourdain Fantosme.

[2] For example, the uncle of Mary Queen of Scots often called " the Cardinal of Lorraine " was a Cardinal, but not " of " anywhere : de Lorraine was his family name.

Introduction

of Anglicized Christian name and Latin cognomen is traditional; *Guillaume le Roux* might better convey the "atmosphere" of 1091, though the cognomen would still be inexact, because it means red-haired. Historically his face was red, not his hair, which was yellowish (*subflavus*). As the Old English chronicler correctly puts it, he was William the Red. To give the name Robert of Mowbray to Robert de Montbrai[1] (a village in Normandy) seems somehow to credit him with native English qualities to the possession of which he may not have aspired. Robert was "*de* Montbrai" in a sense in which Simon was not "*de* Senlis" and the Bishop was not "*de* St.-Calais". Before being Bishop of Durham William was Prior of Saint-Carilef, known nowadays as Saint-Calais. He liked to have his old monastic connection recalled and in charter style he is Willelmus de Sancto-Carilepho. Perhaps inverted commas are required: Guillaume "de Saint-Carilef". The Conqueror's Bishop of Lincoln was known there as Rémy, but in official documents he appeared in Latin, as did every Thomas, Ricardus and Henricus in the diocese who might have to be mentioned. That on ordinary occasions "Remigius" went by the name of Rémy appears from an incident related by Giraldus Cambrensis,[2] known in private life as Giraud de Barri (but he adopted a pen-name meaning "Gerald of Wales" and his pen wrote Latin). To call the Bishop "Remigius" at all times and in all circumstances is unhistorical in so far as it stresses his absorption in the Church Universal at the expense of his reputation as a recruiting agent at Fécamp for Duke William's expeditionary force, or in so far as it conveys an impression of prelates in eleventh-century England as vague "churchmen", conversing in mediaeval Latin and coming from anywhere except France. Similarly in real life the Archbishop of

[1] But cp. *Molbraium* in Orderic's Latin, *Molbrai* in the French form adopted in the Pipe Roll of 1130, and see below, p. 64, n. 3.
[2] See Freeman, *Rufus*, I, p. 312, n. 5.

xxiv

York now called Thurstan answered to the name of Toustain, as did his very numerous namesakes in Normandy.[1] Whatever reasons there may be for Anglicizing his name, there can be none for Anglicizing the name of his brother Oudin, who did not settle in England but stayed where he was, at Bayeux, as Bishop. In English writings on the Norman Conquest the scene may shift at any moment to Normandy, where there were stay-at-homes uninterested and un-Anglicized. In short, a mixture of French and English has become inevitable—and is not entirely to be regretted, because a mixture of French and English is precisely what the Conquest was.

As a general rule it seems best to call Normans in Scotland by the French names they received from their parents, as: *Eustache* for " Eustachius " or Eustace ; *Geoffroi* for " Galfridus " or " Gaufridus "; *Hugue* for " Hugo " or Hugh ; *Raoul* for " Radulphus " or Ralph ; *Renouf* for " Ranulphus " [originally Ranwulf] or Ranulf.[2] The present work deals with a comparatively short period. During that period the incomers were foreigners bearing foreign names, and their interest lies largely in the fact that they were Frenchmen. When people who, though in some ways different from their present-day counterparts, are very recognizably French settle in the English countryside and move from there to strath and glen, there is a certain piquancy in the situation and it is apt to be lost when their Frenchness disappears under Latin forms once employed by scribes or English forms since evolved incorrectly by popular tradition or artificially created by historians. Moreover the sole evidence of Norman origins is often the Norman name. No doubt within a generation or two after 1066 Norman names were

[1] Toustain (Tostein, etc.), Latinized to Turstinus, Anglicized to Thurstan, re-Latinized to Thurstanus. Cp. " Turstinus filius Rollonis vexillum Normannorum portavit " [at Hastings]—Ord. Vit. III, xiv.

[2] Radulphus and Ranulphus were often confused with Randulphus by scribes.

given to English children and Norman children even before 1066 were baptized Edward or Edith. Eventually the fashion of giving French names—in honour, for example, of a feudal superior or a well-known public figure—spread among native English families. But the eleventh-century examples quoted are few and seem dubious, and French names are a sure enough indication of French parentage till well into the twelfth century. It must, however, be borne in mind that some may be names in religion, and that scribes were quite capable of turning a native Scottish Gillebright into a French-looking "Gillebertus" or Gilbert.

In the case of constantly recurring names such as *Esteven* or *Étienne, Guillaume, Henri* consistent or persistent use of the French form would probably prove irritating, and therefore we have generally accepted the English forms which have become as it were stereotyped. In the interests of accuracy it may often be desirable that a name should be given both in the Latin form of the original document and in the French or English form in which it is commonly quoted in works of reference. We then add alternative forms in square brackets and give scribal or purely conventional forms in inverted commas.

The Normans suffered throughout their history from a dearth of Christian names. Of the stock names there were only a dozen or two to go round and often one sufficed for two or more brothers—to the discomfiture of the genealogist, though he is seldom lacking in stoutness of heart or strength of imagination. Nomenclature was by patronymic, with the use of " filius ". In charter style the father is, for instance, " Robertus filius Gulielmi " ; the son is " Herbertus filius Roberti ", and outward connection with the grandfather is lost. Even when the son is given the fuller style " Herbertus filius Roberti filii Gulielmi " this may be insufficient for purposes of identification, such was the number of individuals possessing these names. When the names are handed down in

French the form is *fils*, Old French *fiz* (pronounced *fitz* and often so written), and though it may save trouble to call the son Herbert fitz Robert this is not yet a fixed surname; his own son is fitz Herbert. If, however, the family founded by the original Guillaume or William became important its members, or the early genealogists, or the early historians, gave prominence to his name, and the family became generally known as fitz William. That is what happened to the fitz Alans. The founder was Walter, son of a Breton called Alain. Walter migrated to Scotland and was there known as Walter son of Alain; the French form *Alain* is engraved on the seal of his son, who describes himself thereon as Walter son of Walter son of Alain. But the ever-lengthening patronymic could not be continued indefinitely. The last element, the most ancient, *fitz Alain*, was felt to be essential and it was retained. In the matter of consistency there seems to be no reason for Anglicizing *Alain* to Alan in the case of the father, who did not migrate from Brittany to England till he had reached years of maturity. Nor is there any compelling reason in the case of the son. But as the son, the first Hereditary Steward of Scotland, is the founder of the family well known as fitz Alans till they became even better known as Stewarts or Stuarts, it is convenient to call him Walter fitz Alan.

" *Scotland* " *before Malcolm Canmore*

The Kingdom which Malcolm Canmore recovered by the sword consisted of Scotland, Lothian and Cumbria. Scotland was the land north of the Firths of Forth and Clyde. The original Scots were Goidels or Gaels who had long been crossing over from Ireland when, towards the year 500, they set up a kingdom, Dál Riata, corresponding roughly to the modern Argyllshire, with the adjacent islands. The Gaels were what have been known as

Introduction

" Celts " since the French archaeologist Pezron in 1703 conveniently classified them as such : " Celtic " denotes a certain community of language and customs rather than of race.[1] The Gaels had Fergus Mór, son of Erc, for their first King ; their citadel was Dunadd, at the head of Loch Crinan, and from there they spread inland through the glens, gradually establishing an ascendancy over the Picts, whom they found in possession and who have not yet been classified. The Picts eventually united with the invaders and adopted their language, Gaelic. Political union took place when the King of Dál Riata, Kenneth MacAlpin, inherited the throne of Pictland in 844. The native name of the thus united Kingdom was Alban.

But the Gaels (and also their kinsmen in Ireland) were given by early mediaeval writers the name *Scotti* or *Scoti*, for reasons unknown, and " Alban " came to be superseded by a purely literary form *Scotia*, " Scot-land ".[2] The religious centre of all *Scotti* was Iona. Those of Dál Riata had owed much of their success to their possession of the sacred island, and when the relics of St. Columba were translated from Iona to Kenneth MacAlpin's seat of government at Dunkeld, Picts and Scots became truly one people.

For the tourist Dunkeld is the gateway to the Highlands. For the Scottish dynasty it was the way out. Both Picts and Scots cherished an ancient tradition, apparently founded on fact,[3] that they had once held the country south of the

[1] See Professor John Fraser, *The Question of the Picts*, pp. 172-201 of *Scottish Gaelic Studies*, vol. ii.

[2] More exactly *Scotia minor*, as distinguished from *Scotia*, which, till *c*. 1000, normally meant Ireland. " Scotland " was so known to the Norsemen from *c*. 900. Brøgger, p. 57. The Welsh name for the country remained " yr Alban ". From *c*. 1000 the King of Alban or Alba was generally known as King of Scots or King of Scotland, though in 1174 he is still, for Jourdain Fantosme, " le roi d'Aubanie " as well as " le roi d'Escoce ". " Rex Scottorum " is the regular charter style, but " Rex Scotiae " is also used.

[3] In 547 a British monk, Gildas, writes of an appeal sent by the Britons to the Roman governor in Gaul for help against invaders, evidently Picts and Scots, the " Scots " coming from the North-West, *i.e.* from Ireland and Dalriada. The Irish version of Nennius explicitly states that after the Roman evacuation Picts occupied the middle of Britain as far as the Tyne.

Forth as far as the Tyne and had been dispossessed. This tradition formed the basis of the " foreign policy " consistently followed by Kenneth MacAlpin and his successors. " There are hills beyond Pentland [Pict-land] and lands beyond Forth " ; there are rich corn-lands, and the hope of the Highland kings was to derive some practical benefit from that fact. Their objective was Lothian, the wide district between Forth and Tweed wrested from the Britons or Brythonic Celts by Angles who spread north soon after their arrival on the coast of Northumbria. Conquerors and overlords rather than colonists, the Teutonic invaders did not to any great extent displace the native population, which, however, came to be largely English in language and culture. The efforts of the Scottish dynasty to expand southwards failed till 973, when Edgar the Peaceful ceded to Kenneth II all the lands between Forth and Tweed which were then collectively called Lothian. The term included not only the present counties of West Lothian, Midlothian and East Lothian but also those of Berwick and Roxburgh and part of Peebles. If any doubt still remained as to the possession of Lothian, it was removed for ever in 1016,[1] when Kenneth's son Malcolm II and his kinsman Owain, King of Cumbria, defeated Uchtred, Earl of the Northumbrians, at Carham on the Tweed.

The Kingdom known as Cumbria or Strathclyde was formed by a remnant of the Britons, isolated from their westward-driven kinsmen in Wales ; in its early days it had extended from Stainmore and the Cumberland Derwent to the Firth of Clyde. These " Cymry " (hence " Cumbria ") had their chief stronghold at Alcluid, also called Dumbarton, the Dun or Fortress of the Britons. Their history is extremely obscure.[2] Their Kingdom passed into English hands in the seventh century. In the

[1] Usually given as 1018 ; probably 1016. See Stenton, *A-S.E.* p. 412, n.
[2] The most authoritative account is Professor Stenton's, in *Westmorland* (1936).

tenth a native English aristocracy was still in power, but there was extensive Scandinavian settlement, mostly by Norwegians and Gaelo-Norwegians from Ireland and the Isles. Geographically (and perhaps at times politically) the Kingdom was nearly bisected by the Solway Firth. North of that Firth there was an enclave whose mixed inhabitants, known as Gall-gael (Foreign Scots), gave their name to Galloway (in the Norse tongue Gaddgeddlar), a district including, besides Wigtown and Kirkcudbright, parts of Ayrshire and Dumfries. In the tenth-century confusion, possession of the Kingdom was regained by the old Royal House, which had intermarried with members of the Scottish reigning family. Shortly after the victory at Carham, Owain died without issue and Malcolm Mac-Kenneth [Malcolm II] obtained the succession on behalf of his own heir, his daughter's son Duncan. From then (or perhaps before [1]) Cumbria was regarded as the appanage of the heir to the Scottish throne. It was so held by Duncan till his accession in 1034 as head of a new dynasty (in the female line).[2]

The three component parts of the Kingdom differed widely. In Scotland proper the people generally were Gaelic-speaking. Their civilization was Celtic, resembling that of Ireland, the culture-centre from which in the Dark Ages music, literature, piety and learning came. But there can be no question of inviolate Celtdom. Firths unite as well as sunder. Settlement and cultural contact can be made by sea. In Fife and further up the East Coast there had been English infiltration. Norwegians occupied Orkney and Shetland, Caithness and the " Southern Land " ; they

[1] Fordun asserts that in 945 an agreement was made between Malcolm I and Edmund, whereby the heir of the Scottish King was always to hold Cumbria of the English King. That Cumbria was regarded till at least 1152 as the appanage of the heir will be clear from our subsequent pages.

[2] Duncan I was the son of Malcolm MacKenneth's eldest daughter (Bethoc) and Crinan the Thane, hereditary (lay) Abbot of Dunkeld. On the death of Malcolm MacKenneth (Malcolm II) in 1034 the direct male line of Kenneth MacAlpin became extinct.

had settlements all round the West Coast, held the Hebrides and controlled the Irish sea. Thus surrounded, " Celtic Scotland " was permeated with English feudalism and Norse custom.

The Church, however, remained " Celtic ", keeping to the organization and usages which came from Ireland by way of Iona, the mother-house of the numerous monasteries founded. With these the Bishops were closely connected; they considered themselves subject to the jurisdiction of the Abbot of Iona, and afterwards of his successor, the Abbot of Dunkeld. The chief among them, eventually the Primate, was the Bishop of the Scots, *Episcopus Scottorum*; he had his see at Kilrymont, which became known as St. Andrews.[1] The Church was still monastic and missionary, with religious communities serving wide areas. There was probably no diocesan or parochial organization.

Political division was into provinces, traditionally seven,[2] each governed by a Mormaer—a sub-king, one who was a king within his own dominions, but owed tribute and allegiance to the King of Alban, to an Ard Righ, a High King, somewhat as in Ireland. Of these theoretically subject-states the most formidable was Moray. Moray had different limits at different times : it might include the present counties of Moray, Elgin, Nairn, Cromarty and parts of Ross, Inverness and Banff. It possessed practical independence, no doubt because of the need for consolidation against Norse attack, and the Mormaer maintained a claim to be King of Alban.

[1] The relics of St. Andrew brought by Acca to Hexham were, when he was exiled in 732, taken by him to Kilrymont.

[2] According to Skene, III, ii, the seven provinces, " Mormaerships ", afterwards Earldoms, consisted each of two districts and were : Angus, with the Mearns ; Atholl, with Gowrie ; Strathearn, with Menteith ; Fife, with Fothrif ; Mar, with Buchan ; Moray (Muref), with Ross ; Caithness, with Sutherland. When the last named passed into Norwegian hands Ergadia (the old Dál Riata and the entire North-West of Scotland) may have been counted as Argyll, among the Seven. It should be said that doubts are entertained on Skene's Seven.

The people in Scotland proper were mostly pastoralists, consequently somewhat nomadic in their habits. Cattle remained the essential element of personal property. The owners moved themselves, and sometimes their dwellings, as the cattle used up the grass or in summer were taken into the hills. Houses were scattered up and down the land. The Celts in Britain, unlike the Saxons, had always preferred hamlets and lonely homesteads to village life. In the Western Highlands and perhaps elsewhere there was the Celtic grouping by " twenty houses ", but nowhere was there anything quite corresponding to the English nucleated villages—groups of houses built close together, clustering round what was in Norman times to become known as a manor-house.

The two lately-added provinces—all the South-West and South-East of present-day Scotland—had for long periods been part of Northumbria and had been at all times subject to strong influence from the neighbouring Celtic Kingdom, and it is doubtful if in the eleventh century any very strict line of demarcation could be drawn between them. Together they made up a vague general unit, what we shall henceforth call " South Scotland ", rooted deep in England, stopping, though not abruptly, at the line of the two Firths, differing on the extremities, the East and West coasts, fusing together in the middle, more " Anglic " and more agricultural in the low-lying East, more " Welsh " and more pastoral in the hilly West. Cumbria had become in the main English-speaking, but the native language continued in use. It was " Welsh ", that is, the form of Celtic spoken in Wales, Cornwall and Brittany, known as Brythonic, or P-Celtic, in contradistinction to Q-Celtic, which was spoken in Scotland proper, Ireland and the Isle of Man. The land was probably broken up into small holdings, which may be one reason why there is no mention of great leading families rivalling the Prince—why there is so little Cumbrian " history ".

In default of evidence it may perhaps be assumed Cumbrians lived as, according to a twelfth-century observer in Wales, their Welsh kinsmen lived, " on beef, oats, milk, cheese and butter—not bowed down by heavy agricultural labours, but head erect, ready to spring to arms in defence of their homeland, as men in the enjoyment of freedom ".[1]

Strathclyde had been evangelized by a Briton regularly trained at Rome, St. Ninian, who built, *c.* 400, the famous church, *Candida Casa* (Whithorn), on the shores of Wigtown Bay. In the sixth century Christianity was restored by St. Kentigern, affectionately known as St. Mungo, and from 727 there had been a Bishopric of Whithorn, dependent on York, but after 796 it had sunk into obscurity or lapsed. In Clydesdale and Galloway the Church probably had " Celtic " characteristics.

Lothian was the richest, the most fertile part of the Scottish Kingdom. The more important of the inhabitants were dour Northumbrians, farmer folk mostly .The social order was probably as in Northumbria, but with " Celtic " vestiges, and this may also be true of the Church. Ecclesiastically Teviotdale and various localities remained subject to Durham ; the rest of Lothian had come under the Bishop at St. Andrews, whose authority extended along the East Coast towards the north and southwards over Lothian. But if there was any diocesan or parochial organization in Lothian, it was rudimentary.

The Scottish Kingdom thus finally constituted lies in the Highland Zone of Britain—which, from the Highlands, the Southern Uplands and the Cheviots, continues into the Pennine Chain, the Welsh hills and the moors of Devon and Cornwall. The Lowland Zone, the rest of Britain, could be easily overrun by invaders landing on the South Coast or on the much-indented East Coast, where broad slow-flowing rivers open the way far into the interior.

[1] Giraldus Cambrensis, I, 8.

Introduction

The invasions of Britain by Celt and Roman and Saxon and Norman reflect the fact that the easily invaded area lies in the east.[1] Had the uplands been placed in the east conquest would have taken much longer to complete. The waves of invasion generally broke at the approaches to the Highland Zone ; it was unattractive to settlers and hard to penetrate. Both zones belie their description in parts and the Scottish Kingdom included a certain amount of lowland, which the cession of Lothian had greatly increased—a coastal belt of fertile land, from three to thirty miles in breadth, which is fairly continuous from Caithness to the mouth of the Tweed (and thence to Durham).[2] These Lowlands are the parts of the Scottish Kingdom which provided the line of least resistance for waves of Norman settlement coming in from the South.

The Contemporary Sources of Information [3]

The information available from contemporary writers is incidental, indirect, curiously *external*. No one was minded to write a connected account of the dealings of the Normans with Scotland. The known writers best qualified to have done so were : Turgot, Ailred, Eadmer and Henry of Huntingdon.

The most important person in the diocese next to the Bishop, Turgot lived thirty years at Durham with Normans. He also spent some time at Melrose, perambulated Teviotdale as Archdeacon and frequently visited the Court of Malcolm Canmore. From 1107 till his death in 1115 Turgot was Bishop at St. Andrews. He left some historical writings, from which Fordun quoted a few extracts, but which have since been lost, and a *Vita Sanctae Margaritae*, of which we give some critical account in Appendix E, pp. 395-399. Ailred also had connections with

---

[1] Haverfield, pp. 92-95. [2] Sir Cyril Fox, pp. 27-35.
[3] The necessary bibliographical and other details are given in the Bibliography, below, pp. 419 ff.

Durham. From the day when he was sent as a boy to be brought up among them at the Scottish Court till his death in 1166 he was continually meeting David's Normans. All we should like to know about them Ailred knew. But he makes only a few incidental references to them, in his description of the Battle of the Standard and in his eulogies of David and his son Earl Henry. Turgot and Ailred were essentially eulogists, hagiographers, and their evidence is subject to some discount, but as definite terms of comparison are lacking the discounting can only be arbitrary. Both played a considerable part in Scoto-Norman affairs. They come into our narrative by the circumstances of their lives, and then their own personality and their own actions sufficiently indicate the nature and the limitations of their testimony. Eadmer shares with them the advantage of having had some Scottish experience. As Anselm's confidant and biographer he has first-hand information on the circumstances preceding the Royal marriage of 1100. As Turgot's successor at St. Andrews for a short time, he writes with special knowledge on the condition of affairs which facilitated the introduction into Scotland of a Norman hierarchy and clergy. The Archdeacon of Huntingdon could have said much about the Earl (David) and his Norman vassals, the ancestry, the parentage, the home life, the personal qualities of the younger sons in the Archdeaconry who helped to provide Scotland with a Norman aristocracy. Instead, he supplies items of a general nature, mostly with reference to the Wars of Stephen and Matilda.

The *Chronicle of Melrose*, of which the first edition was completed 1178 × 1198, uses as sources chiefly the *Anglo-Saxon Chronicle*, Florence of Worcester, Simeon of Durham and John of Hexham, but is valuable as it contains independent entries concerning Scottish events. As clearly shown in the facsimile edition, there are marginal additions ; they are in the form of an historical summary, and were probably written between 1198 and 1214. The *Chronicle of Melrose* is utilized from 1169 by the compiler of the *Chronicle of Holyrood*, in which original notes appear from 1136, and which *s.a.* 1104, borrows from the *Translatio Sancti Cuthberti*. Apart from these two Chronicles, which to some extent supplement each other, the information provided by contemporary writers consists of isolated or merely incidental references to Scotland by various individuals living elsewhere. Their works or compilations are entered in the Bibliography. They have been so long utilized for the history of the Normans in England or for general Scottish history, and so justly appraised by modern scholarship, that their relative value and importance need not be discussed here. The reader is referred to Sir Frank Stenton's critical survey in his *Anglo-Saxon England*, pp. 679-713, and to Dr. Alan O. Anderson's two admirable source-books. There are, however, certain points which seem to require mention :

The MS. of the *Anglo-Saxon Chronicle* which has the fullest references to Scotland is MS. D (the *Worcester Chronicle*), in various hands, 1050–early twelfth-century. It ends in 1079. The version from which it is derived has some points of resemblance to the chronicle attributed to Florence of Worcester. The latter part of MS. D was probably written by someone in the entourage of Aldred, Bishop of Worcester and Archbishop of York, who till his death in 1068 took a prominent part in events which concern us here. It is thought that in its final form MS. D was destined for the Scottish Court. The reasons are : the fullness, and the nature, of the references to Margaret and her relationship to the Old English House ; the addition, after 1130, of a note on the revolt of Angus of Moray and the tone of the note,[1] markedly hostile to the fallen Angus. MS. E (the *Peterborough Chronicle*) ends in 1154. It is founded on a chronicle which in its earlier portions has a close affinity to MS. D.

[1] See below, p. 230, n. 2.

Introduction

The *Vita Æduuardi Regis*, the chief source of information on the pre-Conquest period, was dated by M. Marc Bloch as later than 1103. It is certainly a bizarre production, but we find no reason to take it for anything else than what it purports to be—a Life of Edward written for his widow Edith by a protégé of hers, between 1066 and 1075. Mr. R. W. Southern, who has convincingly upheld the date 1067, shows cause for believing that the author was Goscelin; he was certainly a Lotharingian or Flemish cleric of similar education and outlook. The *Vita* is instructive as regards the origin of the religious and dynastic considerations to which much weight was given in connection with the Scoto-Norman marriage of 1100.

On Orderic [Ordericus Vitalis] as an authority for Scoto-Norman history we place more reliance than has been customary. " My dear old friend ", as Freeman called him, to Round's great annoyance, is the most communicative of the chroniclers and the most truly informative. No one familiar with the general characteristics of present-day Normandy and Scotland can fail to recognize truth in Orderic's remarks and in the lively detail too often dismissed as " irrelevant ". He makes woeful errors of fact. They are, however, of the sort very easily set right and those which can be rectified from other parts of his own voluminous and discursive work may be mere aberrations. He has the names of Scottish sovereigns in the wrong order. But interavailability of " Malcolm ", " Duncan " and " David " was the cherished belief of reputable Continental writers, of whom one at least, Abbot Suger of Saint-Denis, should have known better, being in correspondence with King David. Several statements for which Orderic is the sole authority among the chroniclers and which at one time met with some scepticism—for instance that the " field " of Hastings was Senlac, that the good Queen Maud's baptismal name was Edith and that the subjugation of Moray in 1136 was complete—have now been confirmed. In his report on Moray he is prompt as well as correct: he ceased writing in 1141.

His account of the meetings in 1091 between Malcolm Canmore and Robert, Duke of Normandy, is dramatized and cast in the form of a dialogue—a practice much in favour with historians, ancient and modern. His King and his Duke are exactly the sort of persons that from other sources they are known to have been. The views on homage, and on Rufus, which Orderic attributes to them are consistent with their historical actions and go far to explain them. His opinion of King Malcolm, which is high, finds strong support in MS. D of the *Anglo-Saxon Chronicle* (possibly for reasons to be deduced from its Scottish connections) and less strong, but solid, support in most of the Chronicles, with the exception of Simeon's (perhaps because of the proximity of Durham to the scene of Malcolm's raiding expeditions). Orderic takes a genial interest in Scotland and the Scots. He interrupts the circuitous flow of his narrative to bestow a word of praise— from which it may perhaps be inferred that he had good Scottish friends and informants.

His known written sources for the Conquest and the family history of the " Conquerors " account for only a small part of the abundant material he offers and it has always been assumed that he owed much to oral " sources ".[1] His informants no doubt included : the veteran knights who had fought in the wars of the Conqueror and his sons and who were living in retirement at Orderic's monastery of Saint-Évroul in the forest of the Pays d'Ouche; numerous travellers and clerkly visitors, some coming on business connected with the revenues which the monastery drew

---

[1] Orderic's written sources for England are chiefly: the annals and charters of Saint-Évroul and neighbouring monasteries ; William of Poitiers, whose Chronicle he utilizes till it ends in 1071 (including the last few folios, which have since been lost); Florence of Worcester ; Eadmer ; a version of the *Vita Comitis Waldeui*. He quotes extracts from Geoffrey of Monmouth's *Prophecies of Merlin*.

from several districts in England; members of the local aristocracy, expert in family history and eloquent on the inadequacy of the share which their own families had received in the spoils of the Conquest; the persons whom he met on his travels—in France (1105) and in England (1115), when he visited Crowland and Worcester. He spent five weeks in the Abbey of Crowland, where he wrote an epitaph for Waltheof's tomb and made a copy of his " Life ", and could have heard much about his widow the Countess Judith and their daughter Maud, recently married to David, and about Normans in Scotland.

Monasteries in Orderic's time were whispering-galleries, and a monastic historian could be well abreast of what was going on in the world. Orderic was born near Shrewsbury, the son of a married priest, who came from Orléans. The mother was English and the boy was sent at the age of ten, knowing no language but English, to the monastery of Saint-Évroul, where he passed his whole life in serving his house and writing his chronicle. Even if he never saw his English friends and relations any more, even if he had never passed beyond the precincts, he could have learned much history that was not to be found in books. That he had some inside information on Scotland seems certain. The circumstances of his life being what they were, it could not have been difficult to obtain.

As to its value, because Orderic was born in 1075, began writing towards 1120 and ceased writing in 1141 it does not follow that his evidence on Scoto-Norman affairs is much less valuable for the period 1090–1120 than it is for the period 1120–1140. As an historian he was at least as interested in the past as in the present. There is no reason for assuming that any Scottish informants he may have had at any time, whether correspondents or authors of memoranda or visitors, were younger than himself and purveyors of only the very latest news. They are just as likely to have been men of his own age or older,

Introduction

consequently subjects of Malcolm Canmore till they were at least eighteen. Quite possibly some were credible witnesses for events in the last few years of his reign.

Much information comes from St. Cuthbert's Church of Durham and not only through Turgot and Ailred. The two voluminous Histories by Simeon of Durham and his collaborators are, though uncoordinated, ill-arranged and too visibly the work of many hands, invaluable for their account of contemporary or recent events in Scotland and the North of England. Significant details are embedded in miscellaneous short pieces, memoranda and narratives connected with Durham, some of them purely hagiographical. We have drawn on these works more fully than is usual, not only because they throw light on the workings of the mediaeval mind but because they contain occasional references to individual Normans. On the miracle or the vision opinions will differ; on the persons and the dates mentioned in corroboration there is, as the Judges say, no reasonable doubt. Naturally the writings coming more or less directly from St. Cuthbert's Church tend to overstress its importance and, like all mediaeval churchmen, the writers make the most of their Saint.

There is something to be gleaned from various works bearing on prophecy, on the supernatural, on the romantic. Whether St. Cuthbert intervened directly in Scoto-Norman affairs, whether Earl Waltheof was a saint and martyr, whether the epoch-making marriage of 1100 was prophesied by bards of old, or by Edward long before it took place, or by the dying Margaret only seven years before— these are matters on which doubt may be allowed to reign. What is beyond doubt is that they are matters which profoundly affected Scoto-Norman relations and which kings, bishops, cabinet ministers, university professors or their mediaeval counterparts made the basis of their policy, their action or their writings. There is even something to be learned from pseudo-historical works, such as those of

Geoffrey of Monmouth, and from avowed Romances, such as those of Chrétien de Troyes or *Tristan* or the early-thirteenth-century *Fergus*. Romances not only influenced the minds of men. They registered what had been passing in their minds, and on details of daily life they are often more illuminating than the writings of the historians. In a general way use of the French vernacular seems somehow to produce a more revealing, if cruder, light than that which comes from the Latin of, for instance, the extremely sophisticated and curiously modern William of Malmesbury. That the Middle Ages should not be romanticized is agreed. But when the Normans settled in Scotland their Conquest of England had been romanticized already. What " conquered " Scotland, or at least her rulers, was not Norman military power but Norman prestige, acquired in England and there much enhanced by considerations of religion, sanctity, legend and romance.

In default of contemporary Scottish writers attention must be given to those of later times who may be supposed to have been more interested in some aspects of the period covered in this book than the well-intentioned but alien twelfth-century chroniclers. Unhappily their works not only suffer from the lateness of their composition, but are seldom available in critical editions. Fordun [John of Fordun in the Mearns] was a serious-minded historian. In 1363 he set out on his quest for the lost memorials of early Scottish history and continued his travels till 1385, making " copious notes in a book carried in his bosom ". His Chronicle (to 1153) contains five books and appears to have been concluded by 1387. On our period he quotes, copiously, from William of Malmesbury, sparingly from a lost work of Turgot, and has comparatively little of his own to say. But what he does say merits credence. His work was amplified and continued in the *Chronicle of Inchcolm* (1447) or, to give it its more familiar title, the *Scotichronicon*, by Walter Bower, Abbot of Inchcolm. Fordun's

Introduction

text was freed by Skene from accretions due to Bower. But Bower drew from sources which have been lost and of the accretions there is no critical text. While it is useful to know what is by Fordun and what is by Bower, the latter's contributions are not necessarily of much less value. Andrew of Wyntoun, Canon of St. Andrews and Prior of St. Serf's in Loch Leven, a dull man but an honest, may often be faithfully reporting well-accredited tradition. Of the corpus of writings represented by Fordun, Wyntoun (*c.* 1425) and Bower only a comparatively small portion relates to the years 1042–1165.

Hector Bois or Boys (Latinized Boethius, retranslated Boece), who was born at Dundee *c.* 1465, belonged to the family of Bois of Panbride in Angus. Perhaps because of his own French ancestry, his views on the French in Scotland are indulgent. Though Principal and Professor of Theology at Aberdeen, he has a well-established reputation for mendacity, but may sometimes be giving scraps of true history, preserved in oral tradition or taken from works since lost which were better than his own. Unfortunately some of those which he quotes seem to have been even worse.[1] In the sixteenth-century translations of Boece, by John Bellenden into Scottish prose and by William Stewart into Scottish verse, there are occasional interpolations which have the ring of truth. In this matter it is possible to be over-critical. When what late Scottish writers say is credible, enlightening and uncontradicted by known fact they need not be assumed to be romancing. But except for picturesque detail, local colour and pawky phrase their works have yielded a lean harvest.

Contemporary record also is incidental and indirect, but from 1094 it is no longer external. Scotland's entire stock of mediaeval documents is small. Of the public

[1] See *Lectures*, by W. Douglas Simpson, *Hector Boece*, and J. B. Black, " Boece's *Scotorum Historiae* ", in *Quatercentenary of the Death of Hector Boece* (Aberdeen University Press, 1937).

records little escaped the hand of time or of depredators, of whom the sorry list is headed by Edward I. Hardly anything remains of the vast mass of documents in existence at the death of Alexander III in 1286: the six hundred or seven hundred great rolls, one of them made up of sixty-two pieces of skin. Apart from the *Book of Deer* there is no extant writing earlier than 1094.[1] But it is possible that before then—as in Ireland—diplomatic documents never did exist in quantity. Ireland, and presumably Celtic Scotland, did not share the tradition by which written records were used for official purposes and which all the States that were heirs of the Roman Empire inherited in some degree.[2]

Of the extant charters the earliest is that recording Duncan II's grant to Durham in 1094; it was written by a Norman scribe.[3] They remain rare till the accession of David in 1124. All those which are prior to his death in 1153 were collected, edited and assigned approximate dates by Sir Archibald Lawrie, in his *Early Scottish Charters*. (Our references to this work being very numerous, only the name Lawrie and the number of the Charter are given.) David's charters are undated and laconic, but can be usefully supplemented from the confirmations by Malcolm IV and William the Lion. Their own charters are more explicit and more communicative and some bear dates. Not all are to be easily found and we have had to take a few on trust, chiefly from the monumental work of Cosmo Innes, *Origines Parochiales Scotiae* (abbreviated to *O.P.*).

The chartularies of Scottish religious houses, and also the registers of certain dioceses, are published, mostly by the Bannatyne Club, under their varying and cumbrous original titles (which for convenience of reference we have reduced to the place-name, printed in italic). They contain Royal,

---

[1] See Sir Henry M. Paton, *The Scottish Records* (Historical Association of Scotland, 1938).

[2] See Kenney, p. 5.   [3] See below, p. 63.

episcopal and private charters and confirmations and various other documents in which mention is made of Normans, usually in connection with their gifts of churches or of land. They record names of Norman witnesses in profusion but only occasionally actual grants of land to Normans. The chartularies richest in such material prior to 1153 are : *Dunfermline, St. Andrews, Kelso* and *Melrose.*

Relevant facts, generally relating to Norman family history, are to be found scattered here and there in Collections of non-Scottish charters, such as those by J. H. Round and H. W. C. Davis, and in the volumes of *Early Yorkshire Charters* (abbreviated to *E. Yks. Ch.*).

The nature and scope of the charter evidence we discuss in Chapter IV, but a general observation may be made now : that charters were written for quite another purpose than that for which they have been utilized here. The authenticity of those so utilized is, however, seldom in doubt. The few which are manifestly spurious are disregarded. Others which some authorities, not always on very strong grounds, have considered to be dubious are used, with caution. A document may itself be dubious and yet its contents, or part of its contents, may be true.

The entire information available, that which is matter of record and that which is merely matter of report, is thus in one sense or another incidental and indirect. It is intermittent. It is often scanty, but it is sometimes surprisingly full and it has the merits of its defects, being unlikely, at least in the questions at issue here, to be much affected by prejudice, personal or national, or by ulterior motives. It has to be sought for in nooks and crannies, but in the mass it is impressive. Although there are lamentable gaps, which make continuity of treatment difficult, contradictions are few and items appearing in documents of dubious authority usually find some corroboration elsewhere.

CHAPTER I

MALCOLM CANMORE, MARGARET AND THE NORMANS

★

§ 1

Celtic Prince : Hungarian Princess

DESPITE all that Shakespeare so poetically says to the contrary, Duncan I, surnamed the Gracious, died young, after a reign as brief as it was unhappy. Succeeding in 1034 the venerable but still mighty Malcolm MacKenneth, *Malcoloun mac Cinathà*, whom the Irish annalists entitle " Lord and Father of the West ", Duncan marched on Durham and was repulsed with heavy loss.[1] In the North of Scotland he was defeated by his Scoto-Viking cousin Thorfinn, Jarl of the Orkneys, and on August 14, 1040, he was defeated and slain by another kinsman, Macbeth, Mormaer of Moray, who after leading the Royal armies against the Norse had transferred his allegiance to Thorfinn. By the Celtic rules of succession, and also through his wife Gruoch and his stepson Lulach, Macbeth had a claim to be King of Scots which was sound enough to be widely accepted. Making large concessions to Thorfinn in the North and West, he governed Scotland with such ability and success that the comparative prosperity of his seventeen years' reign illumines the bleak annals of her early history with a ray of pale sunshine.

Soon after the death of Duncan his two young sons were sent away for greater safety—the elder, Malcolm " Canmore " [Bighead], to England, the younger, Donald Bane [*Bán* = White], to the Isles. Malcolm, a boy of about nine, was entrusted to the care of his maternal uncle Siward the Dane, one of Cnut's warriors who had been Earl of Bernicia since 1038 and was from 1041 Earl of all

---

[1] Sim. Durh. *H.D.E.* I, p. 90.

3

Northumbria.[1]   The limits of Bernicia and Cumbria were vague, and during Malcolm's minority Cumbria was probably governed by Siward more or less nominally on his behalf.   The unhappy Duncan could claim to represent the MacAlpin line, but only on the spindle side, and had been well aware that he might be supplanted. If he could not have his elder son formally recognized as his eventual successor on the throne, he could at least place him in possession of Cumbria, and this he had done.[2]

The Earl of the Northumbrians was no courtier and no politician, but he was one of the most powerful supporters of the new King, Edward, and had frequent occasion to come to his aid.   On an early occasion [3] he came accompanied by his youthful ward and nephew, whose fourteen years of exile in England were partly spent at Edward's Court.   There Malcolm was joined by Macduff and other nobles opposed to Macbeth and the House of Moray.   It is related of " Lady Macduff " that when she was questioned by Macbeth she made many excuses till she saw her husband safely out at sea, and then said : " Do you see yon white sail upon the sea ?   Yonder goes Macduff." [4]   He was going to a court which was thoroughly French,[5] to a king who was French in all but name.   We cannot tell to what extent Malcolm Canmore and his companions in exile were affected by their French surroundings, by contact with the numerous Frenchmen already

---

[1] Malcolm Canmore was probably born *c.* 1031, Donald Bane *c.* 1033. The authority for their flight and for their relationship to Siward is Fordun, IV, xlv, pp. 188-191, where it is said that their mother was a kinswoman of Siward.   Siward's wife was a daughter of a former Earl, Ealdred, son of Uchtred, son of Waltheof, members of a native Northumbrian family, the head of which was often appointed Earl by the King.   Malcolm's mother belonged to this family.   She was probably a sister of Siward's wife.

[2] As Boece puts it, XII, p. 249, Malcolm's father " presented him " with Cumbria.

[3] Wyntoun states that Malcolm, on arriving in England, at once went to Edward.   [4] Wyntoun, VI, xviii.

[5] See J. H. Round, *E.H.R.* XIX (1904), pp. 90-92.

4

settled in England,[1] or with the King's Norman officials and counsellors on whose help their chances of restoration depended. At the least the Prince of Cumbria learned some French [2] and his subsequent career suggests a young man of understanding and adaptability on whom the dignity of Edward's life, the distinction of his Court and the interest of its French ways would not be entirely lost. Mutual regard was certainly achieved. It was " by the King's command " [3] and for the purpose (though there must have been others) of restoring Malcolm to his father's throne that Earl Siward collected a cavalry force and a fleet, and in the summer of 1054 invaded Scotland by land and sea.[4]

It was Malcolm Canmore's destiny to be confronted by Normans all his life. At that early date there were Normans in Scotland. It would have been remarkable if there were not, after fifty years' peaceful penetration of the neighbouring kingdom by the sons of an adventurous and wandering race. Those whom he now encountered were not, however, apostles of peace. They were the most bellicose of Edward's military men, who, two years before, had been driven out of their " castles " in Herefordshire in consequence of the compromise settlement after Earl Godwine's revolt. The Norman " castle-men " took the

---

[1] Their numbers were such that the Conqueror had to make special provision for Frenchmen domiciled in England before 1066. There are only three short pieces of legislation preserved in the form in which they were issued by the Conqueror. In one of them, No. 3 of the ten articles affects " omnes homines quos mecum adduxi aut post me venerunt ". The next, No. 4, continues : " Et omnis Francigena qui, tempore regis Eadwardi propinqui mei, fuit in Anglia particeps consuetudinum Anglorum ".—A. J. Robertson, p. 328.

[2] According to a quotation ascribed to Fordun (Surtees ed. of Sim. Durh. I, p. 258), Malcolm had learned English and French as perfectly as Gaelic : " Anglicam linguam simul et Romanam, aeque ut propriam plane didicerat cum post patris sui mortem quattuordecim annos in Anglia mansisset ".

[3] " Jussu regis "—Flor. Worc. I, p. 212 ; Wm. Malm. p. 237.

[4] Flor. Worc. I, p. 212.
  " Li quens Syward fist nefs mener.
  Son ost i enveiad par mer
  E il menat grant ost par terre."
  —Gaimar, ll. 5047-5049.

road to Scotland, apparently in considerable numbers, under the leadership of Osberne, surnamed *Pentecôte*, and Hugue, his ally. They were henchmen of Raoul [Ralph], son of Edward's sister Godgifu and her first husband Dreux, Comte de Mantes. Raoul, who was Earl of Hereford from 1050 to his death in 1057, had adopted French methods in his defence of the border county against the Welsh. He built " castles ", installed French garrisons in them and " contrary to custom made Englishmen fight on horseback ".[1] The occasion for the expulsion of the " castlemen " was Godgifu's second husband Eustace II, Count of Boulogne, known as " Eustache aux grenons " because of his moustaches. In 1051 there had been a brawl at Dover between his retainers and the townsmen. Edward, perhaps impulsively, ordered the Earl of Wessex, Godwine, to execute reprisals on the town. Godwine refused, and was forced into exile in Flanders. Next year he came back and this time found general support. A compromise was effected and he was reinstated. It was agreed that the King should keep such French friends with him as he might wish, but that the new Norman Archbishop of Canterbury and a few other Norman prelates should go home and that certain of the French " castle-men " in Herefordshire should be expelled. We are told that the Archbishop's French escort " took their horses and went to Pentecost's castle "[2] and that " Osberne surnamed *Pentecôte* and Hugue his ally gave up their castles and, reaching Scotland, were taken by King Macbeth into his service ".[3] They were allowed by Leofric (husband of

---

[1] Flor. Worc. II, p. 213.   [2] *A-S.C.* MS. E, *s.a.* 1052.

[3] " Osbernus cognomento Pentecost et socius ejus Hugo sua reddiderunt castella et . . . Scottiam adeuntes, a rege Scottorum Macbeotha suscepti sunt."—Flor. Worc. I, p. 210. Osberne's castle, which took its name *Pentecôte* from him, has been identified as Ewias Harold, at the southern entrance to the Golden Valley. Round, *F.E.* pp. 321-326. Harold of Ewias was the son of Raoul [Ralph] and his (Danish) wife Gytha. *Pentecôte* was one of the familiarly bestowed cognomens then coming into use among Normans. Hugue is known only as Osberne's " ally ".

" Lady Godiva ") to pass through his Earldom of Mercia, but their selection of Scotland as a place of refuge and the approval of the authorities on the line of march have never been explained.

On the Day of the Seven Sleepers (July 27), 1054, in the single battle of Siward's campaign Macbeth's Normans perished to a man.[1] The battle, fought traditionally at Dunsinane in Perthshire, was bloody but not decisive. Macbeth was driven off the field.[2] Siward, whose eldest son was among the fallen, went home " with booty such as no man had before obtained "[3]—a remarkable testimony to the excellence of Macbeth's government and the soundness of whatever economic policy he may have followed. Next year Siward was gathered to his fathers, grieving that he had failed to meet death in battle and having his steel panoply put upon him for his last hours, like the indomitable old Viking that he was. His nephew, whom, " as Edward had commanded, he had set up as king ",[4] but whose authority was effective only in South Scotland, continued the struggle alone. In the North he slew his father's slayer and after him, in 1058, King Lulach, and thus reached the throne.[5] In 1059 he visited the English Court, the first King of Scots to do so for more than eighty years. As he was accompanied on his way by the new Earl of the Northumbrians (Godwine's son Tostig), the Bishop of Durham (Æthelwine) and the Archbishop of York (Cynesige),[6] and as these were the officials who regularly " convoyed " the Scottish kings, it

---

[1] " Multis millibus Scottorum et Nortmannis omnibus quorum supra fecimus mentionem occisis."—Flor. Worc. I, p. 212.

[2] *A-S.C.* MS. C, *s.a.* 1054.   [3] *A-S.C.* MS. D, *s.a.* 1054.

[4] " Siwardus Malcolmum, regis Cumbrorum filium, ut rex jusserat, regem constituit."—Flor. Worc.

[5] Macbeth was killed at the battle of Lumphanan, August 15, 1057 ; Lulach the Fatuous, at Essie, near Rhynie (all in Aberdeenshire), March 17, 1058. Like Duncan I, they were buried in Iona. Fordun, pp. 206 and 223.

[6] *Annales Lindisfarnenses et Dunelmenses* (*M.G.H.* XIX, pp. 502-508), *s.a.* 1059. " Kinsius " [Cynesige], one of Edward's (numerous) *English* chaplains, had been Archbishop since 1051. Sim. Durh. *H.R.* II, p. 174.

is clear that Malcolm III went to return thanks and to do homage.[1]

On this ceremonial visit he may or may not have seen Margaret, who had arrived in England two years before from her native Hungary. The childless Edward's solution of the succession problem had been his Norman cousin William, but after the troubles of 1052 his mind turned at last to the Old English House. It was nearly forty years since his eldest half-brother King Edmund (Ironside) had died, leaving two infant sons. They were deported by Cnut to Scandinavia and were afterwards taken to Hungary, where they were brought up at St. Stephen's court. The elder, Edmund, who had married Stephen's daughter, had died without issue. The younger, Edward, was still alive and had a wife and family. In the year of Siward's battle, Aldred [Ealdred], Bishop of Worcester, an experienced diplomat with the reputation of being almost too skilful a negotiator, was sent to Germany with a request that the Emperor should arrange with the King of Hungary, a dependent State, for the Exile's return to England. Circumstances were favourable. The Emperor (Henry III) had married Edward's sister Gunnhild and, though she died soon after the wedding, the two men, who had much in common, remained on terms of cordial friendship as individuals and as sovereigns. Moreover, the Exile's wife Agatha, a German princess brought up in Hungary, was a kinswoman of the Emperor and a niece of Stephen's Queen Gisela. Nevertheless the Bishop, after nearly a year of negotiations at Cologne, failed in his mission. It was not till the spring of 1057 that Edward the Exile at length landed in England, with his wife and their three children: Margaret, then about twelve, Christina perhaps nine, and Edgar probably six.[2]

[1] On homage, real or alleged, of Scottish kings, see Appendix B, p. 385 ff.

[2] Margaret was the elder sister and it is generally accepted that she was born in 1046. According to Orderic, Edgar was of the same age as the Conqueror's eldest son, Robert Courte-Heuse [Curthose]. Robert was

Celtic Prince : Hungarian Princess

It has been the fashion for nearly nine hundred years now to look upon this perhaps somewhat forlorn party, none of whom probably could speak English, as poor relations charitably rescued from want and obscurity in a foreign land by a benevolent, if slightly condescending, Royal uncle. Edward's attitude is unlikely to have been condescending. He had been in exile himself half his life and was spending the other half in vain regrets that he had ever come back. Although he had been legally elected King, he can hardly have helped thinking that if in 1042 primogeniture had been as well observed as in his beloved Normandy, his nephew, and not himself, would be wearing the Crown. So far was the long-lost nephew from being a poor relation that he brought with him gold enough and treasures enough, religious and artistic, to keep Scotland or her chroniclers for centuries in wonder and awe.[1] He was a great noble in Hungary and through his marriage he was a man of exalted state in the Empire. If we may believe a twelfth-century poetess,[2] the Emperor held him in the highest esteem and affection, and it was he who had drawn Edward's attention to his merits and his rights. The nephew must have had his reasons for being so long in coming. The Crown which might fall from Edward's brow in ten years' time or in twenty—his hair and beard

probably born in 1053. William of Poitiers, p. 141, and Ailred, *G.R.A.* p. 734, describe Edgar as " puer " in January 1066. William of Jumièges uses the same word of him in 1068. To make him much older than fifteen in 1066 is to strengthen his case for election as King considerably : to make him much younger is to give him the role of a mere figurehead in the armies of resistance. Most probably he was the youngest child and born *c.* 1051.

[1] " Imperator . . . Edwardum . . . cum maxima gloria ac divitiis . . . ad Angliam mittit."—Ailred, *G.R.A.* p. 366. Fordun (V, p. 213), quoting Turgot, says that Margaret, though an Esther, arrived in Scotland as no captive maiden, but with great riches which the Emperor and King Edward had given her father. The artistic treasures no doubt came partly from Winchester, partly from Hungary, where the goldsmiths and silversmiths working for the Church set a style that was famous for centuries.

[2] A nun of the Abbey of Barking who wrote a Life of Edward, *c.* 1173 ; see P. Meyer, *Notice du MS. Egerton 745, Romania,* XL (1911), pp. 41-69 ; also A. T. Baker, *La Vie de Sainte Foy d'Agen, Romania,* LXVI (1940), and G. E. Moore, *ME. Life of Edward,* p. 1.

were white as snow, but he was little more than fifty—was not a firm offer. In a country inhabited by two peoples, one Saxon and submissive, the other Dane-descended and aloof, differing in language, law and social order and held together by little more than acquiescence in Edward, the throne to be some day vacated was of dubious stability. There was, there could be, no guarantee that in case of predecease young Edgar would have special consideration or preferential treatment. If the conditions governing the Succession in 1054 were explained to the Exile as they are explained by the historians to us, the wonder is not that he took three years to come, but that he came at all. When he came he died, just after reaching London. His children were thus left to their grand-uncle's care. He brought them up " benignly as though they were his own offspring ",[1] and gave them an education above the standard of the times. That it was a French education seems likely from what is known of Edward's very marked French sympathies.

Margaret from childhood was noted for piety.[2] She brought with her from Hungary the Black Rood or Holy Rood,[3] which became Scotland's most sacred relic, but was only one of many which had accompanied her from afar.[4] Her piety must have owed something to the passionate faith of a country but recently evangelized. Queen Gisela had greatly aided her husband in his work of founding monasteries, creating bishoprics and not only Christianizing but Romanizing his kingdom—to the point of endeavouring to make Latin the language of the Court and the nobility—and during the reaction which followed his death in 1038 and lasted till " the Christian party "

---

[1] Ord. Vit. I, xxxiv.   [2] " In primaeva aetate."—Turgot, *Vita*, p. 238.
[3] A gold casket having on the outside a crucifix carved in ebony and containing within a portion of the True Cross. Ailred, *G.R.A.* p. 715.
[4] " Attulit plurimas Sanctorum reliquias, omni lapide vel auro pretiosiores : inter quas fuit illa sancta crux, quam nigram vocant."—Fordun, p. 258.

came into power again in 1046, she preserved much of her influence. Like her, Agatha her niece must have lived in an atmosphere charged with religious fervour, vibrant with theological discussion. In Hungary the choice had lain not only between paganism and Christianity, but between the Western and the Eastern Churches. The choice had been made, but it continued to provoke violent political struggles. These peculiar circumstances, in which the Roman Church and Christianity itself were subjects of novel and all-absorbing interest, are reflected in the names which Edward and Agatha gave their two daughters. The selection of the Latin name which the elder was one of the first historical personages to bear in Western Europe and which owes much of its popularity to her, was inspired by the cult of the Saint of Antioch (Marina in the Greek Church, Margaret in the Roman) which reached Hungary from Italy with the Christian religion, bringing thoughts of the *margarita* or pearl of great price.[1] The younger daughter's name, Christina (sometimes given also as Christiana), tells its Hungarian tale with a sublime simplicity. In England Margaret was, as Lanfranc expressed it, " regaliter educata ". The French influences permeating the Court, the Church and the Convent were certainly not without their effect on the able and religious-minded girl who was Edward's ward for nine impressionable years.

[1] These thoughts recur in the early references to Margaret. Turgot, *Vita*, p. 236, and Gaimar, l. 4647 : " La preciose gemme, Margarete l'apelat l'om ". William of Poitiers makes the same allusion when (p. 105) he speaks of the other contemporary Margaret [Marguerite] (also noted for her extreme piety), the daughter of Hugh II, Count of Maine († 1051). She was betrothed by her brother Herbert II to the youthful Robert Courte-Heuse [" Curthose "], but died before the marriage and was buried at Fécamp. The use of the Latin form Margarita as a personal name spread from Italy. The Life and Acts of the Saint of Antioch were well known in England from the tenth century. St. Margaret's, Westminster, first mentioned in a Charter of Abbot Herbert (1121 × 1140), may originally have been a private chapel dedicated to St. Margaret of Antioch with secondary reference to St. Margaret (of Scotland), by her daughter Queen Maud († 1118), whose residence was Westminster.

§ 2

Malcolm Canmore's Early Reign

BY birth and upbringing the new King of Scots had much to commend him to a mixed population. Paternally, he was a Celt; maternally, a Northumbrian; and we can assign what racial origins we please to his great stature and physical strength,[1] his high colour, vivid face,[2] irascible temperament and his curious oscillations between " perfervidum ingenium " and extreme caution. His name (in Latin *Malcolumus*,[3] less formally *Malcolmus*) was Celtic and religious—early Gaelic *Mael Coluimb*, servant or devotee of Columba—and he " had the Gaelic ",[4] but perhaps usually spoke English, with a good Northumbrian burr. All the kings before him had been, like Shakespeare's Duncan, " touched by steel, poison, malice domestic ", some slain in war, some murdered by a kinsman and suc-

---

[1] Implied in the correspondence of 1257 quoted in *Hist. Northumberland*, VIII, pp. 51-52, concerning the discovery of a body supposed to be that of Malcolm Canmore.

[2] Malcolm " the florid of lively visage "—*The Duan Albanach*, a short metrical chronicle in Irish (eleventh century), in *Chronicles of the Picts and Scots*, p. 62, ed. W. F. Skene (Register House, 1867).

[3] A fourteenth-century English genealogist explains (*Illustrns. Sc. Hist.* p. 138) that the name has four syllables in Latin verse, *Malcŏlŏmus*, but elsewhere is generally *Malcolmus*. Malcolm in his son Duncan's charter to Durham (1094) is *Malcolumb*. In *A-S.C.* MS. D the form is *Malcholom*. In the Old French of Gaimar and others it is *Malcolumb* or *Maucoloun*. Malcolm IV in his charters is Malcolomus : so also in William of Newburgh, I, xxxv, MS. C.

[4] " As he knew the language of the English perfectly in addition to his own, he distinguished himself in this Council as a most alert interpreter for both sides."—Turgot, *Vita*, VIII, p. 243. At the Council in question, part of the " business " was to convince argumentative Celtic churchmen that Queen Margaret's calculation of the proper number of days in the Lenten fast was right, and theirs wrong. Malcolm must have had a good knowledge of English and Gaelic to distinguish himself thus, " figures " being usually the linguist's last achievement.

ceeded by him on the throne.[1]   Malcolm had a troubled
heritage of bitter feud and dynastic vendetta and had
himself a blood-stained past.   But he was gifted enough,
" Celtic " and " English " enough, to live it down and to
reign nearly thirty-six years without much internal opposition, or without much that is recorded.   No foreign ruler
ever attempted to treat with anyone in Scotland but King
Malcolm.   His Royal authority he owed to his ancient
Celtic lineage.   But his upbringing and his outlook were
" Southern ".   Coming to the throne as Prince of Cumbria,
and as effective ruler in Lothian for some years, he placed
his reliance chiefly on South Scotland, and he took up his
abode accordingly, not at Scone, Abernethy or Dunkeld,
but in the extreme south of the original Kingdom, at Dunfermline, by the Forth.

It was perhaps as a result of his old English associations that he became Earl Tostig's " sworn brother " and
in this capacity joined what might colloquially be termed
the Conquest family party.   Earl Siward's surviving son

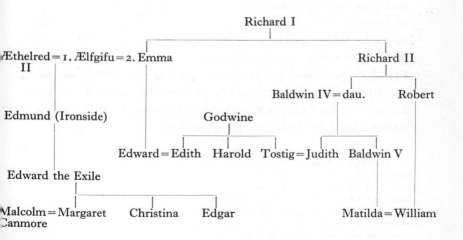

[1] Thus Malcolm I (943-954) was killed by men of Moray, Constantin III
(955-997) by Kenneth III (997-1005), who was killed by Malcolm II.

Waltheof (Malcolm Canmore's cousin) being too young to govern,[1] a successor had been found in the person of Godwine's third son Tostig. Earl Tostig's brother in the flesh was Harold; his sister Edith was Edward's wife; his own wife Judith, granddaughter of a Norman Duke, was an aunt, probably a young aunt, of William's wife Matilda. William's cousin Edward was a distant relative of Matilda, but he was Judith's grand-uncle, and grand-uncles were not as distant then, or as venerable, as might be thought. Tostig's relationship to Edward by marriage (besides that of brother-in-law) was the same as was eventually attained by Malcolm Canmore: husband of a grand-niece. Matilda and Judith were daughters of a Count of Flanders, but none the less " French " for that.[2] William's wife is said to have been of Scottish descent, but this may be only a legend, and is best relegated to Appendix A. Tostig's wife could have inspired the picturesque relationship which he had formed with the King of Scots. She was an enterprising person—much interested in local customs and beliefs—who acquired relics of St. Oswald and St. Oswin and figured in a typical Northumbrian incident which was to become constant in Norman times. She was devoted to St. Cuthbert and made gifts to his Church, but regretted that no woman was permitted to visit his tomb. She therefore promised to give more land to the Saint, but on condition that the regulation should be relaxed in her favour. This being refused, she sent one of her women under cloud of night on an experimental visit, which, if

[1] " Quia Walteof adhuc parvulus erat."—H. Hunt. p. 196.

[2] Tostig had married Judith before he accompanied his father Godwine in 1051 into exile in Flanders, where the family seems to have had property. She was a daughter of Baldwin, fourth Count of Flanders, by his second marriage to a daughter of Duke Richard II, and was the sister of Baldwin V († 1067), father of Matilda, whom Duke William married, probably in 1049. Matilda descended from King Alfred through his daughter Elfrida, wife of Baldwin II. Judith was the niece of Edward's mother Emma, daughter of Duke Richard I. After 1066 Judith took a second husband, Welf II, Duke of Bavaria, and lived in Southern Germany till her death, *c.* 1095. P. Grierson, *England and Flanders*, p. 110.

successful, she herself would repeat. But her emissary, setting foot in the precincts, was overthrown by a rushing wind and died soon after. Brotherhood, sworn in a church on the relics of a saint, was an institution in vogue among the Northern French as well as the Northumbrians [1]

In 1061, during the absence of the Earl, who had gone to Rome with Judith and Aldred, still Bishop of Worcester and now also Archbishop of York,[2] Malcolm invaded Northumbria, for reasons unknown. Perhaps he had only local claims. Or perhaps he had assumed the ancestral task and had hopes of territorial expansion to the Tyne or, in moments when " perfervidum ingenium " was in the ascendant, to the Tees. The Tees was the division between the old Anglian provinces of Deira (the northerly part of the present Yorkshire) and Bernicia, which had extended to the Forth and to the Irish Sea—Bede speaks of " Whithorn in Bernicia "—but had shrunk almost to the present counties of Northumberland and Durham; the chief citadel was Bamburgh; the religious centres were Lindisfarne and Hexham. Together, the two provinces made up " Northumberland ", in Latin *Northumbria*, a term which (like *Cumbria* for the old " Cumberland ") is useful as avoiding confusion with the later (and in both cases much smaller) county. The inhabitants of Northumbria (originally all England beyond the estuaries of the Humber and the Mersey) still held sullenly aloof from the rest of the English Kingdom. In institutions and language they were

---

[1] A pre-Conquest Norman immigrant, Guillaume Malet, was Harold's *compater* and, having fought against him at Hastings, interred him next day : " Quidam, partim Normannus et Anglus, compater Heraldi "—William of Poitiers ; Ord. Vit. III, xiv. The Orestes and Pylades of French romance, Ami and Amiles, were sworn brothers. The Conqueror's Knights Roger d'Ivry and Robert d'Oilly at Oxford were " sworn brothers, united by faith and oath " and also, what was very unusual, joint-founders of monasteries. Sim. Durh. *H.D.E.* I, p. 94.

[2] Aldred had succeeded Archbishop Cynsige († January 22, 1060), but retained the comfortable see of Worcester, as several predecessors in the ill-endowed archdiocese had done. He had set out for Rome, hoping to justify this procedure and to receive the pallium.

nearer to the Anglic population of Lothian than to the Southern English, and in 1061 the late Earl's nephew Malcolm, ruling in the north of the old Bernicia and perhaps hopeful of ruling in the south, was no foreign invader.

All we are told of his incursion is that he " ruthlessly devastated the land of his sworn brother Earl Tostig and that the peace of St. Cuthbert was violated in the Island of Lindisfarne ".[1] Whatever may have been the matters in dispute, they were amicably settled at a conference with King Edward in the North of England, and Malcolm, " much honoured " by his benign neighbour, went home laden with gifts.[2] At this or some earlier meeting of the monarchs there seems to have been question of a marriage with Margaret.[3] If so, nothing came of it and Malcolm married Ingibiorg instead. She was the daughter [4] of his father's old enemy, Thorfinn, son of Sigurd the Stout (Jarl of the Orkneys and Caithness, Conqueror of the " Southern Land ") by his second marriage to King Malcolm MacKenneth's second daughter. Thorfinn was a boy at the Scottish Court when news came out of Ireland

[1] " *Sui conjurati fratris.*"—Sim. Durh. *H.R.* II, p. 175. Perhaps some right of sanctuary had been infringed. Edgar, instituting the King's Peace at Coldingham, defined it as that observed in Islandshire, including Lindisfarne. Lawrie, XX.

[2]
> " Li reis Eadward encontre vint
> Od Malcolub parlement tint,
> Presenz li fist, mult l'onura."
> —Gaimar, ll. 5092-5094.

[3] Orderic, VIII, xxii, purporting to quote Malcolm himself, says that Edward gave him his grand-niece in marriage. The *Genealogia Regum Anglorum* possessed by the monastery of Saint-Évroul and probably utilized by Orderic [printed in Le Prévost's edition, V, pp. li-lv] has : " Edvuardus . . . Margaritam Melcomo regi Scotorum dedit ". In a speech on the delicate matter of his own succession Henry I told his assembled barons the same thing, in the same words. The speech is reported by Wm. Malm. *H.N.* p. 690.

[4] Ingibiorg (Norse Ingibjorg, Mod. Danish Ingeborg) was said, in the *Orkneyinga Saga*, to be the *widow* of Thorfinn. Thorfinn's wife was undoubtedly called Ingibiorg, but it is now clear (see Henderson, pp. 25-27) that Malcolm married her daughter and namesake. The marriage took place between 1059 and 1061. The latter date seems the more probable.

that Sigurd was slain at Clontarf. The King, with political intentions no doubt, obtained the succession to the Earldoms of Caithness and Sutherland for his youthful grandson,[1] who, however, went further than was intended, going indeed from strength to strength till he won, say the sagas, nine more earldoms, all the Hebrides and a kingdom in Ireland.[2] It was Thorfinn's custom to spend the winter in the agreeable climate of the Orkneys and devote the summer to the purposes of plunder on the West Coast of Scotland, or in the Isle of Man, or on Welsh or on Irish shores. He warred on Macbeth as he had warred on Duncan. In the end, having come to terms with his Royal overlord in Norway and, like Macbeth,[3] visited Rome, he settled down to the quiet government of his northern lands, established a Bishopric of the Orkneys, and in 1064 died and was buried in his island cathedral.[4] The marriage brought Malcolm Canmore political advantages : conciliation of the Norse element within and bordering on his Kingdom and neutralization of Moray, thus caught (cartographically) between an upper and a lower millstone, the Norse and the Scottish power. The marriage was said by Anglo-Norman chroniclers to have been irregular. That it was perfectly regular is sufficiently shown by the status invariably accorded to the eldest son (afterwards Duncan II), and to William fitz Duncan, and by the fact that for generations no claimant to the Scottish throne failed to find adherents if he was, or gave himself out to be, a descendant of King Malcolm and Queen Ingibiorg.

For the next few years no more is heard of Malcolm's southern interests. In August 1065 Tostig's rule, or perhaps misrule, in Northumbria came to an end, by

---

[1] The sons of Sigurd's first marriage shared Orkney and Shetland. Malcolm MacKenneth's hope was perhaps to split the Norse dominion and then attack Moray, Thorfinn assisting from the north.

[2] Worsaae, p. 238.   [3] Flor. Worc. I, p. 204.

[4] Christ Church Minster, probably on the site of the present Birsay Parish Church, in Mainland, Orkney. See Kendrick, p. 310 ; Brøgger, p. 150.

reason of revolt against exorbitant taxation, and on November 1, with Judith and a few faithful adherents, he left England as an exile, to live with her relatives in " Baldwin's Land ".[1] " Taking a rest-cure " [2] at Saint-Omer, he was meditating reconquest of his Earldom and vengeance on Harold for inadequate brotherly help against rebels when an historic event occurred which brought him once more into close contact with the Scottish King.

On January 5 half-Norman Edward died and half-Danish Harold Godwineson was crowned and anointed next day. Margaret's brother Edgar Atheling [3] had been set aside. He was only a boy, and only half-English. Nevertheless he was the sole legitimate heir to the throne, the last surviving representative of the House of Cerdic in the male line. Historians are now agreed that Harold, probably in 1064, had " become William's man " and sworn on relics of Norman saints to support his English claim, though we confess ourselves unable to see what Harold could have done for the Norman cause or could have been expected to do. If he had unavowed Royal ambitions, abandon them ? Concert preparatory measures with Edward ? Say a word in season to trusted friends, conduct a little discreet propaganda and, when the time came, address the assembled Witan in William's favour ? But whatever may have been the arrangement made at the mysterious interviews in Normandy, it was made over young Edgar's head and at his expense. To the modern mind it may seem unimportant whether the rights of this or that princeling at a given time were or were not respected. The sequel regularly shows that the mediaeval mind worked otherwise. In a moment of indifference

[1] *A-S.C.* MSS. C and E, *s.a.* 1065 ; Flor. Worc. I, pp. 224-225.
[2] " Morari et quiescere a tot laboribus "—*Vita Æd.* l. 1233.
[3] Ætheling, French *Adelin*, in mediaeval Latin *Adelinus*, more usually *Clito*, meant Noble, often Prince of the Blood Royal, though not necessarily heir apparent. Modern usage fluctuates between " Edgar *the* Atheling " and " Edgar Atheling " ; cp. " Cnut King ".

among the people and panic among their leaders injustice was done which was remembered. Juridical reasons could always be found which might satisfy the plain man for a time. But his sense of justice returned and the rancour lasted for generations.

Perjury, however, not failure to uphold the West Saxon dynasty, was the charge brought against the son of Godwine. Great was the scandal when news reached the Continent of Edward's death and burial, and of Harold's election and Coronation, all within some twenty-four hours. Duke William was certainly not a dispassionate observer; nor was the exiled Tostig, who, when he learned that to his brother's iniquities perjury had now been added, proposed to his relative and neighbour the dead King's cousin that they should seek vengeance together.[1] Tostig was given a roving commission and in May, having got together a fleet manned by Flemings and Normans, he set sail from the Cotentin for the Humber. His descents on the coast of his lost Earldom proving disastrous to himself, he sailed on to Scotland, where he spent the whole of the fatal summer preparing for an anti-perjury campaign, to be conducted, he hoped, from various points of the compass, by himself, by the Duke of the Normans, by the King of Scots and by Queen Ingibiorg's famous uncle, Harold " Hardrada ", King of Norway.[2] Malcolm gave Tostig his protection and aided him with supplies,[3] pending the arrival of the Norwegian King, whose war-fleet was soon signalled to have put in at the Orkneys. It seems obvious that a general attack had been prearranged and carefully timed,

---

[1] Ord. Vit. (III, xi) mentions as a determining factor the relationship between William and Tostig through their wives.

[2] Magnus, King of Norway, who had made a succession treaty with Harthacnut, laid formal claim to the English throne in 1045 and an invasion by him was generally expected then. When he died, in 1047, he bequeathed his Kingdom, and his English claim, to his uncle Harold " Hardrada ", St. Olaf's half-brother, who, before 1066, launched several formidable invasions. Queen Ingibiorg's mother was a sister of Harold Hardrada's wife.

[3] *A-S.C.* MS. C, *s.a.* 1066 ; Flor. Worc. I, p. 225.

and that Malcolm Canmore was involved in this War of the English Succession. But he took no part in the actual operations. When the King of Norway arrived in the Tyne,[1] Tostig sailed south with him. On Monday, September 25, both met death and disaster at the hands of Harold Godwineson at Stamfordbridge, near York. On Wednesday at Saint-Valery-sur-Somme the wind changed. On Thursday morning William effected an unopposed landing at Pevensey.

[1] Flor. Worc. I, p. 226.

§ 3

The Norman Conquest and the Royal Marriage

THE Norman conquerors made contact with Scotland by war, and the *casus belli* was Edgar Atheling. On Harold's death any objection which may have been taken to Edgar on the score of youth nine months before suddenly vanished and he found himself supported by certain magnates, notably Archbishop Aldred, who at Cologne had done his best for the Old English House and who (in the continued absence of Stigand, the dubious Archbishop of Canterbury) was prepared to crown Edgar as expeditiously as he had crowned Harold. But support proved disappointing, and Edgar had to make submission. He was received paternally, " because he was a gentle boy and without guile ",[1] and he was probably given lands and allowed some status.[2] Next February he was taken on the triumphal tour round Normandy, with many other Englishmen of importance; among them was Malcolm Canmore's cousin Waltheof, whom Edward had lately provided with an Earldom, comprising the shires of Huntingdon, Northampton, Bedford and Cambridge. At the Thanksgiving Service, Fécamp, Easter 1067, and at the Dedication of Jumièges, July 1, close-cropped, clean-shaven stay-at-homes could feast their eyes on English nobles, half-guests, half-hostages, " youths of the North long-haired, lovely as girls ",[3] and on a glittering display of loot. The Atheling spent nine months in the

[1] Ord. Vit. III, xiv.

[2] " Athelinum . . . post Heraldi ruinam . . . amplis terris ditavit, atque in charissimis habuit eum "—William of Poitiers, p. 148.

[3] " Crinigeros alumnos plagae Aquilonalis ; nec enim puellari venustati cedebant "—William of Poitiers, p. 156. Ord. Vit. borrows part of the phrase.

Duchy. Meanwhile his mother and sisters were under Norman protection, probably generous, possibly at the convent of Romsey or in the city of Winchester, not far away, where Edward's widow Edith basked in the Norman favour.

William had been inured to feudal warfare from early youth and would certainly not have gone home in six months unless he had been satisfied that his Conquest was secure. He left capable lieutenants in charge, notably his half-brother Eude [Odo], Bishop of Bayeux, whom he made Earl of Kent, and impressed on them the necessity of " building castles in appropriate places ".[1] But Kent rose in favour of the mustachio'd Eustace of Boulogne, who, though he was the late English King's brother-in-law, had distinguished himself in command of a Flemish contingent in the invading host. William had to come back in a hurry early in December. Soon afterwards Exeter defied him. He led a mixed force of French and English to the town, captured it and built a " castle ". These events are typical of the times. In spite of his unfortunate associations with Dover, the men of Kent preferred the Count of Boulogne across the water to the Atheling.[2] When William marched on Exeter, Englishmen marched with him, presumably Anglo-Saxon and Anglo-Danish fighting-men with pre-Hastings equipment and training. Resistance remained local, unorganized.

Shortly after Whit Sunday (1068) William learned that Edgar and his relatives had left for the North, where there was a rising in his favour. The Conqueror marched on York and the revolt collapsed. At York he received a deputation from Malcolm Canmore, headed by the Bishop of Durham, Æthelwine, in whose diocese the King of

---

[1] Flor. Worc. II, p. 1.

[2] William of Poitiers, p. 157, maintained that the men of Kent, by choosing Eustace, proved that they had no hatred of " Normans ". The remark shows how little distinction was made between Normans and Flemings.

Scots was the chief layman. The Bishop brought back terms which were accepted.[1] Evidently they did not preclude harbouring of refugees, for Edgar Atheling, with many other Englishmen of note, and probably with his mother and sisters, spent the winter in Scotland.

The Conqueror had been bent on conciliation and his hope had been that Northumbria, or at least that part of it which lay north of the Tees, could be ruled indirectly, through a native Earl. Soon after his Coronation he had appointed one—a friend and doubtless a companion-in-arms of the fallen Tostig, named Copsi, who, without delay and "much to the grief of William and all good Normans", was slain by fellow-Northumbrians.[2] The first Norman Earl, Robert Comin, met a similar fate at Durham on January 28, 1069. An avenging force of Normans was sent, Simeon tells us, but when they reached North Allerton [Northallerton], so great a mist arose that they could go no further and, making inquiries, they learned that the men of that land had a Saint to protect them, and so they returned whence they came.[3] This was the Normans' first acquaintance with St. Cuthbert's power. They had trespassed on his Land, for Northallerton was in Yorkshire only as an enclave and belonged to the Saint, to Durham.[4] The fate of Comin made the Conqueror revert to the idea of a native Earl, and he appointed Malcolm Canmore's cousin Gospatric, who, as grandson of a former Earl and great-grandson of a King of England, had a certain hereditary fitness for the office.[5] But he already ruled in parts of Cumbria

---

[1] Ord. Vit. IV, iv. The complimentary remarks on Scotland and the Scots which are made here in Orderic's text belong to his account of events in 1080: see below, p. 51, n. 2.

[2] William of Poitiers, p. 151. [3] Sim. Durh. *H.D.E.* I, p. 100.

[4] Allertonshire; cp. Islandshire, etc.

[5] Gospatric, son of Maldred, son of Crinan [Crinan was Duncan's father, Malcolm's grandfather], claimed the Earldom as his mother's heir. She was Ealdgyth, daughter of Earl Uchtred and Ælfgifu, daughter of Æthelred II. Sim. Durh. *H.R.* II, p. 199; *Hist. Northd.* VIII, p. 15. After the accession of Duncan I in 1034, Maldred his brother may have ruled for some time in Cumbria. *V.C.H. Cumberland*, II, p. 235.

under King Malcolm, who resented the appointment and hostilities broke out between the cousins.

At some ill-determined stage in these latter events Malcolm met with Margaret. That the meeting was romantic the chroniclers agree, but they are at variance on time, place and circumstance, and sometimes it is difficult to take their details quite seriously. The version favoured by Ailred, and consequently by Fordun and Wyntoun, is that the Atheling and his relatives in despair had taken ship with the intention of returning to Hungary, but a storm arose and the wind blew them on to Scotia's shores, " at the place since called St. Margaret's Hope " [in the Forth, near Rosyth].[1] Gaimar also blames the wind.[2] Simeon gives Wearmouth as the meeting-place, and supplies a lurid background of carnage and flaming churches, and in the harbour calamitous craft bearing high-born fugitives from the Norman wrath.[3] Among these were Edgar Atheling, his mother and his two sisters, " beautiful girls and of Royal descent ", states Simeon, and the fact may not have escaped Malcolm's notice. But wherever their first meeting may have taken place, Malcolm, at Dunfermline, probably towards the end of 1069, married Margaret, Queen Ingibiorg having died at some unrecorded date.[4]

The customary moralizings on this most celebrated of marriages seem unfounded. The Royal Widower (age about thirty-nine) and the Distressed Princess (age about twenty-four) are familiar and pleasing illustrations on the

---

[1] Ailred, *G.R.A.* p. 734 ; Fordun, p. 257.   [2] l. 4658.

[3] The inconsistencies and self-contradictions in " Simeon " are firmly dealt with by the editor of the Surtees text, Sim. Durh. I, Introd. pp. xxix and 86. His views are combated on some points by J. C. Hodgson, *Hist. Northd.* VIII, p. 22, but the evidence for Malcolm's alleged atrocities remains unconvincing.

[4] The date of the marriage is fully discussed by Freeman, *N.C.* IV, pp. 783-789. The fact that Queen Ingibiorg's death is unrecorded aroused his suspicions, but everything that is known of Margaret and her relatives indicates that they had none. The air of vague reproach adopted by the modern historians when referring to Malcolm Canmore seems unnecessary.

page of history, and little is gained by making one of good King Edward's interesting protégés a wild Highland cateran and the other an English martyr. The son of the gracious Duncan had benefited by a lengthy sojourn in the gentler South and may even have been a Northamptonshire country gentleman.[1] He had further benefited by converse with England's sainted King, her courtly Archbishops and the most cosmopolitan of her Earls, not to speak of his own cousin Earl Waltheof, whom Orderic commended as having been "*elegans*". On the testimony of an Old English chronicler Malcolm was a "very sagacious" man,[2] and by all accounts he was a most impassioned wooer and most devoted husband. The bride's mother-tongue was not English and her stay in England was not nearly so long as the bridegroom's. Her intention had been to take the veil—as her sister did, though not till over thirty. Circumstances had altered. Margaret changed her mind. There was, of course, a political side to the marriage, but the dynastic hopes attributed to her or her relatives [3] were in reality slender. So long as her brother Edgar lived no son of Margaret could have any reasonable claim to the English Crown by kinship, and even if Edgar were to die unmarried the claim would only be on the spindle side and remote. As for Scotland, Malcolm Canmore had an able-bodied brother and a son, both of whom could lawfully succeed him on the throne—and did.[4]

But marrying the English claimant's sister looked like espousing his cause, and provision of military aid may indeed have been a condition of the marriage. In the

[1] See Appendix B, p. 387.
[2] *A-S.C.* MS. D, *s.a.* 1067 : " swa he full witter waes ".
[3] According to *A-S.C.* (MS. D), Edgar and his advisers were opposed to the marriage, but felt themselves in Malcolm's power. A few lines of verse follow, to the effect that Margaret was unwilling to marry Malcolm or anyone else, but saw a providential design in the marriage. Giving what purports to be a confidence received from Margaret herself, Turgot, *Vita*, p. 238, says that she yielded to pressure from her relatives.
[4] Donald III [Donald Bane], in 1093, by the Celtic rules of succession ; Duncan II, in 1094, by primogeniture.

spring of 1070 a Scottish invasion of Northumbria took place, but soon dwindled down to the proportions of a raid—a recurrent feature of Scoto-Norman relations. Raids were no new thing. Land-hunger was the prime cause—as of the Norse emigrations and of their sequel, the Norman Conquest. On what became afterwards known as the Border annexation was the larger hope. But it usually proved impracticable because of social and geographical conditions, and the issue narrowed down to one between local landlords rather than between Kings. In 1070 it was further obscured because Gospatric had once again changed sides. He had been reinstated by William as Earl in Northumbria after receiving from Malcolm the lands which afterwards supported the Earldom of Dunbar, a dignity his descendants long enjoyed. Similar complications attended all Malcolm's raids, five in number. It is very doubtful if they were " invasions "—if they extended beyond what he and many others considered the limits of his Kingdom. His right to Southern Cumbria, the land from the Solway to Stainmore,[1] was admitted (till 1091) by the Kings of England, but not always by their Earls, of whom he was either the near relative or else the bosom friend. He was the cousin of Gospatric and Waltheof, and the " sworn brother " of Tostig and of Morel, who was Earl Robert de Montbrai's Sheriff, right-hand man and nephew. Such close personal relationships might have sudden and unexpected consequences. The territorial problems involved were extremely complex and perhaps beyond pacific solution. The strict lines of demarcation between countries which railways and custom-houses have made familiar to us were beyond mediaeval conception. There was always a certain fluidity and nowhere was it greater than in the North of Britain, and never was confusion more confounded than in the years round 1066. He

---

[1] Whether as heir to the rulers of Strathclyde or in virtue of a cession in 945 or by unrecorded conquests of his own.

would have been a bold man who would have said then where Northumbria ended and the Scottish Kingdom began. Northumbria was *ex hypothesi* north of the Humber. But how far north? And how far north-west? Beyond the Tees and the Westmorland Fells there was a vast stretch of debatable land which was to be deemed outside the scope of Domesday. Southern Cumbria, as held by Malcolm, was honeycombed with English settlements.[1] Gospatric ruled alternately or concurrently in Cumbria at Carlisle, in Lothian at Dunbar, in England at Durham. So long as vast indeterminate regions were governed, with extensive local independence, by near kinsmen and " sworn brothers ", many were the reasons which might bring the King of Scots with fire and sword across the Border. One reason was the difficulty of ascertaining precisely where it was. Even in much later and more settled times, the Tweed with its windings never accounted for more than twenty miles of it, from Berwick up to Carham, after which the boundary wandered indefinitely away into the hills. In 1070 culturally the Border was non-existent; ethnographically it was nowhere, for the Anglic population extended from the Humber to the Firth of Forth, the Cymric population from the Severn to the Firth of Clyde.

Wars took the form of raids, for historical, geographical and social reasons. Neither side had a standing army. Lands which were overrun could not be held. With the revolving seasons the occupying forces melted away as the men went back to their families and their fields. In the beggar-my-neighbour tactics the Scots had the less to lose and stood to gain, on balance, by seizure of livestock and transference of population for cheap labour. In Scotland there was land to spare for all. But land without cattle to stock it and labour to work it was valueless; hence the cattle-reiving and the long lines of peasants, men and boys,

---

[1] See Stenton in *Westmorland* and H. W. C. Davis, *Cumberland before the Norman Conquest, E.H.R.* XX (1905), p. 63.

women and girls, led in captivity into a far country, where even Simeon admits that no worse fate awaited them than agricultural employment or domestic service. According to Simeon, though it is unlikely that he had been there to see, in all Scotland there was hardly a home, were it ever so humble, but had its captive English handmaiden.[1] Turgot, with equal simplicity of mind and absence of humour, avers that Margaret maintained a staff of inspectors who went round the country inquiring discreetly into the lot of prisoners and captives, and when hardship or ill-treatment was reported paid their ransom herself and set them free.[2] His word *captivi*, however, excludes handmaidens and he is not discussing prisoners of war below ransom level. Serfs in England remained serfs in Scotland. Their best chance of regaining home, not liberty, was a counter-raid, when they might be brought back with the recaptured or the stolen beeves. Traffic was not one-way. In the matter of devastation, as between Northerners and Southerners, honours were easy.

[1] Sim. Durh. *H.R.* I, p. 192. This provision of domestic help in Scotland is alleged to have been made in 1069 and was not renewed. At the time when Simeon wrote, the efficiency of the scheme must have been impaired by advancing years.

[2] Turgot, *Vita*, IX, p. 247.

§4

The Conqueror at Abernethy

AFTER Malcolm's raid William took no retaliatory action for two years. In 1072, being at length master of England, he determined to clarify the situation in the matter of Edgar Atheling and in that of the Scottish King's feudal relationship to himself. Like Earl Siward (and like King Athelstan of old),[1] he decided on a combined naval and military expedition. Mustering all his resources, he assembled a fleet and, calling on his tenants-in-chief throughout England, even the bishops and abbots, to furnish their " debita militiae obsequia ",[2] he collected a great force, consisting in the main of cavalry.[3] After the Feast of the Assumption (August 15) he set out for Scotland. There are only two military approaches, those known as the West and East Coast routes. The former proceeds from Chester over difficult ground to Carlisle, guarding the western end of the Tyne and Solway isthmus. This stronghold was not in William's kingdom or in his possession. He took the East Coast route. It passes through Durham and thence to the eastern end of the isthmus. He met with no organized opposition in Lothian. Thence the way north runs from the head of the Forth estuary by Stirling to the crossing of the Tay near Perth

[1] " Athelstan went into Scotland with both a land force and a ship force and ravaged a great part of it."—*A-S.C. s.a.* 933. Also, like William, he made gifts to the shrine of St. Cuthbert.

[2] The ecclesiastical *servicia debita* were fixed in 1070. H. M. Chew, p. 3. The writ of summons to Abbot Æthelwig of Evesham is connected by Round with the Scottish expedition. The knights concerned, those of Worcestershire and Staffordshire, were ordered to assemble at Clarendon, near Salisbury, probably because they were to go by sea.

[3] Flor. Worc. II, p. 9.

and, beyond that, to the broad strath between the Grampians and the Sidlaw hills. In the words of the *Chronicle*, " King William lay about the land with ships on the seaside, and himself with the land force went in over the Wath [the Forth] ".[1] Devastating the country so far as possible—which was not very far, for he found little to destroy and nothing worth taking away [2]—he advanced, still unopposed, through Scotland proper, reaching Abernethy, south of the Tay where it is joined by the Earn. He had certainly hoped to engage and defeat the enemy before then, but probably his objective had become Scone and his plan was—like Earl Siward's eighteen years before—a two-pronged attack by land and sea, the ships to be used as a means of penetrating into the interior of the country by the Firth of Tay.[3] These operations, however, proved unnecessary because Malcolm Canmore presented himself at Abernethy and " became his man ".[4] On that undefined condition Malcolm retained his " English possessions ", whatever these may have been,[5] but undertook to send away the Atheling and gave hostages. They included Duncan, a boy of about eleven, the eldest of Malcolm's sons by his first marriage (a sure enough sign that its validity was unquestioned).

Of this remarkable meeting only a meagre account can be gleaned from the sorry fragments of surviving record. We learn that " the barons " of both sides were present, but the only names given are " Guillaume de Percy " and " Edricus Silvaticus ", Edric the Wild. The former had just arrived from the Duchy to settle in Yorkshire, where

[1] *A-S.C.* MS. D, *s.a.* 1073. "Wath", a ford, is also used as the proper name of the river Forth. O.E.D. Cf. *De Situ Albanie* (c. 1165) in *Chron. Picts and Scots*: " that best water which in Scots is called Froch, in British Werid, in French Scottewater, that is the Water of the Scots " ; see also below, p. 56, n. 2.
[2] This appears to be the meaning of an obscure phrase in *A-S.C.*, MSS. D and E, *s.a.* 1073. *Scalachronica* has : " mouoit un grant ost par tere et mere en Escoce, qui grant destrucion en fist ". [3] Skene, I, p. 409.
[4] *A-S.C.* MS. D ; " in loco qui dicitur Abirnithici ", Flor. Worc. II, p. 9. [5] See Appendix B.

his descendants lived for generations before their name became permanently associated with the county of Northumberland. He is of varied interest: as the first Norman " baron " known to have reached Scotland, as the founder of Whitby and as the name-father of all the Algernons (through his cognomen *al grenon* or *aux grenons*, which he shared with King Edward's brother-in-law Eustace of Boulogne and which they owed to their moustaches; in Northern France at the time it was the fashion to be clean-shaven).[1] Edric, so far as his cognomen " Silvaticus " is concerned, might be an English outlaw who had taken to the woods, or might be only a Welshman.[2] He was a little of both, a Herefordshire thegn with a Welsh following, who had put himself beyond the law by conducting guerrillas against Edward's Normans and then against William's. After a heavy defeat at Stafford in 1069, he had recognized the futility of further conflict and made his final submission to the Conqueror, but why he should have accompanied him to Strathearn there is nothing to show.[3] Who Malcolm's " barons " were we cannot even imagine, but if Macduff still lived, his presence would have been appropriate, for he was lay lord of the monastery at Abernethy, Earl of adjacent Fife, and he and his successors had been given, on Malcolm's restoration, the right to lead the King's vanguard in battle.[4] Only the monarchs stand

[1] Guillaume de Percy came to England in 1067 with Hugue d'Avranches, afterwards Earl of Chester, who then obtained Whitby, which Guillaume held under him. *E. Yorks. Ch.* II, p. 154. " Algernon " was revived four hundred years later in the Percy family as a Christian name and transmitted by marriage to other families.

[2] *Silvestris* was used of Welsh people, " Wild Welsh ". Giraud de Barri was " Giraldus Cambrensis alias Silvestris ". " Silvester et montanus " was a common term for a Scottish Highlander; the Sennachy at the Inauguration of Alexander III was so described.

[3] Whether because of his adventurous career or because of his picturesque cognomen, Edric the Wild lived on in popular imagination. He was Lord of Ledbury (Herefordshire), and the story (related by Walter Map, *D.N.C.* II, xi) was that, coming home through the woods one night, he saw fairies dancing and not only fell in love with one of them, but married her and, to satisfy the Conqueror's curiosity, presented her at Court.

[4] See *Early Sanctuaries*, p. lxvii.

out clear—the enterprising yet cautious Norman, the canny and only on occasions perfervid Scot, each as capable as the other of taking a realist view of the situation.

The Conqueror was not conquering, only conducting a punitive or a precautionary or a dynastic expedition, and it must have been for some time painfully apparent that the Scots were a scattered folk, with no chief stronghold on which to retreat, no town in which they must make a last stand. It was a long way from Salisbury to Strathearn and the campaigning season was far advanced. It is unlikely that he wished to seize the Scottish Kingdom, but even if he had had the will, he had not the power. When the greater part of an island has been conquered there is an urge to conquer the rest and, as a definite geographical unit, an island calls for political unity under one government. The appeal of sentiment or symmetry William had the strength to resist, and probably he was strategist enough to see that the physical features of Britain were such as to put complete conquest beyond the bounds of possibility for many years to come. The Welsh could be watched from Shrewsbury and Chester. Subjugation of their country might some day be possible. Meanwhile defence and retaliation seemed enough and individual warriors could take what they could hold. But the problem presented by Scotland was altogether too difficult, if only because of the immense distances and the lie of the land. The invader has on his left flank an ever-increasing expanse of moss and mountain, parallel ridges and long lochs defying penetration, yet providing a safe base for sudden attack and retreat. Unless the great mountain mass is occupied or neutralized, his left flank is exposed, and the further he advances, the more deadly the threat to his ever-lengthening line of communications. The key to the subjugation of Scotland is control of the Highlands—a military truth which Cromwell was the first to realize.[1]

[1] Simpson, *Mar*, p. 57.

But the Roman and the Norman had glimmerings. If strategic reasons stopped William at Abernethy, near the Tay, they were those which at Inchtuthil on that river brought the legions to a halt.[1]

He had not the resources for a conquest. He could hardly keep knights with him for much more than the regulation period of service (forty days). He had not the troops to ravage the land ; the accepted theory of war was that epitomized by a later Scottish monarch's Continental ally : " Primes guaster la terre et puis ses enemis " [2] (" First waste the land, deal after with the foe "). Behind him William had no encampment or fortress to meet his needs for long, no invasion base from which to receive reinforcements and supplies. Durham had no *castel* ; Richmond was only a frontier post ; York was far in the rear, and in country too well devastated by himself in the pitiless Harrying of 1069. Indeed, even Salisbury, Winchester or London could still be only an advanced base. His real base was Rouen. It was his original starting-point, his headquarters, his home, and all sorts of considerations, including the sentimental sort, made him a Conqueror of the home-keeping order, content with such parts of the Island as were readily conquerable from Normandy and could be governed or exploited from there. These coincided with his late cousin's possessions, which geographically were extensive enough to tax the resources of any eleventh-century monarch and could by no exercise of legal ingenuity be held to include Scotland. Probably William's objectives were diplomatic, feudal, dynastic, rather than military, and had been attained. He had arranged for the expulsion of the troublesome Atheling, taught the neighbour monarch a sharp lesson, secured homage, as he

[1] Inchtuthil (a peninsula in the Tay above Kinclaven, some ten miles north of Perth) was the last important Roman camp before the most northerly identified, Auchterless (Aberdeenshire).

[2] Philippe d'Alsace, William the Lion's ally in 1174. Jourdain Fantosme, l. 1680.

understood it, and reasserted as Edward's successor the dim old English claim to overlordship of all Britain. He was more interested in the Duchy, where his presence was much more urgently required.

The King of Scots could also see things as they were. We may be certain that he did not attend at Abernethy till he had made sure that his presence would be welcome and his person safe. The place of meeting was appropriate. It was an ancient residence of kings, bishops and abbots, and there were priests or Culdees at the Round Tower,[1] men of religion who could receive envoys from either side, transmit a formal request for negotiations and obtain full guarantees. On Malcolm's side, time and place seemed suitable for parley. He was an experienced soldier and knew as well as William that in a set encounter irresponsible spearmen on ponies were no match for disciplined cavalry. He could, however, pride himself on having discovered the correct strategic method of dealing with invasions from the South. It became the national practice and consisted of keeping out of harm's way till the accumulating difficulties of time and distance, climate and supplies, brought the invaders to a halt and to thoughts of compromise and dignified retreat. He was not committing himself to much by becoming William's " man ". Homage, the Norman term, was a sacred act. At a solemn ceremony, promises were given, the breaking of which incurred moral reprobation. But much depended on the implications of the act, and at Abernethy they were necessarily vague.[2] As for hostages, Malcolm must have been sorry to see young Duncan go. But departure from home at an early age was normal. In Celtic Scotland it was the regular practice for chieftains to send their sons to be brought up

[1] Abernethy and Brechin possess round towers. They represent a purely Irish type of ecclesiastical architecture. They are thought to have been used for storing treasure. The Abernethy tower (72 ft. in height, internal diameter 8 ft. 2 ins.) may date from the middle of the eighth century. See McGibbon and Ross, I, p. 27.   [2] See Appendix B.

34

in the household of other chieftains and perhaps it was somewhat in this way that Donald Bane, thirty years before, had been sent to the Isles.[1] The thought that a son was in enemy hands or ex-enemy hands never weighed unduly in the councils of mediaeval rulers. They paid heavily for his maintenance and instruction, and hoped for the best. The best was of frequent occurrence. When Malcolm, six years later, contravened the Abernethy convention the sins of the father were not visited on Duncan. Theoretically, hostages reinforced the sanctity of treaties. In practice, their bargaining or minatory value lasted a year or two and then diminished rapidly. After fifteen years Duncan came home well Normanized. Hostages made friends.

Realities probably clear enough to both parties in 1072 have become clearer to us since 1940. " Armaments ", prepared long beforehand and in full view of the victims, won the day at Hastings and in all the operations leading up to Abernethy. Edward was always well abreast of affairs on the Continent; Harold was a frequent visitor. Five invasions—from France, Flanders, Scotland, Norway and Denmark—had long been considered probable, and from the death of Edward, imminent. Yet adequate defence measures had not been taken. Harold's hasty improvisations succeeded brilliantly at Stamfordbridge, where the Norwegians were caught unawares and, moreover, are said to have left their coats of mail behind in their river-boats, " because of the warm weather ".[2] But when he arrived at Hastings with admirable promptness and engaged too promptly not a Scandinavian, but a really "Continental " army, the composition and the equipment of his force were fifty years behind the times. Obsolete weapons

---

[1] On the important place of fosterage in the social life of Ireland and Scotland, and the elaborate rules, *e.g.* for clothes and food for sons of chiefs, see Cameron, *Celtic Law*, p. 62; on the similar practice in Wales, see J. E. Lloyd, I, p. 310.

[2] *Agrip af Norégs Konúnga-sögun*, in Anderson, *E.S.Sc.* II, p. 14.

imposed out-of-date strategy and tactics. He was defeated by superior "armaments"—trained archers and cavalry—and by the skilful handling of both which came from long experience. The English used the bow for the purposes of the chase, the Normans for the purposes of war. These implied discipline, drill, special practice. The English used the horse for the conveyance of men or goods —ploughing was the province of the ox—and for the rapid transport of the host from place to place. They did battle on foot. A thegn might ride to the field, but there he must dismount and with the two-handed axe fight upon the ground which it was his sacred duty to defend.[1] This, the oldest of insular prejudices, precluded the creation of the trained cavalry which was regularly used in Normandy and the adjacent states half a century before Harold, fighting on foot, and commanding an army with few archers and fewer horsemen, was shot through the eye by a Norman shaft.

The Conquest was consolidated by means of the *castel* or "castle". At Pevensey, carpenters and smiths had waded ashore, carrying the tools of their trade; the necessary timber—the beams and the planks with holes in the proper places for bolts and hinges—was landed with a D-day promptness and efficiency and before evening the "pre-fabricated" fort stood complete.[2] It is depicted in the Bayeux Tapestry and entitled a *castellum*. In the districts overrun, this rudimentary device—a ditch, an earthen mound from the upcast, palisades and wooden defence works—was immediately employed. It required little expenditure of time or money. The main thing was to capture a sufficient number of rustics and make them dig. Such improvised wooden forts served to consolidate a Conquest which had been made for want of them on the other side. A commander operating from a larger "castle", built on a still modest and inexpensive scale,

[1] D. C. Douglas, *Norman Conquest*, p. 4.
[2] Wace, *Rou*, II, ll. 6490-6550.

36

could hold a wide tract of subjugated country with a handful of mounted troops. As Orderic observed, the English were conquered because they had too few of those " fortifications which the French call *castella* ". More precisely, they were overthrown in a single engagement by means of archers and cavalry, and then held down by means of " castles " which they could have made for themselves and which were not to be captured by men on horseback.

The methods of warfare so successfully employed by the Normans from Hastings to Abernethy were not of their own devising. They knew, but no better than their Continental neighbours, the uses of the sword and the hauberk, and the fact that well-trained men-at-arms, riding horses also well trained—for otherwise they would have turned tail in the din of the battlefield—could ensure initial victory over an enemy superior in numbers and the rapid occupation of his country. It was in horse-craft that the Normans excelled. Their superiority in this, perhaps slight in France, proved decisive. The rich pastures of the Seine valley produced, with selective breeding, nobler steeds than England could rear or could withstand.

In Scotland the Normans were at a still greater advantage, immediate and permanent, on all these points, except that their *castel* system was not, and could not be for many years, extended far enough north to be militarily effective. In a pitched battle the chances would have been heavily in their favour. But time and distance were against them and victory in the field could hardly have led to military occupation. Even for the purposes of a rapid incursion they had difficulty in bringing their " armaments " to bear so far north, in solving a hard problem of logistics. They had naval power, rarely a Scottish achievement. The shipping which (as illustrated in the Tapestry) could transport men and horses to Pevensey over seventy miles of water in one voyage, and had since been much increased from English harbours, could take them coastwise from the Channel to the Firth of Tay. But it was an arduous and a perilous enterprise. The overland route was hardly less trying for troops on the march. For the moment all was well. William had taken great risks. But he had arrived, his ships were in the Tay, his horsemen and archers at Abernethy, and a peace treaty had been arranged. There must have been a day of splendour, with a cavalry display, a glitter of shields and mail-armour, and a moment of triumph when the King of Scots knelt bare-headed, put his hands in his lord's hands and became " his man ". It was a remarkable feat of naval and military organization that William had performed, but it was one which could rarely be repeated and from which little benefit could accrue. He was aware of this and his terms were easy. To arrive had been difficult; to stay was impossible. His ponderous expedition after all was only a raid.

§ 5

Invasions through Durham

THE raid had not lasted long. The Conqueror was at Durham again by November 2. On the way north he had beheld " the White Church with the two stone towers standing high into the air, the one continuing the choir, the other at the west end, which were of wondrous size ".[1] Entering with great devotion, he had " heard from its priests how Bishop Aidan had come from Scotland and established his see at Lindisfarne and how Cuthbert, at the instance of King Ecgfrith, had reluctantly left the life of a solitary to become a Bishop ". . . . William " gave one gold mark and a costly *pallium* to St. Cuthbert the Confessor ", confirmed the grants of former kings and " made the gift of Waltham to Durham and to Bishop Walcher ".[2]

Waltham Abbey was a pre-Conquest foundation, by Harold, and some of its first occupants were Lotharingians. Walcher, successor to Æthelwine,[3] was also a Lotharingian. When he was consecrated at Winchester the widowed Lady Edith, on whom Edward's prophetic powers were thought to have devolved, had felt impelled by his commanding figure, snow-white hair and ruddy countenance to exclaim

[1] The Church, consecrated in 999, is thus described by Reg. Durh. XVI, p. 29—" as they that saw it have told us ".

[2] *Cronica Monasterii Dunelmensis* (1072 × 1083) in the *Red Book of Durham*, ed. H. H. E. Craster, *E.H.R.* XL (1925), pp. 504-532. William afterwards enriched the Church of Durham with many further gifts. Sim. Durh. *H.D.E.* I, p. 100. " Ego Willelmus Dei gratia rex Anglorum hereditario jure factus " is the donor of much land, in the *Liber Vitae*, p. 76.

[3] Æthelwine, the only Bishop known to have resolutely resisted the Conquest (which, however, he had at first approved), was outlawed and driven from his see. He died in monastic custody at Abingdon. Roger of Wendover, II, p. 7.

39

that he " would make a lovely martyr ".[1] This perhaps
ill-considered remark proved to be true, though not immediately. William, however, took his precautions. He
gave orders for a castle to be built upon the Rock of
Durham as a protection against eventual attack, not only
from Scotland, but from nearer, and as a stronghold from
which the first " Norman " Bishop could administer a sullen
diocese. Then William addressed himself to the problem
of St. Cuthbert. The Normans were at first sceptical about
English saints, finding it hard to believe that there could
be quite so many and having difficulty in associating
sanctity with names which were unknown to the Christian
world as a whole and seemed to them uncouth and improbable. The sainthood of Cuthbert, however, was not
in doubt; it stood recorded in Bede.[2] All it can have
seemed desirable to ascertain was whether the relics of the
Saint, which had been removed by Bishop Æthelwine in
the turmoil of the Conquest, had been restored to the
tomb, and for that purpose William went to the church,
accompanied by bishops and abbots. But his inquiry was
suspended, and his departure much hastened, by a supernatural and peremptory warning—to go at once and not cease
spurring his steed till he had crossed the Tees,[3]—till he had
quitted the Diocese of Durham, bounded in the south by
the Tees. In the north it was bounded by Jedburgh and
Melrose and the warning could have been delivered there.

What William was told at Durham was in part a Scottish
story. Four centuries had gone by since Cuthbert, " feed-
ing with other shepherds his master's flocks near the river

---

[1] " Pulchrum hic martyrem habemus "—Wm. Malm. II, p. 331.

[2] Papal canonization was then a very recent use. The first known case
is in 993, when John XV canonized Ulric of Augsburg. Kemp, p. 14. In-
corruption was one of the signs of sainthood. Bede, *Hist. Eccles.* I, p. 14,
states that the body of Cuthbert was found uncorrupted when being translated on March 20, 698.

[3] *Chron. Melrose, s.a.* 1072. William's presence at Durham is authenti-
cated on November 2. Davis, *Regesta*, Introd. p. xxii. The story of his
visit to the tomb is given by Sim. Durh. *H.D.E.* I, p. 106.

which is called the Leader ", saw a vision of St. Aidan and heard the call to the religious life. It did not at first take him very far, only to where the Leader falls into the Tweed, only to Melrose, a daughter-house of the monastery which the Celtic Saint had lately founded at Lindisfarne from Iona.[1] Succeeding as Prior Boisil (whose name lives in the adjacent St. Boswells), Cuthbert carried the Gospel through Lothian and Cumbria. His transference to Lindisfarne took place as the result of the Synod of Whitby. The Teutons in Northumbria had received Christianity from two opposite quarters : the mission brought from Rome to Kent by St. Augustine in the year of St. Columba's death (597) and the mission brought by St. Aidan in 635 from the little island off the west coast of Mull where it might have been thought that there would never be anything of more interest than the ocean waves, the white sands and the seagulls. When in 664 the Synod of Whitby recorded its decision against Celtic custom as regards tonsure and the date of Easter, most of the monks at Lindisfarne returned to Iona. Cuthbert joined the remainder as Prior. When he became Bishop of Lindisfarne, Ecgfrith, King of Northumbria, made him an extensive grant of land, to which through the centuries more was added, till at length the *Terra Sancti Cuthberti* comprised nearly the whole district from the Tees to the Tyne.

The *Terra* belonged in men's minds not to " St. Cuthbert's Bishop ", whose see was moved from Lindisfarne by many stages to be finally fixed at Durham in 995, but to the Saint himself and to him gifts of land were made in person. He had outlying properties further north, notably Coldingham, Tyningham, Jedburgh and Melrose. The control exercised in Lothian by St. Cuthbert's Bishop may have been slight ; nevertheless portions of his diocese

[1] In 635 Melrose lay on the regular route between the two island monasteries. It was not a difficult journey, up the Tweed into Strathclyde and thence to Dumbarton. For the rest, see O. G. S. Crawford, *Arthur and his Battles*, p. 282, n. 10.

lay within the Scottish Kingdom. Now he was a Norman, and a Norman connection with Scotland through Durham was established which was to be rich in consequences. Where the Conqueror passed the Norman Prelate was never far behind. Before William set forth for Scotland the relationship between his two Archbishops had been settled after much argument.[1] By a "General Council" and with Papal sanction York was definitely subordinated to Canterbury and the Northern Province defined as extending from the Humber to the ends of Scotland, with Durham as a suffragan see. The hope was then expressed that Scotland would in due course provide other sees and, though Archbishop Thomas I of York afterwards remarked ruefully that none were ever forthcoming, meantime Bishop Walcher may have cherished the hope. The Normans regarded the Church in England as lacking in vigour, its organization as incoherent and religious life as standing in need of reform, particularly by means of closer approximation to the monastic ideal. Reform was in progress, approved by the Pope and zealously furthered by the Conqueror, and doubtless Bishop Walcher thought that it might well be continued into Scotland; the next Norman visitation of Scotland, in 1074, was by a Benedictine mission from Durham.

The prime mover, though he never reached Scotland himself, was one of the Conqueror's knights, Reinfrid by name. While taking part in the Harrying of 1069 or perhaps when on a visit to his son Foulque, who was Guillaume de Percy's Dapifer,[2] Reinfrid had stood upon

[1] One of the Canterbury arguments was that as the Scots and the Danes were wont to come in ships to York, there was a risk of one of their leaders being made King by an independent Archbishop aided by the Northumbrians, "fickle and treacherous folk": "a provinciae illius indigenis mobilibus et perfidis"—Hugh the Cantor, in Raine, *Hist. Ch. York*, I, p. 99.
[2] "Fulco dapifer filius prioris de Wyteby", *i.e.* Reinfrid. *E. Yorks. Ch.* II, No. 859. At the Survey, Foulque held of Osberne d'Arches two carucates of land in Toulston which he afterwards (1100 × 1116) gave to the Abbey of Whitby. *E. Yorks. Ch.* I, Nos. 529 and 530. He held of Guillaume de Percy several manors in Yorkshire, *V.C.H. Yorks*. II, pp. 169 and 182.

the headland at Whitby and meditated on the ruins of St. Hilda's monastery, which had been destroyed two hundred years before by Danes. In consequence of his meditations among ruins in Yorkshire, ancient or still reeking, he forsook the profession of arms, probably in 1070, and became a monk in the Benedictine Abbey of Evesham in Worcestershire. The Abbot, Æthelwig, knew the northern Archdiocese well.[1] He told Reinfrid what he could of monastic history in Northumbria and referred him for further detail to a local authority, an English monk, Aldwin [Ealdwine], in the Priory of Winchcombe a few miles away. Quite unlettered,[2] Reinfrid listened eagerly to the discourse of Aldwin, whose favourite author was Bede the Venerable and who, from much reading in the beloved *Historia*, had acquired a passionate interest in the once-glorious culture of the Northumbrians and in their long-abandoned shrines : York, Whitby, Wearmouth, Jarrow, Hexham and Melrose. Reinfrid made a high resolve. He would relight the Lamps of the North. With the missionary zeal of an elderly novice and the resourcefulness of an old campaigner he set about organizing an expedition. The Abbot had been one of the earliest English prelates to accept the Conquest ;[3] he employed his interest with the Norman Earls and Sheriffs to smooth the path for Reinfrid and Aldwin. They started for York on foot, having with them only such service-books as could be carried on the back of an ass, but it was not into an entirely hostile world that they ventured forth. At York they were welcomed by the Sheriff, Hugue, son of Baudri [Baldric], a personal friend of William's who had been giving him invaluable help in his work of monastic restora-

---

[1] After becoming Archbishop of York, Aldred retained the see of Worcester till 1062. Till then Æthelwig acted as his commissary.

[2] Sim. Durh. *H.D.E.* I, p. 109. Simeon is the chief authority on Reinfrid's mission.

[3] In a remarkably short space of time after Hastings Æthelwig was exercising the authority of a Royal justice over most of the Midlands. See R. R. Darlington, *Æthelwig, Abbot of Evesham, E.H.R.* XLVIII (1933), pp. 1-22 and 177-198.

tion at Selby. The Sheriff sent them on to Earl Waltheof and Bishop Walcher, then working harmoniously together under the new dispensation. With their aid, Reinfrid and Aldwin refounded the ruined monastery at Jarrow, where the immortal *Historia* was written by the Northumbrian monk whose death in 735 St. Boniface had likened to the extinction of a brightly burning light.

Other enthusiasts, French and English, hastened to Jarrow from the South. One of the first to arrive came only from Durham. He was Margaret's future biographer. His name, Turgot, is Danish—which in no wise prevents Simeon's Continuator from describing him as " coming of a good English family ",[1] apparently settled in Lincolnshire, in the Danelaw. When the Normans came Turgot was detained as a hostage at Lincoln, but escaped to Norway, where he spent several years as teacher of psalmody to Harold Hardrada's son, King Olaf. On returning from Norway he had gone to Durham and been well received by Bishop Walcher, on whose advice he proceeded to Jarrow and exchanged " the costume of a clerk for the monastic habit ".[2] But there were other shrines awaiting restoration. Reinfrid departed for Whitby,[3] and there, with the help of Guillaume de Percy, refounded St. Hilda's monastery. Aldwin and Turgot, fortified by the blessing of the Conqueror's Bishop and accompanied by the prayers of the Conqueror's Knight, took their way towards Melrose.

But there they had difficulties with Malcolm Canmore. Their status cannot have been clear. There was room for doubt on the relation in which they stood, or would

---

[1] Sim. Durh. *H.R.* II, p. 202. The name, more correctly " Thurgot " (Old Norse Þorgautr, Old Danish Thorgot), is found T.R.E. chiefly in Yorkshire and Lincolnshire. Feilitzen, p. 393. A " Turgotus " figures prominently in the Lincolnshire Domesday, p. 13. Another, or perhaps the same, who held T.R.E. manors in Yorkshire, was the " lageman " of Lincoln. *V.C.H. Yorks.* II, p. 145. There is a " Torgot " in the signa to a notification (regn. Henry I) of a grant to the brethren at Burwell (Lincolnshire). Round, *Cal.* I, p. 448.

[2] Sim. Durh. *H.D.E.* I, p. 111.   [3] *Chron. Melrose, s.a.* 1074.

stand, to St. Cuthbert's Bishop, to the Bishop at St. Andrews and to the King of Scots. The Benedictines had come to York and Durham with the approval of the spiritual and the lay authorities; all who had welcomed them, archbishop, bishop, sheriff, magnates, were personal friends of the Norman King, and in the matter of monastic restoration were following his example. To Melrose Turgot and Aldwin came uninvited, and the church there was under the jurisdiction of Durham. So soon after Abernethy, the moment was ill chosen. King Malcolm failed to see eye to eye with them on the true relation of spiritual to temporal authority and on property rights at Melrose, and, after much correspondence had passed, came and turned them off his land, even adding insult to injury.[1] In this outburst, suggestive of an irascible laird with military antecedents and vocabulary, the personal element no doubt played its accustomed part. To judge from Turgot's extant literary manifestations, he was not endowed with much tact and his epistolary style may have jarred on the potentate at Dunfermline, never the meekest of men or the most even-tempered. Turgot and Aldwin were recalled by Bishop Walcher and went sorrowfully back to Durham.

In Normandy monasticism, purely religious at first, was fostered by the Dukes (for a time by them only) and had been brought into the feudal system. In England it was one means among many of conquest, appeasement and reconciliation. In their efforts towards monastic restoration the Conqueror and his fellow-workers, clerical and lay, were seconded, perhaps prompted, by individual enthusiasts such as Reinfrid, but what was decisive was official action. As a direct result of the Conquest Benedictine monasteries were refounded in Northumbria. In Scotland the Bene-

---

[1] " Graves ab illo [Malcolmo, ad quem iste locus pertinebat] injurias et persecutiones pertulerunt, pro eo quod Evangelicum praeceptum servantes, jurare illi fidelitatem noluerunt."—Sim. Durh. *H.D.E.* I, p. 112.

dictine mission under Norman auspices had failed. Failure, however, was only temporary. The way was prepared for the monastic restorations in South Scotland at Coldingham and Jedburgh, and for the foundation of the Priory at Dunfermline, where meantime Malcolm and Margaret proceeded with the building of their church,[1] " in honour of the Holy Trinity ".[2]

The following invasion, not till 1080 and only in appearance military, also originated in the diocese of Durham. It was led by the Conqueror's eldest son Robert, bosom friend of Edgar Atheling. In accordance with the terms of the Abernethy convention Edgar had withdrawn to Flanders, but he returned to Scotland in July 1074. He then received a letter from the King of France, offering him the Castle at Montreuil, " so that he could thereafter do evil daily to his enemies ".[3] Philip I, as a boy, had had small satisfaction in seeing his Norman vassal become a king like himself, and he had his own reasons for offering to establish the English claimant on the Norman border at the little port wedged in between the Duchy and Flanders which was the sole Capetian exit to the sea. Edgar accepted the offer. The Queen of Scots consoled her departing brother " and all his men " with rich gifts and strange and precious furs—" skins covered with purple, fur-robes of marten and miniver and ermine, and fine raiment and golden vessels and silvern ".[4] The King made lavish provisions for his comfort and Edgar sailed for France. Shortly afterwards he reappeared in evil case. He had suffered shipwreck and lost his all.

---

[1] Turgot speaks of the church as having been built by Margaret, " in the place of her marriage " and shortly after.
[2] The Church of Dunfermline was endowed by Malcolm and Margaret with lands on both sides of the Forth, enumerated in David's Great Charter of Dunfermline, *c.* 1150. Lawrie, L. It was not a monastery when Turgot wrote his *Vita, c.* 1106, but in 1120 Eadmer, *H.N.* p. 279, refers to a Prior of Dunfermline. [3] *A-S.C.* MS. D, *s.a.* 1075.
[4] " Scynnan mid pælle betogen ", etc., *i.e.* fur-lined purple (cloth), *A-S.C.* MS. D, *s.a.* 1075.

The luckless Atheling then took his brother-in-law's sage advice and sent word to the Conqueror, absent in Normandy as usual, that he was willing to consider terms. William, too, was willing and this time things were better arranged. Edgar was fitted out well-nigh as sumptuously as before, but not again exposed to the perils of the North Sea. He was met at Durham by the Sheriff of York who had been so helpful to Reinfrid and Aldwin and who conducted him all the way to Normandy.[1] Edgar made his peace with the Conqueror and was granted considerable estates and a comfortable pension : one pound silver per day.[2] It was not long before the *Adelin* acquired celebrity as a conversationalist, his chief admirer being the Conqueror's eldest son Robert, a young man of about his own age and almost as good a talker. Edgar's conversational successes were certainly not achieved in the graver subjects, nor in broken French. He had already enjoyed ample opportunities for learning the language of the Normans and appreciating their many qualities. Eight years after Hastings, the "handsome, well-spoken, unmartial" Atheling bowed to the inevitable, gracefully, and became a Norman himself. The

---

[1] *A-S.C.* MSS. D and E, *s.a.* 1075.

[2] As regards the settlement of Edgar in England there is no trace of any provision made by King Edward for his nephew Edward the Exile or for the Exile's widow and children. If, as stated by William of Poitiers, Edgar obtained " large possessions " from the Conqueror after Hastings they were no doubt confiscated in 1068 and returned in 1074, at least in part. In Domesday " Edgar Adeling " holds in Barkway and Goduin holds of Edgar 1½ hides. The same Goduin holds Hormead of Edgar, assessed at 6 hides and 3 virgates. *V.C.H. Hertfordshire*, I, p. 341. Edgar's Hertfordshire property is the only one recorded, but it would be natural that his territorial compensation in England should be greater than his sister Christina's, which (see below, p. 75, n. 1) was very considerable. In the Pipe Roll (vol. I, p. 15) of Henry II, in the fifth year of his reign, under the Northumberland account, " Edgar Aed'eling " renders an account of 10 marks which he paid to the Treasury. The entry, kept inadvertently on the books, may be a belated sign of former possession of land in Northumberland. His extreme ubiquity may indicate, among other things, scattered estates. Edgar's mother Agatha lived in Scotland for some time. She is said, in *Scalachronica*, to have died in a convent in England—Romsey, in Forbes, *Kal.* p. 300. No doubt in 1074 a general family settlement was arranged.

Conqueror " treated him like one of his own sons. Robert loved him like a foster-brother." [1]

Both young men had a strange destiny, of which perhaps the strangest part was their long connection with Scotland. Both made history by the mere fact of their existence and their loss of what the plain man considered their birthright. They had admirable gifts—personal courage, charm, generosity. The charge the historians bring against them is that of not being sufficiently serious-minded, of failing to play the historic role appropriate to the mighty William's first-born and the last of England's ancient line. Perhaps neither young man quite saw himself in this light. Robert may have received too little paternal encouragement. " Short-boots ", " Courte-Heuse ", went through life under that nickname because his father, an austere man who joked with difficulty, once drew attention to the fact that, Robert being very short and very stout, his long-boots were of consequent, yet somehow unexpected, brevity.[2] But in Robert heaviness of body was accompanied by lightness of heart and mind. " Loquax ", Orderic calls him, but credits him with an eloquent tongue, " lingua diserta ", the same phrase as he uses of Edgar. When the Conqueror refused Robert a share in the government, even of Maine, where he was Comte in his own right,[3] war broke out between father and son. Semi-burlesque episodes ensued. Early in 1079, when besieged at Gerberoy in the Beauvaisis, beyond the Norman border, Robert made a successful

---

[1] " Corpore speciosus, lingua diserta, liberalis et generosus, utpote Eduardi regis Hunorum filius, sed dextera segnis erat, ducemque sibi coaevum et quasi collactaneum fratrem diligebat."—Ord. Vit. X, xi ; cp. III, xiv.

[2] " Corpore brevis et grossus, ideoque Brevis-Ocrea a patre est cognominatus."—Ord. Vit. VIII, i. Orderic adds (IV, xix) " Curta Ocrea ", and (X, iv) " *Gambaron* " = Short-legged. Cp. :

> " Petiz fu mult, mais mult fu gros,
> Iambes out cortes, gros les os ".
> —Wace, *Rou*, II, ll. 9369-9370.

[3] By treaty, as intended husband of Marguerite (see above, p. 11, n. 1) whose brother Herbert II had died childless in 1062. Robert in his youth was regularly styled Comte du Maine.

sortie, wounded his father in the arm [1] with a spear and drove him off the field, stripped of much of his military reputation. Severely pricked in body and in conscience, William entered on the paths of reconciliation and when, in the late summer of 1080, after three years' absence, he came over to England, he brought with him his repentant son and, for the first time, entrusted him with an important enterprise—an invasion of Scotland, which had been judged necessary because of untoward happenings in the diocese of Durham.

Feudal agreements were like twentieth-century international treaties: they were valid so long as they could be enforced. The Abernethy agreement had lasted till the preceding August. William being then engaged in military and diplomatic activities against his eldest son and having seemingly left England for ever, Malcolm, perhaps for that reason, made another (his third) raid into Northumbria, as far as the Tyne. The Conqueror, unhappy as always in his dealings with the North, had made the Bishop Earl in succession to the fallen Waltheof.[2] To combine both offices in one person was feasible in Walcher's native city of Liège and theoretically suitable to the needs of a hill-fortress like Durham. But Walcher, though a good bishop, proved a bad earl. He became the object of bitter animosity, as head of a French military household whose violence he failed to control, and as uncle of a French firebrand named Gilbert whose services as Vicomte or Sheriff he unwisely employed. On May 14 (1080), coming out of the church at Gateshead after a meeting of notables, the Earl-Bishop was done to death by an infuriated crowd. The customary punitive measure, the harrying of the district, was carried out by the Conqueror's half-brother Eude [Odo], Bishop of Bayeux. This double discharge of extra-episcopal duties in the Land of St. Cuthbert left

[1] Flor. Worc. II, p. 13 : " in the hand ". *A-S.C.* MS. D, *s.a.* 1079.
[2] For the fall of Waltheof see below, pp. 137-138.

disturbed conditions, and further Scottish intervention was to be expected. The purpose of Robert's expedition was to give both Northumbrians and Scots a sharp warning and to provide an opportunity for conciliation. His mission was not primarily a military one. Spiritual as well as temporal magnates went with him.

His march into Lothian was a demonstration in force rather than an invasion. Malcolm applied his strategic defence method. He avoided combat and, after reaching Falkirk, Robert desisted. " He offered the Scots peace or war—peace if they made submission, otherwise, war." [1] They chose peace. Robert found their King a congenial spirit and, to show appreciation, stood godfather to his infant daughter, the future " good Queen Maud ". The Abernethy convention was renewed. Hostages were again given, and no doubt joined Duncan in Normandy. Scottish Cumbria is said to have been defined as extending to the Cross on Stainmore [2]—the old Kingdom of Strathclyde's southern limit, accepted by William as his northern limit. Probably the sixteenth-century William Stewart, who was no poet, translating into verse Hector Boece, who was no historian, was expressing at least ancient tradition when he wrote that the matter of frontier delimitation was referred to " William Bastard ", who agreed—

> That all the land fra Stanemure inwart la
> North onto Tueid, without ony ganestand,
> All Cumbria and also Westmureland,
> This King Malcolme suld half in peax and rest
> For euirmoir withoutin ony molest.
> —*Bk. Cron. Scot.* ll. 41,974-41, 978.

[1] *Chron. Mon. de Abingdon*, II, p. 9.
[2] Five miles north-east of Kirkby Stephen, near the junction of the counties of Cumberland, Westmorland, Northumberland and Durham, on the Roman road over the Pennines. The Cross, more probably a tenth-century pagan grave monument, stood at the summit of the pass. It was re-erected in 1887. It was long known as the Rere Cross because it was said to have borne the effigies of the Kings of England and Scotland, each symbolically, and wisely looking back on his own territory.

" Molest " errs on the side of optimism, the Cross on Stainmore being within two days' ride of York and unlikely to prove acceptable to the Normans as a permanent boundary post. But a friendly tone marked the proceedings in 1080. Simeon is not altogether pleased. " No business was done ", he says dryly, which may mean that vengeance was not exacted for depredations in the Land of St. Cuthbert.[1] But Orderic has a good word to say of Malcolm Canmore —and of the Scots in general : " though they are fierce in battle, yet they love ease and quiet, decline to let themselves be troubled by neighbouring kingdoms, and are given to the practice of the Christian religion rather than of arms ".[2] On the return march, however, Robert took the precaution of founding a " New Castle " on the Tyne. It was a frontier fortress. The choice of site, admirable in itself, was a tacit admission that the Scottish Kingdom extended to the Tyne. The " New Castle " defended what lay behind, but left as a debatable land in front the fifty miles of country to the Tweed.

[1] Sim. Durh. *H.R.* p. 211.
[2] Ord. Vit. IV, iv—Orderic's sheets, probably never very well arranged, must have become displaced here. His complimentary remarks follow on from the statement that Malcolm " pacem bello praeposuit ". This refers to the events of 1080 and not to his early negotiations with the Conqueror at York, where Orderic ended his brief account with the words: " pro Malcomo rege Scotorum [Praesul Dunelmi] pacis mediator intervenit et acceptas conditiones in Scotiam detulit ".

§6

Rufus and Scotland

Ten years elapsed before another Norman invasion took place. It arose from the irregular accession of Rufus. Contributory causes were the Bishop of Durham and Edgar Atheling.

Walcher's successor was a native of Bayeux, a Benedictine, Guillaume " de Saint-Carilef ".[1] He adopted Walcher's scheme of building a cloister at Durham and, having gone to consult the Pope (Gregory VII) on the project, obtained authority for removing the secular clergy (who lived in the world *in saeculo*, and who could marry and usually did) to make room for regulars (who lived by Rule and were cloistered). Thomas, Archbishop of York, issued a rescript (in which he stated that he himself had spent a night by the tomb of St. Cuthbert and had had a vision and was healed).[2] The seculars were given the choice of remaining as monks, or departing. All save one departed. With Bishop Walcher's help Aldwin and Turgot at Jarrow had restored the twin monastery of Wearmouth, reuniting the two religious houses, only seven miles apart, between which Bede the Venerable distributed all the days of his life. In 1083 the little community, housed partly at Jarrow and partly at Wearmouth — only twenty-three monks in all, several of them French—moved into the new buildings at Durham. Aldwin was the first Prior.

[1] Bishop William I had been Prior of Saint-Carilef, now Saint-Calais (Maine), and Abbot of Saint-Vincent-du-Mans, but the name of his first charge clung to him ; see above, p. xxiv. He was appointed to Durham, November 5, 1080, and consecrated January 3, 1081.

[2] " Canonicos de ecclesia amovere et monachos substituere ", etc.— Thomas, *Epistola ad Archiepiscopos et Episcopos*, in Migne, *P.L.* clv, p. 1627.

When he died, on April 12, 1087, he was succeeded by Turgot.

The Conqueror died in the same year, on September 9. His eldest son Robert, after returning from Lothian, had quarrelled with him again and had fallen on evil days. They were passed in obscure and aimless wanderings which took him as far as Italy. The dying Conqueror, who had apparently made no provision for his sons in England,[1] was with difficulty dissuaded from denying Robert his right to be Duke. In flagrant contradiction of his much-repeated claim to rule as Edward's lawful heir, which logically carried with it the succession of his own next of kin, namely Robert, he designated as his successor in England his second surviving son, Guillaume le Roux [William Rufus], who hastened across to England without waiting for the end, and was crowned seventeen days after his father's death. Meantime the wanderer had appeared from nowhere and been acclaimed as Duke. His first official act was performed for the benefit of Scotland, a country for which the " soft Duke ", as he was all too soon to be called, had evidently a soft spot.[2] The Conqueror had decided, by way of death-bed repentance, that his hostages should be set free. Among them was Malcolm's eldest son Duncan, then completing his fifteenth year of exile. Robert had a gift for doing things with a noble and a chivalrous air, and he carried out his father's last injunctions in the grand manner : he not only granted Duncan his liberty, but knighted him there and then. The accession of a younger son naturally had grave consequences. It caused a revolt among the barons " in favour of Robert ",[3] and it nullified the homage which Malcolm Canmore had

---

[1] " It is remarkable that not a single manor in any part of England or even the smallest portion of land is put down in the Survey as belonging to any of the Conqueror's sons."—Sir Henry Ellis, *A General Introduction to Domesday Book*, 1833, p. 32.

[2] " Omnes ducem Rodbertum mollem esse cognoscebant."—Ord. Vit. VIII, i.   [3] Flor. Worc. II, pp. 21-22.

sworn to the King of England and, by implication if not by more, to his eldest son. The latter difficulty might have been amicably settled if Robert and Rufus had not dealt as they did with Edgar Atheling and the Bishop of Durham.

Edgar, like Robert, had perceived the advantages of Italy in William's declining and none too pleasant years, and in April 1086 obtained his permission to sail for Apulia with two hundred knights.[1] Returning to Normandy on the news of the Conqueror's death, he was granted lands by Duke Robert and lived with him as trusted counsellor and admired table-companion. This privileged position made him a bone of contention among the Conqueror's three discordant sons, of whom Henry, the youngest, now comes into view. Probably intended for the Church, he had had a good education—hence his cognomen "le Clerc", which, only in the fourteenth century and rather oddly, was altered to "Beau-Clerc". His father on his death-bed had given him no land, but much money and a blessing, fortified by a prophecy that he would outdistance both his brothers [2] and by a broad hint to use his wits and fend for himself: "Bide thy time, my son, and thou shalt have all that ever I had ".[3] Henry afterwards displayed an active interest in prophecy and perhaps this early prediction owed something to his own powers of imagination. Meantime he set about making it come true, by bargaining with his ducal and eternally impecunious brother, on advantageous terms—small offer, but cash down—to such purpose that he was soon Count of the Cotentin.

[1] *A-S.C.* MS. E, *s.a.* 1086. No doubt Edgar hoped to win renown in the wars consequent on the death of Robert Guiscard, the Norman Duke of Apulia.

[2] " Henricum quem vulgus clericum nuncupabat, thesauri sui non modica pecunia quam congregaverat dotandum esse decrevit caeterisque fratribus felicius acturum fore quasi praesagio praecinebat, quod et postea contegit."—*Annales de Oseneia*, in *Ann. Mon.* IV, p. 11.

[3] It is reported in full by Orderic (VII, xvi) ; for the other prophecies see below, pp. 110-113.

While all Normandy was ringing with the contentions of the Conqueror's sons, government was in the hands of St. Cuthbert's Bishop. He had sided with the barons in their short-lived revolt and afterwards failed to come to terms with Rufus, who seized the Castle of Durham and had him tried for " deserting his lord in time of need ". The trial, begun at Salisbury, November 2, 1088, before the *curia regis*, was inconclusive and the Bishop was allowed to withdraw to his native Normandy, where Duke Robert received him " more as a father than as an exile " [1] and straightway handed over to him the administration of the whole Duchy.[2] His services were utilized for nearly three years, with great advantage to Durham, for he collected much gold and silver to build his noble Cathedral, but with small advantage to the Duchy, for there pandemonium prevailed. In 1091 Duke and King devoted the whole of Lent to besieging their brother Henry in the abbey-fortress of Mont-Saint-Michel. The siege terminated with the capitulation of Henry. He was allowed to go free and went to the neighbouring parts of Brittany, where he had faithful adherents,[3] some of whom were to help him in the government of England—and, incidentally, to bring Breton names into Scotland. Then, after much violent discussion, Rufus secured the expulsion of Edgar Atheling and the forfeiture of his Norman estates.[4] The Atheling went straight to his brother-in-law in Scotland, whom his account of Rufus must have convinced that a demand for homage was imminent and who in May made his fourth incursion into Northumbria, possibly by way of repudiating any feudal duty towards a younger son and demonstrating sympathy with Edgar, perhaps also with Duke Robert and his episcopal counsellor. Six miles short of Durham, at Chester-le-Street, the Scots were turned back—by the

[1] Sim. Durh. *H.D.E.* I, p. 128.
[2] " A Roberto . . . honorifice susceptus, totius Normanniae curam suscepit."—*De injusta Vexatione*, p. 194.
[3] Ord. Vit. VIII, xvii.   [4] Flor. Worc. II, p. 29.

special intervention of St. Cuthbert, as Simeon relates, though the Old English chronicler speaks only of " the good men who had charge of that land ".[1] Rufus then hastened on the negotiations for peace between himself and his brothers which were being conducted by the Bishop. These completed, the Conqueror's three sons hurried across the Channel *en route* for Scotland.

Preparations must have been on foot for some time. A fleet and a great force, consisting chiefly of mounted men, had been collected, and perhaps the host was already on the march when Rufus and his brothers joined it and he took over the command. With the extreme rapidity which characterized Norman invasions of Scotland he reached Lothian and, according to Orderic, the Forth.[2] But the Red King's troopers were suffering from the Scottish climate, part of his victualling fleet had been wrecked,[3] supplies were running short and, while he was meditating on ways and means of traversing the Forth, messengers arrived from King Malcolm. They intimated that he was willing to do homage to Robert, as the late King's eldest son. A *curia regis* having been held, it was arranged that Robert, who held a strong position in the three-cornered question of homage, should sail across the " Scots Water " with a few knights and negotiate with Malcolm through the medium of Edgar. The Duke of the Normans was thus enabled to renew acquaintance with the King of Scots after ten years. They spent three agreeable days together.

[1] *A-S.C.* MS. E, *s.a.* 1091. The body of St. Cuthbert, on its way through the ages from Lindisfarne to Melrose and thence to Durham, had lain a hundred years at Chester-le-Street, from 883 to 995.

[2] Ord. Vit. VIII, xxii : " Exercitum totius Angliae conglobavit et usque ad magnum flumen quod Scote Watra dicitur, perduxit ". Though Malcolm went into Lothian with an army to meet Rufus (Flor. Worc. II, p. 28, and *A-S.C.* MS. E) and (according to the latter) awaited him there, it has been doubted whether Rufus even crossed the Tweed. But the time-table (start, mid-August; return to Durham, late November) is no more concentrated than the Conqueror's in 1072, and the distance covered in Scotland is much less.

[3] Off Coquet Island, on the coast of Northumberland. *Vita Oswini*, X, p. 22.

Orderic leaves a record of their conversations which at least seems plausible, and we can picture to ourselves the sturdy, if diminutive figure, in the unexpectedly abbreviated long-boots, engaged in animated discussion with the burly monarch of the North. On one of the three days Malcolm took him up to a high place, showed him strong detachments of the Scottish forces in occupation of well-chosen positions and hinted grimly at the fate in store for whosoever might venture to attack. He also explained the position *in re* homage. As a landholder in England, but not as King of Scots, he owed duty to Robert, the Conqueror's eldest son, but not to Rufus, and he quoted the Scriptures in support of feudal theory. No man, he pointed out, can serve two lords.[1] Robert approved, perhaps as a negotiator, perhaps just as a friend, but remarked that things were not what they were in his father's time, which meant, in less diplomatic language, that as regards primogeniture Rufus was a law unto himself. Malcolm had several conferences with that monarch in person and finally accepted approximately the same peace terms as at Abernethy,[2] while Edgar, as honest broker, was restored to the estates in Normandy of which he had been so lately and so unkindly deprived.

The presence of the Conqueror's three sons in Scotland, all at the same time, is a remarkable phenomenon. Rufus was there for retaliation, for frontier-defence, for homage. Henry, as an unattached younger son, might go anywhere. But it is odd to find the Duke so many hundred miles away from his Duchy. Perhaps his experience as leader of a former Scottish expedition was considered valuable. Perhaps as a friend of both Edgar and Malcolm he had been

---

[1] " Nemo, ut Christus ait, potest duobus Dominis servire." Ord. Vit. VIII, xxii. The quotation was apt and many other perplexed monarchs, St. Louis among them, afterwards applied it ruefully to their own case. So long as a vassal had one lord the feudal system operated ; when the vassal had two or more lords, it might defeat its own purpose, for circumstances might arise in which the vassal had to choose between them and join one fighting against the other.   [2] See Appendix B.

cast for the role of mediator. He was a wanderer, fond of far adventure, and Scotland may have held some fascination for him.

Common interest had brought the Conqueror's sons together. Mutual distrust kept them within sight of each other, and they marched away in apparent brotherly love, accompanied by the Atheling and by Duncan, this time of his own free will. Whether the ex-hostage had been living in Scotland or had come with the Norman brothers is unknown, but evidently he was in favour with all three. On the way south he witnessed with them and with most of the chief Normans in England a charter [1] granting certain churches to St. Cuthbert and the Prior and Monks of Durham. During the Bishop's exile the brethren had suffered no evil, " through the merits of the Saint " and through those, perhaps unexpected, of Rufus, who had " defended them like a father from the attacks of wicked men ".[2] Furthermore, on the march north he had shown himself very gracious to a delegation from Durham—he had even stood up to receive the Prior, Turgot.[3] On November 14, in return for good offices as mediator in Normandy, the Bishop was formally reinstated.

Treaty observance was not one of the Red King's strong points. He quarrelled with his negotiators, Robert and the Atheling, who departed for Normandy in displeasure. He had military ambitions and was dissatisfied with his Scottish performance. When the spring came, he marched north again, seized Carlisle, then held for the Scottish King by Gospatric's son Dolfin, and without comment or explanation annexed Southern Cumbria.

---

[1] *Regesta*, No. 318, November 14–December 1091. Its authenticity has been disputed on the ground that the presence of so many notable personages at Durham is not mentioned by Sim. Durh. But his ways are strange and it is mentioned in *De injusta Vexatione* and in *E. Yorks. Ch.* II, No. 938.

[2] Sim. Durh. *H.D.E.* p. 128. Rufus was not without admirers in his day.

[3] " Priori ad se venienti humiliter assurgens benigne illum suscepit."— *Ibid.*

A castle was built at Carlisle, in accordance with strategic considerations. The Cheviot Hills stretch from sea to sea, but leave a narrow gateway at either end for the East Coast and West Coast routes. One route Robert had already barred by his New Castle on the Tyne. Rufus now barred the other. As a further step towards security, and also, it must be acknowledged, towards the reclamation of a long-devastated area, he colonized the annexed region with " a great multitude of churlish folk " from Southern England.[1]

Malcolm protested against this annexation repeatedly, but in vain. Next year, in Lent, Rufus, in the chastened mood induced by his celebrated illness, " vowed many vows to God " [2] and, for once, received Malcolm's envoys courteously. This time he sent them back with a cordial message, inviting him to Gloucester and giving hostages for his safe-conduct. With the returning embassy came the ubiquitous Atheling. At the beginning of August the King of Scots set forth for Gloucester " with mickle worship ", in considerable state. On the way he stopped at Durham. The reinstalled Bishop was proceeding to the erection of the Cathedral which stands to this day as the chief glory of the Northern Romanesque and, on August 11, he laid one of the three foundation stones, the other two being laid by King Malcolm and the Prior, Turgot.[3] It is unlikely that Malcolm was invited to take part in the solemn ceremony merely because he happened to be passing. The Norman Bishop, in the interests of peace and goodwill (and with the help of his silver and gold from the Duchy), was building a majestic shrine for the body of a Scottish and Northumbrian Saint and it may be that the political journey to Gloucester was in some sort an extension of the religious journey to Durham.

---

[1] *A-S.C.* MS. E, *s.a.* 1092. [2] *A-S.C.* MS. E, *s.a.* 1093.
[3] Sim. Durh. *H.D.E.* I, p. 129; *H.R.* II, p. 220; *Tynemouth Chronicle fragment*, in *Hist. Northd.*, VIII, p. 120; Fordun, p. 218 (quoting Turgot).

Malcolm, now past his sixtieth year and anxious for reconciliation, went on " in order that, as was desired by certain of the chief men in England "—and who were they but Normans ?—" peace should be restored and firm friendship be established ".[1] Reaching Gloucester " full of peaceful proposals ",[2] he was not even granted an audience. His plea, he was curtly informed, must go before a *curia regis*. He took his way home, humiliated and distressed. Collecting his forces, he made one last desperate raid into Northumbria. It ended abruptly near Alnwick, in a Norman ambush. Margaret, lying ill in Edinburgh, learned that her husband and her eldest son Edward had been slain. She herself died three days later, on November 16, 1093.

Malcolm Canmore left seven sons, two by Ingibiorg, five by Margaret, but he was succeeded by his brother, by Donald Bane—in strict conformity with the custom followed in the Scottish Kingdom from the earliest times, the custom of tanistry or collateral succession.[3] Donald Bane was elected King.

Half a Celt by birth and wholly one by upbringing, Donald III had reached the age of sixty with his Gaelic sympathies intact. In sullen opposition to his more travelled brother's " Southernizing " policy, he had retired to the Isles, where he had been brought up and where he was among his own people, for though the chieftains were

---

[1] Flor. Worc. II, p. 31.   [2] Wm. Malm. II, p. 336.

[3] By this custom, descent was computed from the founder of the line and not from the last possessor. Brothers had thus a stronger claim than sons. Succession was determined by election ; any adult whose father, grandfather or great-grandfather had been King was eligible. The system, prevalent also in Ireland and Wales, had its merits ; it allowed for the election of the strongest male adult in the kingly house and the elimination of manifest incompetents and it reduced the risk of long minorities, such as those which in later Scottish history were so frequent and so calamitous. By 1093 it may have had its critics in Scotland ; everywhere else the idea of primogeniture was gaining ground, and quite possibly a change in the system of succession had been mooted. It is stated, in *A-S.C.* MS. E, and more definitely in Sim. Durh. *H.R.* II, p. 222, that Malcolm had designated as his successor Edward, the eldest son of his second marriage. But it is hard to see how this procedure could have been justified. The matter was not put to the test. Edward died a few hours after his father.

Norse, the islanders were Gaels. " Put away the luxury of the soft South and resume the ancient virtues of the Gael " was the message he brought back from his Hebridean retreat.[1] That his sentiments were widely shared is shown by the sequel. " all the English were driven out who before were with King Malcolm ".[2] Margaret's sons fled to England, except Edmund, now the eldest, who cast in his lot with his uncle Donald—and has ever since been called the black sheep of the family.[3] His brothers found refuge with their Normanized uncle Edgar, who, fearing that a family reunion of members of the Old English House might displease Rufus, discreetly entrusted their care and education to friends,[4] presumably Norman friends.

Duncan was in England already, as a member of the Red King's military establishment.[5] He was now in his early thirties, he had spent half his life as a hostage for no other reason than that he was King Malcolm's eldest son, and he may well have felt that one who suffered the penalties of primogeniture was entitled to its privileges. In some such frame of mind he went to Rufus and asked for guidance. It was a delicate subject on which to approach a crowned Younger Son, but Malcolm's first-born was a trusted companion-in-arms, barely distinguishable from a Norman, and he was authorized to enrol volunteers. " Having performed such fealty as the King would have of him ", Duncan set forth for Scotland " with a multitude of English and Normans " [6] and, in May 1094, he succeeded in driving out Donald III. But Donald's adherents must have been victims of a surprise attack. " Some of the Scots afterwards gathered together and slew almost all

---

[1] " Nunquam luxu Anglico imbutum, semper severitate Hebridianorum ot iam annos assuetum."—Boece, XII, p. 261.

[2] *A-S.C.* MS. E, *s.a.* 1093.   [3] See below, p. 87, n. 1.

[4] Sim. Durh. *H.R.* p. 222 ; Flor. Worc. II, p. 52 ; Fordun, V, p. 220.

[5] " Willelmum cui tunc militavit."—Flor. Worc. II, p. 32 ; so also *A-S.C.* MS. E, *s.a.* 1093, and Sim. Durh. *H.R.* II, p. 222.

[6] Flor. Worc. II, p. 32 ; *A-S.C.* MS. E, *s.a.* 1094 ; Florence's phrase is : " illi fidelitatem juravit ".

Duncan's men, and he, with few, barely escaped." After much parleying, he was accepted as King, reluctantly, and only " on condition that he should never again harbour Englishmen or Frenchmen in the land ".[1]

If the accession of Duncan II meant anything more than application of superior Norman force, it meant that the old Celtic principle of collateral succession had been formally challenged and was now superseded by the Norman principle of primogeniture. " Duncan, son of King Malcolm, by heredity King of Scotland " is the style he uses in his charter to Durham [2]—a style amply paralleled in the Conqueror's writs, in which legal status as Edward's heir is heavily stressed. Duncan's title must have met with the approval of the witnesses, and these included more than his Norman henchmen. " My brothers " join in the grant ; those who are actually witnesses are his full brother Malcolm and his half-brother Edgar ; clearly Malcolm Canmore's second family admitted Duncan's " hereditary right " and the admission is all the more significant because his wife and children are mentioned.[3] The charter, which remained in Durham because Duncan marching north gave possessions in East Lothian to " St. Cuthbert and his servants ", bears mute testimony to the advance of Norman

[1] " On þa geráð þ he naefre eft Englisce ne Frencisce into þam lande ne gelogige."—*A-S.C.* MS. E, *s.a.* 1094. Florence's phrase is : " ea ratione ut amplius in Scotia nec Anglos nec Normannos introduceret, sibique militari sineret ".

[2] " Ego Dunecanus, filius regis Malcolumb, constans hereditarie rex Scociae."—*National MSS. Sc.* No. II ; Lawrie, XII. The names of the witnesses have been oddly taken for Norse. " Accard ", " Hermer ", " Teodbold ", " Earnulf " and " Ulf " are Norman ; " Hemming ", " Aelfric " and " Vinget " are not Norse. Duncan did in fact give lands to Durham, as is mentioned in later documents, and the authenticity of this charter and the seal, doubted by Lawrie, but not by Raine, is now universally accepted. " Malcolumb ", whose name comes next to " Eadgarus " which heads the list, was the second son of Malcolm Canmore and Ingibiorg. The grant includes that of " Tyningham and all the service which Bishop Fothan [of St. Andrews, † 1093] had therefrom ".

[3] " Pro uxore mea et pro infantibus meis." Duncan II married *c.* 1090 his relative Gospatric's fourth daughter " Octreda ", a Latinized feminine form of Uchtred, the name of her great-grandfather.

fashions. The crosses at the foot, Duncan's first, then Edgar's, served the Anglo-Saxons for the purpose of showing that a charter was genuine. At the bottom there is a seal, the further Norman device for the same purpose.[1] The charter was written by a Norman scribe, as is shown by his name, Grento.[2]

Duncan found " hereditary right " of small avail. He may have had his faults; it was only to be expected that a disciple of Robert and Rufus should be " mair exercit in chevelry than ony administration of justice ".[3] But his promise to dispense with English and Norman help was carried out chivalrously—and disastrously. In November he was ambushed and slain [4] by adherents of Donald Bane and Edmund.

The Son of Ingibiorg sleeps in Iona.[5] Life's fitful fever gave him but glimpses of his native land. The " verdict of God at Hastings " made him a Knight of Normandy, a good soldier and a good churchman. In his seal he is represented on horseback, wearing a conical helmet or *chapel de fer*, with nasal, and a trellised hauberk extending to the knees. A Norman charter, a Norman seal, a grant of land to Dunfermline [6] and one to Durham are the sole memorials of his six months' reign.

Tanistry had won the day. Donald III resumed his Celtic rule, assisted now by Edmund, who was designated as his successor [7] and, according to practice, was placed in

[1] R. K. Hannay, *St. Andrew of Scotland*, pp. 37-38 (The Moray Press, Edinburgh, 1933, 73 pp.).

[2] Cp. *Grentonis mansio* = Grentesmenil, regularly in Ord. Vit., now Grandmesnil (Calvados) canton de Saint-Pierre-sur-Dives. A Grento de Everwic [York] appears in Pipe Roll 31 Hen. I, 1130, p. 32, after the name of Walter Espec.

[3] Bellenden, II, p. 677.   [4] *A-S.C.* MS. E, *s.a.* 1097.

[5] Mondynes on the banks of the Bervie was the scene of Duncan's death. His body was interred at Dunkeld and afterwards taken to Iona.

[6] Mentioned in a charter by King David. Lawrie, LXXIV (1128).

[7] Professor Eoin (John) MacNeill showed in his *Celtic Ireland* that the election of a Tanist, in the sense of a successor chosen during the reigning king's lifetime, is not recorded in Ireland till the thirteenth century. But as Donald III was an old man, Edmund may well have been so elected.

charge of South Scotland, where perhaps his " Southern " upbringing, ineffectual though it had apparently been, made him more acceptable than the incorrigible old Celt, Donald Bane. But not even Donald could avoid Normans. Civil war had broken out among them. It might, he thought, be politic to favour one side, so he entered into an alliance with the nearest of the partisans, the Earl of the Northumbrians, Robert de Montbrai.[1] He was the uncle of Morel, who had slain Malcolm Canmore, a deed which the chroniclers relate with ill-concealed horror because Morel was Malcolm's " gossip " or sworn brother.[2] Earl Robert's vicarious or avuncular triumph over Malcolm Canmore, coupled with succession to the vast estates of his own uncle the Bishop of Coutances, had so turned his head that he set himself up against Rufus and in May 1095 openly defied him.[3] He was joined by other Norman malcontents in a revolt which was not put down till after stern fighting and regular sieges. The Earl was captured at Tynemouth and condemned to imprisonment

---

[1] " Donald invaded England."—Flor. Worc. II, p. 41. According to *Scalachronica*, " Robert se alya au roy Descoce ".

[2] *A-S.C.* MS. E, *s.a.* 1093. See the contemporary quotations (highly favourable to Malcolm Canmore) in Freeman, *Rufus*, II, pp. 592-596. Gaimar, ll. 6121-6123, says that Geoffroi Engoulevant, along with Morel, took Malcolm's life :

> " Ço fu Gefrai en Gulevent [*v.r.* de Gulevent]
> Il e Morel un son parent
> Ki Malcolumb tolirent vie ".

On the name Engoulevant, see below, p. 146.

[3] Montbrai (*Molbraium* in Ord. Vit.) is a village some twenty miles south-east of Coutances. Robert was the " nephew "—the relationship (stated by Ord. Vit.) is not certain—of Geoffroi de Montbrai, Bishop of Coutances from 1049, who had probably taken some part in the government of the Duchy before 1066 and who was rewarded for his administrative, judicial and semi-military services in England by the grant of enormous estates. These, when he died on February 2, 1093, went to Robert, successor of Aubrey de Coucy, who was Earl of the Northumbrians for a very short time after Walcher's death. Morel, Robert's " nephew "—here, too, the relationship is uncertain—was his steward, and was appointed by him sheriff, with headquarters at Bamburgh. The appointment was irregular. Elsewhere the subordination of the Sheriff to the Earl had ceased. W. A. Morris, p. 45.

for life.[1] Morel surrendered at Bamburgh and, in recognition of much double-dealing, was allowed to go free. But his lot was not a pleasant one : " his master being cast into perpetual chains, he left England in sorrow and, wandering through many lands in poverty and detestation, grew old in exile ".[2] No Earl was appointed in place of Robert de Montbrai. Rufus assumed direct control and henceforth " Northumberland " meant not the land north of the Humber, only the land north of the Tyne.

Everything was now conspiring to bring about a " Restoration " of one of Margaret's sons by Norman military power. The death of Malcolm Canmore at the hands of Morel had been a shock to Norman self-esteem. " When the news came, the King and his nobles were greatly grieved and utterly ashamed that a deed so base and so cruel had been committed by Normans." [3] Rufus had made Royal amends by ensuring the succession of the victim's eldest son, and when Duncan II had fallen had endeavoured to hold Donald Bane in check; he sent an expedition against him under Néel [Nigel] d'Aubigny.[4] Rufus could do no more, having his own troubles in Normandy and Wales, but as soon as they had subsided,

[1] He was never released. According to William of Jumièges, Bouquet, XII, p. 572, " It is commonly said (*Dictum est a pluribus*) that this was vengeance for having treacherously (*dolose*) slain the father of Maud, afterwards Queen of the English ".

[2] Ord. Vit. VIII, xxiii. " Moreal factae traditionis causam regi [Willelmo] delexit."—Flor. Worc. II, p. 39. " Moreal ", in that spelling, appears in the *Liber Vitae*, presumably as a benefactor of Durham.

[3] Ord. Vit. VIII, xxi.

[4] The expedition is mentioned, only incidentally, in *Vita Oswini*, IX, p. 21. It is said there to have been sent for the purpose of avenging insults suffered from the Scots. It returned via Newcastle. " Nigellus de Albineio " [Aubigny, near Périers] († c. 1130) was Robert de Montbrai's cousin. By licence of Pope Paschal II (1099–1118) he married the imprisoned Robert's wife Matilda, daughter of Richer de Laigle. Néel d'Aubigny took Duke Robert prisoner at Tinchebray, 1106. He obtained a divorce from Matilda on the ground of consanguinity and then married Gondrée [Gundrada], daughter of Giraud de Gournay [-en-Bray]. Their son Roger, styled Roger de Montbrai, who inherited great estates, will be mentioned later as a founder of monasteries in the North of England, and as a very young warrior at the Battle of the Standard.

in 1097, he made further Royal amends ; [1] he sent the Atheling with an army into Scotland for the purpose of overthrowing Donald Bane and setting up in his place Edgar, fourth son of Malcolm and Margaret. When the host was passing through Durham, St. Cuthbert, it is related, appeared to young Edgar in a dream and, " because it pleased God to grant him the Kingdom ", promised him victory if he would take the banner from the Church and bear it into battle.[2] The fight was hard,[3] but under the banner of St. Cuthbert it was won, and in October 1097 Edgar ousted Donald III. From then onwards, for fifty years and more, the Scottish Kings were Sons of Margaret and reigned by Norman power.

[1] " It was an act of remarkable compassion, such as became so great a man, to restore the son to the Kingdom at his request, forgetting the wrongs done by the father."—Wm. Malm. II, p. 366. So also II, p. 476. William of Malmesbury's comment is noteworthy. At the time of writing, praise of Rufus might seem dispraise of Henry, the reigning King.

[2] Fordun, V, p. 226 ; cp. below, p. 118, n. 2.

[3] *A-S.C.* MS. E, *s.a.* 1097.

§ 7

Norman Influence on the Court

THE Scots had then been in contact with the Normans for a whole generation. Across the most dubious of land frontiers, beyond a wide stretch of hilly, desolate, but not impenetrable country, they had seen all directive power pass to Normans. English society had become French. King, Court, higher clergy, earls, sheriffs, the major and the minor officials, the landowners,[1] were French in language, dress and social usages. Yet in a sense they were " English ", which thus becomes a confusing term in any discussion of the influences or the general ideas emanating from England, or of the personal relations existing between individuals in that country or between them and dwellers in the Scottish Kingdom. It is not to be denied that Guillaume le Roux was an English King, nor that for long years after 1066 life went on unchanged in the country places—

> Where the old plain men have rosy faces
> And the young fair maidens quiet eyes.

The men swinking in the fields, felling trees for the castles, quarrying stone for the churches, never spoke anything but an English dialect, nor did their character or their habits alter because the property had changed hands. But the men who directed their labours were French and directed them to French ends. Native Englishmen might derive much benefit from French enterprises, but it was incidental.

[1] Not more than 1 per cent of the land was in 1086 held of the King by those who held it T.R.E., or by their widows or heirs. Ballard, *D.I.* p. 6. " In 1087, with less than half a dozen exceptions, every lay lord whose possessions entitled him to political influence was a foreigner."—Stenton, *A-S.E.* p. 671.

As a class, they were not represented at discussions on matters of state policy. As individuals, they were not in the counsels of the great. If Rufus had any as advisers, consultants or confidants, their existence is unrecorded. It was not with the native English that the King of Scots or his family or his nobles or his envoys had to deal. Southern influences had become Norman influences. Till 1066 the Scottish Kingdom had borrowed little from England. Afterwards it borrowed much. But what it borrowed was French.

On how much it had borrowed by 1097 there is little contemporary evidence. The little that exists is limited to one family, so strictly do the mediaeval writers confine their attention to kings and princes, warriors and saints.

In its members the absence of hostility to Normans is very marked. Neither for Malcolm nor for Margaret can there have been a hard-and-fast distinction between English as friends and Normans as enemies. While living in England they had been used to seeing Normans in high places and the half-Norman Edward in the highest. Though overshadowed by his second wife in the esteem of the monastic chroniclers, Malcolm Canmore was an able ruler—and therefore not above learning from the enemy. In his unsettled times " enemy " was often but a manner of speaking. To the conquerors of England he had small cause for hostility. From their conspiracies and revolts against their own kings he held aloof. His quarrel was rather with the rulers, Norman or other, of the neighbouring districts. His five raids were local. None can have taken more than a few weeks and they were spread over a period of thirty-five years. As a man of war he must have found much to admire in the Normans, but his dealings with them were not all military. His friendship with the Conqueror's eldest son was cordial and permanent.[1]

[1] " Roberto comite, qui familiarem jam dudum apud Scotos locaverat gratiam."—Wm. Malm.

Among the magnates who accompanied Robert to Scotland in 1080 was Athelelme, the Abbot of Abingdon,[1] where the last English Bishop of Durham had died in his custody.[2] Athelelme was a monk of Jumièges and a Norman of the most uncompromising sort, fond of bringing over relatives and providing them with Abbey lands, never stepping outside the precincts without an imposing bodyguard of armed compatriots and always very free in expressing the poor opinion he had formed of the English and even of their saints.[3] This worthy is said to have returned to Scotland on diplomatic missions: if so, Malcolm must have shown some forbearance. He may be presumed to have joined in Margaret's very pressing invitations to Norman clerics, and the religious and social reforms undertaken by her, some of which were of Norman inspiration, would have been impossible without his approval and his active support.

Unless Malcolm and his family had an extensive acquaintance in North Country Norman society there would be little meaning in the circumstantial account of the proposed betrothal of his elder daughter Edith and the Lord of Richmond, Alain le Noir. Alain belonged to a cadet branch of the ducal house of Brittany and was distinguished by his cognomen from his elder brother Alain le Roux, commander of the Breton corps at Hastings,[4] whose chief residence, the head of the Honour composed by his wide estates, was his castlery of Richmond in the North Riding

[1] " Plures Angliae primates, quorum unus abbas Athelelmus fuit."— *Chron. Mon. de Abingdon*, I, p. 9, and II, p. 283.

[2] Flor. Worc. II, p. 9.

[3] Athelelme († 1084) is reputed to have refused permission for any feast of St. Ethelwold or St. Edmund to be kept, on the ground that all Englishmen were boors. Knowles, p. 408.

[4] " Alanus Niger ", Alain le Noir, was the younger son of Eude, Count not *of*, but *in* Brittany. Alain was a distant relative of the Conqueror and a near relative of Alain IV, " Fergant ", Duke of Brittany, who married in 1076 the Conqueror's daughter Constance († 1090). Eude's elder son " Alanus Rufus ", for services rendered at Hastings, received great possessions in the shires of York and Lincoln. He died unmarried in 1089 and was succeeded by Alain le Noir. See *E. Yorks. Ch.* IV, pp. 84-100.

of Yorkshire. The district was of vital strategic importance, traversed as it was by the ancient ways leading from the North through Durham and from the North-West through Carlisle, and the Conqueror had taken care to place it at once under a strong and capable vassal, his divisional commander, Alain le Roux, who without delay selected a dominating site: on a perpendicular rock, a hundred feet above the river Swale, he raised a " castle ", which he named, appropriately, *Richemund*.[1] His brother and successor Alain le Noir would have found his military problems much simplified by marriage with the daughter of his chief potential opponent, but he died in 1093, before the daughter reached marriageable age.[2]

" The English Margaret " was manifestly a Continental and the traits which emerge from the contemporary descriptions are rather Norman than English. They correspond point by point to those which are enumerated as distinctive of the " Conquerors " by all who have written about them, from Malaterra in her own day onwards. All with one accord note their marked taste for ceremony, for magnificence, for noble and splendid mansions, their love

[1] The castle, built to defend the Vale of York from an enemy in possession of the Eden Valley and the road running from Catterick to Penrith, stands close to the Great North Road and to the point of junction now known as Scotch Corner. The site of Richmond is called Hindrelac in Domesday. The name (*riche* = strong + *mont* = hill, a word of the same formation as *Richelieu* and as *Rougemont*) was first given to the castle and seems unlikely to have been transferred from any site in France.

[2] Orderic (VIII, xxii) confuses the Breton brothers, both Counts, both Alains and both elderly, but there is nothing inherently improbable in the story. It is based on Eadmer, *H.N.* p. 122. Its authenticity turns on the angry remark which, in his account, the quick-tempered Malcolm makes to his daughter: " I had decided you should rather marry Count Alain than go into a nunnery ". Much depends on the intonation of " rather ". Perhaps Eadmer intended the remark to be taken as sarcasm and Orderic, repeating him, took it as a statement of fact. But whether father or daughter looked on Alain as a desirable *parti* or as a bogy-man, they were evidently familiar with his social qualities and personal character. On the whole story, connected with Wilton and extremely complicated, see Dom André Wilmart, *La Destinataire de la lettre de Saint Anselme sur l'état et les vœux de religion*, *Revue Bénédictine*, t. XXXVIII (1926), pp. 331-334, and *Une Lettre inédite*. *Ibid.* t. XL (1928), pp. 319-332.

of colour and gaudy clothes—Margaret's improvements at Dunfermline, her many-coloured furnishings and her sumptuary regulations are discussed later. The Normans won the hearts of critical observers like William of Malmesbury by what in his elegant Latin he calls their " elegantia ", their smart appearance, their good manners, their decorum, their restraint in company—the mundane quality which Turgot most admires in Margaret is decorum. She enjoyed a laugh, but disliked and discouraged laughter which was unrestrained and seemed unoccasioned. There were no wild " skellochs " from the young women at her work-parties.[1] A marked peculiarity of Norman lords was their impulsive, somewhat spectacular charity to the poor, with the consequent spread of the donor's fame. Malaterra says, unkindly, that what made Norman princes most generous was a pleasant anticipatory feeling of the good repute they would obtain [2]—Turgot says, not at all unkindly, that Margaret's munificent alms-giving was extended from the poor of Scotland to " the poor of almost all nations, who came in haste, attracted by the fame of her charity ".[3] The theologian Thiébaud d'Étampes,[4] answering from Caen her invitation to Scotland, employed all the artifices of a style which even in circumstances less gratifying was flowery, and his idea of what would give pleasure was : " The fame of your dignity, munificence and liberality has not only gone out through the regions bordering upon your own, but has spread through almost all the earth ".[5] Margaret

[1] " Nunquam hilaritate nimia in cachinnum soluta." — Turgot, *Vita*, p. 239.

[2] " Principes delectatione bonae famae largissimi."—Gaufredus Malaterra, p. 1102, B. Malaterra, a Norman himself, a Benedictine, was the author of a history, *c.* 1099, of the Conquerors in Apulia and Sicily and is speaking of them.

[3] *Vita*, p. 246. " Nation " has its earlier sense, in which the racial idea is much stronger than the political : ? the peoples of the British Isles.

[4] " Theobaldus Stampensis " =of Étampes [Latin *Stampae*] (Seine-et-Oise).

[5] " Fama vestrae honestatis, munificentiae, liberalitatis non solum per loca vobis affinia propagatur, sed etiam fere per totum orbem dilatatur."—*Epistolae Theobaldi Stampensis*, in Migne, *P.L.* CLXIII, p. 765.

had the " command of eloquent words ",[1] the " lawyer's mind ",[2] the interest in litigation,[3] which are still so noticeable in Normandy to-day. She had the Norman urge to improve the conditions of life in a distant and " barbarous " land, regiment the natives and reform them, particularly as regards their religious practices. The generosity of the Normans to holy places, and their un-wearying zeal for pilgrimages, are paralleled in her institu-tion of " the Queen's Ferry " on the Forth, for pilgrims travelling to and from St. Andrews.[4] All the traditional Norman traits are present in Margaret. So " Norman " is the impression she creates that fourteenth-century writers like Fordun and Barbour quite naturally associate her with the use of French [5] and twentieth-century his-torians wrongly state that she had Norman blood in her veins.

Though the fall of her House was brought about more by Harold's witan than by William's warriors, she might well have borne the conquerors a grudge. But her recorded actions imply admiration for their way of life. The example they set in religion made a profound impression on her mind, perhaps even from her girlhood days in King

[1] " Inerat ei [Margaritae] . . . gratiosa verborum facilitas."—Turgot, p. 238. " Nemo eloquio clarior."—*Ibid*. 241. Cp. Malaterra : " eloquentiae studiis ".

[2] " Ejus consilio, regni jura disponebantur."—*Ibid*. III, p. 238.

[3] Margaret could give her mind to the Scriptures " amid the distractions of law-suits, amid the manifold cares of the kingdom " : " inter causarum tumultus, inter multiplices regni curas ", *ibid*. VI, p. 240.

[4] Margaret erected buildings for pilgrims on both sides of the Forth (North and South Queensferry) and provided means for their gratuitous conveyance. Turgot, *Vita*, p. 241. " She gave hospitality, clothing and food to all pilgrims who came to her."—Flor. Worc. II, p. 32.

[5] When Malcolm first met Margaret he deemed it advisable to address the company in French as well as in English. Fordun, S.S. p. 258. Re-lating how Sir Thomas Randolph was told by a certain William François that the wall of Edinburgh Castle could be scaled, Barbour (*Bruce*, X, l. 746) says that Margaret prophesied this by token. She had a man climbing a ladder portrayed in the castle chapel :

" And wrat owth him, as old men sayis,
In Franch : gardiss wouss de francoiss ".

Edward's time. She chose Lanfranc for her director, " somewhat surprisingly ",[1] and sought his counsels in her projects for Church reform. These were concerned not with organization but with the Christian life, and she consulted him not as Archbishop of Canterbury, but as a Norman churchman, which he essentially was ; he was a " quasi rudis Anglus ", wrote Eadmer, who knew him well, meaning that though Lanfranc came to possess a profound knowledge of Church conditions in England, any English feeling he had acquired was of a rudimentary character.[2] Margaret's appeal for stricter marriage regulations was in conformity with the decisions of Lanfranc's Council, *c.* 1072, and with his condemnation, in 1074, of Irish laxity in these matters. At one of her meetings with the Scottish clergy she quoted Pope Gregory I (the Great), textually, on Sunday observance, in which the Scots lagged behind the rest of the Christian world, though since they have been considerably in advance ; the reason was merely that, with the Irish, they believed the day of rest to be Saturday.[3] Margaret may have owed her quotation indirectly to Lanfranc. His position was that of all the reformers—that he was not attempting to introduce something that was new, but trying to reveal what was implicit in the old decretals— and for that purpose he made great endeavours to provide the bishops and abbots of England with copies of manuals of Church law, especially the manual which derives from the False Decretals and the writings of Gregory the

[1] " Bishops and abbots had always been directors of nuns, but it is somewhat surprising to learn that Lanfranc was chosen as her spiritual father by Margaret."—Dom David Knowles, p. 138. The Archbishop himself in his reply to her request [" In none of his epistles was Lanfranc moved to write in so spiritual a tone as to Margaret ".—Macdonald, *Lanfranc*, p. 195] expresses surprise " that you, of Royal descent, Royally educated should choose me, a man of foreign birth, as your father ". Letter (undated), No. IX in Lawrie.

[2] *H.N.* p. 350, referring to 1079. Lanfranc cannot have been far short of sixty when he landed in England. He died a very old man on May 24, 1089, and the meetings in Scotland to which he sent delegates at Margaret's request must have been arranged considerably before then.

[3] Skene, II, p. 349.

Great.[1] How rare such manuals still were, and how little was yet known of ecclesiastical law, is shown by the fact that in 1088 the Bishop of Durham at his trial dramatically produced his book of the " law Christian ", confuted Lanfranc with it and afterwards presented it to the Cathedral library. Margaret was at an advantage over the Scottish churchmen in that she had a manual from which to quote and they had not.

Among the numerous chaplains at Dunfermline [2] there were certainly French clerks. When Margaret asked Thiébaud d'Étampes, then lecturing on theology at Caen,[3] to accept preferment in Scotland, he declined, most courteously, " because of the inconstancy of the deep ", " maris inconstantia "—in modern and less choice terms, because of the Channel crossing—requesting, however, to be enrolled among her clerks in an honorary capacity. Thiébaud may have been no great loss—he was alleged to be a " *tantillus clericellus* (*Scotice*, a wee priestie), one of those wandering chaplains with pointed beards, curled hair and effeminate dress who are ashamed of the proper ecclesiastical habit and tonsure " [4]—and though he would not let his own light shine in Scotland no doubt other French luminaries came in his stead.

No pre-Conquest Englishman lived to be more " Norman " than Edgar Atheling, yet this in no way lowered him in Margaret's esteem, and indeed nothing in his long and much-criticized career does him greater credit than his devotion to his sisters and nephews and nieces in

[1] The Collection in 74 Titles, *c.* 1050 ; see Z. N. Brooke, p. 162.

[2] Turgot refers to the *capellani* in a way which shows that they were numerous.

[3] " Doctor Cadumensis." Thiébaud was under the impression that Margaret was a King's daughter : " Margaritae praecellenti reginae praecellentis regis filiae ".

[4] Quoted by T. E. Holland, *The Origin of the University of Oxford*, *E.H.R.* VI (1891), p. 241. This, however, was said of Thiébaud at a later stage in his theological career by a possibly jaundiced observer, at a time when the controversy Seculars *versus* Regulars was setting brother against brother, and Thiébaud had come out strongly on the secular side.

Scotland. Christina was provided for by the not un-generous Conqueror with rich lands in the shires of Warwick and Oxford, and though she never married, it was not for want of " tocher ".[1] While her brother was in England she probably lived with him, and on the same friendly terms with the Norman gentry, and when in 1086 he sailed for Apulia, she took the veil at Romsey,[2] where her two very young nieces Edith and Mary were sent without delay to be educated under her care.[3] Even to-day a mother in Scotland bent on sending her daughters to school in England might hesitate at the distance; it is not possible to send them much further. Nor would it have been possible at that time to find a convent where girls would be better educated in a manner which would fit them to take their place in the Norman scheme of things.

Romsey Abbey, founded by Edgar the Peaceful in 967, was one of the Saxon houses to which, in the first few years of the Conquest, Englishwomen crowded, for fear of Norman violence. Perhaps Margaret and Christina had been there themselves. But whatever reasons either may

[1] In the Oxfordshire Domesday " Cristina " (no title given) holds Broadwell of the King . . . (24 hides and 1 virgate, 14 serfs, 52 villeins and 2 mills). *V.C.H. Oxfordshire*, I, p. 499. In the Warwickshire Domesday, p. 244, " Terra Christinae. In Coleshelle [Coleshill] Hundret " forms the heading of a goodly item : 8 hides in Ulverlei [Solihull] (. . . 22 villeins, with a priest . . . woodland 4 leagues long and half a league broad) ; 1 hide in Arlei [Arley]. " In Mereton [Marton] Hundret Cristine " holds Icentone [Long Itchington] . . . 24 hides . . . (83 villeins . . . 2 priests). " Ulverlei " belonged to the forfeited estates of the local Earl—Edwin, son and successor of Ælfgar, Earl of Mercia († c. 1062), son of Leofric. *V.C.H. Warwickshire*, I, pp. 272, 281, 340. " Icentone " was a valuable and extensive estate. Christina's known possessions come to about 57 hides of land, probably a very ample allowance. As Earl Edwin, who had alternately supported and opposed the Conqueror, was killed on his way to Scotland in 1071, some of his lands were no doubt still at William's disposal in 1074. The grant of Solihull to Christina may have been made then as part of Edgar's settlement with William.

[2] *A-S.C.* MS. E and *Chron. Melrose, s.a.* 1086 ; Flor. Worc. II, p. 19.

[3] " Mathildis, inter sanctimoniales ab infantia nutrita et adulta "—Eadmer, *H.N.* p. 121 ; " a teneris annis inter sanctimoniales apud Wiltonam et Rumesiam educata "—Wm. Malm. II, p. 494.

have had for selecting Romsey twenty years later and whatever reasons Malcolm may have had for agreeing to the choice, these can hardly have included distrust or dislike of Normans. For anyone anxious to avoid the sight of them, or the sound of them, Romsey was the worst choice imaginable. At any moment they might come riding by with horn and hound, for the Abbey stood half-way between their headquarters at Winchester and their not very happy hunting-ground in the New Forest —less than ten miles from either. Those who had occasion to call and were approved by the Abbess were received, like other men visitors at any other convent, in the most natural way in the world—if there be any truth or even any verisimilitude in the well-known story of the Red King's visit. He just happened to be hunting in the neighbourhood and had called to pay his respects to the Atheling's sister who was in religion; he would also be glad to meet her niece.[1] French was an " accomplishment " at Winchester long before there was a New Forest, and, by the time Edith and Mary entered Romsey, was probably the chief means of instruction. Edith, and no doubt her sister, afterwards went on to Wilton, only a few miles distant.[2] That great nunnery had profited from the benefactions of Norman Emma and her grand-nephew the Conqueror,[3] and had long flourished under the direction of Lotharingian Bishops and chaplains. In both convents the daughters of conquerors and conquered met on equal terms. Nowhere was the hatchet more decently buried than at Wilton, nowhere was the incipient Entente more securely

[1] The story is related by Herman of Tournai (1127 × 1138) : see Freeman, *Rufus*, II, p. 32 and pp. 600-601. Herman calls King Malcolm " David " and makes one or two other slips, but the story rings true.

[2] Wm. Malm. II, p. 4 ; Ord. Vit. VIII, xxii ; *Ann. de Wintona*, p. 40. Edith's knowledge of literature, which was extensive, was acquired in her convent days. Soon after leaving, at the age of twenty, she displayed a marked interest in French verse and became an enthusiastic patroness of French poets and minstrels. Her education was probably conducted in French.

[3] Dugdale, *Monasticon*, II, p. 316 (London, 1819).

placed on a cultural and educational basis. This is made clear by the hagiographer Goscelin of Thérouanne (Pas-de-Calais), who had a pupil in the convent, a very youthful nun (of Lotharingian parentage) called Eve, and who probably knew Edith. He certainly knew about Margaret, for, when making his report on the Translation of St. Augustine at Canterbury in 1091, he went very far out of his way to describe a supernatural experience which had recently befallen her.[1]

If their daughters' very prolonged stay in England was foreseen it must have been obvious to Margaret—and to Malcolm, whose authority in the household historians seem determined to ignore—that they would grow up Norman ladies, and that if they married the chances were that they would marry Normans—as in fact they did. It may even be that in Margaret's last years her maternal hopes were turning towards alliances such as those which, after her death, united the Conqueror's family to her own.[2] If she set any dynastic hopes on England they were restricted to Edith and Mary. They would present interesting possibilities when they grew up, an expeditious process in mediaeval Royal families. The Conqueror's three sons were unmarried. Margaret maintained cordial relations with them all. She loaded even the ungodly Rufus with costly furs.[3] Robert can be left out of count; a godfather could not marry his goddaughter. But Rufus was not

---

[1] There was a church in Scotland, dedicated to St. Laurence, which women were forbidden to enter. Margaret, having gone to make an offering, was suddenly struck down, but was revived by the prayers of the clergy. This is related by Goscelin (*Historia Translationis S. Augustini*, in Migne, *P.L.* clv, p. 20) as having happened " recently ", " *nuper* ". In another, fuller, account, *Miracula* [S. Laurentii . . .] *Legenda Joan. Capgravii*, *Acta Sanctorum*, February, t. I, p. 296, the locality of this church is said to be " Fortuna " [cp. East Fortune, East Lothian].

[2] Only four of Margaret's eight children married. Of these four marriages, three were with: a son, a granddaughter and a grand-niece of the Conqueror, viz. Henry, Sibylla and Maud (de Saint-Liz). The fourth marriage was with Eustace III of Boulogne, son of a Hastings commander and distantly related to the Conqueror; it was as " Norman " as the others.

[3] Bateson, p. 16.

beyond redemption, nor beyond making himself as agreeable to Margaret as he did to Lanfranc the Lawyer and Anselm the Saint. Henry, when he came to Scotland in 1091, was one of the best educated and most eligible young men of his time.

In Turgot's exuberant description of the Scottish Court there is a thin substratum of credibility and in this Norman elements are discoverable. He relates that the Royal residence was brightened, under Margaret's direction, with *pallia* of many colours. These are the rich cloths used for coverings or hangings, the *pailles* of the earlier *chansons de geste*. They were highly ornamental and they also gave some protection from the damp wall and the invading " haar ". They were multi-coloured, but no more so than they probably were in the adjacent Church of the Holy Trinity, built in the Romanesque style introduced by Edward at Westminster, or than they are known to have been in the Norman Archbishop's similarly named Cathedral at Canterbury.[1] Eventually " the whole house glittered with gold and silver ", some of the glitter coming from " the vessels in which food and drink were set before the King and his nobles ".[2] As a result of Margaret's personal efforts " all the magnates of the realm, and their *ministri* (officers), had their dignity and their splendour enhanced to the utmost ".[3] " These things she did ", Turgot goes on to explain, " not because the honours of the world delighted her, but because her duty compelled her to discharge what the royal dignity required." The

[1] The Church of Dunfermline—the foundations of which have been traced — was in the Romanesque style and consisted of a nave with a square western tower and an oblong choir ending in an apse. The Cathedral Church of the Holy Trinity at Canterbury, destroyed by fire, December 6, 1067, was rebuilt by Lanfranc and decorated " in diversicoloribus picturis, in palliis "—*Gesta P.A.* p. 69.

[2] " Regi et regni proceribus."—Turgot, *Vita*, VII, p. 242. The vessels were " of gold and silver or "—as Turgot adds, rather lamely—" at least gilt or silvered over ".

[3] " Cunctis regni primatibus, et illorum ministris, plurimum gloriae ac decoris ipsa contulit."—*Vita*, VII, p. 241.

age, in fact, was dawning when monarchs must show by the richness of their apparel that they were not as other men. The King of Scots must therefore be visibly a king—one like William, who came out three times a year in full regalia and when the leeches told him his end was near had the Crown, Sword and Sceptre in readiness for Rufus to take away with him on his hurried departure for England, or a king like Rufus himself, of whose wonderful costume parades eye-witness accounts could have been brought to Dunfermline by Duncan and the Atheling.[1] Malcolm took the trappings of a Norman King, perhaps late in life and with some embarrassment, if (as Turgot maintains, with the best intentions) Margaret " gave him " his bodyguard of retainers. They put the Red King's desperadoes to a perpetual shame, being strictly disciplined, douce, well-behaved, " harming neither the rustics nor the poor ",[2] and Malcolm, resembling in this the ultra-Norman Abbot of Abingdon, nevermore rode or walked abroad without his retinue. Wherever he went, he went " cum grandi honore ", with mickle worship.

Not courtiers only, but all Scots, irrespective of rank or station, private fortune or individual taste, were made to benefit by Margaret's sumptuary reforms. At her behest, merchants came " by land and sea from various regions, bringing for sale many sorts of merchandise which till then had been unknown in these parts ", and it is safe to assume that the various regions included England, France and Flanders. After 1066 a multitude of merchants, Norman and Flemish, settling in London and the Channel ports, flooded England with their wares. In the case of the Banner at Hastings trade followed the flag. Merchants arriving in the Humber or the Tyne, pedlars plodding their way to Richmond or Hexham, would have been men of little enterprise had they failed to push their sales further north with Royal encouragement, but their bills of lading

---

[1] See Ord. Vit. VIII, x.   [2] *Vita*, p. 242.

are lost and the burdens of their pack-horses unknown. From such merchants " the natives, urged to do so by the Queen, purchased garments of divers colours and various ornaments of dress ".[1] Margaret had an eye for colour. " New costumes of different fashions were adopted, the elegance of which made the wearers appear like a new race of beings "—perchance like the Norman race, which was renowned for *elegantia*.

Turgot's cruel absurdities must not blind us to the fact that Margaret was a pioneer in a very necessary work, taken up with great success by her son David, that of stimulating the import of better goods and better stuffs than Scotland could manufacture. In her own way Margaret was carrying on the cultural and social work of the Conquest. For the time being, foreign trade was in the hands of itinerant " merchants " selling luxury articles to individual customers. Margaret fostered that trade ; David by creating burghs made it possible for the merchants to settle in Scotland and sell to communities. Margaret was making an honest and sensible effort to raise the standard of living in her adopted country and bring in a little more brightness and colour. Naturally her chief care was for the Church, which received, among other gifts, gold and silver vessels and vestments embroidered by herself and the gentlewomen in the work-parties she had formed. St. Andrews, Dunfermline and Durham were enriched with cross and crucifix and precious gems. Indeed, it is greatly to be feared that Margaret's munificence was only too " Norman " and contributed to her regrettable unpopularity with the Scots. Perhaps they viewed with mixed feelings " the indigent who came with hurrying steps from almost all countries ", the priceless furs, the " vessels of pure and solid gold, the copes for the cantors, the chasubles

---

[1] " Inter quas [rerum venalium complures et pretiosas species] cum diversis coloribus vestes, variaque vestium ornamenta, indigenae, *compellente regina*, emerunt."—Turgot, *Vita*, VI, p. 241. Some translators say " pressed ", others say " compelled " ; " urged " seems sufficient.

and stoles ", and inwardly taxed the Royal Saint with vain expense.

What is the inner meaning of these things, to which the admirably intentioned and humourless Prior of Durham gives such an unhappy twist of ridicule ? It is that in Malcolm Canmore's perhaps originally modest home French ideas were spreading, ideas such as could only be —and still can only be—expressed by French words : " Court " itself and almost all terms relating to it : palace, prince and sovereign ; realm, royalty and rule ; to govern and to reign. In the next generation, when documents have become more plentiful and more precise, the foreign clerics, the sumptuary regulations, the improved furnishings, the dress reforms, the gold, purple and fine linen are all mentioned as characteristics of the Scottish Court. Their Norman inspiration is then beyond doubt. It may well date from Malcolm Canmore's time.

How far French ideas progressed beyond his own family there is no record to show. Scottish History almost succeeds in reaching the year 1097 without mentioning by name anyone outside the kingly house. But even in Turgot's incense-breathing and twilight world the one bright particular star has other satellites than Malcolm, though their names are not mentioned or their attributes described, and the mere recital of events shows that the King of Scots had counsellors and that on the attitude to be adopted towards the Conquest their counsels were divided. Evidently there were parties : a " Celtic party ", content with the life led from of old in Scotland proper and resentful of interference by Saxon or by Norman ; a " Southern party ", particularly strong in Cumbria and Lothian, tending by the force of circumstances to become a " Norman party " and in the end preferring a Norman-supported king to Donald Bane.

Malcolm Canmore did not travel alone when he went to parley with the Conqueror or his sons, to swear brotherhood with Morel, to hold converse with the French Bishop whose Archdeacon perambulated Teviotdale. He went " with mickle worship ", with a great retinue of courtiers and nobles who had these opportunities, as they had others, of becoming acquainted with the Normans and their ways. The tie which bound him and his family to the Normanized Church of Durham was mundane as well as religious: Malcolm and Margaret made it numerous gifts; both Duncan II and Edgar on their accession by armed force made it grants of land, and the help for which gratitude was thus expressed is not without its dynastic, its cultural and its political significance. Gospatric and his sons had property in Northumberland and numerous Scottish landowners in the indeterminate borderland had Norman neighbours, with whom their relations may not have been always unfriendly. Numerous hostages had been taken on various occasions and some perhaps came home as " Norman " as Duncan. Before Edgar's accession he and his brothers, and no doubt several of his supporters, had spent some three years, and his sisters had spent many more, in Norman England.

It had been Malcolm Canmore's settled policy to encourage immigration from the South. After 1066 refugees flocked in and he " received them gladly, one and all, giving them individually as much protection and assistance as he could ".[1] They were genuine Englishmen. But the time is soon reached when incomers need not be anti-Norman or non-Norman. They might be Englishmen more Normanized than they knew or Frenchmen who crossed the Tweed for much the same reasons as their fathers crossed the Channel. It is unlikely that " the English who were driven out and who before were with King Malcolm " were all native Englishmen. As Margaret introduced Norman clerics, so perhaps Malcolm introduced Norman knights. The exaction of a pledge from Duncan II in his

[1] Wm. Malm. II, p. 308.

very brief reign " never again to harbour Englishmen or Frenchmen in the land "—on terms of military service, according to Florence of Worcester—seems to imply that such harbouring was already a practice.

The appearances are that Malcolm and Margaret were more favourably disposed to Normans than has been commonly assumed ; that by the accession of Edgar in 1097 the Court and part of the nobility had become susceptible to Norman prestige and undergone some degree of Normanization ; that there was a body of opinion in the Kingdom favourable to strong government on the Norman model ; in short, that a condition of affairs had been created in which Norman infiltration and settlement could proceed with a rapidity which otherwise would seem incredible.

FIG. I. NORTH-WESTERN FRANCE IN NORMAN TIMES

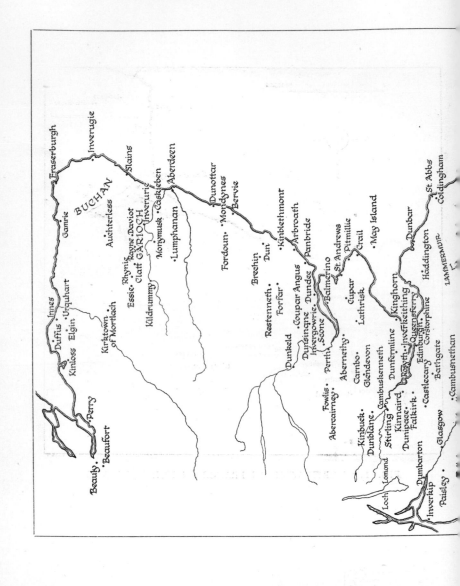

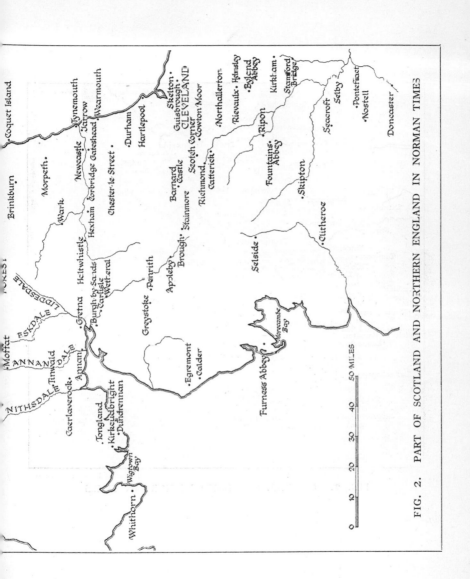

FIG. 2. PART OF SCOTLAND AND NORTHERN ENGLAND IN NORMAN TIMES

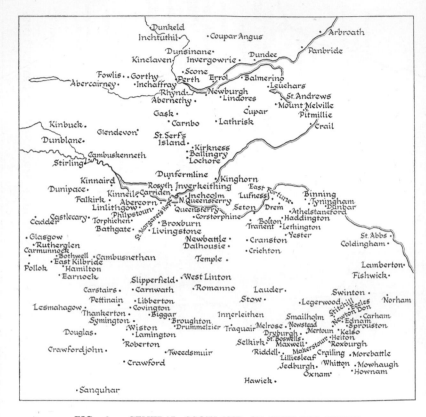

FIG. 3. CENTRAL SCOTLAND IN NORMAN TIMES

CHAPTER II

EDGAR, SCOTO-NORMAN KING
(1097–1107)

★

H

§ 8

Irregular Accessions

EDGAR had given no pledge to send away his foreign followers. They stayed, and order was restored. Donald Bane is said to have been blinded and to have dragged out a pitiful old age as a " launderer ". Capital punishment had been abolished by the Conqueror—the execution of Waltheof in 1076 took place under English law and was a rare exception—and the substituted penalties (blinding and mutilation) were regularly applied. After Robert de Montbrai's revolt they were inflicted on Normans of the highest rank and perhaps the case of Donald Bane, his ally, was assimilated to theirs. But Celtic Royalty was indefeasible. Donald Bane might be old and blind and take in washing, but when he died he was buried in the sacred island where Kenneth MacAlpin lay, with all the Scottish Kings around him. Donald was the last to join them there. He was no vulgar rebel. Nor was Edmund. For him " Margaret's only degenerate son " is a strange epitaph.[1] He was condemned to imprisonment, not death. He died a monk in the Cluniac priory founded by the Conqueror's half-brother Robert de Mortain at the Mont Aigu [Montacute] in Somerset,[2] and, in accordance with his last wishes, was buried in chains, in sign of eternal penitence for the death of Duncan.[3]

Order reigned in Scotland. Edgar " had received his

[1] " Solus fuit Edmundus Margaritae filius a bono degener."—Wm. Malm. II, p. 477.
[2] The Castle was built on the peaked hill (*Mont Aigu*) at Leodgaresburh, near Yeovil (Somerset), and the name may have a secondary reference to Montaigu, near Mortain. The Priory was not built till *c.* 1102. Perhaps before then Edmund had been released and made his profession as a monk elsewhere.   [3] Wm. Malm. V, p. 400.

realm freehold, without tribute ", and financial provision had been made for his attendance at Court on ceremonial occasions.[1] In the new Hall at Westminster, at the Crown-Wearing of Whit Sunday, 1099, the Sword-Bearer was Edgar—by the grace of Rufus—King of Scots.[2]

The task that lay before him and his two brothers who were to succeed him was twofold : to establish the dynasty on a firm basis and to build up on that basis a kingdom comparable to others. The model they knew best was that of Norman England.

As seen not indeed from Dunfermline, but from as near as may be—from Durham—and not by the philosophic historian, but by the plain man of the day, Norman England stands out clearly enough in a vision vouchsafed to one Boson, a Knight of St. Cuthbert.[3] His profession itself bears witness to the changed condition of affairs. Before 1066 England had no " knights " like Boson. Stipulated feudal services there were, and many, but they were not military ; [4] his predecessors were in Normandy. As a King and as a Conqueror, William had been able to apply the Norman system even more strictly than as a Duke. By Boson's time manors in England were regularly held by some form of military tenure, and spiritual tenants

[1]
Li reis Edgar est sis priuez,
De lui son regne ad receü
En franc seruise, sans treü ;
Et li reis bien li otriad,
Ke quant il vers sa curt vendrat,
Seissante solz ait chescon jur.
                    —Gaimar, ll. 6182-6187.

This is the " corrody " ; see Appendix B.

[2] *Ann. Winton.* II, p. 40.

[3] Described anonymously in Sim. Durh. *H.D.E.* I, pp. 130 - 132. " Boso " (in the Latin text) is the very common French name Boson or Bozon ; cp. " Ricardus filius Bozonis ". Writ of Henry I, Easter 1102, to Osbert, Sheriff of Yorkshire. *E. Yks. Ch.* I, No. 14.

[4] Liability to military service T.R.E. was a personal obligation, independent of any contract with a lord. Stenton, *A-S.E.* p. 673. Within a generation after Hastings the Normans had established in Northumbria a system of military service which at every point ignored Old English precedent. Stenton, *E.F.* p. 121.

were furnishing their quota of knights for the King's service. Boson was a member of the Durham contingent (one hundred strong, the Bishop stated at his trial), only a trained mounted soldier, a man of small means and no great consequence.

His vision came to him when he was stricken with grievous illness and lay three days in a trance. What he had seen and heard he would tell no one but the Prior [Turgot, though he is not mentioned by name], and only in secret and in nakedness, so that if he swerved from the way of truth, penance might instantly be applied. The Knight had been led by a mysterious guide through pleasant places and through dreadful to a spot where he could see his own monks of Durham, in procession, all of them perfectly recognizable, in strict ceremonial order, " as is their custom ", and all going straight before them, save only two, who were somewhat out of line. Preceded by a glittering cross and chanting as they went, they were moving towards a wall of immense height in which there was neither door to be seen nor window, and yet they passed within. Pondering on this, Boson at length perceived a very small window and, looking through it, beheld a field full of folk. In the foreground was a troop of Northumbrians " mounted on very fat horses " [1] and carrying, " as they were accustomed to do ", long spears and clashing them furiously together, and great was their pride, but, of a sudden, they vanished into smoke. Then in yet greater pride came *Francigenae*, prancing past on neighing chargers and clad in mail, and they were filling the field with the clatter of horses and the clank of armour when they disappeared, as though the earth had opened and swallowed them up. The field then expanded so as to contain an innumerable multitude of women—a sorry sight, for Boson knew (with some help from his guide) that they were priests' wives, temptresses, stumbling-blocks, soon to

[1] " Equis admodum pinguibus sedentes."

be removed, indeed already on the way to the eternal bonfire. The Knight averted his gaze. When he looked again, the field was a vast and dreary solitude, with only one house in it, of prodigious height and made all of iron. The door was constantly opening and closing, and suddenly Bishop " de Saint-Carilef " looked out and asked Boson where Brother Geoffrey was—which, as the guide explained, portended the death of the Bishop at an early date and of Geoffrey the monk soon after.

All these things Boson was straitly enjoined by his guide to reveal—and did, in tears, reveal. They came to pass. The two monks who were out of line were discovered to be back-sliders and received from the Prior a warning in time. The castle which the Conqueror had built was increasing in iron strength and inaccessible height, while beside it the second Norman Bishop's vast Cathedral was so quickly rising that before he died the processions could circumambulate and enter the unfinished, unvaulted shell. He died on January 2, 1096, and the date of Boson's vision can be placed a little before then or, if our faith in dreams recorded in Latin is not robust, a little after. What he saw—with an approving eye, being *Francigena* or French-born himself— was Normanization in its outward form : first, monks housed, and very quickly housed, in buildings statelier, or at all events higher, than the modest Anglo-Saxon mind had been able to conceive ; disciplined monks, not secular canons sore let and hindered by clergy wives ; trained " knights ", boastful, spectacular, walking with a rattle of ironmongery, but at home in the saddle, hauberk laced, lance in rest, mastering their lean and sinewy chargers, not undrilled spearmen transported to the scene of battle by overfed cart-horses ; real Bishops, controlling a well-organized diocese from grim fortresses in hill-cities, not amiable and possibly inefficient pastors living far from the world in quiet old Saxon villages. These were the results of the Conquest which in his waking hours and daily life had come most prominently into Boson's field of vision—and, no doubt, into Edgar's, Alexander's and David's in their English exile. They were pioneers, reformers. For them reform was imitation : knight-service, military tenure, castle-building, church-building, monastic development, diocesan organization, reconstitution of the Scottish Kingdom on Norman lines.

They have been so long and so touchingly known as the Sons of Margaret that it would seem almost irreverent to give them the correct historical designation which they share with Duncan II—the Sons of Malcolm. Good Kings they were and great praise they won. The twelfth century was the golden age of monarchy and nowhere more clearly so than in Scotland. Yet throughout their reigns a recurrent note of hostility can be detected which is not to be accounted for by " Celtic perversity " or anti-English or anti-Norman feeling. Their tragedy was that for many of their subjects they were only too truly Sons of Margaret : not so much aliens, Southerners, *Sassenachs*, as usurpers. The sporadic revolt against them was dynastic. It is not possible to dismiss the claimants who contended for the throne of Malcolm Canmore, generation after generation, as impostors, visionaries or eccentrics. They found men to die for them. They were ready themselves to die for their cause, and after them it passed to a descendant. Not only had they a cause ; they had a case.

Margaret's fourth son Edgar was a pious and amiable young man, but he had violated both principles of succession, the old and the new. He could not claim to be his father's heir by any right of primogeniture. The heir of line was Duncan's young son William, named doubtless after William Rufus and known to later times as William fitz Duncan. Nor could Edgar pretend to have been elected King. He could of course maintain that Donald III had been deposed. But by whom ?—By foreigners, by Normans. And in virtue of what authority ?

—Only theirs. Edgar's right was might—Norman might. After native resistance had been crushed, he had set aside sons and grandsons of King Malcolm and Queen Ingibiorg, whose title under either system of succession was superior to his own. They might or, like William fitz Duncan, they might not assert their claim. If they chose to assert it, they could always find adherents in the North and West, where the name of Ingibiorg, daughter of Thorfinn the Mighty, grandson of Malcolm MacKenneth, Lord and Father of the West, could not fail to strike a responsive chord. And there was an over-riding claim, that of the House of Moray, which had been maintained by Macbeth, successfully and with popular support, for seventeen years against Malcolm Canmore himself and which could be reasserted with equal justice against any or all of Malcolm's descendants. This claim was not merely legalistic. It corresponded to a territorial and perhaps a racial division. The Macbeth tradition lived on in what was once an independent kingdom—Celtic, originally Pictish, Moray.

The Sons of Margaret had a skeleton in the cupboard, their defective title to the throne. They were sons of a second marriage and they were not elected Kings. To Anglo-Norman lawyers or chroniclers the fact may not have seemed of much consequence. It seemed of more consequence to the Highland Scots, who have long memories, take an interest in genealogy and have a keen eye for Royal rights. The feeling of injustice left by Edgar's accession was one which neither he nor his equally admirable brothers could ever wholly remove. The problem of Norman settlement in Scotland under the Sons of Margaret is thus complicated from the outset by the presence of dynastic factors.

Edgar has been classed as an " English " King, apparently because he descended from Alfred on the mother's side, had a Saxon name [1] and a *Pincerna* or Butler called

---

[1] Edgar's name (or perhaps the note on it by Lord Hailes, *Annals*, I, p. 47) seems to be the basis of Freeman's statement, *N.C.* IV, p. 512:

Ælfric, addressed his charters to " Scots and English " and liked to live in Lothian. The " Scots " are merely dwellers in Scotland proper, mostly Gaelic-speaking; the " English " are Edgar's other subjects. He also liked to live at Invergowrie on the Firth of Tay [1] and no doubt left much of South Scotland to the care of his brother and Heir Presumptive, Alexander.[2] Edgar was a Scoto-Norman King. He looked to England for effective support and there were no native Englishmen in power who could give it. Normans could, and they had their own notions of what a king should be. Edgar had lived for some time among them in England and felt, with his brothers, that some things were better ordered there than at home. In the post-Conquest years there had been an influx of native English refugees. The Anglic element in the Lowland population had been slightly increased and its social value much enhanced. The effect on Scottish life was beneficial. But it has been exaggerated. The English had a great past and a great future, but, demoralized by defeat and foreign occupation, they were at a low ebb. Those who had escaped to Scotland had cut themselves off from their fellows in the South, as unfortunate as they and as powerless. The Normans, not the English, were in a position to exert an influence and one which in an undeveloped country was more beneficent.[3]

" The Kings of Scots who sprang from Malcolm and Margaret were Englishmen, speaking English, often bearing English names, ranking as the highest among English nobles and not wholly without hopes of the English Crown. Just at the moment when England became in some measure French, Scotland became thoroughly English." But, except Edgar, what Scottish Kings who sprang from Malcolm and Margaret bore English names ? And did not Scotland, too, " become in some measure French " ?

[1] Apparently on a property which had belonged to Donald Bane, who is said to have been Mormaer of Gowrie.   [2] See below, p. 114.

[3] A protest against " recent historians who can see nothing but decadence and futility in Anglo-Saxon history of the Tenth and Eleventh Centuries " was made by the late Professor R. W. Chambers, in the Introduction to *Harpsfield's Life of Sir Thomas More*, E.E.T.S. No. 186 (1932), pp. lxiv-lxxxi, *e.g.* p. lxxvii : " Now (January 5, 1066) England possessed a civilization based on Alfred's English prose as the national and literary language. English jewellery, metal-work, tapestry and carving were famed throughout

At home, too, Edgar was among Normans, whom he esteemed for their support and for their personal qualities. For Margaret's able and gifted sons, the Conquerors of the second generation were congenial and fascinating companions : mighty hunters, accomplished horsemen, for ever riding abroad with hawk and hound, fine soldiers, familiar with the methods of cavalry warfare, unafraid of campaigning in the Welsh mountains or on the Scottish moors. They would be misjudged from the Conqueror's short, squat, ill-favoured progeny. Some must have taken after their fathers or grandfathers in the Tapestry—tall, broad-shouldered fellows in their fighting days, fresh-complexioned, with "good" features, prominent nose and high cheek-bones. Some must have been worthy descendants of a race haloed with victories in many lands and famed throughout Christendom for its skill in dealing with subject peoples and its devotion to the interests of Holy Church.

Few charters by Edgar being extant and none of them dealing with grants of land to individuals, it is impossible to know if he made any to Normans. There is documentary evidence, however, of his active interest in land-development. A certain " Thor Longus " records that he received from " Edgar his lord, King of Scots " land at Ednam (near Kelso, Roxburghshire) which was waste (*deserta*) and which he occupied and cultivated with assistance from the King but provided with his own stock (*pecunia*).[1] At Ednam Thor built a church in honour of St. Cuthbert, perhaps helping with his own hands (" a fundamentis fabricavi "), and, *c.* 1105, gave it, with a plough-gate of land, to Durham.[2] He would be unknown but for this, and it seems likely that others, unrecorded, were encouraged

Western Europe. English illumination was unrivalled. . . . Eleventh-century Anglo-Saxon architecture shows an astonishing variety. . . ."

[1] This has been hailed as the first Scottish instance of capital applied to the exploitation of land, on the assumption that *pecunia* means " money " ; it must have its ordinary mediaeval meaning, "stock". Thor's name, which implies Scandinavian origins, perhaps remote, appears as " Thorh Longus " in the Obituary of the *Liber Vitae*, p. 147.   [2] Lawrie, XXIV.

by King Edgar to develop waste land, of which there must have been abundance after so many years of unrest and raiding and counter-raiding. " Restoration " effected with foreign help generally meant rewarding of strangers with forfeited lands, and if the Normans who set and maintained Edgar on the throne had failed to acquire property in his Kingdom they would have been strange representatives of their acquisitive race. One is found in possession of land in Lothian as early as 1099 : a certain Robert, son of Godwin, who came with the Atheling to fight under St. Cuthbert's banner and won renown for having, like the fabled Taillefer at Hastings, left the ranks before the battle and engaged the enemy single-handed. It is true that Robert, to judge by his father's name, was only half a Norman.[1] But it is merely by accident that his ownership of land in Lothian has come to light, merely because he was proceeding in Norman fashion to build a castle on it when " he was surrounded by countrymen and barons of Durham " and, after a stout resistance, which remained famous in the district, was carried off as a prisoner. The Bishop—" Ranulphus " [Renouf], who was called " Flambard " because, as Treasurer to Rufus, he showed a rapacity which the saintly Anselm compared to an all-consuming flame—was apparently at the bottom of the affair : a quarrel among Normans, always sensitive on the subject of frontier fortification.[2] King Edgar was absent at the time, bearing

---

[1] According to Fordun (pp. 220-222), quoting Turgot, Edgar Atheling, being once accused to Rufus of plotting against him by " a certain knight, a degenerate Englishman called Orgar ", was defended by " a knight of Winchester, Godwin by name ", who proved his innocence by a judicial combat. Another, or perhaps the same, Godwin was one of the Atheling's tenants in Hertfordshire ; see above, p. 47, n. 2.

[2] Reported only by Fordun, V, xxv, p. 225. The land was given to Robert by King Edgar, therefore after October 1097. The incident, if " Flambard " instigated it, must have occurred between June 5, 1099, when he was appointed to Durham, and August 15, 1100, when he was incarcerated in the Tower of London. He did not return to Durham till after Robert had gone on Crusade. As Edgar was at Westminster on May 19, 1099, his stay must have been lengthy or his journey home leisurely.

the Sword of State in the Hall of Rufus, and on his way home through Durham he obtained the prisoner's release. The first care of the Normans in Wales as in England was to build castles. In Edgar's realm there must have been other castles than his own at Invergowrie [1] and Robert's in Lothian, and it would only be in accordance with contemporary custom if he settled some members of his Norman garrison on the land.

If he was to govern in a way of which his protectors would approve he required the usual administrative offices and they could be filled only by Normans. That his government was conducted on Norman principles appears from his habit of using a seal—a characteristically Norman practice which Duncan II had been quick to follow. Edgar's seal bore his effigy and the superscription " Imago Edgari Scottorum Basilei ". The title Basileus, used by no other King of Scots before or since, had been affected by the Conqueror.[2] It came to him from the Old English Kings, who had a taste for magniloquence and liked the Imperial resonance of the word. The most picturesque of them, Edgar the Peaceful, had an established reputation in Scotland, being memorable there for proclaiming himself " Basileus of the English World " and circumnavigating the whole Island every summer.[3] His less memorable descendant and namesake was equally peaceful ; his first measure of foreign policy, in 1098, had been to cede the long since nominal Scottish sovereignty over the Hebrides to the warrior-King of Norway who in the course of extensive campaigning in the Isles had taken to wearing the kilt and goes down in history as Magnus Bareleg.[4]

[1] Said by Boece, XII, p. 262, to have been built in stone.

[2] *E.g.* the charter of William I, below, p. 137, n. 3.

[3] Entered in *Chron. Melrose, s.a.* 965. On Turgot's mention of Edgar the Peaceful, see Appendix E.

[4] *Heimskringla*, quoted by Anderson, *E.S.Sc.* II, p. 138. This is said (by Worsaae, p. 288) to be the earliest reference to the kilt—much in evidence some years later on Cowton Moor. Magnus arrived in the Isles in 1098 to assert his supremacy, for all districts conquered by the Norse were claimed

With the Hebrides Iona was lost.[1] Overlordship of Britain
was not one of the Scottish Edgar's ambitions, but the High
King of Ireland, with whom, too, he entered into friendly
relations, was " Imperator Scottorum ", [2] and perhaps there
was some idea of recalling that Edgar was a High King, as
distinguished from a Mormaer or a *regulus*. More probably
the title, together with the seal, was simply borrowed from
the Norman chancery. A royal seal is a sign of changed
times in Scotland. It implies a staff of clerks, scrutiny of
personal petitions to the King, official recording of his
grants, everything done decently and in Norman order,
decisions set down for instant display or future reference
in documents which bear an outward token demonstrating
to all the illiterate world the Sovereign's authentic will.
The keeper and user of the King's seal soon becomes his
chief scribe, an essential officer of his household, eventually
head of the Royal secretarial forces organized into a chancery. The Chancellors of William I, ecclesiastics on the
way to a Bishopric, came from a highly educated professional clerical class which had no counterpart in Saxon
England. It was the creation of Norman lords, efficient,
hard-headed, somewhat crude business men, who liked to
have everything put in writing, but left the actual writing
to specialists, to scribes.[3] Edgar's seal heralds the arrival
of this clerical class. Norman government was essentially
written government. Scotland was taking up the pen.

When the commander of the Norman forces in Scotland
felt that his presence was no longer necessary, he followed
Duke Robert's example and departed on Crusade.[4] With

by the Kings of Norway, though, *de facto*, the Norse chieftains were independent rulers. Magnus was slain in Ulster in 1103, at the age of thirty.
The changed times are shown by the fact that he was the last of the Vikings
and his son was Sigurd the Crusader.

[1] But it does not appear that Iona was ever within the Norwegian see
of the Isles.

[2] A title recorded in Ireland from 1002. E. MacNeill, *C.I.* p. 24.

[3] V. H. Galbraith, *Literacy*, p. 219.

[4] Ord. Vit. says that Edgar Atheling arrived in the East during the siege
of Antioch (June 6–28, 1098), but Wm. Malm., with more probability, places

him went Robert, son of Godwin, and probably no one else, despite William of Malmesbury's minor witticism: when the Pope preached the famous sermon at Clermont-Ferrand the effect was such that in all lands men left their avocations to go on Crusade; " then the Welshman gave up poaching and the Scot fraternizing with fleas ".[1] England also sent few Crusaders, only two of known name,[2] both of Scottish interest and both of the older generation, as Crusaders so often were: Guillaume de Percy, who had been at Abernethy many years before, and Ernoulf de Hesdin, maternal grandfather of Scotland's first Steward, remote progenitor of her ever-famous dynasty.[3] Edgar Atheling, who was to distinguish himself in the East, had already done so in Scotland on this, the last of his many visits. He had placed his nephew and namesake firmly on the throne and, if only through his twenty-five years of intimate association with the Conqueror's sons, he brought about the event which in 1100 settled once for all the struggle between Norman and Gael. This event was the marriage of his niece Edith to the new Norman King.

his arrival with Robert, son of Godwin, at the time of the siege of Ramleh (May 11, 1102). David, *R. Curthose*, pp. 232-233. Robert, son of Godwin, died on Crusade.

[1] " Tunc Walensis venationem saltuum, tunc Scottus familiaritatem pulicum reliquit "—Wm. Malm. II, p. 399. The sermon was preached by the (French) Pope Urban II on November 27, 1095.

[2] David, *R. Curthose*, p. 94.

[3] Hesdin (Pas-de-Calais), arr. Boulogne, canton de Samer. Ernoulf, " the most mysterious personage in Domesday ", was tenant-in-chief in ten counties and must have stood high in the Conqueror's esteem. Round, *Cal.* I, p. 481. He lived at Chipping Norton, Oxfordshire, and is the only landowner in that county who is shown in Domesday as resident on his estates. *V.C.H. Oxfordshire*, I, p. 384. Accused of complicity in Robert de Montbrai's revolt against Rufus, he cleared himself by a judicial duel and left England. He went with Duke Robert on Crusade and died at Antioch. David, *R. Curthose*, p. 222. Ernoulf's daughter Adeline or Aveline married Alain fitz Flaald and became the mother of Walter, who in 1158 was made Hereditary Steward of Scotland ; see below, p. 281.

§9

The Marriage of Maud

EDITH, who took the name Maud on her marriage or perhaps before,[1] had no more than average good looks—in the Monk of Malmesbury's judgment, but he was difficult to please. From the same critical source we learn that she was ill-provided for, being an orphan, and had hardly any household furniture. Yet she had never lacked suitors, all of the highest rank, all related to the Conqueror. The first is said to have been the Lord of Richmond, and the next, the King of England, whose visit to Romsey has ever since been productive of dark hints and sinister interpretations, but seems understandable enough as matrimonial in intent and dynastic in design. When Rufus came to a sudden end in the neighbouring Forest, his place was taken at once by a kinsman, Guillaume de Varenne, Earl of Surrey, son of a Hastings commander, but he, when he spoke of the matter to the new King, learned that a higher destiny awaited the Daughter of Margaret. As the Monk of Saint-Évroul religiously puts it, she was *divinitus reservata*;[2] she was set apart for the Divine purpose of uniting the English and the Norman peoples. But Guillaume de Varenne himself might also be regarded as having been dynastically predestined, for his grandsons were Scottish Kings and the only surname the Canmore dynasty ever had was his, de Varenne.[3]

---

[1] See Appendix D.　　　　[2] Ord. Vit. VIII, xxii.

[3] He was the elder son of Guillaume de Varenne (near Bellencombre, arr. Dieppe) and Gondrée [Gundrada], daughter of Gerbod, Avoué of Saint-Bertin and, for a short time in 1070, Earl of Chester. Guillaume I was a younger son who inherited but little from his father and who, helped

He never quite forgave his successful rival, Henry, in whose favour it should, however, be said that he had been a suitor before, at a time when his own destinies seemed far from brilliant, and only of late, towards the age of thirty-two, had he found his feelings reciprocated. In the interval his fortunes had undergone a dramatic change.

It was on a Thursday afternoon (August 2, 1100) that Rufus was cut off in his prime. His elder brother, Duke Robert, was then coming home from the Crusade in pomp and at leisure—solvent for once, having married on the way a very wealthy and also very beautiful heiress, Sibylla, daughter of one of the Norman princes at Conversano. The younger brother, Henry, was in the New Forest, far enough from the fatal spot to be beyond suspicion, near enough to act with the minimum of delay. He galloped to Winchester, obtained possession of the Treasury,[1] had himself chosen King by " those of the Council who were nigh at hand ",[2] took the sixty-two miles to Westminster at a gallop—and on Sunday was crowned. Elected, crowned and anointed as suspiciously as Harold and (allowing for the distance) as quickly, he maintained his speed much better. A Charter of Liberties was issued almost instantaneously. In this document, addressed " Francis et Anglis ", he referred approvingly to the state of affairs " before my father's time ", undertook to restore the Laws of Edward, with the emendations " which my father made

by a relationship to the ducal house, was the founder of his own fortunes. It was to their English lands that the family owed their importance. See L. C. Lloyd, *The Origin of the Family of Warenne*, in *Yks. Archaeol. Journal*, XXXI (1934), pp. 97-113. Guillaume I supported Rufus in 1088 and was made by him Earl of Surrey, but died a few weeks later (June 24, 1088). Guillaume II did not come to England till after his father's death. His daughter Adeline became the wife of Earl Henry and the mother of Malcolm IV and William the Lion, known to Normans as Guillaume de Varenne.

[1] After a violent altercation with the Treasurer, who had reminded Henry that they had both sworn fealty to Duke Robert, who had long laboured in God's service [on Crusade]. Ord. Vit. X, xiv.

[2] *A-S.C.* MS. E, *s.a.* 1100.

on the advice of his barons ", but, " by common consent "
of his own barons, kept the Forests in his own hands.
IIe then announced that a marriage had been arranged
and would shortly take place between himself and a
daughter of the Old English House, " King Edward's
niece ". From this point onwards, his fortunes and those
of the dynasty set up in Scotland by his late unregretted
brother are linked together for better or worse.

The marriage announced was based on strong mutual
affection, the chroniclers assure us, and it presented further
advantages, the most conspicuous of which was the
strengthening of a weak title to the throne. The case
Henry made out for himself included the argument that,
though the youngest of the Conqueror's sons, he was the
only one born in England and the only one born " in the
purple "—of parents already crowned and not, like the
parents of Robert and Rufus, a mere duke and duchess.
These remarkable qualifications may have appealed to
Henry's English subjects [1] and seem to pass muster with
our historians, in this regard more Norman than the
Normans, who, as their kings came one after another to a
melancholy end, regularly ascribed it to wrongful accession
—an opinion endorsed by " Giraldus Cambrensis " in his
survey of their reigns.[2] It is vain to point out that strict
laws of primogeniture had never governed the succession
to the English throne and not always even to estates in
Normandy. That was no argument for Norman barons.
For them the succession of a younger son was, in principle,

[1] According to Ord. Vit. they did ; see below, p. 112, n. 3.

[2] Gir. Cambr. VIII, p. 138, in the passage (see below, p. 186, n. 1) where
the Norman and Angevin Kings are unfavourably contrasted with the Scottish. Henry I was a Porphyrogenite in the strictest sense, a child not only
" born in the purple ", but born after his father's accession to the throne.
The glory of being one was proclaimed in 1173 by Henry's great-grandson,
the Young King (see below, p. 335, n. 2). But he was a youth of considerable
assurance, aged seventeen, an eldest son and not using an argument against
a brother. He was using one against his father, who was " only a King "
(Henry II), not a Porphyrogenite. His argument would have made small
impression on the ruder barons of seventy-three years before.

subversive. Some of them might defend it for private reasons or on juridical grounds or on English precedents, but it went against the grain. William's younger sons felt that their seizure of the Crown profoundly shocked Norman minds. Rufus brazened it out ; Henry explained it away. There was dire need of explanation. Irregular accession might, as in so many cases, have been quickly condoned or forgotten, had there not been exceptionally dangerous elements in the situation, such as opposition from an outraged brother, who had been passed over once before but after all was Duke of the Normans, and from barons well-nigh as powerful, and as unscrupulous, as Henry.[1] There was an unhappy resemblance to the case of Esau. The new Jacob's legal explanations give the measure of his necessity.[2] He and his friends had to cling to every straw, utilize every shred of argument or of moral support that could be obtained from marriage-connection with the Old English House or could be evoked from the unseen world. Into the maze of argument and haze of dynastic mysticism Malcolm Canmore's second family was inevitably drawn.

As was fitting in the first year of what Maitland called " the most legal of centuries ", the swift events of the autumn proceeded in a legal atmosphere. Monarchy, too, was on the threshold of its greatest century. In the chanceries Royal pedigree was becoming a matter of prime importance. In the *chansons de geste* heroes and heroines were soon to be provided with illustrious ancestors, enumerated with convincing detail. " And I will give you a king's daughter (*fille de rei*) " is the legendary Charlemagne's most dazzling promise, the supreme reward for the bravest of knights. Henry's deficiencies in Royal pedigree were patent to every eye. His ancestry in the male line went up only to Rollo and then came to a mysterious and piratical end ;

[1] Wm. Malm. II, p. 470.
[2] Matth. Paris, *H.M.* I, p. 31 : " jam legisperitus effectus est . . . Jacob resuscitatus, occupator ambitiosus ".

in the female line there was "Arlette". The purple
in which he was born was hardly two years older than
himself, of dubious texture and widely considered to be
stolen property. But deficiencies, regal or legal, could be
partly remedied by marriage with a king's daughter. The
"English Princess, Edward's niece"—she was a Scottish
Princess and Edward's great-grand-niece—would bring
lustre. She might almost seem to bring a Crown Matrimonial.[1]

Henry's marriage had been arranged "on the advice
of his friends and chiefly of the Bishops among them".[2]
"A certain Abbess" who lent her good offices may have
been Christina, who, though she never attained that rank,
was the lady of highest degree in England and, in the eyes
of the world, the chief personage in the sisterhood at
Romsey. Henry's most powerful lay supporter, Simon de
Saint-Liz, Earl of Northampton, was not only a friend :
his wife Maud, daughter of Earl Waltheof and Judith, was
a relative of both contracting parties.[3] Archbishop Anselm
was in France. Old Archbishop Thomas had come up
with all speed from Ripon for the Coronation. But his
speed could not compare with Henry's. He arrived too
late and had to be mollified by the already crowned monarch.[4] He remained a friend. The Bishops known to
have been active in Henry's cause were Maurice (London),
who conducted the Coronation ceremony, Gerard (Hereford), William Giffard, Elect of Winchester, ex-Chancellors,
well able to perceive political merits in the marriage, and
Gundulph (Rochester), who was certainly more interested
in its religious aspect. For earnest minds, Maud was not
so much a descendant of Alfred as a spiritual link with
the Holy King whom the Normans revered, knowing his

---

[1] It would have required a strong effort of imagination. In the line of
succession Edith came after three brothers.
[2] "Suadentibus amicis ac maxime pontificibus."—Wm. Malm. II,
p. 470.   [3] On the relationship see Appendix G.
[4] Hugh the Cantor, in Raine, *Hist. Ch. York*, II, p. 107.

affection for their country and their churches, and whom the English idealized, remembering his goodness and forgetting his failings. There are two Edwards—the Edward of history and the Edward of legend. The Edward of history, son of Norman Emma, grandson of Duke Richard I, cousin of Duke William, the Normans had always considered one of themselves. The Edward of legend—of legend fostered by them—they claimed also for their own. It grieved their spiritual leaders to think that the Norman Kings lacked both the Divine sanction which the French monarchy had received and the religious awe with which the Old English Kings were surrounded and which Edward had renewed, though perhaps only from beyond the grave. In so far as personal considerations entered into episcopal counsels, Maud's education at Romsey and Wilton may have been important, for both convents were closely connected with the Norman episcopate. Anselm, who knew her aunt Christina well,[1] may have spoken of Maud to his inseparable companion Gundulph. But, however the fact had come to be known, Maud was pre-eminently the sort of person whom Bishops in every age have recommended as the perfect Queen.

Her reputation was almost too good. Her forthcoming marriage was no sooner announced than informed opinion declared it an impossibility. Rumour had it that at Romsey, some years before, Maud had taken the veil. The need for an authoritative statement to the contrary was urgent when on September 23 Anselm landed from France and went straight to the King at Salisbury. Maud was in the convent at Wilton, in the immediate neighbourhood, and the Archbishop learned from her how the rumour had arisen.[2] Unwilling to make a pronouncement on his own authority, he summoned a synod—at the Bishop of

---

[1] A few weeks later Maud (perhaps tactfully, to avoid further description of her aunt's strong personality) mentions that Anselm knows her well.

[2] Eadmer, *H.N.* p. 122.

Rochester's manor of Lambeth—of men learned in the canon and the civil law, with archdeacons among them, to take evidence in the case and decide whether Maud had or had not pledged herself to be the Bride of Heaven. After the depositions, the Archbishop withdrew. It was found, unanimously, that the source of the rumour was a cloak, of semi-monastic design and sombre hue, which Christina had compelled Maud to wear in her earlier youth, for the discouragement of unapproved suitors or Norman men of violence. Maud disliked this precautionary, and therefore unbecoming, garment and several times, in the presence of witnesses, had cast it off and trampled on it in fury, on which occasions her strong-minded, free-spoken aunt, acting *in loco parentis*, plied Margaret's rods to the accompaniment of startling expletives.[1] There was sensational evidence that Malcolm Canmore had once seen the cloak and lost his temper; "furore accensus", he had expressed his disapproval in unmeasured terms, going even so far as to declare that no daughter of his should be a nun, could he prevent it.[2] If this remark was held proved, it must have settled the case: at Maud's age parental consent was indispensable.[3] Brought in to hear the decision, she listened to the end, demurely,[4] and then addressed the court with some composure, offering to give further testimony. With equally subdued satisfaction Anselm heard the verdict for which he had hoped and prayed, and with a glad heart he crowned Maud Queen of

---

[1] Maud's deposition runs: "me illum [nigrum panniculum] abjicientem, acris verberibus ac nimium obscenis verborum conviciis saepe cruciare simul ac dehonestare solebat"—Eadmer, p. 122. According to Turgot, *Vita*, V, p. 240, Margaret entrusted her sons' education to a "familiaris minister", with strict injunctions "not to spare the rod". The rod was not spared, and (with the very dubious exception of Edmund) the children were not spoiled.

[2] Though Maud is not known to have returned to Scotland, nor Malcolm to have gone to England, except in 1093, contemporaries find no difficulty here, nor in the meeting of father and daughter mentioned above, p. 70, n. 2.

[3] The Rule of St. Benedict, chapter lix, is adamantine: parents must "offer" a minor.   [4] "Comi vultu"—Eadmer, p. 125.

the English, at Martinmas (November 11, 1100), only three months after the hunting accident in the New Forest.

The subsequent history of the Normans in Scotland flows from the simple fact that the Conqueror's son married Malcolm Canmore's daughter. The immediate effect was to create a pattern which remained constant for many years : two usurpers in mutual support. Usurper is a hard word, and in the case of Henry and the three Sons of Margaret the modern historian finds extenuating circumstances. So did many of their subjects. Others did not; hence most of the troubles in their reigns. For their opponents, there was in England a Norman usurper, liable to be overthrown at any moment, whether in the Kingdom or in the Duchy, by a rightful claimant; personally much obsessed by dynasty; making the most of his wife's Royal descent and her relationship with Edward, which, in fact, was chiefly spiritual; having every reason to uphold her reigning brother—a usurper, who had been aided by Norman accomplices and whose defective title would become no better when it passed to Alexander and, after him, to David. In this delicate situation relationship with Edward, however remote, might be a useful asset. The claim which William established by the sword, being based on kinship with Edward through Emma, passed on death to his own next of kin, his eldest son, but had been usurped by the youngest, who, however, had established for himself a further connection with Edward, by marriage. In the esteem of Normans as of Saxons the Sons of Margaret, descendants of the Old English House and kinsmen of the Holy King, benefited also by this connection.

The marriage of Maud was instantly followed by a marked improvement in the family fortunes. The pious and amiable Edgar reigned unmolested, his throne and his Royal dignity alike secure. The lawyers who filled the centuries with their disputations *in re* Homage of Scottish

Kings passed over Edgar's in silence ; the Norman Queen's brother was no ordinary vassal. Alexander and David, who were boys at the time of the Flight into England and had been living among the Normans as refugees with a dubious future,[1] acquired the style and title which David used for his seal : " Brother to the Queen of the English ".[2] If it was politic to marry " King Edward's niece ", it was politic to have one or two of her relatives about the Court, and Alexander probably frequented it for some time before returning to Scotland. David went into permanent residence [3] and was brought up to be a Norman " baron " ; Mary made a prompt and brilliant marriage. She, too, was a penniless lass with a long pedigree and hardly any household furniture, yet she needed no prophecy, no mention of reservation for any Divine purpose. Evidently her husband was less interested than Maud's in such matters. He was Eustace III, Count of Boulogne, eldest son of the mustachio'd Eustace.[4] His brothers were Godefroi de Bouillon, first Christian ruler of Jerusalem, who had refused " to wear a crown of gold where Christ had worn a crown of thorns ", and Baudouin, first Christian King, who was crowned at Bethlehem on Christmas Day, 1100. Eustace himself was just home from the Crusade, full of honour, having been among the first three who fought their way into the Holy City. He had hardly resumed control of Boulogne when he utilized its convenient proximity to England to help in the invasion inefficiently

[1] Alexander (born *c.* 1077) from perhaps the age of fifteen, David from perhaps the age of nine. David's year of birth is unknown, but from general circumstances it can be guessed as *c.* 1084.

[2] " Davit Comitis Anglorum Regine fratris."—Seal of Charter, *c.* 1117, Lawrie, XXIX.

[3] " David curiae sororii sui inseparabilis inhaesit."—Ord. Vit. VIII, xxii.

[4] Eustace II " aux Grenons ", King Edward's brother-in-law, inherited the English lands of his wife, Godgifu († before 1056). He lost them after revolting against William I in 1067 and, a second time, after revolting against William II in 1088. They were mostly in the Eastern shires. His marriage with Godgifu was childless. Eustace III, son of his second wife Ida, succeeded him in 1093 and died a monk in 1125. See table, below, p. 140.

conducted by his fellow-Crusader Duke Robert, but the efficient and politic Henry, needing all the friends he could find, thought it well to forgive him, returned him the forfeited paternal holdings in England and, in 1102, gave him the Queen's sister in marriage.[1] " King's daughter " was a yet higher matrimonial qualification and this may help to account for the remarkable fact that, though Malcolm and Margaret had ended their lives in ruin and disaster, their two dowerless orphan daughters were yet regarded as the two greatest " heiresses " in the Norman world.[2]

[1] " Maria reginae soror."—Flor. Worc. II, p. 51.
[2] According to the fourteenth-century Book of Hyde = *Liber Monasterii de Hyda* (R.S. 1866, p. 306), which derives some information from sources now lost, Henry had first thought of his own cousin William of Mortain as a husband for Mary. But William was on Duke Robert's side and remained loyal to him. Ord. Vit. XI, x.

§ 10

Mystic Union

THE union of the Old English, the Norman and the Scottish Royal families created around them a strange atmosphere of goodwill, sanctity, mysticism and propaganda. "Mold the gode Quene, Seint edwarde's nece "[1] is indeed one of the most charming figures of the Norman age, full of feminine arts and graces and self-sacrifice, yet pleasantly conscious of having done extremely well for herself and her relations. With Margaret her mother, she was regularly likened to Esther, and if in both cases the comparison overstresses the patriotic self-sacrifice, Maud had at least Esther's gift of " obtaining favour in the sight of all them that looked upon her ". When her godfather Duke Robert, incited by her unsuccessful suitor, Guillaume de Varenne, invaded England in 1101, he landed at Portsmouth and marched on Winchester, but, learning that the Queen was in child-bed there, refrained from acts of war in the neighbourhood and, passing by the city, went on to London by another route.[2] When he came back to England in 1103—this time with peaceful intent and only to the end that Guillaume de Varenne might be restored to his forfeited Earldom of Surrey—it was at Maud's request that he agreed to forgo the annual subsidy of three thousand marks silver which was all he had gained, and rather pitifully, by his late invasion.[3] The venerable Anselm showed her much affection and neither worldly business nor regal pomp could keep her from hurrying to

[1] R. Glouc. ll. 6468 and 7253.
[2] Wace, *Roman de Rou*, II, l. 10,365 ; Farrer, *Itin.* p. 9.
[3] On the political reasons for utilizing Queen Maud's good offices, see David, *R. Curthose*, p. 148.

greet him whenever he passed—so we are told by his biographer and disciple Eadmer, Bishop of St. Andrews.[1] The no less venerable Gundulph was equally charmed and favoured. The Queen frequently sent for him, never wearied of listening to his ghostly counsel and chose him to baptize her infant son.[2]

His birth, in the summer of 1103, was attended by signs and portents and much soothsaying, the most celebrated prediction being King Edward's, that of the Green Tree.[3] The boy became known as Guillaume Adelin. The son born some two years before him to Duke Robert and the heiress of Conversano became known as Guillaume Cliton. Each was, in English, a " William Atheling " [4] and each was a grandson of the Conqueror. By primogeniture, the elder child—only son of Robert, eldest son of William I—had an incontestable title to the throne. But he was not a scion of the Old English House and the honours of prophecy were not with him.

---

[1] *H.N.* p. 183.　　　　　　　[2] *Vita Gund.* p. 288.

[3] " Plures provinciae spectabant nutum pueri, putabatur regis Edwardi vaticinium in eo complendum, ferebaturque spes Angliae, modo arboris succisae ", etc.—Wm. Malm. II, p. 495. This prophecy was discovered in the *Vita Æduuardi*, composed for the widowed Lady Edith by one of her " Flemish or Lotharingian " clerics in 1067 ; see above, p. xxxvi. In an obscure passage towards the end, Edward in his dying moments reveals what had been told him in a vision by two departed monks whom he had known as a young man in Normandy. They had said that after his death his Kingdom would be given over to evil spirits for a year and a day. He inquired when remission could be hoped for and the monks answered that if a growing tree were cut down, and the upper part removed a space of three acres, and if, of its own accord, this severed part returned to the parent stock, grew green and brought forth fruit, only then could there be remission. The prediction is of troubles, mostly ecclesiastical, to be expected after Edward's death. The Green Tree is a simile like the Camel and the Eye of a Needle ; as the author explicitly states, it is a " similitudo impossibilitatis ". But some readers in 1100 took the image as the prophetic part of the utterance. For them the Green Tree was the House of Cerdic ; the three acres were the reigns of Harold, William and Rufus ; the reference was to the marriage of Henry I and Maud. They had three children—1, a child, b. July 1101, who died in infancy ; 2, Maud, b. February 1102 ; 3, William, b. before August 1103.

[4] In English they are indistinguishable. In Latin they were differentiated (*e.g.* by Ord. Vit.) as *Gulielmus Adelinus* and *Gulielmus Clito.*

In the preceding year (1102) the belief that Edward was a Saint and a Prophet had become so prevalent that an Inquiry had been instituted. The Abbot of Westminster, Gilbert Crispin, and Anselm's confidant and suffragan, the Bishop of Rochester, Gundulph, acting as the Abbot's coadjutor, caused the body to be exhumed and found it to be incorrupt. In all the events that were to culminate in the canonization of Edward in 1163 Normans are very prominent. It was in his Normandy days that he was said to have first performed miraculous cures and it was by French witnesses that they were reported ; [1] there were Normans among " the sick who were healed during the three hundred days after his death while the masses, the hymns and the alms continued to be daily offered " ; [2] the first official steps taken were taken by Normans of Normandy, by two prelates born and brought up in the Duchy before the Conquest. An appeal to Rome was not made in 1102 ; it was not yet the custom. All that was laid down by Anselm's reforming Council—which only the marriage of Maud and the consequent certainty of peace with Scotland had made it possible for him to hold,[3] and in the same year (1102) and at the same place (Westminster)—was that there should be no veneration without episcopal authority.[4] He himself had sent an archdeacon to inform the Abbess and nuns of Romsey that they must abandon " superstitious veneration of a man deceased whom they considered a Saint " ; [5] the " man " was Queen Maud's kinsman, Earl Waltheof, who " deceased " in 1076, not far from Romsey, by order of Henry's father.[6] In matters of

[1] *Vita Æd.* l. 1400.

[2] The cripple cured on the eighth day after Edward's burial was a Norman, Ralph—according to the most complete Life of Edward, MS. British Museum, Add. 35298. See G. E. Moore, *ME. Life.*

[3] *Flor. Hist.* II, xxviii, p. 36.

[4] " Ne quis temeraria novitate corporibus mortuorum . . . sine episcopali auctoritate reverentiam sanctitatis exhibeat."—Council of Westminster, 1102, in Wm. Malm. *Gesta P.A.* p. 120.

[5] Anselm, *Ep.* 51, in Migne, *P.L.* CLIX, col. 82.

[6] See below, pp. 137-138.

sainthood the recognized authority was the Bishop, acting with the knowledge of the secular power; furthermore, any such investigation obviously required the assent of the family representatives. In 1102 they were Henry and Maud, with both of whom Anselm and Bishop Gundulph and the Abbot are known to have been at the time in continual association.[1]

Prophecy had become the order of the day. On Turgot's last visit to Margaret she had " foretold certain things in the future ".[2] These things, or those of them which he reveals, are only two in number: her own imminent death and " the elevation of sons and daughters of hers to the summit of earthly dignity. The event proves " —he is writing not later than 1106—" that things are now as she foretold ": Edgar is King of Scots and Maud is Queen of the English. In Turgot's mind, evidently, both facts are surprising. For him the accession of a son of Margaret was an unexpected happening—for others it was plain usurpation—and the marriage of Maud was explicable only by Divine intervention. Similar prophecies referred to Henry's accession and marriage in more detail. After the death of Rufus in the Forest of ill omen predictions were reported. He had seen awful visions in which Bishop Gundulph, who already had warned him to mend his ways, appeared as the herald of approaching doom. Anonymous Britons, or perhaps Bretons, were found to have prophesied in days of old that the doors of the Treasury would open to a king's son born in the purple,[3] and to have made dim but disparaging allusions to Robert and Rufus, cryptic yet promising references to a " Leo justitiae" or Lion of Justice—conceivably Henry, who in his

---

[1] See below, p. 116, n. 5.   [2] *Vita*, pp. 250-251.
[3] " Arx cum regalibus filio regis Henrico reddita est. Hoc antea dudum fuit a Britonibus prophetatum "—*Britones* could be Ancient Britons, or Welshmen, or Bretons. Orderic continues: " et hunc Angli optaverunt habere dominum, quem nobiliter in solio regni noverant genitum ". Ord. Vit. X, xiv.

youth had studied law and in his reign was to apply it with some severity; [1] what was meant by "justice" in those days was suppression of disorder by extremely stern measures. These prophecies are chronicled by authors who wrote in his reign. [2] They did not prophesy themselves; they merely recorded, with some complacency, predictions made by others before them and before 1100, or, as the sceptic may think, very soon after, while the sensational events of that year were still fresh in people's minds. The predictions are of clerkly origin. Unsophisticated as they are in their imagery of trees and birds and animals, they are composed in good Latin and, though they are dim and mysterious, can be readily applied to Royal family matters, consequently to matters of state. Prophesying after the event has been at all times a popular practice. The early twelfth century made it a regular means of political persuasion. The psychology no doubt was that a *fait accompli* appeared more natural or more tolerable when presented as something long foretold. A king seemed yet more kingly when he was found to have been the subject of communications received from the unseen world before he was born. As some of the vaticination in Henry's reign seems to emanate from his immediate entourage, in part Breton and Welsh, it may be that he, too, was among the prophets.

In religious minds high above any such suspicions spiritual union of the three dynasties through " Norman Edward " was already a theme for meditation when at

[1] " A people shall come over in timber and coats of iron who shall execute vengeance for iniquity. Two dragons shall succeed, of whom one shall be slain by the darts of malice and the other shall return under the shadow of a name. A lion of justice shall succeed. . . ."—Ord. Vit. XII, xlviii (from Geoffrey of Monmouth).

[2] Orderic wrote from 1120 to 1141, William of Malmesbury, *c.* 1125. Geoffrey of Monmouth's predictions are in his *Prophecies of Merlin*, incorporated as Book VII in his *Historia* (1136), but published before the rest, probably in 1134. Faral, *Lég. arth.* II, p. 9. Soon afterwards we find the illustrious Abbot Suger relating how the prophecies concerning Henry I came true—in his *Life of Louis IX*, Waquet, p. 98.

Durham, on September 4, 1104, the body of St. Cuthbert was removed from a temporary shrine in the cloister to the partially built cathedral, in presence of Queen Maud's brother " Alexander Comes ".[1] This title, which David also had adopted, was generally used without indication of place and could designate indifferently a Duke of Normandy or of Brittany, an English Earl or a Breton Count.[2] It illustrates one of the insuperable difficulties of our subject. How far people who spoke French or English and wrote Latin drew distinctions not readily expressed in one or other of these languages, it is quite impossible to determine. As used by Alexander and David,[3] " Comes " probably meant what would now be called rather Prince than Earl—a Royal personage, acting, with some independence, as a provincial governor. Alexander, being Heir Presumptive, had no doubt been entrusted with some powers in South Scotland, in accordance with established custom. Margaret had given him a religious upbringing, which, on the authority of Anselm, bore good fruit,[4] and he had some clerkly skill.[5] Ailred praised him as " a man of education (*litteratus*), most zealous in regulating Church matters and seeking out relics of the Saints ",[6] and among the Norman higher clergy he

[1] " Praesente Alexandro comite."—S.S. I, p. 106 ; Ord. Vit. (V, ix) makes him (prematurely) King.

[2] In their charters the Dukes of Normandy frequently describe themselves as *Comites*. It was a title practically reserved to members of the ducal house. The Conqueror is sometimes " Dux " at the beginning of a charter and " Comes " at the end. Robert is generally " Comes " but Henry (Duke from 1106 to 1135) is " Dux ". Valin, p. 52 ; Prentout, *O. et F.* p. 228. " Comes " was used also by the Duke of Brittany. The Lords of Richmond were " Comites ". They were Breton Counts, they were English Earls, but they were not yet styled Earls of Richmond ; see *E. Yorks. Ch.* IV, 97.

[3] So far as his status in Scotland is concerned. From 1114 " Comes " might refer to his English Earldoms.

[4] Letter from Anselm (1107) congratulating Alexander on his accession. Lawrie, XXV.

[5] Raoul d'Escures afterwards, when Archbishop of Canterbury, described Alexander as " ecclesiae Dei utilem, vita et moribus et litteris divinis et, si opus fuerit, saecularibus a pueritia instructum " = " instructed from boyhood in divine literature and, so far as necessary, in secular " ; the tense *fuerit* is odd : ? = " in case need should arise ". Lawrie, XXXVII (1120).

[6] *G.R.A.*

must have already had a certain reputation as a devout layman of sound judgment, well informed on things spiritual, for at Durham he was chosen to act as coadjutor to the celebrated authority on Translations, Raoul [Ralph] d'Escures, Abbot of Séez.[1] " Because of the incredulity of certain Abbots "[2] it was decided that both should view the body of the Saint before the Translation,[3] and Alexander, "because he had permission to take part in so holy an office, had given many marks of gold and silver and caused a shrine to be prepared in which the holy body, clothed in new vestments, was honourably placed ".[4]

Raoul d'Escures had left his Abbey not long before to escape from the tyranny of Robert de Bellême and had been hospitably received in England by two venerable friends, Anselm, his former master at Bec, and Gundulph —and by King Henry. He, too, suffered much from Robert de Bellême, who, having succeeded to the great estates in Shropshire and elsewhere which formed the Earldom of Shrewsbury, had come to England and was openly flouting the Usurper.[5] The Abbot would seem at first to have fallen from Scylla into Charybdis, from Séez into Shrewsbury, where his Norman

[1] Escures was a hamlet beside Séez, Latin *Sagii*, now Sées (Orne), arr. Alençon, from which town Sées is some twelve miles distant. The Abbey was founded by Roger de Montgommeri (Calvados), arr. Lisieux, commune Livarot.

[2] Flor. Worc. II, p. 53 : Wm. Malm. *Gesta P.A.* p. 275.

[3] Ord. Vit. According to the account in *De Miraculis et Translationibus*, in Sim. Durh. I, p. 249, a preliminary investigation was held on August 24 by Prior Turgot and nine monks. They included (according to Reg. Durh. *Libellus*, ch. xl) Simeon and the archdeacons Henry and William Havegrim ; the latter was Ailred's kinsman : see Appendix H.

[4] Flor. Worc. II, p. 53, *s.a.* 1104.

[5] Roger de Montgommeri, first Earl of Shrewsbury (from 1071), died on July 27, 1094. He was succeeded in his English possessions by his second son, Hugh, who, being slain in Anglesey by Magnus Bareleg in 1098, was succeeded in them by the elder son, Robert. He used his mother's style " de Bellême ". The Abbey of Shrewsbury was founded (on the suggestion of Orderic's father, who lived in the neighbourhood) by Earl Roger, who brought monks from Séez.

oppressor, " de Bellême, that man of Belial ", was being attacked by the Royal forces. But sound reasons which escape us must have led the Abbot's steps into Shropshire, for the fugitive who before many years were gone was installed in the Chair of St. Augustine was no aimless wanderer.[1] It was he who conducted the negotiations for the surrender of Shrewsbury in July 1102 ; since then he had been living with the Bishop of Rochester at Lambeth and making visitations of the Abbeys, where he displayed his remarkable social gifts and where, no doubt, he had occasion to note and report on " the incredulity of certain Abbots ". On Translations he had been for some time a recognized authority.[2] His host at Lambeth had yet longer experience.[3] Lanfranc, always the lawyer and never very sure of himself on the subject of miracles, had regularly entrusted him with inquiries into matters concerning sainthood.[4] In 1104 Gundulph was administering the Archdiocese and acting as intermediary between the King and Anselm, who had again withdrawn to France. We may be sure that the Abbot of Séez went to Durham with the goodwill of Gundulph's spiritual daughter Maud and of her husband, without whose express approval little was done in his Kingdom. All these personages were constantly meeting that summer.[5]

As Gundulph was in charge of Canterbury, so Turgot was in charge of Durham. Many years before, Bishop

[1] Raoul d'Escures († 1122) succeeded Gundulph († March 7, 1108) at Rochester. After Anselm's death in April 1109 he acted (like Gundulph) as administrator of the see of Canterbury till he was chosen Archbishop, in April 1114. He was " litteris admodum imbutus, eloquens et jocundus, ideoque amabilis omnibus "—Ord. Vit. VIII, viii.

[2] Since 1092, when he was charged with the Translation of St. Nicholas at Noyon.

[3] At Canterbury, in 1073, Gundulph had presided at the Translation of St. Dunstan : see R. A. L. Smith, pp. 260 and 263 n.

[4] Eadmer, *Ep. ad Glaston.* p. 222.

[5] For example, a charter of 1104 is witnessed, probably at the Whitsuntide Court, by Queen Maud, Gundulph, Abbot Crispin and Raoul d'Escures. Shortly before August 15 Henry left for Normandy, on his first visit after his accession. Farrer, *Itin.* p. 24.

" de Saint-Carilef ", following Northumbrian precedents set by Boisil and Cuthbert,[1] had raised him to a position in the diocese second only to his own. Turgot was not merely Prior. He was Archdeacon, Dean and " Vice-dominus " [2]—a comprehensive term reflecting the historical fact that from 1088 to 1105 the " Dominus " was mostly in Normandy, whose strange Duke pinned his faith to government by Bishops of Durham in distress.[3] Turgot was in charge of the whole temporal administration of the see. In the deliberations preceding the Translation he took the foremost part and the arrangements for the actual ceremony were made by him.

The two Royal families now united by marriage had long been joined in veneration of St. Cuthbert. The Conqueror had made rich gifts to his Church.[4] Queen Matilda had helped to found the Priory.[5] Rufus had almost shown the generosity of a pious soul.[6] The Priory had entered into an agreement with Malcolm and Margaret and their sons " that for the King and Queen while they live they shall nourish every day one poor man and after their death their anniversary shall be celebrated every year with festivity as is King Æthelstan's ".[7] Margaret, besides sending many beautiful vestments, had bequeathed " a copy of the Gospels in letters of silver, and the cross set with

---

[1] Sim. Durh. *H.D.E.* I, p. 129.

[2] " In toto episcopatu decanus et vice-dominus "—Wm. Malm. *Gesta P.A.* p. 273. At Durham the Prior was tenant-in-chief of the Bishop " tanquam dominus " not " tanquam patronus ", in order to avoid the awkward canonical difficulty of an internal feudalization of the Church. Lapsley, *Boldon Book*, p. 311.

[3] Bishop " de Saint-Carilef " was absent for nearly three years (1088–1091), governing Normandy. After his death (January 2, 1096) the see was vacant for three and a half years—till " Flambard " was appointed (June 5, 1099). That worthy was one year in office—till August 15, 1100, when he was under lock and key. After escaping from the Tower, he was at Lisieux, scandalizing the Church and misgoverning the district, and probably did not return to Durham till 1105.

[4] Sim. Durh. *H.D.E.* I, p. 100 and again p. 108.

[5] *Ibid.* p. 121.

[6] Gifts of land by Rufus are enumerated in the *Liber Vitae*, p. 76.

[7] *Liber Vitae*, p. 73.

pearls (*margaritae*), which her dying hands had held ".[1]
Duncan II in his six months' reign had time to convey
much good land in Lothian. In gratitude for the banner
of victory [2] King Edgar gave the church of Coldingham to
" St. Cuthbert, my master ", and confirmed to Durham
parts of the *Terra* which lay in the Scottish Kingdom.[3]
Alexander gave " many marks of gold and silver " and the
shrine. Queen Maud gave the church of Carham ; [4] in
the convent garden at Wilton one of St. Cuthbert's disciples
lay buried.[5] Consigned for ever to the Book of Life at
Durham were the names of Margaret, her mother Agatha,
her husband Malcolm and, as though to remind us that
in the sight of God all men are equal, the names of Margaret's eight children without designation of rank and
without reference to her, and the name of Morel, the
Norman Sheriff by whom their father was treacherously
slain. The foundation-stones laid in the autumn of 1093
by the Norman Bishop, the English Prior and the Scottish
King had been well and truly laid ; when in the autumn
of 1104 the relics of the Northumbrian Confessor were
borne into the Norman cathedral built to receive them,
Malcolm Canmore's last prayer for peace had been heard.

While this or that detail may be legend or hagiography,
it is impossible not to connect this solemn occasion with
the history of the period and the men by whom it was
being made and being written ; in too short a time (August
2, 1100–September 4, 1104) too many strange events had

---

[1] Reginald of Durham (*Cuthb.* I, pp. 217-218), who adds that once on
St. Margaret's Day, when great crowds had flocked " ad ecclesiam Stellen-
sem [?], quae Dunfermelin in eorum lingua dicitur ", the Benedictines of
Dunfermline allowed the relics of St. Cuthbert to be borne in the procession
before the relics of St. Margaret " because they had read in the book of her
life that there was no Saint she loved more than Cuthbert ".

[2] Fordun, V, p. 226. The banner could not be removed from the church
except by express permission of the Prior [Turgot]. By similar permission
it was carried before the English army at Flodden.

[3] " Domino meo."—Lawrie, XVIII (1098) ; XIX (*c.* 1100).

[4] *Hist. Northd.* XI, p. 12.

[5] Mentioned by Herman of Laon, *De Miraculis*, Migne, *P.L.* CLVI, 983.

occurred and in them too many great personages had been concerned. It is possible, indeed it is highly probable, that the actors in the drama were themselves unconscious of its remoter implications, but it is not certain that these escaped the attention of thoughtful minds. Reconciliation of conquerors and conquered was proceeding by religious and by dynastic means, with the Scottish Royal House as the central factor. At Westminster as at Durham, the Norman clerk was acquiring a local allegiance, a loyalty to the land and its past, especially through the saints and the privileges of his own Church.[1] The Norman and the Scottish reigning families were being bound together by spiritual links, in the Communion of the Saints—of Cuthbert, Edward and Margaret. Turgot is not the only historian in question. Simeon walked in the procession; with him went Ailred's clerical and monastic kinsmen. From the ceremonies Simeon must have returned with zeal renewed to his two great tomes, one on the History of St. Cuthbert's Church, the other on doings in the world as seen from the rock of Durham, while Turgot addressed himself to the composition of a *Vita Sanctae Margaritae* at the request of her daughter, the Norman Queen. The theme was interpreted by him or by Maud as threefold: the goodness of Edward's ancestors, the Norman as well as the English; the sanctity of Edward; the sanctity of his grand-niece Margaret. In the next generation the threefold theme was taken up by Ailred of Rievaulx, son, grandson, great-grandson of secular clerks, kinsman of Norman religious at Durham, Household officer and devoted servant of Margaret's son David. What would be known of Scottish events in her time without Simeon's two ponderous volumes? In all that concerns the inner life, what would be known of her and her sons but for Turgot, what of David and his friends but for Ailred? The testimony of twelfth-century writers is coloured

---

[1] Galbraith, *Nationality*, p. 122.

by considerations relating to the dynastic union of 1100. Decolorization may be possible, but it is arbitrary and apt to be affected by twentieth-century prejudice. It will be sufficient to have drawn attention to the existence of the colouring and to its nature.

Under the double aegis of the half-Norman Saint and Cuthbert the Confessor, Edgar's peaceful reign proceeded. " Sweet and lovable was he, like in all things to King Edward, his kinsman, employing no harshness, no tyranny, no greed against his people, but ruling with the greatest charity and loving-kindness." [1] Following in his kinsman's tradition, he " lived as a monk " and gave Scotland no Queen and no Prince. Both peace and enlightenment are implied in the present which he sent in 1105 to his friend the High King of Ireland. It was " an elephant, which is a beast of marvellous size ".[2] Perhaps it came from King Henry, an ardent collector of strange fauna at Woodstock,[3] or perhaps it came from the Atheling, who had covered himself with such glory in the East that the Emperor of the Greeks implored him to stay and made him numerous and, it may be, embarrassing gifts.[4] Alexander's Arab steed [5] furnishes more elegant proof that Norman

---

[1] Ailred, *G.R.A.* p. 735.

[2] " Camall [not a camel] quod est animal mirae magnitudinis."—*Annals of Innisfallen* in *Collectanea de Rebus Albanicis*, Iona Club (1847), p. 279.

[3] It is after noting that " Murcardus " [Muirchertach (†1119), King of Munster and High King of Ireland] had a profound admiration for Henry I that Wm. Malm. (I, p. 485) mentions Henry's custom of requesting foreign rulers to send strange animals for his park at Woodstock. The park is said to have been enclosed in 1114 (*V.C.H. Oxfordshire*, II), but H. E. Salter (*Med. Oxford*, p. 30) believes that the building of the palace and village was begun early in Henry's reign.

[4] Wm. Malm. II, p. 310. Edgar Atheling was seized with home-sickness and returned, though whether " home " was England or Normandy is not clear. After Tinchebray (1106) it was probably England.

[5] On Alexander's Arab steed, see below, p. 172. It is believed to be the only Arab horse recorded in Great Britain till 1616, when James I bought, for five hundred guineas, " the first of that breed ever seen in England ". Ridgway, p. 378. There were Arab horses in the booty taken by the Crusaders, *e.g.* at Jerusalem in June 1099. *Gesta Francorum*, ed. L. Bréhier, 1924, Index *s.v.* CHEVAUX.

participation in the Crusade was introducing Scotland to the wonders of the East.

From a stormy beginning Edgar's reign passes imperceptibly into a quiet transition period, half Celtic twilight, half Norman dawn. He had reigned only nine years when he died, at Dundee,[1] on January 8, 1107. He was buried in the Church of Dunfermline by Margaret's side, his father still lying in foreign soil, at Tynemouth, where he was taken for burial after the ambush at Alnwick.[2] There was no more question of Iona. It, too, was foreign soil. The ancient link between the House of MacAlpin and the island home of Celtic piety had broken for ever. Henceforward the Kings were laid to their rest in Dunfermline.

[1] Fordun; Wyntoun, VII, v, 605; perhaps at Edinburgh : see Skene, I, p. 444.

[2] Malcolm Canmore's body was brought home by Alexander towards 1123 and buried in Dunfermline. Wm. Malm. II, 309.

CHAPTER III

KING ALEXANDER AND EARL DAVID
(1107–1124)

★

§ 11

Family Rule

THE age of seal and charter had come. Edgar left a will. Its provisions were that his dominions should be shared by his two surviving brothers: Alexander, Malcolm Canmore's eighth son, the fifth by Margaret, was to be King; David, the ninth and youngest son, was to have Cumbria and parts of Lothian. This in itself can hardly have required a will. For ninety years at the least Cumbria had been treated as the appanage of the heir to the throne, and unspecified parts of Lothian had gone with it. Edgar was childless, Alexander unmarried, and David's status was perfectly clear—he was Heir Presumptive and entitled to the appanage. But perhaps in the will both " presumption " and " appanage " had been, with Norman assistance, interpreted somewhat generously in his favour. The Normans who had made Edgar King must have approved his testamentary dispositions. These Alexander violently resented, and his angry objections were not silenced till David threatened to march against him with Norman knights in support.

Ailred is the authority for this, and it accords with all we know of David at this stage in his career. He was an energetic young Prince and the outlet for the energy was Norman. In the Monk of Malmesbury's judgment Edgar and Alexander retained vestigial traces of the rugged Scot. David, he thought, was *curialior*, more courtly, better versed in the ways of the *curia regis*. " He had been polished (*limatus*) by living among us; in boyhood he had rubbed off all the rust of Scottish barbarity ".[1] At that time the epithet *barbarus* was very freely bestowed on the Scots, and not only on them, for the Pope condoled with Anselm for being " inter barbaros positus ". It meant "outlandish", from the speaker's point of view. Observed not from Rome, but only from Malmesbury, Edgar and Alexander seemed imperfectly Normanized, whereas David possessed *elegantia* and could be distinguished at a glance from *barbari* or non-Normans. The Monk of Saint-Évroul corroborates : " David was trained among the boys of the household and when he grew up merited a wise and peaceful King's familiar friendship and received knighthood at his hands ". No date is given, but attainment of the age of sixteen would have been a suitable occasion ; there had been opportunities since, and he was certainly a Norman Knight before the death of Edgar. " Court " meant divers things : among others, an essentially social institution and a place to which the King's rights of wardship brought the heirs of many noble families for their education, so that from early youth they were familiar with him and his ministers, and with each other.[2] David all his life enjoyed the advantages of so useful an upbringing ; for the highest-born Normans, and the highest-placed, he was always " one of us ". " Court " also meant law court, and he had only to join his sister Maud on the bench when she sat in the *curia regis*, issuing writs in her husband's absence.[3] She lived at Westminster in great state, bestowing her bounty with more generosity than judgment on " clerks of melodious voice " and French writers of French or Latin verse,[4] " lavishing gifts on all manner of men, but especially on foreigners who spread the fame of her munificence far and wide ",[5] and gaining wide renown by her charity to the poor, her work for the Church, her acts

---

[1] Wm. Malm. II, p. 477. He was evidently pleased with his metaphor of rust and applies it again to the Scots in his *Vita Wulfstani*.

[2] Stenton, *E.F.* p. 32.   [3] Documents in Bigelow, pp. 100 and 137.

[4] We have shown, *Medium Ævum*, XIX (1950), pp. 64-66, that it was for Queen Maud that Benoît made his French translation of the *Navigatio Sancti Brendani*.   [5] Wm. Malm. II, p. 494.

of devotion and penance. Maud had as many Norman traits as Margaret—or as David, who before he was twenty was as busy with legal matters as any Norman baron, attesting charters with the greatest of them, among whom he was himself accounted, his name being sometimes followed by his style and title, " The Queen's Brother ", sometimes given with a splendid simplicity as " D ".[1] For his personal character we must, as so often, turn from the soulless documents to Ailred, who tells us that David, being hurriedly summoned one night to his sister's presence, left the young courtiers with whom he was feasting and found her Hall at Westminster full of lepers, and herself, suitably attired for the occasion, washing and drying and kissing their feet. She was a true daughter of Margaret and he was a true son, but he none the less vigorously remonstrated, pointing out that Henry, should he come to hear of kisses such as these, might well be sparing of his own. Maud informed her brother that she had summoned him in order that he might learn from her example, but he only laughed and withdrew, having, as he confessed to Ailred in maturer years, not yet felt the spirit of God within him.

The knights whom Ailred had in mind when he referred to David's menace of invasion had passed beyond the stage of festive courtiers. They were such as Robert de Brus and Walter Espec, men whom David met at the *curia regis* when it dealt with important business, men who were his personal friends, but were not private adventurers. They were the Norman King's most trusted representatives in the North of England and any offer of armed assistance they may have made was made with his approval. He was then at Windsor,[2] fresh from the field of triumph at Tinchebray,[3] where, on September 28, 1106, forty years

---

[1] Charters so attested by David are numerous in Farrer, *Itin.*, *e.g.* p. 30, August 1105, with Eustace III and Guillaume II de Varenne ; and p. 44, 1107, Confirmation of a gift made by Earl Simon de Saint-Liz to the priory he had founded at Northampton.

[2] David, *R. Curthose*, p. 179.   [3] Orne, arr. Domfront.

to a day after the landing at Pevensey, he had received the final instalment of his father's prophecy. At last he was Duke of the Normans, as he had longed and schemed and fought to be. But before him stretched a long vista of wars consequent on his seizure of the Royal and the Ducal Crowns and the anarchy left by his deposed brother, and already he could foresee much of what did happen : he spent in the Duchy more than half his twenty-nine remaining years of life. Security from attack in the North of his Kingdom was a prime necessity. It had been achieved by marrying Maud, and though he was well disposed to both her brothers and both were peaceably inclined, peace would be doubly sure if as much of South Scotland as possible were ruled by a *persona gratissima*, a good friend of the Northern barons. Henry's chief preoccupation immediately after Tinchebray was to strengthen their hands, give them forfeited manors and support them in their efforts to bring about settled conditions. For them, too, security was vital ; several of them were living on lands lately torn from the Scottish Kingdom. It was a Norman interest that the terms of Edgar's will should become operative and that David should have his full share, and perhaps rather more, in the Scottish patrimony. In the words of the Chronicle, " Alexander succeeded to the Kingdom as King Henry granted him ".[1] This probably means that he did homage to Henry and reigned over the whole of the composite Kingdom, while in the two great added provinces David ruled under him, with fuller powers, perhaps, than had hitherto been exercised by the heir to the throne.

No further quarrel, no contest of authority, arose between the brothers. They had the same (Norman) conception of government and under them for seventeen years Normanization proceeded apace. Things moved faster in the South. If as a liaison officer for the forces of Normanism Alexander had his imperfections, one more enthusiastic

[1] *A-S.C.* MS. E, *s.a.* 1107.

and more efficient than David would have been hard to find.

Since their father's death the southern limits of the Kingdom had been the Solway Firth, the ridge of the Cheviots and the Tweed. Alexander's most direct rule was over the country between the Forth and the Spey. Ergadia or Argyll, Moray and Ross remained virtually independent; Caithness with Sutherland still formed a Norwegian earldom. What came under the King's closest personal supervision was the Scottish homeland. There were the two ancient religious centres: Abernethy, capital of the Picts, Dunkeld, capital of Kenneth MacAlpin; St. Andrews, seat of the Bishop of the Scots; the new Church of Dunfermline; Scone, with the Hill of Belief [1] and the Stone of Destiny. Scone was "the principal seat of our Kingdom".[2] Alexander's own place of residence was occasionally Edinburgh, usually Invergowrie. The land of his choice was the heart of Scotland. As regards Norman influences it was the hard core.

In "Cumbria"—and it may be recalled that this vague term included such places as Ayr, Renfrew and Glasgow—David ruled avowedly under his brother the King, and with such respect for the Royal prerogative, or with such unfailing tact, that no reference to the nature of his rule is anywhere to be found. Styled "Comes", without designation of place, he was Earl of Huntingdon and Northampton from 1114, but what he was in the Scottish Kingdom from 1107 is not clear. Perhaps he had a sphere of influence rather than a territorial earldom or principality forming a definite administrative unit. But the sphere was vast, including (though not Edinburgh) almost the whole of the country south of Clyde and Forth, with overlordship of Galloway, and the

---

[1] Constantin, becoming King of Alban in 900, held a solemn assembly on the Hill at Scone, "in colle credulitatis". See Skene, I, pp. 340 and 351. It was to become the Mote Hill, a Norman name.

[2] Foundation Charter of the Priory, confirmed by Malcolm IV "ecclesia de Scon in principali sede regni nostri fundata". *Scone*, No. V, p. 5.

influence became more and more preponderant as he acquired immense and ever-increasing personal prestige. All the circumstances make it probable that in South Scotland David's word was law.[1]

Alexander was " a man of great heart, exerting himself in all things beyond his strength " [2]—perhaps a somewhat sombre mediaeval monarch, austerely following the Norman ideals, the religious and the military. He held the Norman view of the Royal prerogative. When Eadmer at St. Andrews asked for counsel from those who knew, they told him that Alexander " wishes to do everything in his Kingdom alone, by himself, and will not suffer any interference from any authority whatsoever ". In Wyntoun's words, Alexander's delight was in visiting churches and enriching them with "ornamentis, iowellis, bukes and westimentis" :

> Luffande he was and richt wertuosse
> Til clerkis and al religiousse ;
> Til his legis he was curtusse ;
> In iustis lauchful he was alwayis.[3]

If he loved to visit monasteries and make them gifts of furnishings, jewels, books and vestments ; if he was amiable and very generous to clerks and all religious, courtly to his lieges, and in the administration of justice always adhered to strict legality—then Alexander was a typical early-twelfth-century Norman ruler. Before he acceded, towards the age of thirty, he had been in the public mind the devout Christian Prince of the Translation at Durham, a recluse rather than a man of action, and because he was so

> Diuote and full of religiositie,
> Richt mony man thair demit him till be
> Baith blait and blunt [spiritless and dull].[4]

---

[1] On David's status in Cumbria see Appendix G.
[2] Ailred, *G.R.A.* p. 756.
[3] Wyntoun, VII, vi, 819. He is partly repeating Ailred's phrase : " Clericis et monachis satis humilis et amabilis erat, caeteris subditorum supra modum terribilis ". Norman " courtliness " towards lieges did not preclude considerable severity.   [4] *Bk. Cron. Scot.* ll. 41,822-41,824.

Alexander was not " blate ". Once King, he displayed a
startling efficiency. Early in his reign he was at his
castle of Invergowrie, " withe ane honest cowrt ", when
word came of " a multitude of Scottis men " advancing
on him with hostile intent. The whole " Court " took to
their steeds, routed the assailants and chased the fleeing
remnants through the Highlands into Ross, where the last
of the rebels were rounded up and killed :

> . . . Fewe he left
> To tak on hande sic purposse eft.
> Fra that day his legis all
> Oyssit hym Alexander the Fers to calle.[1]

" Fierce " was a French cognomen (*Fers*, *Fiers*, meaning
strong and bold, not ferocious), and adolescence among
the Normans in England had brought Alexander, besides
strength and audacity, a belief in castles and armour, and
some knowledge of horse-craft and cavalry tactics. His
lieges were backward in such matters. Those who appeared
at Invergowrie—men of Moray, representing the cause of
their House—had been more intent on " laying the proud
usurper low " than on acquiring military equipment for
the purpose. Few can even have had horses, and sorry
nags they must have been, compared with the Norman
chargers. It is no easy matter for an undisciplined body
of men to stand up to a horse at a gallop, and Highlanders
had a superstitious dread of mounted troops which lasted
into the '45. A Scoto-Norman King was at an advantage
over warriors who despised armour and rushed into battle
with no more protection than helmet and leathern buckler.

Alexander was also at an advantage over the Welsh.
As unafraid as any Norman of campaigning in the Welsh
hills and as little burdened with scruples when a chance
came for a cavalry charge, he led an expedition into
Snowdonia which can scarcely have been accounted a

[1] Wyntoun, VII, v, 651. " Alexander Fers, id est fortis ob singularem
in latronibus compescendis virtutem cognominatus "—Boece, XII, p. 262.

Scottish interest. It was a Norman-feudal interest. Alexander had "succeeded to the Kingdom as King Henry granted him "—no doubt on terms which implied provision of military assistance when asked for. On Henry's accession in 1100 the only parts of Wales which were unconquered were in Gwynedd. Since then, Gruffyd ap Cynan, King of Gwynedd, besides holding Eisted-foddau, advancing the cause of poetry in Wales and teaching the Welsh to play upon the harp, had been steadily extending his sway over the country west of the Conway. He knew the Normans well, having long been a prisoner among them, and can have had small cause for surprise when at last, in the summer of 1114, they took energetic action and three armies converged on Gwynedd. But when he learned that the army arriving from Chester was commanded jointly by the Scottish King and young Richard, Earl of Chester and *Vicomte* of Avranches, he may well have felt both astonished and aggrieved. Astonishment still prevails. The Welsh chroniclers undertake no explanation of Alexander's motives: " The Earl [of Chester] was offended by the seizure of his land. . . . The King of England was amazed and opened his treasury and spared no expense on horsemen and footmen, and took with him the King of Scotland. . . ." [1] The present-day Welsh historians assure us that there was no fighting (despite the inevitable prediction by Merlin), but refrain from speculating on what benefits Alexander or his lieges expected or obtained. [2]

Thus, less than fifty years after Hastings, unconquered Wales had been attacked by three Norman-led armies from the rest of Britain: one under the Conqueror's youngest

[1] *The History of Gruffydd ap Cynan*, p. 153, ed. Arthur Jones (Manchester University Press, 1910).
[2] See J. E. Lloyd, II, p. 463 ; O. Edwards, pp. 72-74. Orderic quotes Merlin's prophecy from Geoffrey of Monmouth : " Albany shall be roused to fury and, calling on those who dwell by her side, shall give herself up to the shedding of blood ". Ord. Vit. XII, xlviii.

son ; another, composed of Cornishmen, under the Earl of Cornwall, Gilbert son of Richard ;[1] the third under another Norman Earl and a Scoto-Norman King. Whatever may have been the feelings their peoples entertained towards the Welsh, the two surviving Sons of Margaret found themselves on the side of the " Conquerors ". And perhaps it was just as well. This was Henry's first campaign in Wales ; thereafter, under his guidance, subjugation and settlement went on inexorably, irresistibly and (after a vain revolt in 1116) unresisted till there was hardly a corner left in South Wales under the sway of a native prince and the chronicler of Llanbadarn could write of Henry as " the man with whom none may strive save God himself, who hath given him the dominion ".[2] Scotland was not so conquered. Some will say that the accession of Edgar made such conquest unnecessary. It might be truer to say that the marriage of Maud obtained for her brother's Kingdom a favoured position which was not obtainable by Wales.

By early training, family relationship, common interests and the logic of events, Alexander and David were members of the Norman oligarchy and there can have been little to distinguish Henry's two brothers-in-law from his other relatives, friends, courtiers or vassals, save their higher rank and repute. Heirs to a line of kings which stretched back to the Son of Alpin at Dunkeld, and from him through the Highland mists to Fergus Mór at Crinan, they descended on the mother's side from Cerdic, founder of the West Saxon dynasty. By the marriage of their two sisters they had risen high in Norman esteem. Maud rejoiced to have a daughter Empress,[3] as Margaret would have rejoiced to have a daughter Queen. The only Scottish Princess who ever married a King of England, Maud set an example which could fitly have been followed. She won all hearts, and when she died (May 1, 1118) " evident signs and

---

[1] This Earl has not been identified.   [2] J. E. Lloyd, II, p. 423.
[3] Maud or Matilda, who married, January 7, 1114, the Emperor Henry V.

frequent miracles showed that her soul was in Heaven ".[1]
The scene of these miracles is itself significant : her tomb,
at which they were wrought, was next to Edward's, in his
Abbey of Westminster.[2] Mary, who, like her, died young,
resembled her in all things—in marrying into a House
whose fame was passing into legend, in discharging the
duties of her high estate with much distinction and piety,
and even in having an only daughter, who was a Maud
and a Queen.[3] With such sisters, Alexander and David
could not but be workers in the Norman cause—in the same
cause as their nephew Guillaume Adelin, first-fruit of the
Green Tree, handsome young Richard d'Avranches and
the rest of the bright band of Norman youth who on
November 25, 1120, went down in *La Blanche Nef* off
Barfleur.

The Normans in England necessarily clung together.
They were still an alien minority, a garrison. But of late
their rule had changed for the better. The first reign had
been military occupation ; the second, suppression of revolt
(among Normans) by methods of violence ; the third was
organization on conciliatory lines. The time had gone by
when Rufus' ruffians could proclaim in the subjugated
district of Carlisle that Norman lords were predestined to
chastise Englishmen.[4] But their Divine mission for other
purposes obtained widespread credence. The verdict of
God at Hastings was being accepted in other fields than
the military or the religious or the legal. England was
being conquered anew—by more polished manners, by
smarter clothes, better food and drink, more ceremonious

[1] Roger of Wendover, II, p. 195.

[2] The Register of Holy Trinity, Aldgate, Maud's foundation (see
below, p. 171), shows that she was to have been buried there, but Henry
insisted on Westminster, though he chose Reading (his foundation) as his
own place of sepulture. *V.C.H. London*, I, p. 465.

[3] Mary died May 31, 1115. She was a benefactress of Bermondsey and
was buried there. Her daughter Maud was Stephen's Queen.

[4] " En quel temps [1091] nul riche ome se osa clamer Englès pur hount,
tant estoient en servitude, les seignurs Normaunz qi de Dieux estoient
predestene de lex chastier fourount si couaitous qe . . ."—*Scalachronica*, 19.

service: in brief, by French "*elegantia*". Judged by modern standards, *l'élégance* left much to be desired. Compared with the Anglo-Saxon or the Celtic achievement, it was probably inferior in some respects, superior in others. But this is a matter of taste or of fashion, and the French had performed their historic function in the world; they had set the fashion. *La mode* quickly captivated the women. After them and through them, it captivated the men. On feminine *elegantia* in Scotland the least said may be the soonest mended, and the least that can be said here is that, for the rest of the century and for long after, there was no Queen of Scots who was not French.

Alexander's Queen was one of his Norman brother-in-law's unlawful daughters. Henry's notions on posterity were regal. For him, as the Monk of Malmesbury in a pioneer excursion into psycho-analysis philosophically explains, Royalty was a precious gift, a rare quality, to be generously transmitted to a wide posterity,[1] and the number of Henry's illegitimate children was large. A further reason for having them, or for having so many, was their usefulness for the purposes of diplomacy. The daughters he married not to his own barons, who might presume upon the semi-Royal status so conferred, but to neighbour princelings whose advancement to the rank of son-in-law seemed safe and advantageous. It was his practice to take into consideration the relative value and importance of both parties, and as Sibylla, whom he gave in marriage to Alexander, was not very high on the list of daughters, or possessed of much personal charm, it might seem at first sight that the King of Scots was ranked low among the monarchs. Her shortcomings were in deportment and style,[2] the very matters in which Norman ladies

---

[1] Wm. Malm. II, p. 488.

[2] "Morum modestia . . . corporis elegantia", Wm. Malm. II, p. 476, who adds that Alexander bore her death with composure. Her mother is said to have been a daughter of Robert Corbet of Alcester, Warwickshire. If so, Sibylla (Sibile) was a half-sister—no doubt an elder half-sister—of

were supposed to shine most dazzlingly, but in the twelfth-century view her presence alone sufficed to shed lustre upon a Court and it must be allowed that her double title makes a brave show : " Ego Sibilla, Dei gratia Regina Scottorum, filia Henrici Regis Angliae ".[1] Sibylla was *fille de rei*.

The marriage, of which the date is unknown, was evidently one of the Norman-feudal type, the vassal marrying in accordance with his lord's wishes. It underlined the feudal relationship between the two Kings and had doubtless been arranged when Alexander did homage and received knighthood, events which required personal attendance. Both events are unrecorded, but probably took place soon after his accession.[2] There was no child of the union. None apparently was expected. David was always looked on as the future King and in matters likely to be important his assent was regularly obtained. It was not usual for a mediaeval King to be both brother-in-law and son-in-law of another. Special circumstances may be presumed. On the unanimous testimony of their contemporaries [3] the Sons of Margaret were models of private virtue. They were much preoccupied with contingent problems of homage and succession, and with religious scruples, particularly those so constantly attributed in their lifetime to " Edward their kinsman ". Only two of Margaret's six sons married and only one had children.[4]

David's wife was better chosen—" a wise and excellent

" Reginald of Dunstanville " († 1175), who received forfeited Mortain fiefs in Devon and Cornwall and was created Earl of Cornwall in 1141 by his half-sister the Empress Maud. Sibylla was perhaps related to the Robert Corbet who received lands in Scotland (see below, p. 155, n. 6).

[1] Foundation Charter of the Priory of Scone. Lawrie, XXXVI, *c.* 1120. Its authenticity is disputed (see Lawrie, p. 279), but not on the ground of the Queen's designation. " Regis Angliae ", instead of the more usual " Anglorum ", is not in itself suspect and " Dei gratia " seems well within contemporary beliefs.

[2] Cp. " *When Edgar died* Henry allied to himself his successor Alexander, giving him his illegitimate daughter "—Wm. Malm.

[3] *E.g.* Wm. Malm. II, p. 477.

[4] Wm. Malm. remarks that their sister Maud, after giving her husband "a child of either sex", considered her duty done. Mary had an only daughter.

woman ", Jocelin opines,[1] and brother-monks concur, while dwelling, like himself, rather markedly on the wisdom of the choice and the excellence of *la dot*. For a youngest son born in the generation after the Conquest and neither in France nor yet in England, David had a remarkable share in the spoils. It was secured by marrying into the Conqueror's family. In 1113 Queen Maud obtained the Royal assent to a marriage between her brother and their distant relative Maud de Saint-Liz, who was King Henry's kinswoman and ward.[2] There were at the least four Mauds in David's life. This Maud, widow of Simon de Saint-Liz, Earl of Northampton, was one of the greatest heiresses in England, and not only to lands but to traditions. She was the eldest daughter of the Conqueror's niece, Judith, and Waltheof, son of Siward the Dane, and her family history could still stir tragic memories.

After hasty acceptance of the Conquest,[3] Waltheof had twice changed sides when in 1072 he received from the Conqueror his father's Earldom of Northumbria and a Norman bride, bearing the same name, Judith, as Earl Tostig's wife and, like her, related to William, but more closely. She was the daughter of his sister Adèle and Lambert, Count of Lens, brother of Eustace II, Count of Boulogne. In 1075 Waltheof was, for his misfortune, among the wedding-guests at Norwich :

> There was that bride-ale
> That was many men's bale,

affirms the Chronicler, breaking into verse.[4] At the bride-ale a plot was made against the conqueror. Whether under

---

[1] *Vita S. Waldeui*, p. 252, col. 2.

[2] David's marriage took place between the end of December 1113 and the beginning of February 1114. Anderson, *E.S.Sc.* II, p. 146.

[3] He appears (" Ego Waldief dux consensi ") in a very early charter of William (" jure hereditario Anglorum . . . Basileus "). Round, *Cal.* I, p. 526. Waltheof appears with Abbot Æthelwig in other charters of about the same date : see *Regesta*, Index.

[4] *A-S.C.* MS. E, *s.a.* 1075. In fact the feast was at Exning (Cambridgeshire) in Waltheof's southern Earldom. He had been made by Edward Earl in the Midlands and by William Earl in Northumbria.

the influence of the bride or of the ale, or merely because he was *elegans* and liked to be in the fashion, Waltheof joined in the plot, but he was genuinely astonished when it materialized, and he took no part in the revolt. Twice tried on a charge of failure to disclose the existence of a conspiracy, Waltheof—after long hesitation on William's part—was beheaded on St. Giles's Hill outside Winchester, May 31, 1076. Judith was said to have testified against her husband. She undoubtedly incurred odium at Crowland,[1] where Orderic was a visitor long afterwards and heard the worst and where the Chronicle of the pseudo-Ingulf [2] was compiled which may preserve some eleventh-century local gossip as in amber. Judith may have been unfairly treated by writers who took sides in family feuds dating from the partition of Waltheof's great estates. Whether moved by love or by remorse, she pleaded with the Conqueror for her husband's body, which at length she obtained and accompanied on the long sad journey home to Crowland Abbey in the Fens.[3] It was almost the only religious house in Waltheof's Midland Earldoms and accessible only by water. Belief in his innocence was general, and soon the rumour spread that miracles were being wrought at his tomb. Before long he was venerated as a saint and martyr.[4]

William's judicial decision, justified or not, embittered the rest of his existence. There is no question here of half-brothers or half-sisters, children of the respectably married

---

[1] Crowland (also Croyland : both forms are ancient), in the south of Lincolnshire, close to the boundaries of Cambridgeshire and Northamptonshire.   [2] See Appendix G, p. 409.

[3] *Vita Wald. Com.* p. 101.

[4] Ord. Vit. II, xvi ; Wm. Malm. *Gesta P.A.* p. 322 ; Gaimar, l. 5735. Yet there had been little sanctity about his life : at most he had taken his share in the promotion of pious works at Crowland, Jarrow and Melrose. He had been a man of blood. Not long before the bride-ale he had had the sons of a hereditary foeman sought out and slain. His reputation for goodness probably began with his arrest, with the sudden fall of so great a noble and one so familiar both to Anglo-Danes and to Anglo-Saxons. It spread rapidly with the stories of his fortitude and his humble piety during his protracted trial for treason.

— indeed brilliantly married and re-married — Arlette [Herlève], the tanner's daughter. Adèle was William's full-sister and Judith stood in a relationship to him which was peculiarly sacred to Normans. Her marriage was an event in the family circle and on it fond hopes had been placed. It had ended in blood and tears, and the current belief was that henceforward the hand of God was against him.[1] In historical fact a great career reached its climax in Scotland and in 1076 sank into family recriminations, property disputes, succession problems, trouble with the eldest son, and general anticlimax.

Judith being a young widow with three daughters and owner of a goodly part of the conquered Kingdom, her uncle William received applications for her hand from numerous henchmen able and willing to manage her family affairs and her vast estates. He selected Simon de Saint-Liz, whom she refused, and persisted in refusing, ostensibly because he halted on one leg. After many acrimonious *conseils de famille* it was at length arranged that Simon should wed not the Countess, but in due course her twelve-year-old daughter Maud—which, as regards succession to property, came to much the same thing, since Maud, as the eldest daughter, was her mother's chief heiress. Thus the halting Simon obtained the Earldom of Northampton. One of Henry's earliest supporters, a signatory to his Charter of Liberties, a Crusader, he was the founder of the Priory of St. Andrew outside Northampton, affiliated to the great Cluniac Priory of La Charité-sur-Loire. He died at La Charité in 1111, when for the second time on his way to the East. He left two young sons, whose names, Simon and Waldef (French form of Waltheof), symbolized the Norman present and the English past.

To her second husband, David, Maud de Saint-Liz,

---

[1] Orderic points out that, after the execution of Waltheof, William retained his fortitude, but lost his peace of mind, and thenceforward his luck deserted him in the field.

daughter of the Northumbrian Saint and the tragic Norman widow, and great-grand-daughter of Robert le Magnifique and Arlette, brought (besides properties scattered all over England, some of them in London) two great Earldoms, Northampton and Huntingdon,[1] and a potential claim to a greater. Though Maud was as Norman as her name, her father, whom she had hardly seen, was an English Earl and was venerated as a martyr in the cause of freedom through all the wide lands from Trent to Tweed. Her sons were heirs to his traditions and, as some thought, to his northern Earldom. If they were both to be eliminated (and ultimately they were), the only son of her second marriage, called Henry after his relative the King of England, could, in certain contingencies, put forward the ancient Scottish claim to Northumbria north of the Tees, and reinforce the claim by another, based on immediate heredity, recent tradition and local sentiment.

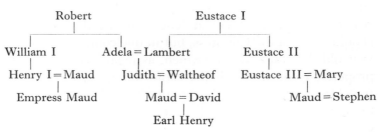

After David's marriage, Cumbria no doubt made more rapid progress in French culture. The Conqueror's grand-niece was a better arbiter of elegance than Sibylla, his granddaughter. She had a *cameraria*, one Hélisende, who was famous for her skill in the weaving of purple and had the reputation of being the best orphrey-worker in England—a reputation of which we should never have heard but for what happened to her at the Tomb of St. Cuthbert. When David and Maud, proceeding north on their honeymoon, broke their journey at Durham, the

[1] See Appendix G.

Countess went religiously to the bounds beyond which no woman must go, but Hélisende went further and was stricken down. She recovered, however, and made atonement by becoming a nun in the convent of Elstow.[1] Having retired to a nunnery (as many ladies did who had not transgressed at Durham), Hélisende may, like them, have spent much of her time on embroidery and needlework and on the training of young women in these accomplishments, and no doubt she had competent successors in Earl David's household, some perhaps trained by herself. The incident, not in itself of much historical significance and by 1114 lacking in novelty, suggests that the arrival of Maud de Saint-Liz in Cumbria provided its inhabitants with object-lessons in courtly splendour and " Southern luxury ".

[1] Reg. Durh. *Cuthb.* I, pp. 151-152. Elstow (*Elnstou* in Domesday, where Judith appears as owner of three vills), about a mile from Bedford, acquired a later fame as the birth-place of John Bunyan. The convent was founded by Judith and greatly enriched by her daughter Maud : see *V.C.H. Beds.* II, p. 353.

§ 12

Earl David's Normans

FROM 1114 David was in right of his wife Earl of Northampton and Huntingdon. He was the greatest baron in England, holding the place of honour at meetings of the *curia regis*, taking his share in the central administration and in the conduct of local affairs, seeing from the inside how the country was governed under the " Lion of Justice ". No one could be an efficient Earl in Norman England— and David was always conspicuous for efficiency—without becoming well versed in three laws : the law of the land, of the Church, of the forest. David spent much, perhaps most, of his time in his Midland Earldoms. His favourite residence on the late Countess Judith's estates was Yardley Hastings [1] in Northamptonshire, the chief attraction there being Yardley Chase, his own private domain in the immense Royal Forest of Whittlewood.[2] The " forest ", the *forestis (silva)*, was properly the " wood outside " [the *parc* or walled enclosure]. But in Normandy the "wood", and the ducal rights, had been extended beyond measure, and in England the hunting-spaces of the Norman Kings became vast tracts of land which were not necessarily wooded over the whole area or uninhabited, but within which a particular body of law was enforced, for the preservation of certain animals *ferae naturae*, " the beasts of

[1] Lawrie, p. 267.
[2] Still an extensive tract of woodland stretching along the south-east side of Northamptonshire and encroaching at one point on Buckinghamshire. It was not a " forest " in the Survey, but was one in the reign of Henry I, who refers to " all his foresters of Whittlewood "—Baker, II, p. 74. " The Yardley Oak " of Cowper's poem—he frequented Yardley Chase when living at Olney, Bucks.—was supposed to have been planted by the Countess Judith.

the forest "—the red deer, the fallow deer, the roe, the wild boar and in some districts the hare. The Chronicle tells us that the Conqueror " loved the tall stags as if he were their father. He also ordained concerning the hares that they should go free." [1] Henry inherited this paternal trait to the full and, from the day he granted his " Charter of Liberties " till the day he died, clung hard to the ferocious forest laws. His own regulations provided for the maiming of all dogs in a hunting district.[2] The sport in Whittlewood must have been excellent. More was to be had in the fiefs composing the Honour of Huntingdon : the valley of the Ouse in which most of them lay was particularly rich in " forest ".[3] David had all the Norman passion for the chase, and his closest friends, those who were his chief collaborators and beneficiaries in Scotland when he became King (and perhaps before), were his hunting companions, generally neighbours or vassals of his own in his English Earldoms. Their names occur in the charters he gave when only " Comes ". Evidently they were men in constant attendance, men on whom he regularly relied for advice and assistance, whether in the ritual of the chase or in the intricacies of feudal administration, estate management, land-distribution, and whether he happened to be in Cumbria or in Lothian or in the shires of Northampton and Huntingdon.

When resident in the North, he cultivated friendly relations with the neighbouring French landowners. They had the same interests ; they were pioneers like himself, men set in authority over a wild and far country sparsely peopled by " natives " living a life of their own and speaking a tongue of which, as William of Malmesbury complained at the time, " we Southerners " could make nothing. The " Northern Counties ", as they were afterwards called, were inhabitable only in the long dales, and

[1] *A-S.C.* MS. E, *s.a.* 1087.   [2] According to Ord. Vit. XI, xxii.
[3] See Moore, *L.Sc.K.* p. 13.

consisted largely of uplands rising to considerable heights, covered with moors over which the red deer roamed. Geographically the whole region was difficult to defend against Scottish attack; historically it was poverty-stricken, disaffected, rebellious. The Conqueror and Rufus in their slow advance to the Tyne and the Solway had created Castellaries, Honours, Baronies, Franchises, Liberties, too remote to be closely controlled by themselves. Such was the Liberty of Redesdale, granted by the Conqueror to Robert d'Amfreville [Umfraville], whose son, or perhaps grandson, Robert was one of David's intimates and afterwards, though still generally resident in Northumberland, received Scottish lands which passed to his descendants.[1] The reason which William of Malmesbury adduced for the backwardness of the people in the North of England was that they dwelt near barbarous folk and far from the control of the kings who, whether English or Norman, always fixed their residence in the South. Indeed civilization, as it was understood by King Henry, came to an end at the Humber, and when he crossed the Humber he doubled his body-guard, notwithstanding that he was probably a Yorkshireman by place of birth.[2] For

---

[1] The original Robert came from Amfreville, but in Normandy there are eight places of that name. He is described as Lord of " Toures ". This has not been identified, but may possibly represent Tourville, near Amfreville-la-Campagne. Robert d'Umphraville witnesses Earl David's Foundation Charter of Selkirk (*c.* 1120) and his Royal charters from 1128, *e.g.* Lawrie, LXXXII and CIV (in connection with the Abbey of Kelso and the Church of Glasgow). Robert's two sons, Odinel and Gilbert, also witness charters, chiefly those given by David's son Henry as Earl of Northumberland. Odinel witnesses the Annandale Forest charter, 1147 × 1153. The family properties in Scotland in King David's time are not precisely known, but Gilbert gave to the Abbey of Holyrood a ploughgate of land in Kinard. *Holyrood*, No. XLII, p. 34. A Gilbert d'Umphraville married *c.* 1240 Matilda, Countess of Angus in her own right. He passed on the title to his descendants till it lapsed, in 1381. Another Gilbert d'Umphraville held (and forfeited) Dunipace in the reign of Robert the Bruce. It is to be supposed that David's friends received from him Dunipace and Kinard (Stirlingshire).

[2] Queen Matilda may have given birth to her " English " son at Selby. The Abbey was founded by William *and* Matilda. Ed. *E. Yorks. Ch.* I, p. 363.

him, as for his father, Northumbria, in particular the more northerly part thereof, was hardly quite " l'Angleterre ". It had become a sort of " Crown Colony " directly dependent on himself, governed no longer through an Earl (Rufus had put an end to that), but through tenants-in-chief, to many of whom, for faithful service elsewhere, Henry had granted estates which were distant outposts of empire. In the first six perilous years after his dubious accession he had scant sympathy from the great Norman families and his gratitude to the lesser men who stood by him then was lasting. From them he formed what constituted a new nobility. Its members, generally pillars of the administrative system which he was elaborating, were endowed by him with confiscated lands. In the North there were many, notably those in Yorkshire forfeited by his late uncle Robert, Count of Mortain.[1] But, extensive though the Mortain fiefs were, they were not of much value and Henry bestowed them on " *novi homines* "—on promoted adherents—not that they might live in comfort ever after, but rather that they might continue their esteemed service, by keeping a firm hand on remote and unsettled districts. The rise of the " new men " was a portent of his reign, duly foretold by Merlin.[2] They soon became great feudal magnates, often possessing large reserves of strength in estates further south. David's chief friends among them were Eustache, son of Jean ; Walter (or Gautier) Espec, and Robert de Brus.

" Eustachius filius Johannis Monoculi ",[3] now conventionally called Eustace fitz John, was the son of a " John de Burgh " and nephew of a " Serlo de Burgh " and

---

[1] (Manche), arr. Avranches, chef-lieu. The grant which William made to his half-brother Robert was his largest : 797 manors, of which 215 were in Yorkshire. Robert's English fief was forfeited in 1088. See *V.C.H. Yorks.* II, pp. 154-155. After his death in 1090 part was restored to his son William, but not the Yorkshire part.

[2] " The men of after times shall aspire to soar aloft and new men shall rise to favour and eminence."—Ord. Vit. XII, xlviii.

[3] *Hist. Northd.* VI, p. 439. John was no doubt one-eyed.

possessed Brough and Knaresborough in Yorkshire.[1] After Tinchebray (1106) he received Alnwick, perhaps through his marriage with the daughter of Yve de Vesci, who held Alnwick, and he was given other lands by King Henry for services rendered. Eustace is described by Ailred as a man of great wisdom and he certainly became a man of great importance, governor of Bamburgh Castle, one of Henry's *Ministri* and, with Walter Espec, Justiciar in the North of England.

Walter was the son of one of the Conqueror's beneficiaries in Bedfordshire, " Wilhelmus Spec ", of whom nothing is known except that all his holdings were in that county.[2] As regards the name, Giraldus Cambrensis remarks that the French for woodpecker is *spec*.[3] It may be further remarked that *sp-* and *esp-* at the beginning of a word are constantly interchanged, and that Espec was a family name in Normandy, and of the same type as the name of the Geoffroi Engoulevent incriminated in the death of Malcolm Canmore : *engoulevent* = nightjar ; Old French *espec* (Modern Norman *épec*, Modern French *épeiche*) = woodpecker.[4] Henry enfeoffed Walter Espec of five knights'

[1] Pipe Roll of 1130, pp. 24 and 31, where " Serlo de Burg " is also mentioned.

[2] In Domesday, I, p. 215, col. 2, " Willelmus Spec " holds 9 hides of the King as one manor in Wardon. [In *V.C.H. Bedfordshire*, I, p. 246, William is erroneously called Walter.] In 1135 Walter Espec founded, as a daughter-house of Rievaulx, the Abbey of Wardon (also called Sartis = *les Essarts* = clearing). The lands mentioned correspond exactly and Walter was certainly the son and heir of William. Walter's wife, Adeline de Beauchamp, was no doubt a relative of the Hugue de Beauchamp who received from William a great part of Bedfordshire. Walter Espec " made Christ his heir " (Ailred), but the constantly repeated statement that his religious benefactions were for the loss of an only son is without historical basis. He is not recorded as having ever had a son. He had three sisters and co-heiresses : Hawise, *m.* Guillaume de Bussy ; " Albreda ", *m.* Nicole de Traylly (Trailli = Trelly, near Coutances) ; Adeline, *m.* Pierre de Ros (Calvados, arr. Caen, canton de Tilly), whose descendants held Wark-on-Tweed. Gaimar, who on a celebrated occasion failed to return a book borrowed from Walter Espec, says of his own work : " If anybody looks into this book, and does not believe what I say, let him ask Nicole de Trailli ".

[3] Gir. Cambr. V, p. 135.

[4] Especs held Kesnoi-Espec (Quesnai, near Saint-Étienne-de-la-Tillaie) in the district of Auge. Delisle, *Cartulaire normand*, p. 257. Lands in

fees in Yorkshire, the chief manors being Helmsley and Kirkham, and also gave him Wark and Carham in Northumberland. It was not possible to give him lands closer to Scotland. While neighbouring places have been now in one Kingdom, now in the other, Carham on the Tweed, whether insignificant hamlet or scene of a victory as decisive as most in history, has never been anywhere but in England. It was not, however, a single unit; few places then were. The church belonged to Queen Maud till she gave it to Durham; Walter Espec held only part of the vill, though he held the barony of Wark,[1] and Prior Richard of Hexham observes that " Carham is called Wark by the English ". Whatever it was called, it was a memorable crossing-place and it was in the interests of peace that the landowners facing each other across the river should be the good friends that Walter Espec and David had always been. Walter's place in Scottish history is assured, but he missed Scottish domicile by a few yards.

Robert de Brus acquired it with a margin of a few miles. His name is that of the commune of Brix in the Cotentin, some six miles from Valognes,[2] where the Conqueror spent part of his boyhood. Brix is an Old French spelling, *x* being merely a scribal flourish for -*us*; the forms in the Latin documents are Brius, Bruis and Brus, and the last became customary in designating the Robert de Brus who fought at Hastings. He died towards 1090 and his son, David's associate, probably much older

Herpaiz-Mesnil were held by the sons of Renouf Espec. Charter of Henry I, Sign. Robert of Gloucester, confirming endowments to the Abbey of Lessay. Round, *Cal.* Index. The definite article and the preposition freely bestowed by modern writers have no justification : " l'Espec " is found only in much later charters of Rievaulx : " a " is as excrescent as in the name of Thomas Becket. See *Cart. Riev.* p. xlix. " Walter a Espec " (David's charter, 1132, Lawrie, XCVIII) must be a modern clerical error.

[1] *Hist. Northd.* XI, p. 31 ; *V.C.H. Yorks.* II, p. 155.

[2] Brix (Manche), arr. Valognes. See Palgrave, *N. and E.*, III, p. 103, for a detailed and recent account (by his son) of the Château of Brix and the family ; also *S.H.R.* II, p. 424.

than David, is first named as a witness to a charter
(1094 × 1100) by Hugh, Earl of Chester.[1] For reasons
presumably connected with the difficulties following on his
accession, the ruler of the Cotentin who had suddenly
become King made the son a grant of some eighty Yorkshire manors which in Domesday form part of the " Terra
Regis ". This, the original fee of Brus, was augmented,
probably soon after Tinchebray, by thirteen Mortain
manors, including Guisborough.

Lord of Guisborough, Skelton, Cleveland and Brix,
Robert had for a neighbour Bernard, Lord of Bailleul in
Picardy, Bywell on the Tyne and Marwood in Teesdale,
where he built " Barnard " Castle. Bernard was soon to
be a landowner in Scotland, and already the stage was set
for the long series of Bruce-and-Balliol episodes.[2]

David himself might almost be said to have been one
of his brother-in-law's " new men ", having, as a baron,
given him valued assistance and counsel, in acknowledg-
ment of which he had received knighthood, the hand of a
Royal ward and two Earldoms. In spirit he was with the
" new men ". He was no less active than they in religious
works : Augustinians were brought by him to Jedburgh,
as by Walter Espec to Kirkham and by Robert de Brus to

[1] *Cart. Gyseburn*, I, p. v. Robert de Brus attested a charter (1103 × 1106)
of William, Count of Mortain, no doubt as a tenant of the fee of Mortain,
whether in Normandy or in England, and a charter (1109) of Henry I, confirming certain possessions to Durham. *E. Yorks. Ch.* II, p. 11. Robert
held estates round Hartlepool from *c.* 1119. *V.C.H. Durham*, III, p. 256.
His wife Agnes was probably a daughter of Geoffroi Bainard, Sheriff of
York, 1089–1094.

[2] The founder of the family, a Picard, Guy de Bailleul, is not in Domesday and may not have come to England till the reign of Rufus, from whom
he received, *c.* 1093, Bywell and the forest of Marwood. He was Lord of
Bailleul-en-Vimeu, in Picardy (Somme), arr. Abbeville, canton de Hallen-
court. His son Bernard († 1167) shared with Robert de Brus in the gift by
Henry I of forfeited manors in Cleveland (*V.C.H. Yorks.* II, p. 167). Bernard
had become King David's " man " before 1138 and apparently had received
grants of land in Lothian before then. He gave to Kelso a fishery in the
Tweed pertaining to Wudehorne, called Wadehorne. Lawrie, CCLVIII ;
King David's Confirmation, CCLIX, 1153. See also *Hist. Northd.* VI, pp.
16-24.

Guisborough.[1] David was a "chief man" in the Midlands; his friends were "chief men" in the North, important landholders, inspiring general confidence, often called in to settle difficult problems, ecclesiastical or other, at Durham or elsewhere, not necessarily in any official capacity.[2] Walter Espec and Eustace fitz John became Justiciars. They were constantly moving about Yorkshire, Durham, Northumberland and "English Cumbria", holding pleas, inquiring into the state of the King's lands, seeing to the restocking of his manors and the refortification of his castles.[3] In North and North-West England David's friends were the depositaries of Norman power. All along the Border his lands marched with theirs, and some of theirs had belonged to his late father's Kingdom, as neither David nor they can have pretended to forget.

The pioneer work which fell to him in "Scottish Cumbria" his Norman associates were doing, and conscientiously, in "English Cumbria", the annexed land from the Solway Firth to the Derwent and the Rere Cross on Stainmore, which was afterwards to comprise the counties of Cumberland and Westmorland. It was an all but inaccessible district, where the mountains, the highest in England, were impassable with forest and swamp, wild

[1] The date of the foundation of the Priory at Jedburgh is given by Wyntoun as 1118. It was made an Abbey *c.* 1150. David's Augustinians were brought from Beauvais. They were settled at New Jedburgh, four and a half miles down the valley of the Jed from Old Jedburgh, which belonged to the monks of St. Cuthbert. See *O.P.* I, p. 368. Kirkham, some sixteen miles north-east of York, was founded in 1122. Letters of protection, issued then in favour of Kirkham, are attested by Earl David. Farrer, *Itin.* p. 102. The first Prior was William, rector of Garton, a relative of Walter Espec. Guisborough in Cleveland was founded 1110 × 1124 (or perhaps × 1129).

[2] It was just because Robert de Brus and Walter Espec happened to be at Durham on other business that in 1121 they were asked to adjudicate on a long-standing dispute about the church of Tynemouth. The matter was discussed " *coram magno conventu principalium virorum* "—Contin. Sim. Durh. *H.D.E.* III, p. 261.

[3] Presumably long before 1130, when the first extant Pipe Roll is full of references to the activities of Eustace fitz John and Walter Espec, working in conjunction, *e.g.* p. 24.

beasts and wild folk. The whole region had been occupied by miscellaneous incomers at divers times. It had been overrun in the tenth century by Norsemen from Ireland, Man and the Isles, and by Danes from their Kingdom of York, with which for a period it was loosely linked. Everywhere in the coastal districts from the Solway to what is now Lancashire there had been Norse settlers ; their memorials are the sculptured stones. The tide of Norman immigration had spent itself in " English Cumbria ", which in Earl David's time was held for the Norman King by a military governor with headquarters at Appleby, a friend of David's, Renouf Meschin or le Meschin [= *Mesquin* = " Junior "], leader of the van at Tinchebray.[1] His great lordship, described by himself as the *potestas* of Carlisle, had superseded as the northern outpost of Norman power Alain le Noir's castlery of Richmond, which it closely resembled in organization.[2] Scattered here and there were other " Conquerors " of the second generation, installed, like the Morville family at Burgh-by-Sands, as members of a military colony on the extreme confines of a conquered land. Carlisle, which Rufus had restored from Danish desolation,[3] now belonged to the group of lordships which, like Richmond, Durham, Clitheroe, Pontefract and Lancaster, formed administrative districts dependent on a Royal castle, and was, with the other outlying regions of the North and North-West, being rapidly brought into line with the rest of the English Kingdom. Organization was the order of the day. A great, indeed a noble, work of reconstruction, reclamation of waste land, colonization was

[1] Renouf [Ranulf] was the son and heir of Renouf [de Briquessart], hereditary Vicomte of the Bessin, by Maud, sister of Hugue " le Gros " d'Avranches († July 27, 1101), first Earl of Chester, after Gerbod's temporary appointment in 1070. The second Renouf († 1129) was lord of Carlisle, and had charge of English Cumbria till 1121, when he resigned his lordship to the King on being made third Earl of Chester, in succession to Hugue's son Richard (1094–November 25, 1120), his cousin. See Round, *D.N.B.* art. RANDULF LE MESCHIN, and Cronne, p. 104.

[2] F. M. Stenton in *Westmorland*, p. liv.   [3] Flor. Worc. II, p. 30.

in hand. Barons were constantly returning south to report, and to receive instructions. For them the centre of civilization was the centre of England, in those days Northampton,[1] where their Scottish neighbour was Earl.

For all his ancient Celtic and English ancestry, he too was a " Norman baron ", sharing the tastes of Norman barons, speaking their language, having the same outlook on life, the same feudal mind, spending as much time as he could among them and undertaking similar public duties.[2] More particularly, he was a " Norman Earl ", to wit, a personage of the most exalted rank (usually, till Tinchebray, a member of the Conqueror's family), possessing great influence in the county, but no very definite administrative or military status. That may be what David was in South Scotland. When he came home, he was no doubt attended by the Normans who, to judge by their prominence in the charters given by him before he became King, were constantly in his counsels and his company. Some must have been simply members of his household; it moved with him, whether to Roxburgh, Selkirk, Yardley Chase or Westminster, and on his travels he would no more have changed his dapifer or his chamberlain than he would his confessor. Some of his Norman companions were at his side when, proceeding in due legal form, as befitted one so experienced in Norman administration, he restored the Bishopric of Glasgow, and it is reasonable to suppose that they included men knowing something of the district, or even landholders whose interests might be affected by decisions regarding Church properties.

The inquiry or *Inquisitio* which Earl David caused to be made into the rights and properties of the old Church of Glasgow is recorded in a memoir or *notitia*, an unofficial

[1] H. E. Salter, *Med. Oxford*, p. 90.
[2] Earl David is found, *e.g.*, attesting Notifications issued at St. Albans, Holy Innocents' Day, 1116; Westbourne, 1116; Winchester, 1120–1122; York, 1122. Farrer, *Itin.* pp. 72, 77, 94, 102. He was present at Henry's second marriage, at Windsor, January 29–30, 1121. Round, *G.M.* p. 249.

and later document. It enumerates the lands which had been recognized as belonging to the Church of Glasgow, and the names of persons who had taken part in the inquiry.[1] It has not the value of a contemporary record, but the names seem to be given in all good faith. The native names come first, then the Norman names. This separate classification appears again in Malcolm IV's Kelso Charter of 1159, but there the native names come last and are few in number.[2] " The older and the wiser men of all Cumbria " gave evidence on oath, stating what they knew of the local tradition and belief. The body which took their evidence and of which they were themselves members appears to be simply the Conqueror's Jury of Inquisition.[3] The ancient Bishopric instituted by St. Kentigern

[1] In the *Inquisitio*, the *juratores* summoned by David to give sworn evidence on the possessions of the Church of Glasgow are : " Uchtred filius Waldef " ; " Gill' filius Boed " ; " Leysing et Oggo, Cumbrenses judices " ; " Halden filius Eadulf ". The witnesses (" testes audientes et videntes ") are, besides " Matildis comitissa " : " Willelmus nepos ipsius principis " ; " Cospatric frater Dalfin " ; " Waldef frater suus " ; " Cospatric filius Uctred " ; " Cospatric filius Alden " ; " Osolf filius Eadiue " ; " Maccus filius Undewyn " ; " Uchtred filius Scot " ; " Ulchel filius Alstan ".

After these (native) names come : " Paganus de Brausa " ; " Osbert de Ardena " ; " Gervasius Ridel " ; " Guido de Caynes " ; " Berengarius Engaine " ; " Robertus Corbet " ; " Walterus de Lindeseya " ; " Robertus de Burnevilla " ; " Reinaldus de Muscans " ; " Walterus filius Winemari " ; " Willelmus Venator " ; " Alanus de Perci " ; " Walterus de Broy ".

[2] Below, p. 366.

[3] Cp. the " Inquisitio Eliensis ", a document of William I (1071 × 1075) concerning the losses of lands and jurisdiction which the monastery of Ely had suffered since 1066. It calls for the attendance from all the shires " . . . of those who can come of the barons and those who hold lands of the Church. When they are assembled, there are to be selected several of those English who know how the lands of the Church were lying T.R.E. and what they report is to be attested by oath." Similar commissions had functioned before then in Normandy. Adams, *C. and C.* p. 85 and p. 90 n. David's " Inquisitio " appears to reflect Norman practice, as introduced by the Conqueror and developed by his sons. See Jolliffe, p. 199. When Bishop " de Saint-Carilef " introduced monks at Durham, his counsellors were similar to Earl David's : " senes et prudentiores totius episcopii homines, qualiter in initio apud sanctum ageretur Cuthbertum a me exquisiti "—*Liber Vitae*, p. 74. As the Bishop's Inquiry went back to St. Cuthbert, so no doubt the Earl's, which was protracted and probably, like the rest of his work, conscientious, went back to St. Kentigern. Early " Lives " were in existence and were afterwards incorporated in the " Life " written for Bishop John's successor, Herbert ; see below, p. 361, n. 2.

(Mungo) was restored, and the see fixed at Glasgow, a small place which owed its existence to the earthen and wattled church which the Saint built by the Molindinar Burn. The Cathedral church was partly endowed with lands in Northamptonshire;[1] David was not a "sair sanct" to Cumbria. The first Bishop, Michael, appointed by him, and apparently before the completion of the Inquiry, was a native of Westmorland.[2] His successor John, elected before January 1118, was David's old tutor,[3] "a most intimate friend because of the excellence of his virtues".[4] His birth-place may have been in France and he may have had previous connections with the Tironensians lately come to Selkirk.[5] He is found in 1122 faring to Rome and Jerusalem, and next year faring home again, having been turned back by order of Pope Calixtus.[6] Bishop John, possibly with his former pupil's discreet approval, steadfastly declined to admit the primacy of York and was the object of many more Papal objurgations.

Normans mentioned in Earl David's charters and in the account of the *Inquisitio* but not known to have had any subsequent connection with Scotland may be omitted from consideration here. They include one or two possessors of great names—such as "Paganus de Brausa",

[1] Parts of Hardingstone, near Northampton. Earl David's Charter, *Glasgow*, p. 8, No. II: Lawrie, XLVI. The witnesses are described as "proceres et milites mei". They are: "Robertus de Brus", "Robertus filius Nigelli", "Hugo de Moruilla", "Hugo Bret" and three already mentioned in the *Inquisitio*: "Robertus Corbet", "Walterus de Lindeseia" and "Walterus filius Winemerij".

[2] "David Comes Michaelem episcopum constituit." Hugh the Cantor, p. 127. Michael was consecrated at York by Archbishop Thomas II, therefore before February 1114.

[3] "Religiosum virum qui eum educaverat."—*Inquisitio*.

[4] John of Hexham, referring to Bishop John's death (in 1147).

[5] His own name John may indicate either France or Britain. Anselm was the name of his nephew: "Anselmus nepos Johannis episcopi". Charter by Earl Henry, *c.* 1141. Lawrie, CXXXV. This Anselm was perhaps the father of the "Henry son of Anselm" who *c.* 1180 gave the church of Carmunnock to the Abbey of Paisley. Bishop John is afterwards mentioned several times in connection with the Tironensians and eventually retired to Tiron.   [6] Sim. Durh. *H.R.* II, p. 264.

Payen de Briouze, a neighbour in Bedfordshire [1]—and need not be supposed to have been anything more than distinguished visitors present at a moment when Earl David was dealing with Cumbrian business. Of the remainder the most important were apparently Hugue de Morville, Gervais Ridel and Robert Corbet. The first was Earl David's chief man of business, a constant signatory of his charters, whether relating to Cumbria or not. He held in demesne manors in Rutland and in Northamptonshire, to which county his wife, Béatrice de Beauchamp, belonged. Her surname must indicate relationship, though perhaps distant, with the wife of Walter Espec ; his own surname probably reveals kinship with the Morville family at Burgh-by-Sands. At what may be presumed to have been an early period in their married life Hugue and Béatrice de Morville were already sufficiently interested in the Scottish Kingdom to have their second son baptized Malcolm. Hugue de Morville acquired great estates in South Scotland. He became, before 1140, King David's Constable and towards the end of his reign, evidently with his help, founded the Abbey of Dryburgh.[2] Gervais Ridel, who gave the church

---

[1] " Paganus de Braiosa."—Pipe Roll of 1130 under Bedfordshire, p. 103.

[2] Morville is near Valognes. The Richard de Morville at Hastings was perhaps Richard, Constable of Shrewsbury in 1084. Families of the name were early established at Burgh-by-Sands and in Devon, Dorset and Surrey. Palgrave, *N. and E.* III, p. 414, where it is stated that Hugue de Morville belonged to the Burgh-by-Sands branch. This seems probable ; he owned lands near Shap (Westmorland). Both he and his son Richard had lands in the North Riding of Yorkshire, part of which they afterwards gave to the Templars. Lees, *Temple*, p. 128. Hugue de Morville's lands in Northamptonshire and Rutland passed to his son Richard's daughter Helena and, through her marriage to Roland of Galloway (see below, p. 310, n. 1), to Roland's son Alan. Bishop Robert of St. Andrews confirms, 1150 × 1158, donations made " ecclesie sancte Marie de Dryburgh quam Hugo de Morevilla fundavit ". *Dryburgh*, p. 9. In all the circumstances the Bishop's statement seems likely to be correct. But David's Foundation Charter bears " quam fundavi ". *Dryburgh*, p. lxix. Hugue de Morville's grants to Dryburgh Abbey show that he held lands in Berwickshire between the Gala and the Leader, at Dryburgh, St. Boswells, Lauder, Newton (now Newton Don), Mertoun, Lanark, Pettinain. *Dryburgh*, pp. 6, 51, 194.

Béatrice de Beauchamp owned the church of Bosyete in Northamptonshire till she granted it to Dryburgh. Lawrie, CCXIX, *c.* 1150. They had

of Abbotsley Huntingdon to the Priory of Jedburgh,[1] was closely related to the Ridels of Northamptonshire, typical members of the new official class,[2] and to the well-known Geoffroi Ridel, who, in the year before he perished in the "White Ship", was witnessing grants by the King of England which were addressed to Earl David and other Midland magnates.[3] The Ridel family came from Blaye in Guienne. Gervais Ridel owned Cranston in Lothian and Wittering in Northamptonshire. His wife "Christiana" [Christiane] owned land near Old Jedburgh and gave part of it to the Priory, to which he retired in his old age, then becoming an Austin Canon.[4] Robert Corbet, possibly a relative of Alexander's Queen, belonged to the family which held Drayton in Northamptonshire.[5] His name recurs in David's Royal charters till 1138. Perhaps he was the father of Walter Corbet, Lord of Makerstoun (Malcarveston) in Roxburghshire and of Glendale in Northumberland, a benefactor of the Abbey of Kelso. But Corbet was a very common Norman name and though many Corbets held lands in Scotland, their descent from Robert has not been traced.[6]

Probably those of Earl David's associates who, as soon

three sons: 1, Richard, who on his father's death in 1162 succeeded him as Constable: see below, p. 310, n. 1; 2, Malcolm, who when hunting was accidentally killed by a brother of Alexander de Saint-Martin; 3, Roger, and a daughter Ada, who married a Roger Bertram. *Dryburgh*, p. 106.

[1] Morton, p. 51; Moore, *L.Sc.K.* p. 40.

[2] *V.C.H. Northants.* I, p. 286; Round, *G.M.* p. 418.

[3] *Ramsey*, I, p. 245, No. CLXVIII. Geoffroi Ridel was lord of Wittering.

[4] Cranston-Ridel remained with Gervais' descendants till the reign of Edward III. As the family on account of their Northamptonshire estates mostly sided with England they finally lost Cranston and returned to Northamptonshire. The line ended in female succession in the reign of Edward IV. Joseph Bain, *Gen.* N.S. VI, pp. 1-2.

[5] Moore, *L.Sc.K.* p. 31; Lawrie, p. 338. Corbet (Lat. *Corbatus*) is a name associated with Shropshire by Ord. Vit., who was born in the county.

[6] Walter Corbet witnessed charters of Malcolm IV, notably *Kelso*, No. I (1159), in which his gift to Kelso of the church of Malcarveston is confirmed. He, or a son, was one of the hostages in 1174. A namesake lived till after 1200. *Inchaffray*, p. 305. A Robert Corbet gave to Kinloss some land near the church of Gamrie (Banffshire), as appears from a later confirmation by Alexander II in 1227. *Kinloss*, pp. 114-115.

as he becomes King, are found in possession of land in Lothian and Cumbria—whether in large tracts or only in bovates, carucates and tofts [1]—were younger sons (though not necessarily young) of his tenants in his Midland Earldoms or of landowners in neighbouring districts. " Robert, son of Nigel [Néel] " cannot be identified. " Osbert de Ardena " came from the celebrated Forest of Arden in Warwickshire.[2] He is not known to have settled in Scotland, but he is found witnessing one of King David's charters after 1143, again with " Hugo Brito ", *alias* " Hugo Bret ", of whom nothing is known save the self-evident fact that, like so many " Norman Conquerors ", he was a Breton ; [3] " Robertus de Burnevilla ", Robert de Bourneville ; [4] all of these were to be for many years in attendance on King David. " Walterus filius Winemari " may perhaps be the father of Winemers afterwards found settled in the Scottish Kingdom.[5] "Alanus de Perci "will be discussed later.[6] "Walterus de Broy", who appears occasionally in David's Royal charters, may have been a brother or a son of the Robert de Broy who at the point of death restored Crawley to the Abbey of Ramsey in Huntingdon.[7]

[1] The bovate or oxgang contained 13 acres : 8 bovates made a carucate or ploughgate, 104 acres of arable land : a toft was the site of a house with its outbuildings.

[2] He is no doubt the Osbert de Ardena who appears under Warwickshire in the Pipe Roll of 1130, p. 105.

[3] Hugue Bret witnesses King David's charter granting to Dunfermline a fishing called Aldestelle and a toft in Berwick (with Osbert de Ardene). Charter to Melrose 1143 × 1146.

[4] Bourneville (Lat. *Burnenvilla*), Eure, arr. Pont-Audemer, canton de Quillebeuf. The Latin form in David's charters is sometimes Burnetvilla : cp. Burne*l*villa, once (1157) in Round, *Cal.* I, p. 268. Robert appears in charters to Coldingham (1147) and Holyrood. Lawrie, XCIII, XCIX, CLIII. A Robert de Bourneville, presumably a son of this Robert, was one of the Scottish sureties for the Treaty of Falaise in 1175.

[5] In the reign of Malcolm IV a Winemer is a witness to the Countess Adeline's grant of land in Crail to the Canons of St. Andrews. *St. Andrews*, p. 208. A " Johannes Winemer " appears somewhat later. *Ibid*. pp. 269, 271 and 272.   [6] Below, pp. 262, 266 and 291.

[7] " Robertus de Broy, *in articulo mortis*, feeling that he had grieved St. Benedict and the Abbot of Ramsey, sent his son Walter to give back Crawley to the Abbey."—*Ramsey*, I, p. 257, No. CXCVII, 1133 × 1160.

" Berengarius Engaine ", Bérenger Engaine, a future benefactor of Jedburgh and landowner at Crailing (Roxburghshire), was certainly a scion of the Northamptonshire
hunting family and a near kinsman of Richard Engaine,
forester in the county. Bérenger comes into Earl David's
charters—possibly also into possession of lands in Cumbria
—to the sound of the horn, with a Christian name borne
by one of Charlemagne's paladins and a surname acquired
in Normandy in the pursuit of game and already famous
in the annals of the Pytchley Hunt.[1]

Earl David's associates were in great part gentlemen
adventurers, soldiers, land stewards, surveyors, foresters,
whose fathers or grandfathers appear in Domesday, mostly
under " Northamptonshire ". But it is seldom possible
to ascertain their Continental home, whether in the Duchy
or in Flanders or in Brittany or elsewhere, and the
precise connection which their forebears had with Duke
William's Breton, Lotharingian, Flemish, Picard, Artesian,
Cenomannian, Angevin, general-French and Norman Conquest. Thus he who is called " Walterus de Lindeseia "
in the *Inquisitio* and " Galterius de Lyndeseia " in the
Foundation Charter of Selkirk (1120), but does not appear

[1] Bérenger Engaine is soon found, *c.* 1128, witnessing charters to
Coldingham. Lawrie, LXXXIX and XC. He gave to the Priory of Jedburgh one mark silver out of the profits of the mill of Crailing, with two
oxgangs of land, and, for the maintenance of the chaplain of Crailing, two
other oxgangs and two tofts. See below, p. 290. " Ricardus Engaine "
and " Willelmus Engaine " received from the Conqueror lands in Northamptonshire which were held T.R.E. by Alwin the huntsman. *D.B.*,
V.C.H. Northants. I, p. 294. Richard was one of the King's chief huntsmen,
and appears among the Royal *ministri*. *V.C.H. Oxfordshire*, I, p. 386.
William held lands in Pytchley. Round, *F.E.* pp. 154-156. He had two
sons, Richard and " Vitalis " [Viel]. Bérenger Engaine was no doubt their
relative and probably the knight of that name who, with other neighbouring
knights, had settled disturbances in the district of Ramsey in Huntingdonshire " in our own time "—*Ramsey*, p. 160, No. C (1146 × 1153), *De funda-
tione abbatiae de Sautreia*. There were also Engaines at Burgh-by-Sands
and Lazonby. *V.C.H. Cumberland*, I, p. 338; II, p. 153. The name is
more correctly spelt Engaigne, *e.g.* in a charter (before 1164) in Round, *Cal.*
I, p. 77. Cp. also the modern Northants. forms, Inganny, Ingany, etc. It
is OF. *engaigne*, a snare, a trap, and was originally a nickname, appropriate
enough in a family of foresters.

in the Royal charters, was head of the family which made its home in Lothian and Upper Clydesdale and which, as Lindsay, became, at least genealogically, one of the greatest in Scotland.[1] But the canny Andrew de Wyntoun's comment is :

> " Of England came the [= de] Lyndysay,
> Mair of them I can nocht say ",

and it may be doubted if the modern genealogists can truthfully say much more. The conjecture that the name comes from Limesay in the Pays-de-Caux, near Pavilly, is phonetically improbable. In its Latin forms it is identical with *Lindisseya*, etc., Lindsey, the district in Lincolnshire, where large numbers of Normans were established very soon after 1066. King Henry addresses mandates to Earl David and the Bishop of Lincoln ; between Lindsey and Huntingdon contacts would be easily made, and it may be supposed that Walter was a member of a family in Lindsey which had come to Earl David's favourable notice. The peculiar derivation of the name from a district, not from a village, may be accounted for by an ancestor who held land in Lindsey and had to be distinguished from a land-owner of the same name in another district. But no such

[1] For the souls of King David, Earl Henry and " Walterus de Lindeseia ", Walter's nephew and namesake gave, *c.* 1160, the church of Ercheldune (Earlston) in Lauderdale to the Abbey of Kelso. Lawrie, CCLXX. The charter is witnessed by his son William. The nephew Walter also witnesses the Annandale Forest Charter of 1147 × 1153. William and Walter de Lindesei witness charters of Malcolm IV. *St. Andrews*, p. 197. It has not been possible to identify the " Randulphus de Lindesai " who, along with " Lamberton dapifer ", attests a document of Gospatric II before 1138. Lawrie, CXVII. There were three branches of the family, probably descendants of the second " Walterus ", one holding Lamberton, another, Luffness and Crawford, and a third, The Byres. *Complete Peerage*, III, p. 508. The father of the first Walter may possibly have been the " Angodus de Lindsay " who gave land to the monastery of St. Albans in 1077. See Lord Lindsay [afterwards Earl of Crawford], *Lives of the Lindsays*, 3 vols. (1849), I, pp. 18 and 20. Or he may have been the " Baldricus de Lindissi " of 1081 who was put forward by Sir George Sitwell (*Gen.* N.S. XII, p. 1), but failed to meet the sterner requirements of J. H. Round (*ibid.* p. 75), viz. evidence of a son Walter and recurrence of the name Baldric in the Lindsay family.

persons have been identified. As to Walter's forebears in France nothing can be said.

These are the Normans classed vaguely by Earl David as " my nobles and my knights ". The attendant clerks and chaplains, like Aldwin and Osbert, who were to be Abbots of Holyrood, are less identifiable, being given no surname. They were not less numerous, nor less influential, nor were they to prove less active in completing the Normanization of Scotland.

§ 13

Normanization till 1124

On the extent to which the Kingdom was Normanized
before the death of Alexander in 1124 the surviving documents can throw little light, being few in number and
almost exclusively ecclesiastical, as the chief events in his
reign seem also to have been. The Court at least was
partially Normanized. The Conqueror's granddaughter,
who lived till 1122,[1] must have had an imposing suite and,
though not herself a very impressive person, she took some
part in ceremonial, for instance, at the reception of Eadmer
at St. Andrews. Certain of the Norman great officers of
state are found already installed. These at their full
complement were seven in number : Chancellor, Chamberlain, Seneschal (or Dapifer), Butler (*Bouteiller* or Pincerna),
Constable, Marshal, Hostiarius (*Huissier*, Usher or Door-
ward). Some of the seven, with varying names and
attributes, had long existed among the Anglo-Saxons ;
there is a door-ward in *Beowulf*. Edward assigned French
titles and duties, and added other officers from France.
The Conqueror made his own changes. It is possible that
at the Court of Malcolm Canmore some of the Norman
officers were already to be found. In every country the
Court and the administrative system originated in the
domestic household of the Sovereign ; all ministers began
as his servants. *Ministri* are mentioned by Turgot.
Originally Malcolm's " ministers " may have been simply
friends, men of confidence without any very definite status.

[1] Queen Sibylla died on July 12, 1122, on the little island in Loch Tay
which Alexander gave to the Augustinians of Scone, that a church might be
built to her memory. *Scone*, No. II.

" Persons of a higher position were appointed for his service. . . . They were given more ceremonious duties (*obsequia*)." Turgot's words may reflect a change from unofficial assistant to Court functionary. The relative importance attaching to officers of state varied with social conditions and neither Malcolm Canmore nor Alexander may have required all seven. In Alexander's reign those actually recorded are : a Chancellor (Herbert, a Norman),[1] a Chamberlain or Treasurer and a Constable (Edward, a relative of the King).[2] The Constable was the chief officer of the Household ; he commanded the Royal army in the field and under his cognizance came all offences committed within the precincts of the Court. The rise of these officials must have been accompanied by some decline in the status of the Mormaers, who, too, had been officials in " Celtic Scotland ". In Alexander's Foundation Charter to Scone they are styled " Comites ", without designation of place ; it is a title which, though given in connection with a territory, usually implies more a personal dignity than an office.[3] Assimilation of Mormaers, and also of Earls and greater Thanes, to *Comites* (*Comtes*) may

[1] Lawrie, XLVII. Herbert apparently became King's Chamberlain (till 1160). In *Holyrood*, No. XIV, he confirmed to the Abbey his grant of the church of Kinel with consent of his sons Stephen and William, " salvo tenore domini Willelmi nepotis mei quamdiu ipse praenominatam Ecclesiam tenere voluerit ". The grant is confirmed by Malcolm IV (*Holyrood*, No. XV), one of the witnesses being " Willelmus clericus, nepos Camerarii Herbert ".

[2] Edward witnesses David's general Confirmation to St. Andrews. *St. Andrews*, p. 191. He was perhaps a son of Siward Barn, who was probably a younger son of Siward the Dane. Siward Barn took refuge in Scotland after 1066 and went from there by ship in 1071 to join Hereward in the Isle of Ely. Edward, who is described by Ord. Vit. as David's " consobrinus ", cousin, would then be a distant relative of Alexander and David, a cousin of Maud de Saint-Liz and a nephew of Waltheof. The relationship between this Edward [presumably " Edwardus filius Siwardi " (*c.* 1150 : *Dunfermline*, p. 4)] and other Edwards of David's reign, such as his Chancellor, afterwards (from 1150) Bishop of Aberdeen, is not clear.

[3] This charter is too dubious to warrant confident conclusions. See Skene, III, p. 62, n. 6. It is granted with the consent of nine persons, two of whom have the simple designation of *Episcopus* and six of whom have the word *Comes* after their name. They can be identified ; *e.g.* " Mallus " was

have already begun under Malcolm Canmore, for he in later and resentful Scottish minds bore the blame, that of substituting empty foreign titles for the ancient designations of native worth.[1] Further decline in the status of existent officials is foreshadowed by the arrival in South Scotland of the " Vicecomes ", who, in Norman theory, represented the central government locally and collected the Royal dues. The first to be recorded, in 1119, was not a Norman, though possibly he was Normanized; he had his headquarters at Roxburgh, where the office must have been created by Earl David.[2]

How far Norman infiltration was actively encouraged by the King cannot be determined. There was certainly little to prevent it. Complete peace reigned between the

Mormaer, afterwards Earl, of Strathearn. The seventh, Gospatric, who is given no description, was afterwards *Comes* (of Dunbar) and probably represented the part of Lothian which came under Alexander's more direct supervision.

[1] " Cesti Maucloun, qi esposa la dit Margaret, fist chaunger les nouns de thains en countes."—Extract from Leland's transcript from a fuller MS. of *Scalachronica*, p. 320.

Hector Boece's sturdy denunciation in 1527 is translated (*con amore*) by John Bellenden in 1536 : " Be chance of sindry seasonis, specially about the time of King Malcolme Canmore, al thingis began to change. For quhen . . . we began to have alliance, be proximite of Romanis, with Inglismen . . . we war gevin, efter the arrogance and pride of Inglismen, to vane glore and ambution of honouris, and began that time to seke new names of nobilite ; howbeit afore thay dayis, he was maist nobil that was decorit mair with virtew than riches, confiding mair in his awin dedis than in ony dedis of his eldaris. Than began, in Scotland, the maneris of Dukis, Erlis, Lordis and Baronis ; for afore thay dayis, the principall men of Scotland under the king war called Thanis, that is to say, Gadderaris of the Kingis malis ; and war ay rewardit be the king as their faith and virtew deservit." Quoted Hume Brown, *Scotland before 1700*.

Boece is in error as regards the Dukes—there were none in Scotland till 1398—and persistent in his belief that the ancient Scottish virtues suffered contamination from England. The Normans are exonerated, except as transmitters. It was only " through proximity to Frenchmen " that contagion occurred.

[2] " Cospatric Vicecomes " is a witness to the Foundation Charter of Selkirk (1119–1120). No place-name is added, but his residence was clearly Roxburgh. He is identified by Professor Dickinson, *Sheriff*, p. 37, as the son of the Uchtred whom Bishop Æthelwine T.R.E. had appointed Prior at Hexham. Cospatric's early career may have been somewhat similar to Ailred's and as little " Saxon ".

two Kingdoms.   It is even surprising that " Flambard ",
a great builder in his reformed old age, should in 1121 have
thought it worth while to fortify the North Ham of St.
Cuthbert's Bishops, one of the resting-places of the Saint's
body, so strongly that ever afterwards

> Day set on Norham's castled steep,
> And Tweed's fair river, broad and deep.[1]

It is hardly less surprising that in the following year the
King of England should have journeyed north to refortify
Carlisle.   But fortification was explained or explained away
as a protection against Border robbers, and Renouf le
Meschin's departure to be Earl at Chester did necessitate
some redistribution of military and other duties in his
Potestas.   Cordiality remained unimpaired; Renouf gave
his niece to William fitz Duncan, nephew of Alexander
and David.[2]   Probably Norman soldiers, courtiers, administrators, clerks, were drifting north in some numbers,
making themselves useful and receiving due recompense
in grants of land, more freely perhaps from Earl David
than from King Alexander, whom we know, however, to
have fully maintained the family reputation for partiality
to foreigners and coolness towards native talent.   He was
" generous beyond his means to all new-comers "; [3] " no
man was more devoted to clerks, more severe towards men
of his own land ".[4]   He brought French Augustinians to
Scone [5] and it is scarcely to be supposed that his household
cavalry, his Chamberlain Herbert and the members of the
Queen's Norman suite were all left without territorial
means of subsistence, or that Invergowrie, Stirling and
Edinburgh were the only Royal *castella*, or that their occu-

---

[1] The chronicler's Latin prose is as worthy of the site as Scott's verse
(*Marmion*) : " Condidit castellum in excelso praeruptae rupis super Twedam
flumen, ut inde latronum incursus inhiberet et Scottorum irruptiones ".—
Sim. Durh. I, p. 140.   [2] On this marriage see Appendix F, p. 401.
   [3] Ailred, *G.R.A.* p. 756.   [4] Fordun, V, xxx, p. 230.
   [5] Below, p. 171.

pants were persons of Scottish birth. In the matter of distribution of land among Normans both brothers probably went as far as they could, but Alexander ruled with difficulty [1] and it may be doubted if in Scotland proper, except perhaps in Fife and Angus, he could go very far.

That Earl David went further, and even to great lengths, is highly probable, but there is nothing to prove it. Happy the land that has no history, and Cumbria has hardly any. The extant charters given by him when Earl are not addressed to " Cumbrenses ",[2] and they are not concerned with lands in Scotland. On earlier practice we have only the case of " Thor Longus ".[3] It is in accord with what can be supposed on general grounds to have been the conditions obtaining from 1107—much " deserted " land, whether derelict or without a recognized owner; small holdings which could advantageously be extended by clearance and development of marginal land. In Tweeddale and Teviotdale there were wide areas of mountain and waste, as well as arable valleys, and everywhere in Cumbria there must have been ample scope for the energies of a business-like Heir Presumptive actively interested in land-development. It is easy to imagine David seconding the efforts of pioneers like Thor, winning their confidence and gratitude, and generally commending himself to a mixed population with an ancient tradition of fidelity to a single Prince and used from of old to the arrival and settlement of strangers no more " strange " to Cumbrians than many Cumbrians were to each other.

Though undoubtedly aided by a Head Quarters Staff of Normans, Earl David had Scottish counsellors whom even the scant documentary evidence proves to have been numerous and influential. He has two " judices Cum-

---

[1] " Regnum laboriosissime tenuit."—Sim. Durh. II, p. 275.

[2] " Cumbrenses " is not used in the Address of charters till later (*c.* 1139. Lawrie, CXXIII) and then it means only inhabitants of the " Cumberland " occupied by David in the reign of Stephen.

[3] Above, p. 94.

brenses " at his *Inquisitio*, he addresses charters to " my Thanes " and " my Drengs ",[1] and in the documents preserved there are as many native witnesses as Norman. Of these the most important (afterwards loyal subjects of King David) are : " William my nephew ", " Gospatric, brother of Dalfin ", " Cospatric, *vicecomes* ", " Colbanus ", " Maccus " and Alwyn Mac Arkil. No more than William, son of the ex-hostage Duncan II, and related by marriage to Renouf Meschin, are the other witnesses likely to have been hostile to Normans, as such. " The brother of Dalfin " [2] [Dolfin who held Carlisle till expelled by Rufus] was Gospatric II, son of the Conqueror's Earl. He held estates in Northumberland and had a daughter baptized Julienne, who married a landowner in the county, Raoul de Merlay. "Cospatric, *vicecomes* " must have been well versed in Norman ways, as a native of Hexham, as one of Earl David's officials or simply as a " vicecomes ", the representative of Norman rule everywhere, and notably in Wales at this time.[3] Colban, who gave his name to Covington (Upper Lanarkshire), found also in the form Colbaynstoun, apparently was, or soon became, to some extent Normanized.[4] Maccus, son of Undewin, obtained from David lands on the south side of the Teviot and called his residence there Maccusvill [now Maxwell]. Probably he was the Maccus who gave a Norman name, Herbert, to his son and his own name to Maccuston [now Maxton] on the right bank of the Tweed some seven miles

[1] " Cospatrico . . . et omnibus fidelibus Tegnis et Drengis de Lodeneio et de Teuegetedale "—Lawrie, XXX, *c.* 1117.

[2] Dolfin was the eldest son of the Conqueror's Earl of the Northumbrians, Gospatric, whom it is convenient to call Gospatric I. Gospatric II was a younger brother of Dolfin, and first Earl of Dunbar.

[3] J. E. Lloyd, II, p. 424.

[4] " Colbanus " appears with " Macchus " among the witnesses to the Foundation Charter of Selkirk. His name is Norse (ON. Kolbeinn). He may be the Colban who married the daughter and heiress of Gartnach, Mormaer of Buchan, and was styled " Comes " or Earl of Buchan. The son and heir, who succeeded before 1176, had a French name, Roger. A Thomas de Colbainstun witnesses a charter by William the Lion, *c.* 1187, confirming certain churches in Dumfriesshire to the see of Glasgow.

from its junction with the Teviot.[1] Alwyn Mac Arkil's Christian name and his patronymic alike betoken Northumbrian origins, but in his *signa*, very frequent till well into the reign of Malcolm IV, " Mac ", save for an occasional lapse into " filius ", maintains itself so persistently as to indicate Celtic rank or status and a sturdy pride therein. He was a relative, probably the grandson, of Arkil, a great landowner in Yorkshire and Northumbria north of the Tees, who had, at the same time as Malcolm Canmore, come to terms with the Conqueror and given him his son as a hostage.[2] But Arkil changed his mind and after strong, but unsuccessful, resistance withdrew in 1070 to Scotland, where he was welcomed by King Malcolm and given lands which afterwards supported the Earldom of Lennox, held by his descendants.[3] If David's Alwyn Mac Arkil, whom we take to be the son of the hostage, had any family prejudice against Normans, he evidently overcame it early in life.

There seems no reason to suppose that influential personages in Cumbria co-operated with David and his Norman companions less cordially or would have acquiesced in the distribution of land among Normans less readily when he was " Comes " than they undoubtedly did when he was " Rex Scottorum ".

As " Queen's Brother " in England and " King's Brother " in Scotland, David in 1107 was a powerful personage whom it is easy to imagine arriving on a favour-

---

[1] See *O.P.* I, pp. 445-446. Herbert of Maccusvill [afterwards Maxwell] was Sheriff of Roxburgh. He gave the church of Maxwell to Kelso before 1159, when the gift is mentioned in Malcolm IV's Confirmation. *Kelso*, No. I. The name Maccus, common in Yorkshire, T.R.E. and T.R.W., is Scandinavian (Feilitzen, p. 323), but is soon found used by Normans, *e.g.* " Petrus filius Macus ". *E. Yks. Ch.* I, No. 545.

[2] Ord. Vit. IV, iv. Unspecified Arkils, Gospatrics and Dolfins appear together in the *Liber Vitae*, p. 48.

[3] After the death of two Alwyns, father and son, the Earldom of Lennox was held by David, brother of Malcolm IV, presumably in wardship, during the minority of an heir, Aldwyn, who was the second Earl, and who died before 1225. Ed. *Levenax*, Introd. p. x. See also *Complete Peerage*, *s.v.* LENNOX.

able field of experiment and exploitation with the younger, or the more forceful, of the knights who secured him his ample patrimony and, as occasion offered, providing them with land. The grant need not have been large, or have implied more than receipt of dues or rents in kind formerly payable to David himself. From 1114 the Earl of Huntingdon and Northampton was a man of great wealth and power, constantly moving about with a formidable retinue, preceded by dapifers and assistant dapifers preparing his way before him, having the *castella* set in order for his reception and brief stay, seeing to commissariat and other practical matters connected with the crops and the land—all of which presupposes in Cumbria Norman caretakers, land-stewards, foresters, resident in the district. The *veltrarii—veltriers*, huntsmen with their packs of *veltres* or French hounds [1]—no doubt under the charge of "Willelmus Venator", mentioned in the *Inquisitio* must have had permanent quarters in Cumbria.

In South Wales, at this time undergoing intensive Normanization, the arrival of French religious in a district is a sure sign that the process is complete, that the Norman in the castle bears undisputed sway and that Normans possess the surrounding land. One example is the foundation of the Tironian monastery of St. Dogmael's by the Norman who held the castle at Cardigan. This took place in 1113 [2]—only three or four years after Bernard of Abbeville founded his reformed Benedictine community in the woods at Tiron on the marches of Maine and Picardy. [3] In the same year as the Norman castellan in Wales Earl David brought monks from Tiron to Selkirk, settled them

[1] " Veltrarius (Vautrarius), veltricibus omnibus praefectus ; canis veltris = canis gallicus."—Ducange, VI, p. 756.

[2] *c.* 1113. Knowles, *R.H.* p. 33 ; *c.* 1115, J. E. Lloyd, I, p. 431. The first Abbot was instituted *c.* 1120.

[3] The settlement at Tiron is mentioned in *Chron. Melrose, s.a.* 1109. It was made provisionally in 1107, permanently in 1110. Tiron is now Thiron-Gardais (Eure-et-Loir), arr. Nogent-le-Rotrou.

beside his forest castle and richly endowed the monastery with lands and revenues.[1] Among other grants enumerated in the Foundation Charter is " a tithe of the hides of stags and hinds which my *veltriers* may take ".[2] Men of all sorts and conditions had hastened to Tiron ; Bernard of Abbeville encouraged them to exercise in the community the arts and crafts they had followed in the world,[3] and no doubt the Tironensians who arrived at Selkirk were practical men, used to a life of hardship while building themselves a habitation in the woods. But it would have been inconsiderate, and unlike David, to bring a colony of French monks from over the seas unless he was in a position to assure them that the great hinterland of Royal Forest was under efficient, possibly under Norman, supervision and that the promised tithe would be regularly forthcoming. Similar conclusions could be drawn from the acceptance by French Augustinians at Beauvais of his invitation to settle at Jedburgh.

The foundation of French religious houses, the exist-

[1] Sim. Durh. gives the date of foundation as 1113. Some expressions in David's Foundation Charter of 1119 or 1120 suggest that his Abbey was founded on the site of an ancient religious house. *O.P.* I, p. 267. David gave " rich lands and revenues ", according to " Gaufridus Grossus ". The endowment included lands in Hardingstone (Northampton). *Kelso*, No. I. The first Abbot, " Radulfus ", resigned in 1115, according to *Chron. Melrose* (facsimile edition, p. 31, margin). The second Abbot, William, went back to Tiron in 1118 or 1119 and was succeeded by Herbert. In 1128 the monastery was transferred to Kelso on the advice of the third Abbot, Herbert, and Bishop John, whom Herbert was to follow in the see of Glasgow. Henry I, who greatly admired Bernard of Abbeville, made an annual grant to Tiron of fifteen marks silver (Haskins, *N.I.* p. 106 ; Round, *Cal.* I, p. xxxviii), but St. Dogmael's was their only settlement in Britain besides Selkirk. David is stated to have journeyed to Tiron to see Bernard, but arrived after his death (April 25, 1116). We have, however, no confirmation of this statement, made by Bernard's disciple, " Gaufridus Grossus " [*Geoffroi Le Gros*], *Vita B. Bernardi Tironensis*, Migne, *P.L.* clxxii, p. 1426.

[2] " Decimam coriorum cervorum et cervarum quos veltrarii mei capient." —Foundation Charter, Lawrie, XXXV. The phrase is repeated, and the right confirmed, by Malcolm IV in 1159. *Kelso*, No. I. The whole district, comprising the forests of Selkirk, Ettrick and Traquair and popularly known as " the Forest ", was Crown property. *O.P.* I, p. 241.

[3] Ord. Vit. VIII, xxvii.

ence of a *castellum* at Selkirk, the installation of a *Vicecomes* at Roxburgh—all suggest that the Normanization of Cumbria was in active progress. The terms of David's first known Royal Charter (to Robert de Brus in 1124) imply that the *castellum* at Annan was already in being,[1] and the explicit reference to the rights enjoyed at Carlisle by Renouf le Meschin, who had in fact left Carlisle some years before,[2] suggests that what was new in 1124 was rather Robert's charter than his possession of Annandale.

All the elements which contributed to extremely rapid Normanization under King David are found assembled under King Alexander: the French counsellors, the French prelates, the Norman officers of state, the knights, the *vicecomes*, the castle, the castle chapel, the French monastery—all the elements save one, the distribution of land among Normans, on which there is only the Silence of History. Silence may mean anything, even consent, even acquiescence in territorial awards to Normans. When we reflect that lands were continually conveyed without charters, that in general King David's Normans are the same persons as Earl David's and that their Scottish estates which are first heard of are in Cumbria, it seems reasonable to suppose that when, immediately after his accession, David announces in an extant charter that he has granted certain lands to certain Normans, he is only giving formal recognition in a few cases to a state of affairs already general. When we further reflect that usually we have no announcement at all, but merely find ourselves in presence of a *fait accompli* revealed later on and quite incidentally by the mention of a subsequent donation to a religious house, it is difficult to resist the conclusion that Earl David's Normans had not to wait seventeen years for their territorial acquisitions in Cumbria.

---

[1] See below, p. 186. The words are " illam terram et suum castellum ".

[2] In 1121 ; see above, p. 150, n. 1.

As for Norman influence in the religious sphere, we find Alexander's reign ending with the installation of a French Bishop at St. Andrews and a spectacular demonstration of his own devotion to Norman ideals. Within a few weeks of his accession in 1107 he had had his colleague at the recent Translation of St. Cuthbert elected to the see of St. Andrews, vacant since 1093.[1] Turgot wished the jurisdiction of York to be acknowledged. Alexander held strong views on Scottish ecclesiastical independence, and the relations between King and Bishop became strained. On August 31, 1115, Margaret's biographer died at Durham.[2] Alexander then requested his other colleague at the Translation, Raoul d'Escures, now Archbishop of Canterbury, to assist in the choice of a successor and after considerable delay one was found, in the person of Anselm's biographer, Eadmer. He was not elected till June 1120.[3] When he arrived he pleaded for the jurisdiction of Canterbury. But, as he writes, " Alexander would not have the Church of Canterbury placed before the Church of St. Andrew of Scotland ". Eadmer went back to Canterbury in dissatisfaction and resigned, probably soon after the death of the Archbishop in November 1122.[4] Alexander was within a few weeks of his own death when he had

---

[1] Church reform had been under consideration in Edgar's reign, and Anselm had sent brethren to Scotland at his request, as Lanfranc had done at Margaret's; see Anselm's letter (1107) to Alexander (Lawrie, XXV). Turgot was elected on June 20, 1107.

[2] Turgot, whose health had been affected by his troubles with Alexander, had returned to seek healing at the shrine of St. Cuthbert. At Durham he received a visit from the new Archbishop of York, Toustain [" Thurstan "], and promised him obedience should God restore him to health. Turgot was buried in the chapter-house between Bishop Walcher and Bishop " de Saint-Carilef ".

[3] In the interim the diocese had been administered by a monk of St. Edmundsbury, named William. Perhaps he was the cleric [often assumed to be William, Bishop of Man, 1109–1114] who (see Kenney, p. 434) caused copies to be made of a poem on St. Columba written at the request of King Alexander and his Queen by a monk named Simeon. Or perhaps he was the William mentioned on p. 261, n. 4. In any case the interim Bishop, having a French name, was presumably French.

[4] It has been generally thought that Eadmer died at Canterbury on January 13, 1124, as stated by Sim. Durh. *H.R.* II, p. 275. But recent

Robert, Prior of Scone, elected. Thenceforward St. Andrews had French Bishops.[1]

When in 1114 Alexander had rebuilt the Culdee monastery at Scone as a thanksgiving for his victory over the men of Moray, he had stipulated that the Culdees, who were in some ways similar to canons regular,[2] should share the new buildings with Augustinian canons, an order lately introduced into England from France by his sister Queen Maud and her beloved Anselm. She was the foundress of their first important house in England, at Aldgate (1108).[3] Earl David settled Augustinians at Jedburgh and was a good friend to St. Oswald's Priory at Nostell (1113), near Pontefract in Yorkshire. Thus Alexander was acting promptly and in full accord with family sentiment when in 1114 he invited brethren from Nostell to Scone.[4] Though Augustinians lived in community, according to Rule, and were bound by the monastic vows of chastity, poverty and obedience, they were not monks. They were priests, which monks might be or might not, and they served

publication by Dom André Wilmart of works attributed to Eadmer and dating from *c.* 1130 seems to show that he only resigned in 1122 and died several years later. Foreville, p. 68 n.

[1] On Prior Robert's French origins see below, pp. 197-198.

[2] Skene, II, p. 227 ; Kenney, p. 470.

[3] The Priory of the Holy Trinity, to which in 1108 she granted two-thirds of her life interest in the Exeter fee-farm rent, paid to the Queens of England. *Misc. Deeds*, No. 1288. Dugdale, *Monasticon*, VI, 155.

[4] Fordun, V, xxviii. In England canons regular of St. Augustine appeared first in 1106 at St. Botolph's, Colchester. The Priory at Carlisle was founded by Henry I " per industriam et consilium Mathildis reginae ", according to the Ingilby MS., published by Professor Galbraith, *Anonimallie*, pp. xlvi-xlvii. This would dispose of the hitherto accepted date, 1123, though that given [1101] is too early. Hexham was founded in 1113, Nostell probably in the same year, though the full regular life was not perhaps introduced till 1122. Knowles, *R.H.* p. 87. Connections between Nostell and the Scottish Royal House were pointed out by the Reverend James Wilson, *Foundation of the Austin Priories of Nostell and Scone, S.H.R.* VII (1910). Maud de Saint-Liz made a gift of rent in Bedford to Nostell, renewed after her death in 1131 by King David and Earl Henry, who made a further grant from their silver mines at Carlisle. Her elder son Simon was a benefactor of Nostell, where her younger son Waldef joined the community. The Notification (at Winchester, 1120 × 1122) to the Canons, of liberty to alter the site chosen for their church at Nostell, is attested by Earl David. Farrer, *Itin.* p. 94.

churches in the neighbourhood of their houses.[1]   The
brethren from Nostell could thus be installed at Scone
with Culdees, as Benedictines could not have been.   In
the ancient seat of the monarchy they were well placed
to extend their activities [2] and they had been established at
St. Andrews for some time when their Prior became Bishop.

The public act of Norman symbolism which Alexander
performed in the last year of his life was one which he
evidently felt his lieges would understand.   The ceremony is taken by Scottish historians for " Celtic " and
considered unimportant.   It is Norman and it illustrates
the spread of Norman ideals in the Scottish Kingdom.
Granting to the church of St. Andrews a piece of land in
the immediate neighbourhood known as the Cursus Apri [3]
or the Boar's Raik, Alexander came in state and, with all
his lords around him, " in witness and token " of the
gift, made his men bring up to the altar " his comely
steed of Araby ", richly caparisoned, his " costly armour
of Turkey . . . and shield and spear of silver white ".[4]
Normans liked to emphasize a grant of land, especially
one made to a church, by the gift of some concrete object,

[1] From their first appearance in Britain the Augustinians—or Austin
Canons or Black Canons or Canons Regular, as they were variously called—
were popularly confused with monks ; their houses were regularly known
as " monasteries " (*e.g.* in the Foundation Charter of Holyrood), and they
themselves were described as an " Order ".

[2] Alexander gave them the island in Loch Tay for a church to be built
" pro anima regine ibi defuncte " (*Scone*, No. II), and in 1123 founded a
priory on the island in the Forth called St. Colum's Inch or Inchcolm because it was believed to have sheltered St. Columba.   See Wyntoun, VII,
v, 605.   [3] Fordun, p. 227.

[4]   " Befor the lordis al the kynge
         Gert than to the altar brynge
         His cumly steide of Araby,
         Sadillit and bridillit costlykly
         Cuverit withe a fayr mantlet
         Off preciouss and of fyne weluet,
         Withe his armouris [*v.r.* armys] of Turky,
         That pryncis than oyssit generally,
         And cheyssit mast for thar delyte,
         Withe scheylde and spere of siluir quhite."
                             Wyntoun, VII, v, 693.

such as a book or a knife, not necessarily of much intrinsic value, and they knew how to enliven inexpensive giving with a dash of poetry, as when the transference of land was accompanied by the branch of a cherry-tree.[1] The gift of a horse had a tragic significance. Towards 1061 the sorrowing parents of Roger de Laigle came to the monastery of Saint-Évroul and offered his best horse to God and to the monks and, because the horse was of great price, one Ernaud begged that he might have it and made the monastery a grant of land in return. About the time that Alexander gave his Arab steed to God and the canons of St. Andrews, the aged Ansoud, Lord of Maule,[2] on his death-bed, sent to the monks of Saint-Évroul his best palfrey, which, in accordance with his last wishes, his son Pierre redeemed, by granting them a piece of land.[3] Alexander was not old, but he knew that his fighting days were over and death was near.

Twelfth-century morality had its strictnesses and its laxities, and there were few monasteries in Christendom but would fabricate or falsify a charter, so might possession of a little more land be proved, or a contested privilege retained. One fraudulent document after another had been produced, challenged and exposed during the late contentions between Canterbury and York—as none knew better than he whose reign had been largely devoted to keeping St. Andrews out of the jurisdiction of either. This time, this last time, he would make sure. He had taken all ordinary precautions, obtained the assent of the Heir Presumptive, expounded the purpose of his gift to

[1] Whether observing a native custom or, more probably, a Norman one, King Edgar, when he attended the dedication of the church of St. Mary at Coldingham, placed some unspecified symbol upon the altar and gave lands at Swinton near Coldingham to the monks of St. Cuthbert. Lawrie, XX (c. 1100). The Lord of Richmond in 1135 placed a knife on the altar of St. Edmund at Bury when making a gift to the Abbey of all his land within the borough of Cambridge, *E. Yorks. Ch.* IV, No. 11. A long list of objects thus used by Normans from early times will be found in the Index to Round, *Cal.* I.   [2] Seine-et-Oise, arr. Versailles, canton de Meulan.
[3] Ord. Vit. V, xix.

the French Bishop, the Black Canons from France, the native churchmen and the Culdees. But when he was gone, dissensions might arise, a false document be shown and the laity perplexed. Like his brothers, he put his faith in written evidence, but collective memory seemed still to have its value. He was " devoted to clerks ", but they might conveniently forget. The inhabitants of St. Andrews, if they could not read, could see, and they would understand. They and their descendants, he hoped, would remember, and some inhabitants still do.

The ceremony had a further significance. The horse, unimportant in Celtic and Saxon history, was the basis of Norman greatness—and of chivalry, as the word *cheval* is of *chevalier* and *chevalerie*. The Normans, who owed much of their success to their efficiency as mounted soldiers, loved horses, understood them and, while exploiting their military possibilities to the full, admired them for themselves, for their strength, their beauty, their grace. The horses which conquered England or pursued Malcolm Canmore to Abernethy were not of the heavy lumbering sort which imagination associates with the corpulent Duke of Normandy. Their counterfeit presentment in the Tapestry shows a light nimble breed, of Spanish origin, with a Moorish or Arab strain—blood relations to Alexander's " comely steed ".[1] Normans " delighted in the splendour of horses and of all the instruments and habiliments of war ".[2] They knew the symbolic power of arms and armour. Helmet, Saddle and Spear were the symbols which, fifty years afterwards, a more " Norman " and a more tragic King of Scots than Alexander laid sorrow-

---

[1] L. Champion, *Les Chevaux et les cavaliers de la tapisserie de Bayeux*, Caen, 1907 (156 pp.), p. 35. The author was a cavalry remount officer, an expert judge of horses. " Ce sont des chevaux orientaux " was his remark on first seeing the Tapestry. William and his commanders ride Spanish horses, direct descendants of the " orientals " bred by the Moors in Spain.

[2] " Equorum caeterorumque militiae instrumentorum et vestium luxuria [gens] delectatur."—Malaterra, p. 1102, B.

fully down upon the altar of the church at York.[1] In
Alexander's lifetime the *miles*, the *chevalier*, the mailed
horseman, had become the god of battles, invincible in the
field and moving through the days of peace in a cloud of
glory. *Miles* had of course two senses, according as the
profession itself or the personal qualities associated with it
came to mind. Who shall say when " miles " in Scottish
or any other early documents is to be translated as
" soldier " and when as " knight ", or, in the latter case,
when it means a man rendering certain feudal services or
a man credited with possessing those qualities which in
English, and that only in recent English, are hardly de-
finable except as " chivalrous " ? When Henry, at the age
of sixteen, received breast-plate and helmet from the
Conqueror at a service conducted by Lanfranc, Knighthood had already a religious significance,[2] and ten years
later the French Pope in his celebrated sermon enunciated
the doctrine that a Knight was peculiarly bound to obey
and serve the Church. When Alexander was King the
best Knight was he who fought for Christ's sepulchre and
the acts most pleasing to God were thought to be taking
the Cross and endowing a monastery. Alexander the
Fierce had founded Austin Priories. He had not taken
the Cross. But in spirit he was a Crusader and, in the
eyes of all men, in the belief that all would understand,
with pomp and circumstance, Arab steed, ornamental
panoply, silver shield and spear, he invested his last gift to
Holy Church with the mystic symbols of the Norman faith.

[1] In the *Anonimallie Chronicle, 1333 to 1381*, there is the following
marginal note (f⁰ 176ᵛ) against the account of the peace made in 1175 between
William the Lion and Henry II, after the former's release from captivity :
" en remembraunce de le accorde le roi Descoce offrist soun chapel, sa cel
et sa launce qe sont en la eglise Deverwick en lour tresuri ".

[2] " Se cyng . . . dubbade his sunu Henric to ridere."—*A.S.C.* MS.
E, *s.a.* 1085. Ord. Vit. (VIII, i) states that Lanfranc placed Henry's breast-
plate, set the helmet on his head and girt him with the belt of knighthood.
Anselm's Council of Westminster, on September 29, 1102, discussed the
question whether Abbots could make a Knight, and it was decided that they
could not. Wm. Malm. *Gesta P.A.* I, p. 120.

CHAPTER IV

SCOTLAND'S "NORMAN CONQUEST"
(1124–1130)

★

§ 14

David the Conqueror

ALEXANDER died childless on April 23, 1124, and was succeeded by the Earl of Huntingdon and Northampton. David must have then been about forty. He had power, wealth and goodwill, such as his brothers had never known. The respect of his own countrymen he had long enjoyed. In England he stood next in rank to the King and was held in much honour by all Normans. At Malmesbury the Monk rejoiced that " David, famous for his meekness and wisdom, was now King of Scots ". The bonds of friendship, sympathy and mutual admiration remained unsevered. Still " one of us ", still Earl of Huntingdon and Northampton, he would always be welcomed back to his spiritual home and surest source of revenue. A Scot by birth, a Norman by adoption, a knight, a man of law, a man of conscience, anxious to do what was chivalrous and right and just, he naturally wished to improve the conditions of life in his native land and, as naturally, he identified improvement with adaptation to the Norman institutions he knew so well and so honestly admired. Endowed himself with great organizing ability, he was seconded in his efforts by the soldiers, administrators, officials, men of business, landholders, country gentlemen, whom he had had about him for many years. They were aliens. The more important of them were placed by him in possession of Scottish lands. They came into power with the new King and in the changes that were made Norman England was taken as the model.

It was still a conquered country. Normans ruled

supreme. English had ceased to be a literary language. It was a welter of patois, each barely intelligible beyond its own district. English-speaking society had foundered and English literature had gone the way of the patrons and readers. Old English prose was running underground, emerging on Sundays and feast days in pithy Sermons for Rustics. The *Anglo-Saxon Chronicle* staggered on a few years more. Writers were of French or mixed parentage and wrote in Latin. Teachers were French. By 1117 the theologian at Caen who had so politely and so firmly declined Margaret's invitation to come over and help in Scottish regeneration was at Oxford and, by his own account, holding large classes spellbound.[1] For social purposes English was inadmissible. The King knew little, if any.[2] Courtiers and high officials knew no more. The few Old English families that had weathered the Conquest had assimilated themselves to the surrounding gentry and taken to using French. The process continued far down the social scale.[3] Intermarriage was common and children of mixed parentage had an opportunity of making themselves bilingual which some of them may have utilized. For practical purposes many people acquired a working knowledge of a second language. When only one was learned or retained, prospects in life favoured French. Circumstances varied greatly with individuals and localities,

---

[1] Before 1117 and after 1119. Rashdall, III, p. 117. Thiébaud d'Étampes is only *magister* at Oxford, whereas he was *doctor* in his letter to Queen Margaret, written at least twenty-five years before. But *doctor* stressed scholarship and also led up to stylistic effects, whereas *magister* indicates status as a teacher. Thiébaud describes the attendance at his prelections rather oddly as " sixty to a hundred clerks, more or less ". Thiébaud perhaps should not be taken too seriously.

[2] Cp. Round, *G.M.* p. 426 : " The belief, so dear to Mr. Freeman's heart, that Henry I was, more or less, familiar with the English tongue ", and Bateson, p. 22 : " The story of ' sac ' and ' soc ' does not bear the interpretation that Henry knew English ".

[3] The contemporary evidence is collected by R. M. Wilson, *English and French in England, 1100–1300*, in *History*, XXVIII, No. 107 (March 1943), pp. 37-60. It is so conflicting and so confusing that we are reduced to probabilities and the exercise of common sense.

but in the country as a whole the pre-Conquest cleavage between " haves " and " have-nots " had widened into a gulf. The " haves " were French and French-speaking. Norman government was written government and the documents were written in Latin. French was still hardly more than a spoken tongue, but it was the language of the free, not of men who might be free or might be serfs,[1] and all conversation, all social intercourse, with people of any importance had to be conducted in French.

These people, however, came of families domiciled in England for two generations and they would have been dense indeed had they remained impervious to the subtle charm of English life. In some ways and in some degree they were becoming acclimatized, though not enough to qualify for the title " Anglo-Norman ", which modern scholarship has prematurely bestowed. Officially they were never called anything but what they were, viz. *Francigenae* or *Franci*. But the institutions of the country can by 1124 be called Anglo-Norman. All conquerors are conquered in the end. Those of England realized more quickly than most that many things are best done in the native way. They readily adopted ancient customs, local practices, general ideas of government, and they never abrogated Old English law. Their only revolutionary innovation was in the matter of land tenure. They made knight-service the dominant and distinctive tenure, and thus established in England their cardinal feudal doctrine : all land is held of the King ; all other occupiers of land are tenants either of the King himself or of some lord who holds of him ; the tie between the lord and his tenants is hereditary ; the extent of each man's holding and the nature of his tenure determine in the main his civil and political rights. The application of this theory made

[1] In the official documents which Henry I was addressing, at the same time as Earl David and in the same formula, " Francis et Anglis ", the *Franci* are all free ; the native-born Englishman requires a qualifying word : *Anglicus liber*. Bateson, p. 103.

England, which had long been feudal, a Norman-feudal state.

All that concerns David's kingdom is Norman government in England at the stage which it had reached by 1124. Henry was still elaborating a centralized administrative system, built up on English foundations out of Norman and English elements. He was probably himself its chief artificer and to work it he had created a professional body of administrators who were French and employed French methods and nomenclature. As able a man as his father and as despotic, Henry was before all things an organizer, and from the outset he put his faith in the wise selection of subordinates. His achievement was introduction of order and method into the government of a country which, before him, was under an improvised military regime. This he accomplished by the exercise of his personal power, which was unlimited, and with the help of personally selected administrators.

While the Norman principle of dependent tenure in return for definite service remained inviolate, it was no longer interpreted as strictly military. Not only had scutage, the commutation of military service at a fixed rate, come freely into use,[1] but estates could often be held by performance of a specific service which might be trivial or formal. A Norman King's decisions were professedly made " cum consilio baronum " and the Conqueror's primitive *curia regis* had been organized into what was in the fullest sense the King's Court (" Court " is a word of many senses),[2] a body managing the business of his great property, the state. It met when and where he wished —almost anywhere in Normandy or England, for king-

---

[1] Scutage is mentioned *eo nomine* in a writ of the first year of Henry I. A. L. Poole, p. 41.

[2] French *cour* (Latin *cohort-em*) meant a " cohort ", a company of soldiers, a crowd of attendants, a retinue, but at an early date was associated with Latin *curia*, an assembly. *Cour* thus acquired a series of senses (see *O.E.D. s.v.* COURT, *sb.*[1]), for which *curia* is the regular Latin equivalent.

ship was still ambulatory and a Norman monarch was as likely to be on one side of the Channel as on the other. In a single session advice might be given to the King on any matter—on taxation, on the making or revising of a law, on a suit betweeen two of his vassals. But gradually the financial business had been set off from the legislative and the judicial, and a distinction drawn between the King's Court as a whole and the Exchequer Court, a board of barons charged with the duties of auditing the sheriffs' accounts and trying causes which concerned the collection of the King's revenue. His officers remained unspecialized. His judges, *justitiae regis* [1] or *justitiarii regis*, were simply men of experience, members of his household, or " barons " whom he thought fit to summon to meetings of his *Curia* and some of whom, like Walter Espec and Eustace fitz John in the North, went on circuit, dealing with much other business than the purely judicial. The central administration was thus carried down into the counties and a Royal system of local justice operated in conjunction with the shire court and the barons' courts. In the shire court the *Vicomte* sat in the seat of the English Sheriff, making what he could of the Laws of Edward, as amended under three Norman Kings, introducing such French procedure as occurred to him and further extending the financial duties inherited from his English predecessor. " Baron " was still a vague term. A baron might have a court or might not. A baron's court was for his dependants ; when disputants were vassals of different lords the case went before the shire court ; cases of unusual difficulty or importance could be referred to the Itinerant Justices. Norman methods of trial were being more and more generally applied ; the native ordeal of water or hot iron was being superseded by the judicial duel or wager of battle. The Jury had its uses extended from criminal

[1] Richard de Courcy is *justitia regis* in the Winton Domesday. D.B. Add. 534.

cases to civil. The King, who had reached the throne with the help of Bishops, worked in close alliance with the Church, holding himself free, however, to differ on occasion, and violently, with Archbishop or Pope. Long years of peace and settled conditions had brought increased trade and favoured the development of the towns. Boroughs, trading centres with privileges and monopolies, had been growing up beside the castles and the religious houses.

King David's achievement was simply to establish in Scotland this manner of government, these institutions (*Curia Regis*, Justiciar, Sheriff, Jury, Borough)—in short, this Anglo-Norman System. He had a profound admiration (shared by twentieth-century historians) for the methods of government devised by King Henry and, like him, he relied on personally selected advisers. David implanted the Anglo-Norman system in a soil which had been prepared for its reception by his father and brothers, and by himself. He came to Scone as they had come—as a travelled Scot, a reformer from the South—but with a much fuller training in Southern ways and the certainty of support from the South. He had more belief in government, more zest for reform, and he came accompanied by a phalanx of " new men ", Normans all. What made his accession tantamount to a " Norman Conquest " was that he immediately granted them extensive lands, to be held on Norman-feudal terms. The doctrine he thus established was never seriously challenged. Perhaps it was not even formulated. Men of David's time did not reason much about their government or their system of land tenure. He and his Norman associates felt vaguely conscious of an organizing mission and carried it out by continuing the practices they had followed in England all their lives. Their set of ideas contained the belief that the King possesses all the land, or rights over all the land, and that landholders are merely his tenants, either directly or through a larger or smaller number of intermediaries.

He grants estates to individuals, or confirms them in estates they already hold, the evidence for the grant, or for the confirmation, being his written charter; in return, these individuals undertake to render him military or other service. Written evidence was not always considered necessary. The King's word, spoken before witnesses, or the ceremony of investiture, or actual possession, could suffice.

Only a few such charters given by David have come down to us. As it is unlikely that the Conqueror after Hastings was asked for a charter by his chief beneficiaries, so it is unlikely that Hugue de Morville requested one for himself. He was too demonstrably a *beatus possessor* for his tenure to be called in question by any man. It is not possible to imagine the Earl of Fife, Constantin, son of Macduff, wishing to have his estates confirmed to him by a son of Malcolm Canmore and accepting from him what the stalwarts of a later age scornfully described as a " sheepskin title ". But in practice, as the demand for written evidence, fostered by the Normanized Church, steadily increased, the use of charters became general. In theory, from the accession of David onwards, all who received land in Scotland, Frenchmen or natives, " held by charter " and were, directly or indirectly, the King's vassals.

Every age is entitled to its theory on the ownership of Scotland.[1] In Scots Law the theory followed, consciously or not, by David and his Normans still holds the field. Scotland is still in the Age of Charters.[2]

Accompanied by well-tried Norman friends, David went to Scone, not to be crowned—the Scottish Kings

[1] In 1300 Pope Boniface VIII declared that Scotland belonged, and always had belonged, to St. Peter. Edward I maintained that the Scottish Kings had held of King Arthur, apparently by sergeanty; Wyntoun (in the Prologue to Book VI) argued that they were tenants-in-chief of the Almighty. See G. Neilson, *Knight-Service*, pp. 183-184.

[2] " Not only are almost all estates held on tenures dating back to charters of the oldest form, but new charters are being granted every day which both in form and in substance are their lineal descendants."—Duke of Argyll, p. 82.

were neither crowned nor anointed [1]—but to be installed, perhaps to be robed in white and to place his foot in the imprint of one graven in the Stone of Destiny, vowing to walk in the ways of his predecessors.[2] Norman baron though he was, and usurper though to many of his subjects he seemed, he descended from the old Highland Kings, and yet he was reluctant, Ailred tells us, to assume the Royal dignity, and the Bishops had much difficulty in inducing him to undergo the ancient rites.[3] He was not backward in dispensing Royal favours. At Scone, probably just after the Installation, he granted Robert de Brus the territory of Annandale, extending to some two hundred thousand acres. In the charter Robert is " to have and to hold the land and its *castellum* with all its customs, to wit, with all those customs which Renouf le Meschin ever had in Carlisle and his land of Cumberland ".[4] Apparently Annandale was to be a *Potestas*. Thenceforth the high road from Carlisle to Glasgow ran many a long mile through the lordship of one of the King of England's great barons, a lordship stretching from Gretna to the sources of the Clyde at Moffat and rich in places since famed in Scottish song and story. There was as yet no nation, in the modern sense, consequently little question of national security or of national susceptibilities.

[1] In their seals the Scottish Kings are represented crowned, from Edgar (1097). But they wore a crown as an ornament ; its imposition was no part of the solemnities at Scone. Giraldus Cambrensis states categorically, and as a point in their favour (VIII, *Liber de Principis Instructione*, p. 139), that they were neither crowned nor anointed, and this is accepted doctrine with all who have written on the matter, *e.g.* Lord Bute, p. 16, and Schramm, pp. 243-244. That in the period ending in 1165 there was no coronation must be obvious to anyone reading Ailred and Fordun, from the vagueness of their references to " rites and ceremonies ", where *coronatio* would be the expected word. David II was the first Scottish King to be crowned and the first to receive unction (on November 24, 1331).

[2] According to Lord Bute, p. 12, the Stone at Dunadd, the ancient fortified hill in the Moss of Crinan which was the citadel of the Dalriadic kings, has the graven imprint of a human foot. It has been maintained that at Scone Edward I was hoaxed by the " underground movement " of the time, and went off to Westminster with the wrong Stone.

[3] *G.R.A.* p. 713.   [4] Bain, *Cal.* I, p. 29 ; Lawrie, LIV.

The document recording this prodigious donation is small : to be precise, $6\frac{1}{2} \times 3\frac{3}{4}$ inches. There is no room for explanations and perhaps no need for any. Definition is by means of reference to previous established rights—those which had till lately been enjoyed by Renouf le Meschin at Carlisle and were familiar to his friends in Scottish and English Cumbria and elsewhere, Earl David and Robert de Brus among them. There is no detailed specification of boundary lines. They are assumed to be well known : Renouf le Meschin's on the one hand, Dugald of Nithsdale's on the other—which may mean that if Cumbria had primitive characteristics, uncertain delimitation of estates was not one of them.[1] No feudal service is provided for. The matter is left to common knowledge, to use and wont. But knight-service is implied, as can be seen from the confirmation, which becomes explicit.[2]

The charter, the first known document of the new reign, is addressed by David, King of Scots, " omnibus baronibus suis et hominibus et amicis suis Francis et Anglis ". It is attested by French witnesses whose names occur in the charters he gave when Earl, the only new-comers being " Randulphus de Sules " and " Willelmus de Sumarvilla ". Both friends were well rewarded for their attendance at Scone. Randolf de Soules[3] perhaps attended from

[1] The area is described as " Estrahanent " [= " Strathannan " = Annandale] and all the land from the marches [*divisae*] of " Dunegal de Stranit " [= " Strathnith " = Nithsdale] to the marches of " Radulfus Meschin ". The initial *E* in " Estrahanent " betrays the French scribe.

[2] Annandale was confirmed by William the Lion to Robert's second son, Robert de Brus [le Meschin], for the service of 100 knights. *National MSS. Scotland*, I, with facsimile.

[3] The fief of Soules, held of the Honour of Saint-Lô in 1066, was granted soon after to the chapter of Bayeux. The de Soules family was established in Oxfordshire and Kent. Palgrave, *N. and E.* III, pp. 426 and 488. As early as 1125 " Randulphus de Sules " witnessed, with John, Bishop of Glasgow, a mandate by King David at Perth, regarding the payment of tithe to Dunfermline (Lawrie, LXI). He witnessed, *c.* 1138, the grant to Tiron, and many subsequent grants. He gave to Jedburgh several churches before 1152, and the church of Castleton, near the Mote of Liddel, before 1165. He was " *Pincerna regis Scottorum* " when he gave land to Newbattle, Walter fitz Alan and " Gaufridus de Malwyn " being witnesses. *Newbattle*,

Northamptonshire, where he held Doddington, the church of which he gave to the Abbey of Jedburgh ; [1] he is found before long in possession of Liddesdale. Guillaume de Sommerville had probably come from Yorkshire ; [2] he was granted, no doubt with equal promptness, Libberton (Lanarkshire), a wide domain, including the whole tract of land known as Carnwath—in all, thirty-nine thousand acres.[3]

David proceeds by implication, not statement, but more often utter silence prevails, whether because a charter has been lost or because none ever existed. His charters bear no date, and even if there were a date, his formula, " I have given and by this my charter confirmed ", would not necessarily mean " I have this day given " or " I have recently given ". He states an accomplished fact, not when or where it was accomplished. It can only be surmised that it was in the early years of the reign that Robert de Bourneville obtained his possessions in East Lothian, Bérenger Engaine and Robert Corbet theirs in Teviotdale, and Hugue de Morville received Cunningham [mid-Ayrshire] and extensive lands in Lauderdale and elsewhere.

p. 29, No. XXXVII. He died without issue *c.* 1170. He was succeeded in Liddesdale by his nephew " Randulphus " or " Ranulphus " de Soules, whose father, William, and brother, Richard, appear in charters of William the Lion. The nephew was slain by his own domestics in 1207 (*Chron. Melrose, s.a.*). Before 1214 " Fulco " [Foulque] de Soules was King's *Pincerna* and representative of the family, which provided a Competitor for the Throne in 1291, but became extinct in Scotland *c.* 1320.

[1] Moore, *L.Sc.K.* p. 40.

[2] He was probably a son of the Robert de Sommerville who gave land in Seacroft to St. Clement's Chapel, Pontefract (*E. Yorks. Ch.* III, No. 1651), and perhaps a relative of Gautier de Sommerville, who held Wichnor in Staffordshire. An old family tradition is associated with Wichnor. See *O.P.* I, p. 431. Guillaume de Sommerville witnesses numerous Scottish charters, from *c.* 1130. In 1157–1158 and 1159 the Pipe Rolls bear testimony to his Yorkshire connection. In Yorkshire he owes 20 marks silver, " sed manet in terra regis Scotiae in Loeneis ". *E. Yorks. Ch.* III, No. 1651. The family continued to possess the greater part of Carnwath till the reign of James VI, *O.P.* I, p. 127. The name probably comes from Sémerville, now Graveron-Sémerville, commune du canton d'Évreux nord ; Latin *Semervilla* (1209) ; 13th c. spellings, Semerville and Soumerville. See *Scots Peerage*, vol. VIII, *s.v.* SOMERVILLE, and Blosseville, *Dict. Topographique de la France (Département de l'Eure)*, 1877, p. 210.

[3] J. T. T. Brown, *S.H.R.* XXV (1928), p. 220.

As early as 1127 King David's gift to the Church of St. Cuthbert in Edinburgh [1] is witnessed by " Willelmus de Graham ", who had probably arrived from Grantham in Lincolnshire and been given lands in Scotland. He retained his original territorial designation, Graham, an old spelling of Grantham,[2] and thus brought into Scotland the name which is written variously as Graham or Graeme.[3] But it is not known what lands he received or who were his immediate descendants. Lesser awards, soon afterwards to be revealed in profusion, may be assumed to have gone to lesser men. It is highly probable that in 1124 the tide of Norman immigration was flowing in full strength and it is certain that the wholesale distribution of Scottish land among Normans was briskly proceeding.

It proceeded so smoothly, or at least so silently, as almost to imply a preconceived plan. Duke William, before he set sail from Saint-Valery, had allocated to his chief confederates, albeit in very general terms, their several shares in the proceeds, as though he had been launching a limited liability company. When Earl David rode up to Scone from Northampton, or perhaps only from Roxburgh, he knew infinitely better than Duke William what land was available for distribution or could be made available, and had had fuller opportunities for discussing matters with prospective recipients beforehand. In 1124 his " Norman Conquest " was still only theory

[1] Lawrie, LXXII.

[2] *E.g.* Pipe Roll of 1130, p. 114: " Burgenses de Graham ".

[3] Dr. G. F. Black, *s.v.*, suggests " Old English *graegham* = grey home, from the manor of that name (temp. Domesday Book) ", but does not say where the manor was or what connection the Graemes may have had with it. There seems no reason to doubt that, like the Lindsays, they came from Normandy to Scotland via Lincolnshire. The name may have been affected in later times by *Grim* and *Gryme*. As an illustration of the various spellings and the contentions which they have aroused, Dr. Black quotes:

> " I'm damned if I will sail with you, Sir Graham,
> Though I may seem uncivil,
> But Graham is Graeme, and Graham is Grim,
> And Grim, sir, is the Devil ".

> (*Old Ballad.*)

and might have come to little in practice had he reigned
but a few months. He reigned for almost thirty years
and his two grandsons, half-Norman by blood and born
to bear rule in a Scoto-Norman State, reigned, and not
without distinction, for sixty. The " Conquest " of 1124
was permanent. What followed that date was not of
course " inevitable ". Much might have happened that
did not happen. What did happen was that the charter
proved as mighty as the sword. If William conquered
England in a battle without a morrow, David "conquered"
Scotland by a scart of the pen.

§ 15

Royal Family Matters

AFTER only two years, in the early autumn of 1126, David the Conqueror went back to England, leaving his Norman lieutenants to their task of consolidation and castle-building, somewhat as in 1067 William went back to Normandy with the parting injunction : " Build castles in appropriate places ". Both were men of caution and would not have withdrawn prematurely. On both occasions much remained to be done, but Conquest had been permanently effected : in the later case, social and theoretical and bloodless, in the earlier case, military and practical and bloody. David's " Conquest " was a secondary one, consequent on Duke William's and starting from Huntingdon and Northampton, but even if we reckon from Hastings, the lapse of time was short. In manuals of British History 1126 and 1066 belong to utterly different periods. Oceans roll between. In reality the gulf was one easily bridged by the span of human life. Malcolm Canmore's throne, like the Conqueror's, was occupied by a son. Many of the historical personages who flourished before 1066 were still going about their ordinary avocations and everywhere there were men still living and still talking whose memories went further back. They could talk to David ; he was the most affable of kings. " Priest, soldier, monk, citizen, pilgrim, merchant, rustic, he conversed with them all and sent them on their way rejoicing." [1] If on his own way south, passing through Lothian, he conversed with the local worthies and the conversation happened to turn on

---

[1] Ailred, *G.R.A.* p. 714.

the Norman monarchy, there were ancients among them who could have muttered : " I mind the biggin' o't ".

The remark could have been repeated in the courtly tongue by several of the people on the Royal traveller's visiting-list. Aunt Christina, who could have married in King Edward's time, was a vigorous old lady and there is nothing to prevent us imagining her bustling about the convent at Romsey, apple-cheeked, hale and hearty, pleasantly expectant of a visit from " young David ". Uncle Edgar, who was very nearly crowned before William, was still to the fore. In 1106 the campaign of Tinchebray occupied only the months of August and September, the battle was over in an hour and, though Edgar was not in at the beginning, he arrived in time to be captured with Duke Robert. But no one could bear the Atheling a grudge for long ; he was the good Queen Maud's uncle and all was forgiven him. Still in enjoyment of his English estates, he was " a hoary-headed old man living quietly in the country " when William of Malmesbury was putting the final polish on a well-turned paragraph of faint praise.[1] Robert was a prisoner at Devizes, completing the twentieth year of his life-sentence. David's Normans could have been born, like himself, in the Conqueror's reign and been still under forty. They had been brought up in French homes in the Midlands, where relatives were constantly coming in from the Duchy and a hero of Hastings was as likely to be out hunting as sitting by the fire.

One of David's first duties in England was to discuss ex-Duke Robert's sad case with the King's daughter Maud, Robert's niece and David's. A young widow, styled " Emperis " in French, though the Imperial diadem had not actually been placed on her brow, she was now at home in her father's Kingdom, waiting to be recognized as his successor. Uncle and niece reviewed the case of

---

[1] II, p. 310—either *c.* 1120 (his first edition of *G.R.*) or *c.* 1127 (his second edition). Christina also is mentioned.

the Scottish Royal family's fallen friend, and Henry, *de retour* from Normandy, found himself confronted with a joint request to do something for Robert. All he did was to provide new prison quarters, further west, further away. He had his unfortunate brother taken from the custody of Roger, Bishop of Salisbury, at Devizes and handed over to Robert, Earl of Gloucester.[1] Robert of Caen, *alias* of Gloucester, the eldest of Henry's illegitimate sons, ruled like a vassal king over the western shires and the Welsh marches. He had his uncle Robert removed to Cardiff Castle in his Welsh lordship of Glamorgan. In that wild frontier fortress the ex-Duke of the Normans was to spend the long remainder of his old age.

Family succession matters kept David a whole year in England.[2] Since the wreck of *La Blanche Nef* in 1120 Henry had no male heir. The dangers he had foreseen in 1100 had proved very real. His position, as Duke and as King, was fundamentally as unsound as ever, and he went in fear of his captive and septuagenarian brother's only son, Guillaume Cliton, *Anglice* Atheling, who at any moment might appeal to right and justice, obtain full ecclesiastical sanction and take the field in Normandy with the most formidable of allies.[3] Henry thought it would be good policy to nominate a successor provisionally— should he have no heir by his second wife. His choice

[1] " That was all done through his daughter's counsel and through the Scot King."—*A-S.C.* MS. E, *s.a.* 1126.

[2] " And then after Michaelmas came the Scot King David from Scotland to this land ; and King Henry received him with great worship and he then abode all that year in this land."—*A-S.C.* MS. E, *s.a.* 1126.

[3] The case of Robert's only son, William Clito, was a main cause of Henry's wars from 1109 to 1113. From 1117 Louis VI and the Counts of Flanders and Anjou were banded together to place him on the ducal throne. In October 1119 Louis VI appeared with him before the Council of Reims, and the Pope went to Normandy to discuss his case with Henry. The reason why Henry, who had persistently refused to allow a Legate to enter England, allowed John of Crema to hold a legatine Council at Westminster in 1125 was possibly that he felt under an obligation to him for helping to have the marriage of William Clito with the daughter of Foulque of Anjou dissolved on the ground of consanguinity. Henry's anxieties ceased only with the death (in the monastery of Saint-Bertin) of William Clito, on July 27, 1128.

was limited : either his only surviving legitimate child, Maud, or else a sister's son. But on Maud's legitimacy grave doubts were felt, for the rumour still ran that her mother was a professed nun. Anselm's handling of the Romsey case had been severely criticized and his biographer at St. Andrews had vainly devoted many pages to dispelling the criticisms and the doubts. So long as Maud was in Germany, her father had contented himself with the idea of nominating Esteven [Stephen], the son, but only the third son, of his cultured sister Adèle and the Comte de Blois. Henry had all the Norman partiality for a sister's son, and held a high opinion of Stephen, a most charming young man, to whom he had given the forfeited Comté of Mortain, great Mortain estates in England, notably in the present Lancashire, and the hand of a niece. She was another Maud, the only child of Eustace III and David's sister Mary, and since her parents' death she was Countess of Boulogne in her own right. Both Mauds were granddaughters of Margaret and thus in either case Henry, still harping on dynasty, could maintain his ancient thesis that the Queen of the English ought to be a descendant of the Old English line, whatever her husband might be. David, always the upright judge, weighed the claims of both his nieces with impartiality and concurred in his brother-in-law's decision : that the widowhood of the Empress and her return to England had altered the situation in her favour. At the Christmas Council (1126) Henry made his barons swear allegiance to her. The first to take the oath was David, as Earl of Huntingdon. The next two, after a little altercation between them about precedence, were Robert of Gloucester (half-brother of the Empress) and Stephen (her cousin, and husband of her cousin and namesake, the Countess of Boulogne). Family matters were matters of state. In Norman-feudal society they transcended frontiers and the Normans in Scotland were soon to find themselves drawn into the family affairs of Esteven de Blois, later known as King Stephen, and those of David's two nieces, Mahaut, usually differentiated as the ex-Empress Matilda, and Stephen's Queen Maud.

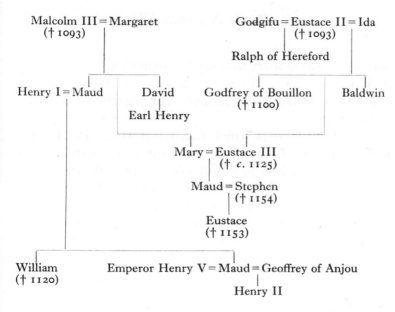

§ 16

Scotland's Norman Clergy

THERE was a corollary to every Norman Conquest, whether in England, Sicily, Wales or elsewhere: introduction of a Norman clergy, ecclesiastical reorganization, monastic settlement.

The family affairs which had taken David to England had before then brought him the visit of a Legate,[1] whose mission extended to Scotland because of the controversy between York and St. Andrews. The Legate, John of Crema, was received by the King at Roxburgh and held a Council on the matter, which David when in England further discussed with Henry. Bishop Robert at last came to an understanding with his fellow-countryman Toustain [" Thurstan "], in whom his own long struggle with Canterbury had perhaps induced a certain fellow-feeling.[2] A formula saving the dignity of both York and St. Andrews was devised. A sign of the times is that the witnesses to the written agreement on the Scottish side included three Normans and that one of them, Robert de Waterville, was a Norman of Huntingdonshire.[3] In 1127 Bishop Robert

[1] See above, p. 193, n. 3.

[2] The Archbishop, a native of Bayeux, where his brother Oudin was Bishop, succeeded Thomas II († February 24, 1114). But Raoul d'Escures, Archbishop of Canterbury since April 1114, refused to consecrate him and controversy continued till Raoul died, October 20, 1122.

[3] " Aymarus miles ", in David's Declaration (Lawrie, LXXV), appears in the Archbishop's Declaration (*ibid*. LXXVI) as " Almarus miles " and is there accompanied by " Robertus de Waterville " and " Rogerus Coyneres ". " Aimarus " [Aimer] had already been mentioned in David's Confirmation of Coldingham to Durham (*ibid*. LXV), 1126. Robert was evidently a relative of " Ascelinus de Waltervilla ", who between 1125 and 1128 holds 3 hides of the Abbey of Peterborough at Orton Waterville. *V.C.H. Hunts*. I, p. 331. This Huntingdonshire family is represented in 1130 by " Hugo de Walterivilla " (Pipe Roll, pp. 83 and 86) and in 1160

was consecrated at York.[1]   In the same year, before David
and many prelates of England and Scotland, at the door
of the church of St. John the Baptist at Roxburgh, Bishop
Robert declared that, although out of consideration for the
monks of Durham he would not insist on certain rights
over the priory of Coldingham, that church, and all other
churches in Lothian, were, and always had been, subject
to the Bishop of St. Andrews.

No doubt because of the notorious shortcomings of
Bishop " Flambard ", the connection between Durham
and the Scottish Kingdom had of late become looser [2]
and this firm declaration shows the new prelate stout in
his defence of Scottish ecclesiastical independence.   The
Scottish historians, with a unanimity rare among them
when the mediaeval Church is under discussion, describe
him as an Englishman, and incontrovertibly he came to
Scotland from Nostell in Yorkshire.   But why was he
called Robert ?   To have been Prior of Scone in the reign
of Alexander he must have been born at a time when few
English boys were baptized with any such Norman name.
And how came it that his parents, in accordance with
a Norman custom, gave his brother and himself the same
Christian name,[3] that his three nephews, who are very soon

by Ascelin and Geoffroi de Waterville (*Red Book of the Exchequer*, p. 35).
The latter is in 1178 a witness to David of Huntingdon's Foundation Charter
of Lindores.   *Lindores*, Appendix I.   The name means Walter's vill.

[1] Sim. Durh. *H.R.* II, p. 278.   Robert was consecrated by Archbishop
Thurstan, assisted by the Bishop (" Flambard ") of Durham († 1128) and
Raoul Novel, titular Bishop of Orkney, of whom more will be heard in 1138.
Contin. Flor. Worc. II, p. 80 ; Lawrie, LXXV.

[2] According to the Continuator of Sim. Durh. *H.D.E.* I, p. 139, the
Bishop of Durham [" Flambard "], because of his quarrel with Henry I,
failed to recover the appanages of his diocese, viz. Carlisle and Teviotdale,
" which certain of the Bishops had attached to their Churches during his
exile ".   The see of St. Andrews had apparently asserted its rights.   After
the death of " Flambard " in 1128 the see of Durham was vacant for five
years.

[3] " Rodbertus frater meus " witnesses the Bishop's Charter of July 17,
1127.   Lawrie, LXXIII.   He became Prior of St. Andrews.   For the
common Norman (and Breton) custom of giving two or more brothers the
same Christian name, cp. Alain (above, p. 69).   " Willelmus de veteri

found attesting his charters in Norman company, bore the names Raoul, Roger and John, and that Roger exercised the as yet un-English profession of *miles* ? When Robert went to Scone there cannot have been many Augustinians of English birth and the natural presumption is that he, like the other Canons, had come to Nostell from France. He had a Dapifer, a Chamberlain and several Norman chaplains and, whatever his parentage may have been, lived for thirty years as a French Bishop of St. Andrews. Where two English-born prelates had failed, Robert succeeded. He was Scotland's Lanfranc. Without Lanfranc's status of Archbishop, and with or without his commanding gifts (for nothing is known of Robert's personality), he worked with the temporal ruler as closely and much longer, and reorganized the Church in his adopted country in as thorough and as Norman a fashion.

David's idea of a chaplain, Bishop or Abbot, was a Norman cleric, of the type he knew and admired in England. He brought into his Kingdom, with Bishop Robert's approbation, churchmen belonging to the same social class as his barons and knights or actually to the same families. With them came others of lesser degree, like Thurold, Archdeacon of Lothian, brother of a Norman skipper. Though Norman ecclesiastics could not found landed families, they were seldom short of lay relatives who could, and in Norman England the Bishop's nephew or the Abbot's nephew was to be found in all positions of honour or at least emolument. This social type, already discoverable at Glasgow,[1] now makes its appearance at St. Andrews [2] with Bishop Robert's two nephews. It reveals the Norman trait of nepotism, but Bishops and Abbots in a strange land must have been thankful when they had a

ponte " [Vieux Pont, in Scotland Vipont] had three sons of his own name, distinguished as " Willelmus primogenitus ", " Willelmus medius " and " Willelmus junior " in a grant by the eldest. *Holyrood*, p. 33.

[1] Above, p. 155, n. 3.

[2] For further illustrations of the nexus Bishop-Abbot-Brother-Nephew at St. Andrews, see below, p. 368.

capable lay relative on whom they could depend for assistance in practical matters, book-keeping, military tenures, the collection of tithes and dues or the operation of the secular arm.

Everywhere, even in England after all Lanfranc's reforming efforts, secular and ecclesiastical affairs were inextricably interwoven. Churchmen were almost the only literates of the time, and the Royal administration was dependent on them for the transaction of public business. It may be supposed, on the analogy of Ireland, that the old Celtic state had little need to employ clerks and that Bishops and Abbots were not generally called on to act as such. But things had changed with the accession of Edgar and it is significant that Eadmer had promised to be useful at St. Andrews in executing writs and records. No doubt Bishop Robert worthily discharged these duties. Such services were sometimes rewarded by a grant of land. Under David Norman clerics rapidly attained to high office in the State as well as in the Church, and some of them, though more modestly and in an official rather than in a private capacity, shared with their lay kinsmen or other fellow-aliens in the distribution of Scottish lands.

The diocesan system became definitely established. Bishoprics were considered as territorial. Reorganization on Norman lines was facilitated by the introduction of a territorial archdeaconry. In 1128 and for many years after, Archdeacons, who as a class came over with the Conqueror, were represented at Glasgow by one with the fine old Norman name of Ascelin, and in Lothian by one who bore the same name, Thurold, as the author, or the scribe, of the *Chanson de Roland*.[1] Some advance was

---

[1] Archdeacon Ascelin was in office before April 1127. (Lawrie, LXV.) He held the church of Old Roxburgh with all its pertinents till his death in the reign of Malcolm IV, and he received land at Partick from King David. *O.P.* I, p. 452. Archdeacon Thurold († 1163) appears frequently in documents from 1128. (Lawrie, LXXXI.) He was the son of one Mauger and had a brother Guillaume, a master mariner, of whom Reginald of Durham tells a story.

made towards the division of the country into parishes, each served by a church sustained by tithes. When the demarcation of the parishes becomes known, somewhat later, it corresponds closely with the parcelling out of the land among Normans, and probably most were coextensive with the fief of the new Norman lord.[1] Apparently, before David's time no tithes had been paid, or at least there had been no appropriation of ecclesiastical dues to a particular church, but the duty of giving tithes to the secular clergy was being zealously inculcated throughout all Christendom and David's Normans were good churchmen and good church-builders. The new lord of the manor made a grant of the tithes of his estate to the manorial church, and the manor tithed to its church became a " parish ".[2]

Usually, if only for strategic purposes or for convenience of supplies and maintenance, the Norman castle was set up in an ancient centre of population and therefore of religion. Fortress and shrine had long existed side by side in Edinburgh when towards 1127 David granted " to the church of St. Cuthbert beside the Castle all the land beneath the said Castle, *videlicet* from the spring that rises at the corner of the King's garden. . . ."[3] (The grant recalls incidentally the importance which David attached to gardens and gardening, whether this was or was not the result of his acquired Norman tastes.[4]) When there was no church the Norman built one, near his castle or inside, as in the earliest days of the Conquest Robert d'Oilly had done at Oxford, thriftily incorporating his church in the defensive works, and as King Alexander had lately

---

[1] Thus the fiefs of Simon Loccard, Robert, brother of Lambin, and John, stepson of Baldwin, gradually came to form respectively the parishes of Symington, Roberton and Crawford John ; for details see below, p. 376.

[2] But " parish " was at first used in various senses : see *O.P.* Introd. I, pp. xxvi-xxvii.   [3] Lawrie, LXXII.

[4] For David's official support of gardening in Scotland see below, p. 252 ; for his own gardening see below, p. 283.

done at Stirling [1] and Earl David at Roxburgh. [2]   Under the new dispensation parochial church and Norman castle grew up together in places long sacred to the native population. But the first parish priests were French. [3]   The fact, when realized, is apt to be deplored.   It is not peculiar to Scotland.   Everywhere in the English-speaking world many words (such as " parish ", " priest ", " parson ", to " preach " and to " pray ") recall the ancient labours of a French-speaking clergy.

The Norman lord's attitude to the church on his lands was frankly proprietary.   The compilers of Domesday dispassionately listed among Christina's properties :   " 24 hides of land . . . 83 villeins . . . 2 mills . . . 2 priests ". It was silently assumed that there were no spiritual rights a lay lord might not bestow ; ecclesiastical boundaries thus adapted themselves to temporal—bishoprics to provinces, parishes to vills or manors ; the gift of a manor carried the church with it ; churches could be subdivided, tithes given away, at will.   There was the same silent assumption behind the charters of Christina's reigning nephews.   Their grants of land carried with them any church already built, except when specially withheld. [4]   This, whether it was an old custom or an innovation, corresponds to Norman practice in England, where lords of manors gave their churches at their own will and pleasure to whatever religious communities they preferred.   David's Normans had no sooner taken over the church on their lands, or built one, than they gave it to a monastery.   The erection of parishes was hardly begun when the rapid spread of monasteries and their

[1] " De capella Castelli de Striulin eo die quo Rex Alexander fecit capellam dedicare."—*Dunfermline*, p. 8.

[2] There was a " Church of St. John *in* the Castle of Roxburgh ", which received the oblations of inmates and visitors.   Lawrie, LXXXIII, *c.* 1128.

[3] The first parish priests recorded seem to be Henry, of Coldstream, and John, of Legerwood (Berwickshire).   They witnessed Bishop Robert's charter to Coldingham of July 17, 1127.   Lawrie, LXXIII.

[4] King Edgar had granted Swinton and Fishwick to the monks of Durham and a later confirmation shows them holding the churches of both vills ; see Morgan, p. 136.

ever-increasing need of endowments confronted Bishop Robert with the difficult problem of monastic appropriation (or, as afterwards it was also called, impropriation).

The year 1128 alone saw some remarkable monastic developments. " Acting on the advice of John, Bishop of Glasgow, and of his nobles ", David removed his Tironensians from Selkirk, " because the place was not suitable for an Abbey ", settled them " in the church of St. Mary at Roxburgh on the River Tweed, in the place which is called Kelcho [Kelso] ",[1] and provided them with further rich endowment;[2] founded the Augustinian Abbey of the Holy Rood with Alwin his confessor as its head;[3] had the Benedictine Priory at Dunfermline raised to the rank of Abbey, bringing Geoffrey, Prior of Canterbury, to be the first Abbot; and gave audience to the Master of the Temple. He was a French Knight, Hugue de Payns,[4] who, while Baudouin (brother of Mary's husband Eustace) reigned uneasily over Jerusalem, had gathered round him a little band of Crusaders, sworn to the defence of pilgrims in Palestine. They were given by Baudouin the Temple enclosure for their quarters. After many difficulties and many years their Society, early in 1128, had, on the enthusiastic recommendation of Bernard at Clairvaux,[5] obtained formal sanction as an order, and at once Hugue de Payns, as the first Master, set forth on a journey through the western kingdoms, exhorting their princes and nobles to help the new brotherhood and send succour to the Holy Land. In Normandy Henry showed him much favour and sped him on his way to England. There " he was received

[1] Confirmation of the charter by Malcolm IV in 1159. *Kelso*, No. I. The early form is Calchou (=A.-S. *cealc* =chalk + *how* =hollow).

[2] Sim. Durh. *H.R.* II, p. 281.

[3] The first abbot, Alwin [" Alwinus Abbas " in the Foundation Charter], and his successor Osbert were the chaplains who witnessed several of Earl David's charters. Alwin's name is English, but his nephew and niece had Norman names ; see below, p. 368, § 28.

[4] (Aube), near Troyes.

[5] At the Council of Troyes Abbot Bernard provided the initial suggestions for the Rule which the Templars adopted.

by all good men, and all gave presents to him; and in Scotland in like manner ".[1] It was doubtless as a sequel to this visit, though not perhaps till some years later, that David gave the brethren, together with property at Yardley Hastings and at Great Stukeley (Huntingdonshire), those lands at Balantrodach (now Temple), on the South Esk in Midlothian, which tradition represents as his chief benefaction to their Society.[2] Templars owed allegiance to no country. They were the soldiers of Christendom. But the first of them were French. Legates had long been proceeding from Rome and religious leaders from France. Now they were beginning to arrive in Scotland, for many reasons, one of which was that in the French world David had the name of being a great Christian prince.

The same year, 1128, is the probable date of the first known settlement of a property dispute between members of a Scottish religious community and a Norman landholder. They were the Culdees of St. Serf's Island in Loch Leven; he was their new Norman neighbour, a knight, Robert le Bourguignon or Bourgoin.[3] He had laid claim to a fourth part of their lands of Kirkness, and they, on the advice of the Augustinians at St. Andrews, appealed to the King to adjudicate on the matter. David sent his couriers through the province of Fife and Fothrif,[4] " summoning a great number of men " to meet Constantin, Earl of Fife, " magnum judicem in Scotia ". Constantin, the son of Macduff, is characterized as " vir discretus et facundus "

[1] *A-S.C.* MS. E, *s.a.* 1128.
[2] Lees, *Temple*, p. 116; Aitken, *K.T.* p. 3.
[3] " Robertus Burgonensis miles ", who from 1126 appears in several charters thus, or as " Burgeis ", " Burgunnus " (*Dunfermline*, p. 4, *c.* 1150), " Burguillus " (*Dunfermline*, p. 10), is supposed to have held Lochore in Ballingry parish, south-west of Loch Leven. Haddan and Stubbs, II, i, p. 209. The French form underlying the Latin may have been *Bourguignon* or *Bourguillon* or *Bourgoin* [cp. the *chanson de geste, Auberi le Bourgoing*]. The number of Latin variants shows that it is not a fixed surname. Robert or his parents must have come from Burgundy.
[4] Fothrif was the western part of the modern Fife and Kinross. Ballingry and Lochore are in Fife; Loch Leven is in Kinross.

and his official designation need mean no more than it says—someone exercising high judicial functions north of the Forth, not supreme judge.[1] The " army of Fife " marched to the meeting-place, probably Cupar.[2] The Bishop of St. Andrews sent at least the leaders and " lumnarchs " of " his army ". With Earl Constantin were " Dufgal, judex senex justus et venerabilis " and " Maldoinneth, judex bonus et discretus ". Their names are Celtic, but there is nothing to show whether their functions resembled those of a Saxon *judex* or those of an Irish *brehon*, who was essentially an arbitrator, a consultant, an expounder of the law, and had no fixed territorial jurisdiction. Various native *clerici* whose names are enumerated stated on oath what they knew of the boundaries of Kirkness. The case went against Robert. By agreement of the court, judgment was delivered by Dufgal, " because of his great age and knowledge of the law ". The verdict may have been put in writing, but all the Austin Canons possessed was a note, made by themselves, giving the names of the judges and witnesses and stating that Knight Robert, " firebrand of all iniquity ", had been publicly confuted. What they had was a written record of oral collective testimony.[3]

The circumstances, as set forth by them, recall the practice of the Norman Kings, who sent a special judge to hold a local court for the trial of a specific case. He acts

[1] Constantin († 1128 or 1129) is the third known Earl of Fife, the first being Macduff, the second, David's brother Ethelred. The principle of succession is obscure. But there seems no reason to doubt that Constantin was the son of Macduff; cp. " filii Magdufo, Constantini " in Edgar's (dubious) charter to Durham. Lawrie, XV. Macduff and Ethelred were apparently lay Abbots—of Abernethy and Dunkeld respectively. In 1609 Skene writes, *Reg. Maj.* 58 : " It is statute, that Justitiars salbe beath vpon the southside, and the northside of the water of Forth ". But we are unaware of any evidence showing that in 1128 there were two Justiciars and that Constantin was the one who had jurisdiction north of Forth.

[2] The meeting-place may have been the Cross Macduff, a mile southwest of Newburgh, on the watershed of a wide pass through the Ochils from Fife to Strathearn. But Wyntoun states that those claiming the privilege of the Law of Clan Macduff were required to appear before the judges assembled " at Cowper in Fife ".

[3] Record, in *St. Andrews*, pp. 117-118, and Lawrie, LXXX.

for the King—" in meo loco " (William I)—and though he may be a local magnate, he is an officer of central, not local government.[1] In David's charters *Justitiae* had appeared two years before. Constantin, though not styled a *Justitia* or *Justitiarius regis*, was already acting as one. Whether Knight Robert was a firebrand of all iniquity there is no way of determining, but it is reassuring to see Culdees and Augustinians standing shoulder to shoulder in defence of property rights, and equal justice meted out to Celt and Norman in the King's name.

Bishop Robert's " army " no doubt included tenants holding by military service. He and the Abbots of Kelso and Dunfermline had their own courts.[2] The Church in Scotland was being rapidly brought into the Norman-feudal complex. By 1128, if it be permissible to pursue the metaphor of Conquest, two armies of occupation, one spiritual, the other mundane, acting in liaison, had advanced as far north as St. Andrews and were consolidating their positions. The distinction between them was one which the twelfth century found it difficult to draw.

[1] The practice is said by Adams, *C. and C.* p. 93, to be without precedent in Saxon England, but reasons for believing that it was known to England before William I have been shown by G. O. Sayles (*Select Cases in the Court of King's Bench under Edward I*), Selden Society, 1936, pp. xviii-xx. Under William I and William II it was applied only intermittently. Under Henry I it was much extended and became regular.

[2] Charters of 1128 × 1136. Lawrie, LXXIV and CLIII.

§ 17

Scotland's Norman Aristocracy

THE men who had attended the Earl in the counties of Northampton and Huntingdon, and presumably in " Cumbria and parts of Lothian ", continued to attend the King of Scots. In his, now Royal, charters, given in the most varied and unexpected places, the old familiar names recur with the inevitability of a refrain. After the brief intimation of a grant of land, scribbled on an exiguous strip of parchment, the same list of witnesses drags its slow length along : " Robertus Burnevilla, Gervasius Ridel, Hugo de Morevilla, Hugo Brito, Berengarius Engaine . . .". Who were these " Norman Conquerors ", of the second or the third generation, so industriously engaged in attesting charters at some half-built castle or some lonely farmhouse on the moors ? They were simply David's personal friends. But, as he was now a King, they, when thus engaged, had *ipso facto* a certain status in the realm.

A charter [1] was in essence a letter informing those to whom it was addressed of a transaction already passed and recording the names of the more important people who had read the contents or had heard them read. The more witnesses the better ; some might be included who were not actually present but afterwards adhibited their *signum* or cross. The men whose names recur in David's Royal charters were not, however, like modern bystanders witnessing a signature and incurring no responsibility for the document signed in their presence. David did not sign (the deed was completed by affixing his seal). But he had

---

[1] At first *carta*, later often *scriptum* ; *e.g.* Lawrie, CXCI.

previously discussed the contents with the signatories, taken their opinion, assured himself of their approval—and their active support, should the need for it arise. When called together for such discussion, they were in effect counsellors and might find themselves expected to act as executive officers. Some acquired an official status : Hugue de Morville, besides being David's right-hand man, became Constable ; Guillaume de Sommerville apparently was only a friend, not even one from Northamptonshire, and held no known office, but when the King towards 1130 issued a mandate regarding ships trading at Inveresk, he witnessed it, one might almost say " countersigned " it, and was perhaps expected to see that its terms were observed.[1]

Behind the formal charter there is a meeting, a discussion, presumably in French, some general agreement arrived at, and an instruction to chancellor or scribe to put it in Latin ; hence, perhaps, the vagueness of the resulting document, the product of men speaking one language among themselves and leaving what they had had in mind to be put in writing in another language by someone else. Accuracy was not a mediaeval virtue. Figures are unreliable. References to time are couched in very general terms or omitted. It is not merely a question of avoidable error. In the mediaeval world there were two sets of human beings : the great unlettered majority, and a handful of clerkly persons, more or less bilingual, using now the vulgar tongue, now the learned one, but writing only in the latter, which, not being their own, might leave a subtle discrepancy between inner thought and actual expression. David's scribes belonged to the latter set, and probably most of his Normans did not. They were men of action, men of experience and resource, to whom when Earl he had turned for practical advice on questions of custom or finance or administration and now turned for

[1] Lawrie, LXXXVII : so also CXIX.

help in all manner of urgent business, inevitable at the beginning of a new reign. No more than Henry's advisers were they members of a Council. They were not Councillors, only counsellors. But (being what they were, namely Normans, and surrounded by scribes and all the paraphernalia of written government) when they were gathered together they constituted what was practically a *curia regis* and what became the single organ of state in the Scottish Kingdom, as it already was in England.

No doubt there was something of the kind before. Every mediaeval monarch was supposed to rule under God, responsible only to Him, but also to have counsellors, and any grievous errors made were ascribed to evil counsellors. The old Celtic Kings had a council, though how much attention they paid to it is not known. No doubt it consisted of Mormaers and other chiefs and, after 1016, also of Earls. Perhaps Bishops and Abbots were called to the meetings, though probably as in Ireland they took little part in state business. David when King had native counsellors, as he had had when Earl. The name of Alwyn Mac Arkil is writ large in the extant Royal documents. " Comites " (ex-Mormaers and Earls) attest David's charters and give charters of their own. There is no reason to suppose anything very " constitutional " about his *curia regis*.[1] Nevertheless it was one ; it was very similar to Henry's. Its novelty lay largely in the fact that the " personnel ", as it is now called, was French and employed French methods of government. David's *curia regis* was drawn from the Household officers, mostly Normans ; the Bishops and Abbots, more and more of them Normans as time went on and attaining an importance in the State which had not been customary in Scotland whilst

[1] " The Constitution of Scotland is more obscure in its origin and progress than that of most other countries. . . . But it is scarcely reasonable to expect to trace the first steps of the rise of a government which are made among men not aware of the consequence that is afterwards to be attached to them."—Cosmo Innes, *Act. Sc. Parl.* I, Preface.

little stress was laid on written record;[1] " Comites " and other native personages, some of them in process of being Normanized; Normans, never so designated, but tending to be marshalled among the witnesses to documents in a group by themselves. They were evidently felt to be *different* but what they were "constitutionally" we are not told. Their names predominate in the documents preserved. We do not know, we can only suppose, that they were the persons whom David most frequently summoned to his meetings and to whose advice he gave most weight.

His *curia regis* was a body meeting informally and not so much in permanent session as permanently on the move, a group of men accompanying or encountering the King on his peregrinations, helping him to discharge state business amid the toil of war or the pleasures of the chase, on a tour of inspection, on a perambulation of boundaries, on a round of visits to vassals, half-castellans, half-farmers, or on a pilgrimage to some distant shrine. Like his brother-in-law of England David had favourite residences, but no fixed capital. Personal government meant personal contact. A King had to see things for himself. He was an itinerant. The Court, the Household, most of the administration, moved with him. Mediaeval majesty was in a state of perpetual motion. Economic pressure was often the motive force—there was, for instance, the necessity of providing a large retinue with adequate maintenance. Money payments could be made; David had a coinage—he is the first King of Scots known to have had one. It consisted, as everywhere else, of silver pennies; the mints were at Berwick and Roxburgh; the moneyers were French, the Roxburgh coins bearing the impress of one Hugue. It was thus possible to convert into money rents renderings in kind; probably the separate

[1] Written record played no part in Old Ireland. " Only very rarely do we hear of a churchman holding the position of a King's minister."— Kenney, p. 6.

items and the total sum always had been calculated in money terms. But coins were rare. In the permanent shortage of currency the produce of land had generally to be remitted to an overlord or to the King in uncommuted form. Transport difficulties were such that it might have to be consumed on the spot or perish. The business done, the hunting ended, the boundaries perambulated, the produce consumed or the welcome outstayed, and favourable advices coming in from elsewhere, there was early one morning a great folding-up of tents, neighing of steeds, blowing of horns and cracking of whips. Two-wheeled carts rattled over ill-made roads and the Scoto-Norman Court, accompanied by a considerable section of the armed forces of the Crown, passed on its way to other quarters for man and beast, fresh food and pastures new.

David still describes his Norman companions as " my barons " and " my knights ". But with his accession these terms had acquired a fuller meaning. Till then he had " barons " and " knights " as the Earl of Chester had, or the Lord of Richmond, or the Bishop of Durham. " My barons " had meant " the more considerable among my tenants, those I am in the habit of occasionally convening for consultation ". " Baron " is a term which was never closely defined in Norman times. It is a French term, meaning etymologically a "man", as such ; hence a manly man, a man of confidence, in battle or in council ; any feudal relationship it indicated was that of a *man* to the *lord* of whom he held. It came to imply rank, power and wealth, but the quality enabling a baron to play his distinctive part in feudal society was a sense of responsibility, the faculty of giving a reasoned opinion for his lord's guidance, of using experience and elementary knowledge of law or custom in his lord's interest.[1] That interest was assumed to be identical with his own and the advice expected of him was *favourable* advice, such as suggestion

[1] Stenton, *E.F.* pp. 82, 84, 87, 94.

of ways and means by which a proposed course of action could be put into effect. He might be a comparatively small landholder or he might be what was afterwards called a great baron, one of the main buttresses of the realm. He might have high military status and discharge administrative and judicial functions in his own locality, but essentially he was a counsellor and his importance varied with that of the person whom it was his duty to counsel. In England the term " baron " was now coming to be restricted to lords who held great fiefs of the King and for that reason also the rank of David's barons rose with his own. As he was now more than Earl, so were they more than the barons they had hitherto been.

Between barons and knights there was no hard-and-fast distinction. Technically, knights were professional soldiers ; as such, they were asked for counsel chiefly on military matters. When David was Earl, " my knights " might mean " my tenants and under-tenants holding by military service ", " my *milites feoffati* ". Or it might mean " my *milites domestici* ". At first most of the knights he brought into his Kingdom were probably of the latter class—men well born and of high repute, who were bound to their lord only by a personal tie, who became his vassals but received no fief, or not till after a period of service. The lord whom David's knights now served being a King, territorial recognition could come more quickly and be more substantial.

Barons and knights did not live on air, nor did their horses, and if David's Norman supporters were to support themselves and to render the services expected of them, they had to be placed in possession of Scottish lands and allowed to build castles. The reason why he preferred Normans as landlords was no doubt that they seemed to him the sort of men best suited for dealing with the situation as he saw it. He had a very loose hold over great stretches of territory, and a few determined men with

Norman equipment and horses could keep a grip on a large district from an improvised castle, in the manner practised in England from 1066. Under the Anglo-Norman system landlords had duties as well as privileges, and the best among them had a sense of responsibility to one another, to those above them and those below, to the whole society of which they were members. But proper performance of their duties depended also on training and experience which, as David may have thought, Scotland could not yet provide. To be a baron required some knowledge of feudal custom and current military practice, and the gift of asserting sufficient authority over knights and men-at-arms to ensure discipline in the castle and order in the district; to be a knight implied skill in equestrian warfare (acquired only by long and expensive training from boyhood) and ability to lead soldiers, mounted or not. Armour and steed were costly and without the assistance of one or more serving-men they were useless. Knightly requirements meant money, which in those times meant land.

David had need, or thought he had need, of barons and knights for the purposes of government, administration, defence and the maintenance of order. He no doubt felt that the Norman would be as good an overlord, general overseer or supervisor as the Saxon or the Celt, and as acceptable locally to natives who, though they might equally resent the presence of all three (for dislike of strangers is not love of one's fellow-countrymen), could yet discover advantages in the protection of life and limb and security for the fruits of their labour. What he asked of Normans was to exercise supervision from their wooden forts, develop the resources of the country, perfect the organization of the peaceful districts and pacify or overawe the wilder, as Walter Espec, Eustace fitz John and so many other old friends were doing in the North of England—and as (it may be shrewdly suspected) others had been already doing for some time in the South of Scotland under his own direction. David is apt to be imagined as issuing forth from a small district in the South-West to rule at Dunfermline or Perth, whereas his "Cumbria" was the larger and the richer half of the Kingdom. His accession meant removal not to a more central position, but to a higher status. Except for return journeys to England and tours in Scotland proper—infrequent, to judge from the place-names in his documents—he stayed where he was, at Roxburgh or Selkirk, and continued his Normanizing activities from there.

It was doubtless for material support as well as for moral that he gave lands in South Scotland to Robert de Brus or Bernard de Bailleul, who had military resources in their North of England possessions, or gave lands beyond Forth to Robert the Burgundian, evidently a self-assertive individual well able to look after the King's interests or his own. Robert de Brus could keep watch on restive Galloway. The barons and knights, the only Normans who appear in the earliest charters, were members of a military aristocracy who migrated to Scotland, accompanied or followed by clerical friends or kinsmen, on the King's invitation. They came as counsellors, as assistants, one might almost say as technical assistants, persons with special knowledge of the methods of civil and military administration practised under the Anglo-Norman System. They received great reward. We know too little of them to know if it was excessive. Some may have been "favourites". But foreign administrators, military men or clerical advisers were generally brought in by mediaeval monarchs for much the same reason as foreign workmen are imported by employers of industry—because they had, or were supposed to have, special qualifications. In all likelihood some of David's collaborators had the Norman faults —intense individualism, turbulence, petty jealousies, sudden enthusiasms and sudden depressions—and others of them had the energetic Norman temperament and the Norman genius for organization and leadership. But whatever their individual faults or merits may have been, he evidently felt he could rely on all for that personal loyalty on which the whole fabric of Norman-feudal society depended. They had been gathered round him for several years. Some had been " discovered " or brought to his notice in the North of England. Most came from his Midland Earldoms. Loyalty to the Earl of Northampton and Huntingdon was their guiding-star.

On their remoter origins information is lacking. David in his charters gives none. He only gives his greetings " omnibus hominibus totius regni sui, clericis et laicis, Francis et Anglis et Scottis presentibus et futuris ". The last are apt to be omitted. When all three appear in the Address the French invariably lead the van, English-speakers come next and Gaels bring up the rear, pending the arrival of " Galwenses " or Galwegians. After the Address David intimates that a certain person has been granted certain lands. To take an example from a later period in his reign—but only then does he become comparatively explicit—he announces : " I have given and by this my charter confirmed [1] to Alexander de Saint-Martin Alstaneford [Athelstaneford, East Lothian] and the land which . . ." David states that the grant made was a half-knight's fee, but not when or why the grant was made, who or what Alexander was, where he came from, where he lived, what lands, if any, he already held in Scotland or anywhere else, when or how he or his family was, or had been, connected with Saint-Martin, or where Saint-Martin is.[2] Where it is, one cannot so much as guess, for all the region west of the Seine was evangelized by St. Martin of Tours and the number of the churches and

---

[1] " Me dedisse et hac mea carta confirmasse "—Lawrie, CLXXXVI.
[2] Saint-Martin-de-Bon-Fossé (Manche) ? Or Saint-Martin du Bosc, or du Bec, or de Bocheville (all Seine-Inférieure) ?

parishes to which his name was given is such that they pass far beyond identification. As the old saw has it:

> Saint Martin et Sainte Marie
> Se partagent la Normandie.[1]

As to why Normans migrated to Scotland without delay (and, as will appear further on, in considerable numbers), reasons probably varied with individuals. Successful Royal government then depended on personal relations, and across a distance of eight centuries it is clear enough that whether as a penniless refugee, or as " The Queen's Brother ", or as Earl in the Midlands or as ruler in Cumbria, David had the gift of inspiring intense personal loyalty. Praise comes from quarters too many and too close to be insincere or ill informed. The Archdeacon of Huntingdon, who must have met the Earl many a time and was in a position to judge Royalty, being one of Henry's intimates, speaks warmly of that " most urbane King of Scots ".[2] The gentry of the Honour endorsed archidiaconal opinion. Some of them followed their Earl to Roxburgh or Scone as they would have followed him to Antioch or Jerusalem, whither he was often minded to proceed. Others went with him for personal aggrandizement, for financial gain, for an ampler, richer life. Some went simply to make a career. Probably most went for land, the main source of wealth in a still rural society. Where there were Normans there were younger sons to be provided for. They hived off from David's Earldoms as from William's Duchy. The case of some might be likened to that of a modern Northamptonshire gentleman with Army experience, managing a property for his brother the Squire and accepting an appointment abroad with good opportunities for acquiring land of his own. Others had moved northward by stages with the Conquest, and with their parents, into Yorkshire, Northumberland or " English Cumbria ", and had seen

---

[1] Prentout, *O. et F.* p. 38.
[2] H. Hunt. p. 190 : " urbanissimi regis Scottorum ".

attractions on the way or on the horizon. The attractions were real, and a Conqueror mentality still subsisted. Yet Orderic tells us that a Conqueror's life is not a happy one ; that many of William's companions-in-arms became home-sick and restive, and that he, being beholden to them and still dependent on their support, had to induce them to stay in England by ever-increasing grants of land ; that he thus went farther than he had originally intended and in the end went much too far. So may it have been with David. Sometimes he may have had to offer inducements, and the scale of remuneration may have been pitched too high. Gentlemen from Northampton or Huntingdon might move readily enough into the northern Kingdom, but their en-thusiasm might not always be shared by their womenkind. Robert Corbet prematurely disappears from the records, perhaps because he died, perhaps because he went home to Northamptonshire and left colonial effort to younger or more energetic kinsmen. All Normans were not Nor-manizers, Conquistadors, exponents of efficiency, land-improvers, missionaries of culture, arbiters of *élégance*, social reformers. Some stood in need of reform themselves and moved to Scotland because they were in trouble at home. Others went for a change of scene, for adventure, or for the mere pleasure of chasing the wild deer and hunting the roe.

Essentially the incomers were country gentlemen ; to employ rather differently the term which a mystified Old English chronicler used of Macbeth's Normans, they were " castle-men ". For some of them Scottish " deer forests " held the same attraction as for sportsmen from the South in our own times. This may partly account for the case of such as Robert de Brus or Bernard de Bailleul, who had no pressing need to add to their extensive estates in Yorkshire, but were pleased to hold more in South Scotland, for themselves, for a younger son and successor to outlying properties, or for the benefit of the monasteries they founded in haste and adequately endowed at leisure.

Robert de Brus had a very long way to go, from the Yorkshire coast across to Carlisle and a few miles more to
Annan. He must have left a son or a Dapifer in charge
at Annan or at Guisborough. Though probably his
residence in Scotland was seasonal and even more intermittent than David's, he evidently thought the journeys
worth while. Perhaps he considered his two hundred
thousand Scottish acres not so much a great castellary, a
Potestas in embryo, as an immense sporting estate, for
Annandale was given to him " in forest . . . no one to
hunt in the said forest save himself ".[1] The names of
many places in the region, such as Thortonwold and
Tinwald, indicate the presence of " wald " or wood where
now there is none.[2] Lower Annandale in early times was
cumbered by damp oak woods of excessive size and density[3]
and some parts must have had a close enough resemblance
to the " forest " of the Norman Kings, which contained
woodland and covert for the shelter of its wild inhabitants
and also open areas of browsing pasture or "vert". It
is appropriate that in the speech which Ailred attributes
to him before the Battle of the Standard[4] the Lord of
Annandale and Guisborough should feelingly remind the
Scottish King of the " manly games ", the " hunting of
birds and beasts ", the outdoor joys they had shared in
their younger and much happier days.

As the seventeenth-century ballad says :

> Ettricke Foreste is a feir foreste,
> In it grows manie a semelie trie ;
> There's hart and hynd, and dae and rae,
> And of a' wilde bestis grete plentie.

---

[1] In an even smaller charter ($5\frac{3}{4} \times 2\frac{1}{4}$ inches) his second son Robert de
Brus was expressly granted forest rights by David (Lawrie, CXCIX, 1147
×1153), and the limits of the forest were then defined. It marched with
Nithsdale and the valley of the Clyde, and stretched eastward till it met the
Royal Forest of Selkirk. But the grant was clearly due to some untoward
incident in either forest and it was only a confirmation of the original rights.

[2] J. Ritchie, p. 310.   [3] Childe, p. 20.

[4] Ailred, *D.B.S.* p. 195.

In the twelfth century the land of brown heath and shaggy wood was in great part shaggy wood, primeval forest denizened by " beasts " more formidable than those to be encountered on Yardley Chase. " The cuntre wes more geuin to store of bestiall than ony production of cornys ", wrote Bellenden, relating how David's inspiration to found an abbey as a shrine for Margaret's Holy Rood came to him when he was miraculously saved from a wild stag—when he had gone hunting in the " forest " under Arthur's Seat at the Feast of the Exaltation of the Cross (September 14), having listened to " mony young and insolent baronis " and ignored the remonstrances of " Alkwyne . . . quhilk wes lang tyme confessoure to Kyng Dauid in England, the tyme that he wes erle of Huntingdoun ".[1] This stag, represented in the ancient emblems of Holyrood, is believed by naturalists to have been " taller " than those which the Conqueror " loved as their father "—in fact an elk. This giant among deer, the huge ungainly elk, became extinct in Scotland only when the sheltering forests were laid low. Not climate but felling of trees has made an end of other " beasts " which are now in the fairy-tales, but were a real danger for all, as well as a tempting target for Norman Nimrods: the woodland reindeer or caribou, the lynx, the wolf, the brown bear, descendant of the Caledonian bears which made a Roman holiday in the ancient arenas. The wild cat, the red deer, the roe are with us yet, and, thanks to David's Normans, the cony, since known by another French name, " rabbit ".[2] They introduced the rabbit for utility, not

---

[1] Bellenden, XII, xvi.

[2] OF. *conil*. The " rabbit " [Northern French; cp. Walloon *robett*] has no native name in Celtic or Teutonic and there is no mention of it in English before the Norman period. It was not found, at any rate as a wild animal, in eleventh-century Britain. References to it in the twelfth century are frequent and steadily increasing. By the thirteenth, the rabbit is as common in Scotland as in England, which suggests contemporaneous introduction. J. Ritchie, pp. 248-249 and 346-349. See, for bibliography on the subject, the note in *Westmorland*, p. xxxv.

sport, judging the creature unworthy of their skill and fit only to be snared, though perhaps their young sons judged otherwise. Big game, perilous sport, was what appealed to David and his friends ; for his gift to Abbot Suger at Saint-Denis he chose the tusks of a narwhal.[1] The fame of Scottish wild life was well spread in the French-speaking world, and lost nothing in the telling. Moreover, in England, though an almost incredible proportion of land was forest, hunting was severely restricted : Henry considered it the sport of Kings, discouraged his barons from aping their betters, even on their own estates, and made them groan under the Forest Laws almost as loudly as the common folk.[2] Scotland had no Forest Laws so severe and has had no Robin Hood, but has never lacked amateurs from the South. All forest was the King's. David was a generous sporting owner, which may in itself account for the migration of a few Normans. In the days when he was Earl, at the end of the long list of witnesses comes the " venator " or *veneur*, indispensable for the proper ordering of the hunt. For some immigrants the conclusion of the whole matter may be in the final flourish of his signum or the last notes on his winding horn.

Some of the new landlords may have had the propensities of the idle sport-loving laird, others of the improving proprietor. There is no need to impute unduly altruistic motives. David was perfectly well aware that better estate management would mean increased revenue for the Crown. His Normans were equally well aware that to settle in his Kingdom would be to their material advantage. Exploitation was his aim and theirs, but often in the more favourable sense of that term. In England they had seen great tracts of land reclaimed from the

---

[1] " David religiosus Scotorum Rex exenia illi cum epistolis familiaribus direxit marinae scilicet belluae dentes mirae magnitudinis, et non parvi pretii."—*Vita Sugerii Abbatis a Willelmo San-Dionysiano*, in Bouquet, *Recueil*, XII, p. 105.

[2] See Ord. Vit. XI, xxii.

ravages of the Conquest or the Danish incursions; clearings made (as on Walter Espec's Bedfordshire property at Wardon, called also Sartis = *Les Essarts*, the Clearings); boundaries permanently fixed; law and order brought into the countryside. Some of them had probably joined in the task and were prepared to carry on such beneficial activities elsewhere. Even from the extant documents, where all personality seems lost in legal formula, there emerges a type of country gentleman, genuinely interested in land development, who likes to see things done properly, who feels that land should not be wasted, but made to give its full yield, who has a certain enthusiasm for ditching and draining and fencing.

The Norman of the charters seems rather a professional land-surveyor than a land-grabber. For instance, there is the never-ending perambulation of boundaries. David's continual references to " lands which I myself perambulated " with various personages, mostly Normans, all punctiliously named and carefully enumerated, bring clearly before us the little party making its way along the ploughed field and down by the burnside, stopping to consider the lie of the land, give ear to " the older and wiser inhabitants " and decide on soul and conscience before God whether the boundary is on this side of the rowan-tree or on the other, starting off again, possibly in the rain, calculating distances, " measuring up ", with the King of Scots stepping out in front. These are men who take things seriously, leave nothing to chance, establish the facts and have them noted down by attendant scribes. Thereafter the marches are set forth for ever on good parchment in formal Latin, in full detail, " ascending as far as the cross near the green fosse and by the green fosse as far as the cross which is placed above Sprouisdene and thence descending to the spring near the hawthorn and thence to the willows and crosses and ditches which have been placed in the middle of the hill to the top of the same, on which King David caused the ditches to be made, and thence descending westward to the place ", etc.[1]

When, before departing for the hunt or the perambulation or on returning, the most influential of David's Normans attested charters, they were in effect registering each other's eventual admission into a new aristocracy of barons and knights which in the process of time would fuse with the old nobility. They did not themselves become nobles. David referred to " my barons " as our present monarch might refer to " my Privy Councillors, my Judges ", but not to " my Marquesses, my Viscounts ". " My barons " meant important persons, rendering the King certain services, which in some cases need not mean much more than good advice, good neighbourliness, moral support, loyal co-operation. In other cases, barons were in effect the King's representatives in a district—stewards, as it were, undertaking general supervision, seeing that sufficient order prevailed for the Royal dues to be regularly collected. At first the tenure of David's Normans and the services he expected of them were probably vague ; at all events they were left undefined. Scutage must have been usual from the first ; so also sergeanty (tenure by peculiar service of special duty to the person of the lord). Sergeanty, which made a considerable breach in the feudal structure of barons and knights, must have been the usual way in which members of the Royal Household were recompensed for their services. Some small estates could certainly be held on trivial terms, as afterwards when Malcolm IV gave his clerk Serlo land in Sprouston to be held by the service of presenting certain gilded spurs annually.[2] But only a much later Scotland can produce actual evidence of such

[1] There was a controversy in 1202 between the monks of Kelso and of Melrose concerning the marches of the lands they had respectively received from King David. King William, having first bound both Abbots to abide by his decision, decided that the marches were as above. *Kelso*, No. XII.

[2] *Kelso*, pp. 24 and 178.

holdings as a barony for a mass or broad acres for two blasts of a hunting-horn.[1]

Important service passed imperceptibly into office. A " man ", a good man, a man of importance, could be a " baron " without having a barony in any geographical sense. He had rather rights and privileges and enough land, not necessarily in one district, to support a person of importance. But he tended to acquire powers, military, administrative or judicial, in a definite area and then his service constituted in effect an office held under the Crown, comparable, in this regard, with that of sheriff. The office and the territorial district could then have been called a " barony ". The term, which came to mean technically a fief held *in capite* of the King, is said to be unrecorded in Scotland till the fourteenth century,[2] but what Robert de Brus held in Annandale in 1138 John of Hexham calls a *baronia*, which probably is just what it was.[3] Definition lags behind fact. Walter de Ridale [Rydale (Yorkshire)] was granted by David, *c.* 1150, Whitton, the half of Lillies-leaf, the half of Eschetho (afterwards called Riddell) and pertinents from an unidentified Richeldoun, these lands (in Roxburghshire) to be held " in feudo et hereditate " for the service of one knight " *as one of my barons*, his neighbours ".[4] Walter died without issue. But he had a

[1] Neilson, *Knight-Service*, p. 173. The service of holding the King's stirrup on his birthday is recorded in the reign of Alexander II (1214–1249). Elizabeth M. Kimball, *Serjeanty Tenure in Mediaeval England*, Yale Univ. Press, 1936. Instances of jocular tenure are hardly found till the reign of James V, when part of the reddendo for the barony of Carnwath was the price of two pairs of stockings, to be given to the winner of a race. *O.P.* I, p. 127.

[2] But we notice " terra illa que fuit de *baronia* patris mei comitis Wyntonis " [in Strathearn] in a charter duly confirmed by Alexander II. *Inchaffray*, No. LXXXI.

[3] " Rodbertus absolvit se ab homagio quod ei fecerat pro *baronia* quam tenuit de eo in Galewegia."—John of Hexham, p. 293.

[4] Lawrie, CCXXII. Whitton, now divided into Upper Whitton in Hounam and Nether Whitton in Morebattle, was apparently for many centuries an undivided lordship or barony. Walter de Ridale comes into David's charters in 1142. His brother Aschetil was succeeded in the estate, 1175 × 1199, by Patrick of Ridale, who was probably his son. See *O.P.*

brother Aschetil, a knight, who inherited his lands and his status of baron—and what was in effect his " barony ".[1]

Office and territorial district formed a unit and, as such, passed to a single heir on the same, or on more rigorous, terms of service and only after confirmation by the King, who, reasonably enough, on the death of a baron took the unit into his own hands and kept it till he was satisfied that the heir was capable of performing the requisite duties. The heir to any fief would usually be the eldest son, who, if only by his age, was, on the average, the best fitted to succeed, and from the first years of David succession by primogeniture was permanently established. Save in exceptional cases,[2] his barons were succeeded in their lands and office by their eldest sons, who, or whose descendants, gradually became indistinguishable from " Scottish nobles ".

By a similar process knights came to form the nucleus of a landed gentry. As in England, knight-service was provided for in multiples or fractions of ten.[3] A baron could arrange for the specified number of knights by means of sub-enfeoffment, *i.e.* he could assign a certain portion of his fief to an under-tenant, to be held by the service of one or more knights. In theory a baron who held his land for the service of, say, twenty-five knights could provide the contingent by two methods. Either he could collect the requisite number of knights and maintain them

---

I, pp. 407-408. This Roxburghshire family, which invariably used *de*, is to be distinguished from the Ridels of Lothian, whose surname was a personal one and who never used *de*. See Joseph Bain, *Gen.* N.S. VI, p. 1.

[1] Confirmation by Pope Adrian IV in 1156, to "Anchitellus miles", of his brother's will. Lawrie, *Ann. M. and W.* No. XV. It is not easy to see why the Pope should have been brought into the matter.

[2] The choice between sons might be a matter for family arrangement, sanctioned by the King. Thus Robert de Brus was succeeded in his Scottish estates by his younger son, Robert, though in exceptional circumstances ; see below, p. 278. When there was no son, a fief passed to the eldest daughter or to the daughters as co-heiresses. They must marry as the King wished, because he must assure himself that the husband was able to fulfil the obligations resting on the fief.

[3] *E.g.* five, in the case of Walter fitz Alan.

in his castle from the produce of his estates, or he could grant them fiefs in return for service. The latter method had been generally preferred in England, and it was adopted in Scotland. A baron could then either grant twenty-five fiefs, each large enough to support one knight —what had been called in Normandy a *fief du haubert* (*haubert* = coat of mail = *lorica*) and was termed in England a knight's fee—or else he could give to five vassals fiefs able to support five knights and then let each vassal find his quota as he thought fit.

The King, as well as his barons, granted lands to knights, who held directly of him. To Alexander de Saint-Martin David granted only half the amount of land considered adequate to support a knight : a half-knight's fee. Alexander and his heirs are granted lands at Athelstaneford to hold " de me et heredibus meis in feodo et hereditate per servicium dimidii militis ", but the King undertakes to give him from his Treasury ten marks silver per annum " until such time as I complete for him a full knight's fee ".[1] Evidently a knight's fee was then considered roughly equivalent to a money value of twenty marks silver per annum, and apparently there was no suitable land immediately available for full territorial recognition of Alexander's merits.[2] Not till the next reign are conditions of tenure specified in charters and such obvious duties as castle-ward actually stated.[3]

A knight's fief was heritable property. He was succeeded in his estate and in his service by the eldest son. The landed gentry being thus formed by the knights was afterwards represented by Willame le Valeys [William Wallace]. A descendant of the baronial class was Robert the Bruce [= de Brus].

[1] " Usque donec perficiam ei plenarium feodum unius militis "— Lawrie, CLXXXVI.

[2] For Alexander's fortunes in Scotland and also for the greater precision afterwards shown, at least in private charters, see below, p. 275, n. 4.

[3] In the case of Berowald the Fleming at Elgin ; below, p. 377, n. 1.

CHAPTER V

NORMANS AND SCOTS *v.* NORMANS AND ENGLISH

(1130–1139)

★

§ 18

Scottish Acquiescence

By 1130 surviving documents are sufficiently numerous to cast a flickering light on the state of matters obtaining after six years of rule by David, of which one complete year had been spent outside his Kingdom. Adhering strictly to information supplied by the charters of the years 1124–1130, we note the following : a native King, reigning by the grace of God,[1] intimates the Royal will to " French and English " and to " *episcopi, abbates, comites, barones, justiciae, vicecomites, praepositi* " in documents witnessed by " *equites* " and " *archidiaconi* "—designations of which the last six are hitherto unrecorded in Scotland.[2] He possesses burghs (" my burghs ") ; four of them are specified.[3] He is surrounded by men of Norman name, transacts public business with their help and makes them considerable grants of land. He sends Norman knights to represent Scotland at important proceedings at York. In a word, he rules as no predecessor is known to have ruled, but as the Norman King is ruling in England. A few years afterwards, when the light of record improves, it illumines a land with Normans to be seen everywhere, the great men in authority over their Liddesdales or their Lauderdales, the lesser men in enjoyment of their ploughgates of land, their

---

[1] " Dei gratia " is generally omitted in the later charters of David, in the reign of Malcolm IV and the earlier years of William the Lion. This corresponds to the practice in England at the same periods.

[2] *E.g.* Lawrie, No. LXVII, *c.* 1126, *vicecomitibus*; *ibid.* XC, *c.* 1130, *justiciis*. There had been one solitary *vicecomes* before, introduced probably by Earl David.

[3] " In burgo meo de Dunfermelyn . . . Struelin . . . Perth . . . Edenesburge "—*ibid.* LXII, *c.* 1125, witnessed by Robert, still only Bishop-elect of St. Andrews.

half-ploughgates, their one-tenth share in the profits of the church or the mill. And nowhere in contemporary record or charter, history or chronicle is there a trace of opposition or resentment to be found, or a note of criticism or even surprise to be detected. If in 1130 all Normans had been driven out of Scotland never to return, even so this period of six years would be a most remarkable episode in her history.

They were so far from being driven out that David in 1130 could freely indulge in another of those lengthy absences which his exalted station in England entailed. As Robert de Brus had duties and privileges, sympathies, interests and revenues in both Kingdoms, so had he, being in all these respects as much Norman Earl as Scottish King. He could go to Court with the more ease and pleasure as official hospitality was provided all the way and his travelling expenses were defrayed by the King of England's extremely well-organized Treasury.[1] In 1130 David was combining pleasure with business. He was going on a judicial mission. Easter found him at Woodstock " in the Court of King Henry diligently inquiring into the charge of treachery brought against Geoffrey of Clinton ".[2] This French Geoffroi with an English estate called Clinton was none other than the Treasurer himself, an old acquaintance of David's, a neighbour of his in Northamptonshire, one of the " new men " who had served a clerical or financial apprenticeship and by their skill and zeal of office had helped to bring the Exchequer into being. Like so many of them, he was new to England, a native of the Cotentin, whose *Comte*, becoming King, had raised him from the dust to wealth and honour—as Orderic superciliously says.

---

[1] H. Hunt. p. 252. In the sheriffs' rolls, extant from 1130, there are numerous indications of David's journey to Court, the sheriffs charging their respective accounts for the corrody. Farrer, *Itin.* p. 130.

[2] Ord. Vit. VIII, xxii: " Goisfridus de Clintona." The name is also given as Glinton. It is either Clinton (Oxon.) or Clinton (Northants, near Market Deeping). Both have old G-spellings. *Complete Peerage*, III, p. 312.

Geoffrey was, among many other things, a Sheriff, and never did loyal service in the Duchy or the Kingdom preclude Châtelain or Vicomte or Sheriff from interpreting the Custom of Normandy, the Laws of Edward or the *Leges Henrici* [1] to his own advantage, provided some discretion were observed in the process. Geoffrey may not have started from quite so low as the dust, nor have overstepped the bounds of discretion on the upward way, but he had undoubtedly climbed to dizzy heights.[2] His trial was thus a sensational one and, as his official net had been cast wide over English shires and Norman châtellenies and the alleged treachery was of a financial character, the case must have been extremely complex. Imagination retires baffled before the prospect of the moves with the counters in the squares of the Exchequer tablecloth. It needs less effort to perceive that among the Norman lawyers David had a reputation for integrity and clearheadedness. Membership of the *curia regis* was not yet an office, and he, like his colleagues on the bench at Woodstock, was merely a man of affairs, a public man, an experienced and trusted " baron ", sitting, as they did, by invitation and certainly not as a distinguished stranger or ornamental assessor. There was a highly technical case to be tried and a need for competent judges. The Normans were nothing if not lawyers, and when they chose David to be a judge among

---

[1] An unofficial compilation (1109 × 1118) by a professional jurist, probably French, living perhaps at Winchester.

[2] Geoffrey was born in the neighbourhood of Saint-Lô (Cotentin), where he had a castle. He appears at the *curia regis*, c. 1110. W. A. Morris, pp. 85-86. He was a considerable landholder in Northamptonshire, in Hampshire and in Warwickshire, of which county he was Sheriff. His nephew Roger had been made Bishop of Coventry on December 22, 1129. Wm. Malm. *Gesta P.A.* p. 311. Geoffrey had frequently had dealings with David, *e.g.* 1120–1124, when winding up the estate of Henry's Justiciar, Geoffrey Ridel, who was drowned in the " White Ship ". Stenton, *E.F.* p. 34. David, Geoffrey, Walter Espec and Robert de Brus appear together in a document, 1124 × 1130 : below, p. 230. The trial at Woodstock appears to have resulted in an acquittal. Some years later Roger, Earl of Warwick, gave his daughter in marriage to the defendant. Round, *Ancestor*, XI, p. 153.

them they paid him their highest compliment : they took him for one of themselves.

While he was pursuing his judicial inquiries at Woodstock thus " diligently ", a dark secret of the Sons of Margaret was brought unpleasantly to his mind. News came that " Angus, Earl of Moray, with Malcolm and five thousand armed men had entered Scotland and was endeavouring to master the whole country ".[1] There was more in these names than meets the eye. Angus was the grandson and heir of King Lulach, whom David's father had slain. Malcolm's father no one knows. He himself was surnamed MacEth or MacHeth, but mysteriously ; perhaps Eth or Heth was the name of an unknown mother. A Royal force, with a stiffening of Norman knights, surprised and routed the rebels at Stracathro in the Mearns. Angus fell in the fighting.[2] Malcolm escaped—to be hailed Earl of Moray and to wage successful war, till at last, in 1134, the King of Scots sent a despairing appeal to the barons in the North of England.

Walter Espec called them together at Carlisle. He and Robert de Brus and Eustace fitz John had often met Earl David at the *curia regis*. They were still meeting King David on important business, not only in the North of England but in the shires of Huntingdon and Northampton,[3] and they looked upon him as a Norman governor in difficulties with his natives. Robert de Brus, Bernard de

[1] Ord. Vit. VIII, xxii.

[2] " Battle between the men of Alban and the men of Moray, in which four thousand of the Moravians were slain along with their King Angus [Oengus], the son of the daughter of Lulach ; one thousand of the men of Alban, however, were slain in that battle."—*Annals of Ulster, s.a.* 1130, in *Collectanea de Rebus Albanicis,* Iona Club, 1847. A note was added to MS. D of *A-S.C.* : " In this year [1130] Anagus was slain by the Scottish army and there were many slain with him. There was God's right avenged on him because he was all forsworn."

[3] *E.g.* when the Abbot of Ramsey in Huntingdonshire and Simon de Beauchamp settled their controversy concerning a wood in Crawley and Henry I confirmed the agreement, his precept (1124 × 1130) was addressed, among others, to David, King of Scotland, Geoffrey of Clinton, Walter Espec and Robert de Brus. *Ramsey,* I, p. 244, No. CLXVII.

Bailleul and others with them stood in a relation to David which was more than that of personal friendship. The Lord of Cleveland held of him Annandale and Exton in Rutland. Bernard de Bailleul had become his " man ". Such " men " were bound to him by the most sacred ties of feudal duty—and by common interest, having no wish to see their Scottish holdings taken from them or their friends by any Gaelic claimant, arguable though his case might be. North and south of Tweed the same (Anglo-Norman) system was in operation. Its administrators and beneficiaries were interconnected and interdependent. Their sense of solidarity was completely unaffected by the national feeling which in the process of time was to make the Tweed one of the broadest rivers in the world—so broad that to this day those born north or south of it seem foreigners on the other side. Barons on either side were bound together by spiritual ties. They were all working for the Church, often for the church of St. Cuthbert at Durham; some had taken their share in creating the diocese of Carlisle in the preceding year and, long before then, the diocese of Glasgow, which in the opinion of Bishop John—and of his successors a century later—extended to the Rere Cross on Stainmore. Barons were constantly consulting and aiding each other in matters concerning the foundation, endowment and upkeep of their religious houses.[1] In particular, Walter Espec and David vied in pious emulation.

At the meeting convened at Carlisle it was resolved that preparations should be set on foot for aiding David by land and sea. As obviously as twenty-seven years

[1] In 1132 Walter Espec, Robert de Brus and Hugue de Morville attest David's charter (Lawrie, XCVIII), giving the Church of Tottenham to the Canons of the Priory of the Holy Trinity in London, " for the salvation of the souls of Queen Maud, my sister, and Queen Maud, my wife, and Earl Simon " [her first husband]. On Walter Espec's foundation of Rievaulx, in 1132, and David's, of the daughter-house at Melrose, in 1136, see below, pp. 254 and 334. Walter Espec's Foundation Charter is witnessed by Eustace fitz John.

before, the Norman barons were intervening in his favour with full authority from King Henry. A fleet might have sailed from the Tees or the Tyne for the Moray Firth, but such was the renown of Norman arms that when the news from Carlisle reached Malcolm's adherents they felt that all was lost. They abandoned his cause and he fell into the hands of David, who " obtained possession of Moray, and thus, with his power increased, was he exalted beyond his predecessors, and the land of the Scots honoured by his zeal for religion and by the presence of men of distinction and learning ". So wrote Orderic soon after, and excused himself for a long digression " because the Scots from ancient times adhered to the Catholic faith and cheerfully practised Christian simplicity ".[1] In Moray they were now sustained in their practice by the presence of Benedictines at Urquhart and Normans on confiscated lands. Elgin was made one of " my burghs ".[2]

The only settler whose name is recorded was a Fleming, Freskyn, who held of David Strabok in Linlithgow [Broxburn], Duffus near Elgin and a vast territory in Moray.[3] He is not designated as " Flandrensis ", but his name indicates Flemish origins and his sons are recorded in the company of Flemings. A " Fresechinus fil Ollec "[4] is mentioned in 1130 along with persons of Flemish name who were evidently members of the very large Flemish colony settled *c.* 1108 by Henry in the district dominated by the castle of Pembroke. David's Freskyn may have been a

[1] Ord. Vit. VIII, xxii.

[2] David went to Moray in person. At Banff he made a grant to the monks of Urquhart from the rent of the burgh of Elgin. The charter (Lawrie, CX, *c.* 1136) is addressed, among others, " praepositis et omnibus probis hominibus totius Muref et Scotiae ". The grant was twenty shillings annually " de firma burgi mei et aquarum de Elgin ". The priory of Urquhart was attached to Dunfermline, perhaps later.

[3] All we know of Freskyn is that his son William was confirmed by Malcolm IV in these lands; they were " terrae quas pater suus tenuit tempore regis David, avi mei ". See *O.P.* II, pp. 626 and 654, and *Moray*, Introd. pp. xii-xiii.

[4] Mentioned, with " Witso Flandrensis ", under " Pembroke ", Pipe Roll Henry I, 1130, p. 136.

soldier of fortune or only the leader of a band of colonists like Henry's; they formed in Pembroke not a military aristocracy, but a community of farmers, traders and woollen manufacturers. Their settlement involved a complete displacement of the native population [1] and the general circumstances may have some bearing on happenings in Moray which have always remained mysterious. Freskyn founded the great house known as *de Moravia* (Moray) [2] and was closely related to the founder of a greater, that of Douglas.[3] It seems likely that Freskyn was only one of many " praepositi " and " probi homines " and new landed proprietors, Norman and other, and that the subjugation of Moray was complete. Soon afterwards Moray sends her sons to fight for David at the Battle of the Standard.

A dangerous situation had been ended, but Malcolm MacHeth was not executed. He was taken to Roxburgh, kept in confinement there for twenty-three years and then brought forth and made Earl of Ross. What can have been the reason for so singular a proceeding? Perhaps that for

---

[1] See J. E. Lloyd, II, p. 424.

[2] Freskyn's eldest son Hugh († before 1226) succeeded him in the lands of Strabrok and Duffus, and either inherited from him or received from the Crown the territory of Sutherland. He granted, 1203 × 1214, lands in Sutherland (" faciendo seruicium vnius sagittarii ") to his brother William's son Gilbert [Archdeacon of Moray 1203–1222, Bishop of Caithness 1223–1245, and a Saint in the Aberdeen Breviary] and to those of Gilbert's *parentela* whom he might appoint as his heirs. *Moray*, No. I. *Hugh* Freskyn's son, known as " Willelmus de Moravia, miles " and " dominus de Suthyrlandia ", became, *c.* 1237, the first Earl of Sutherland.

Freskyn's second son William, who witnessed documents in 1160 as " W. filius Frisgin " and a Royal charter *c.* 1170 as " W. filius Fresekin ", became head of the de Moravia family of Duffus and Petty.

[3] William of Douglas witnesses a charter by Jocelin, Bishop of Glasgow 1175–1199 : see *O.P.* I, pp. 152-156. William was either the brother or else the brother-in-law of Freskyn of Kerdal, referred to by [Bishop] " Bricius " of Douglas as " avunculus meus ". The relationship between Freskyn of Kerdal and David's Freskyn is unknown, but was evidently close. Wyntoun, preserving his usual caution, says (VIII, vii) that the House of Moravia or Moray [descendants of David's Freskyn] and the House of Douglas had the same armorial bearings and were commonly believed to be of the same kin. On the rise of the Douglases, which began in Moray, see below, p. 332.

which Donald Bane died blind, but free, and was buried with the Kings in Iona. Perhaps that for which, in the year of Malcolm's incarceration, the venerable octogenarian who had been Duke of the Normans died in the wild frontier fortress on the Severn Sea.[1] Later generations remembered

THE HOUSE OF MORAY AND THE REIGNING DYNASTY

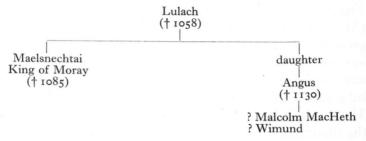

Lulach
(† 1058)

Maelsnechtai
King of Moray
(† 1085)

daughter

Angus
(† 1130)

? Malcolm MacHeth
? Wimund

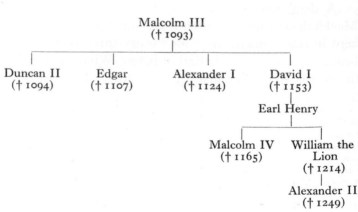

Malcolm III
(† 1093)

Duncan II   Edgar   Alexander I   David I
(† 1094)   († 1107)   († 1124)   († 1153)

Earl Henry

Malcolm IV   William the
(† 1165)   Lion
(† 1214)

Alexander II
(† 1249)

only the Crusader. Here we may recall the poet; Robert learned Welsh to while away the time in the last long years of his captivity and acquired a remarkable skill in the composition of Welsh verse.[2] He, like Donald Bane, had Celtic sympathies and, like him, passed for a rightful

---

[1] Ex-Duke Robert died at Cardiff in February 1134 and was buried before the high altar in the abbey church of St. Peter at Gloucester—the city of his nephew Earl Robert.

[2] See David, *R. Curthose*, p. 186.

King deprived of his throne by a usurper. So perhaps did
Malcolm of Moray.

The treatment of his case suggests dynastic rivalry, a
guilty conscience, tardy compensation, but not suppression of a revolt against Norman-feudalism. Its introduction
into Moray can hardly have seemed imminent when Angus
and Malcolm took the field in 1130. They were the
assailants and they waited till David was out of the country
before they launched their attack. Angus was head of the
rival House, with a claim to be King which, when he fell
in battle, passed to Malcolm MacHeth. Their movement
seems primarily dynastic, directed not so much against
David the Norman as against David the Usurper. In the
end his throne was saved for him by Normans, but the attack
on it was evidently not inspired purely by feeling against
them or by resentment arising from the distribution of
land among them. Dynasty is a guiding-thread of Scottish
History from Kenneth MacAlpin to James VI and Prince
Charles Edward, and in 1130 no very definite political or
economic issue need have been involved.

We can find no historical evidence of feeling against
Normans as such anywhere in Scotland. It would have
been easier to believe in its unrecorded existence had there
been a trace of enmity in the fertile regions where lands
were given them with so lavish a hand—in the valleys
among the Border hills, in the dales of Teviot, Tweed or
Clyde, in the seabound Lowlands or on the golden fringe
of the beggar's mantle, Fife. In 1130, as in later years,
the attack came from afar. It was led by men of mystery,
heirs to their unnamed fathers' wrongs, heirs to Royal rights
handed down from Kenneth MacAlpin, heirs to a legacy
of hatred and vendetta dating from times when there were
no Normans and no Normandy. Even if the battle-cry
had been " Scotland for the Scots ", the mode of action
was dynastic. The appeal was to men loyal to a former
line of Kings. Certainly the claimants and their followers

must have had grievances which, well or ill founded, economic or political, were probably aggravated by dislike of Norman-feudalism and fear of Norman encroachment. But they were anti-Margaretsons first and anti-Normans afterwards.

Of Scotland's Norman Conquest or Tenurial Revolution all that the scanty documents can tell us is that in 1124 the country had a new King and Governor, whose hereditary claim to the throne, though considered by many unsound, was plausible, whose advisers and executive officers were mostly Normans and whose Royal functions and relationship to the land in his Kingdom were given by him and by them a Norman interpretation. It was accepted, first by the Lowland nobles and people without any known opposition and then by the rest of the Kingdom without any fierce or sustained resistance.

The apparent quiescence or acquiescence is hard to explain, except perhaps in the domain of theory. There Scotland probably had not far to travel before reaching the assumptions at the base of the Norman-feudal system —no further than Northern England had travelled (under some compulsion, it is true) after 1066. In Lothian and Cumbria there were Celtic customs with an admixture of Scandinavian, but till 1066, as regards either land-tenure or collection of the rustic dues of the homesteads or the fields, Lothian cannot have differed much from England north of the Tees, or Cumbria much from England north of the Ribble.[1] Moreover, Lothian was the natural refuge of exiles from the South, migration of individuals was a marked characteristic of the age, exile was often voluntary and, by 1124, in Lothian, Fife and the coastal districts further north there were incomers for whom Norman land-tenure and Norman methods of government or finance

---

[1] Many of the customs which had been considered peculiar to Old Northumbria have been found to be closely paralleled in early Scottish records : see Jolliffe, *C.H.* pp. 33, 37, etc. So also for the old Cumberland ; *e.g. cornage* was very similar to the Scottish *can* : see R. R. Reid, p. 187.

can have had no novelty and no terrors. In Cumbria the illustrious Earl David had long been setting a brilliant example, perhaps a forceful example, of Norman ways.

Celtic Scotland had not so far to travel as might be imagined, not nearly so far as Ireland when her time came. What is known of " Celtic Scotland " in 1124 is largely what can be divined from actual knowledge of Ireland at that time (but Ireland was isolated, literally) and from modern survivals in the Highlands (but they may be deceptive). If all has been correctly divined, then Normanization in Celtic Scotland must have been easy enough. Within the clan the sense of kinship was strong. The headship was, however, confined to one family and the chiefs had come to form a hereditary nobility. There was extensive feudalization of the Anglo-Saxon type, dating perhaps, as Fordun affirms, from the accession of Malcolm MacKenneth in 1005. As in pre-Conquest England, there was a form of military service, probably similar.[1] There were Thanes—indeed it is mostly north of the Forth that they were to be found. There were greater Thanes and lesser Thanes, and it is not at all certain that they differed widely in status and functions from Anglo-Saxon Thegns, who, like them, were properly officials and might be unimportant or highly important.[2] The titles of Thane and Toisech were becoming interchangeable. Chiefs had a

[1] According to Skene (III, p. 232), the *Feacht* or expedition and the *Sluaged* or hosting (*expeditio et exercitus*) consisted of a general obligation upon the possessors and occupiers of land to follow their superiors and chiefs as well as the King in their expeditions and wars.

[2] Thegnage means no more than service, *ministerium*. In pre-Conquest England it was the normal expedient for getting any work of exploitation done which could not be conveniently left to the reeves of the shires or boroughs, or for discharging such public duties as could be discharged by deputy. Every great Royal estate and every great private franchise had its thegns. The King's Thegns were officials of high standing, *ministri* below the rank of ealdorman, and some were very important persons through whom the King controlled the provinces. The lesser Thegns (*læss-thegns*) had functions which varied endlessly according to locality. Jolliffe, pp. 93-94. In Moray there were very numerous thanedoms, some smaller than a parish, and many persons of extremely modest condition bore the title of Thane. See *Moray*, Introd. p. xxviii.

double capacity : they were officials and they were landed proprietors. The province or *Mor Tuath*, composed of *tuatha*, originally tribes, was governed by a *Mor Maer* or great *maer*.[1] A *maer* was the steward of a chief's rents, but he was also the representative of the Scottish King and discharged duties similar to those afterwards discharged by the Anglo-Norman Sheriff. A Mormaer was regarded by his own people as a King, but by the King of Scots merely as his steward—as an hereditary Royal official. The Tuath was the territory, or rather the people, of a Toisech. He had originally been a " captain " or " leader " (*dux*), but had become the hereditary chief of a *clan* (the name given to a *tuath* in later times) ; officially he was a collector of dues or of tributes in kind, payable, some to the King, some to the Mormaer. There were *tuatha* which were very small. There were important Toisechs and unimportant, as in Ireland and Wales.[2] Land belonged in theory to the clan, but was in fact held only by the near kin of a *flath*, the head of a sept, by those who were within three degrees of him. Thus in the course of a few generations descendants of the *flath* became landless,[3] and at any given time land and power remained in the hands of the Chief and his near relations.

Everywhere in the Scottish Kingdom there were magnates performing many of the functions of a Norman lord ; in Cumbria and Lothian governors of districts must have been, as in Old Northumbria, deputies of the King, sub-Kings, resembling to that extent at least the Mormaers of

[1] It should be said that in the opinion of some Celtic scholars this obvious etymology is wrong and the short syllable *Mor* of *Mormaer* has nothing to do with the long syllable *mór* = " great ".

[2] " The tywysog might be the lord of a single cantref playing with all ceremony and dignity the part of monarch on that narrow stage or the master of the fifteen cantrefs of Gwynedd."—J. E. Lloyd, I, p. 309.

[3] Gradually, not at one fell swoop on the demise of the flath. A man's heirs were a family group, the descendants of one great-grandfather, and as the older members of the group of joint heirs died out, each group, in the course of nature, resolved itself into a new group of the same kind. See E. MacNeill, *C.I.* p. 6.

the North. Celtic social grading was strongly official in character,[1] but office none the less tended to pass from father to son—as in later days when the Lords of the Isles had hereditary physicians and the Macleods of Dunvegan hereditary pipers. In " Celtic Scotland " nobility by office had developed into nobility by birth. In theory the passage from Celtic chief to Norman feudal lord was simple. In practice it could be a mere matter of arrangement between the head of the clan and the King ; the clansmen would follow their chief, and when the change did at length take place it is doubtful if they suffered by it. On the old Celtic burdens or exactions, of which little is known, opinions differ : " The one essential feature which distinguished them from rent properly so called was the uncertainty of their amount and the consequent liability to unlimited extension at the hands of those who were possessed of supreme power ". Such was the opinion of the Victorian Duke of Argyll, himself a Celtic chief and a stout defender of the Normans in Scotland.[2] Nor did the introduction of charters necessarily make much difference in patriarchal rule. In the centre of the parish of Killean in Kintyre may still be seen the rude remains of Dundonald, the residence of the Chief when visiting the district. His charters are said to have run : " I, Macdonald, sitting upon Dundonald, give you a right to your farm from this day till to-morrow, and every day thereafter, so long as you have food for the great Macdonald of the Isles ".[3]

The native landowners who came, or were brought, into the Norman-feudal nexus were not dispossessed. They became the tenants of an overlord. They held of him ; he, tenant-in-chief, held of the King. Theoretically they went down one step, in that they had a third party interposed between them and the King—a person acting

---

[1] Jolliffe, *C.H.* p. 35.   [2] P. 31 : see also Skene, III, p. 230.
[3] *O.P.* II, p. 27.

as his servant. Such an arrangement may, however, have sometimes been considered one of practical convenience : possession of lands dubiously acquired in a remote past could be ratified ; small proprietors could assure themselves of protection. Protection against whom ?—The enjoyment which, under a Norman landlord, " was common to the Few was an enjoyment absolutely exclusive of the Many. And the many were always quite near enough to make this a continual presence in the mind. From across some rough hill, or over some dreary moor or from beyond some firth or bay of the sea, outsiders, representative of the Many, were always ready to rush in on the Few who were protected in the exclusive enjoyment of good natural meadows, of sheltered woods with fine pastoral glades, stocked with sheep and swine and cattle." [1]

The highest and the lowest social classes remained comparatively unaffected :

David's Normans were not made Earls. The native holders of that recent title—*Comes* in the charters, *Counte* perhaps in everyday life—retained their ancient dignity intact. Charters which concern their parts of the country are attested by them. Probably nothing of importance was done without their assent. They were evidently present at important meetings of David's *curia regis*. For long, perhaps even from some date in the reign of Malcolm Canmore, whether by enactment or by custom, " Comes " had been used to designate a King's son (Alexander, Ethelred, David himself), a Mormaer, a greater Thane, an Earl. Perhaps this was merely the result of using Latin. (The term " Mormaer " is not found in any charter.) Or perhaps " Comites ", consciously or not, had begun to act as such—as persons who had exalted rank, but not necessarily administrative status, and to let part of their old official duties, consultative powers or functions of government pass to " King's friends " who had become

[1] Duke of Argyll, p. 61.

transformed, perhaps in Queen Margaret's time trans-
mogrified, into "Ministers", Court officials, great officers
of State. If so, David only hastened the process, following
in this the policy of the Norman Kings, who, while consistently upholding the dignity of Earl and granting it
only to the most blue-blooded of Normans, considered it
as devoid of military or administrative significance and as
indicating rank rather than political power.[1] That was
David's own status in England and he, and apparently
everybody else, found it satisfactory. There is much virtue
in a name. It is conceivable that a Mormaer was not ill
pleased to be a " Comes " and his wife positively charmed
to be a " Comitissa "; never since has an Earl's wife
wished to be called anything else.[2] French titles have given
permanent satisfaction, all the way down to Esquire and
plain Mr. and Mrs.—a remarkable testimony to the success
of the Norman Conquest. There is proof that towards 1130
Thanes, Toisechs and Drengs were finding themselves
designated as " Barones " or as " Vicecomites ", according
to their relative importance.[3] There is no proof that they
disliked the designation.

What had taken place was an aristocratic influx, an
overflow from the dominant class in England, and the
number of native land-holders or office-holders whose

[1] Stenton, *E.F.* pp. 226-227.

[2] *Counte* was regularly used in Anglo-French documents as the equivalent of Earl, but did not find its way into English till the sixteenth century.
In the Journals of the House of Lords the title *Comitissa* is still used, and
the Earl is still *Comes*.

[3] Drengs, originally Thanes, are found in England, chiefly in Old
Northumbria and only where Norse influence had been strong. They were
free tenants, holding by a tenure the nature of which was partly military,
partly servile. Bishop " Flambard " addresses a charter to all his thegns
and drengs of Islandshire and Norhamshire. Details on drengage appear
in the *Boldon Book*, pp. 285-286. It seems likely that in Scotland thanes
were but drengs (and, for that matter, toisechs) renamed. David was not
long in assimilating them all to " barones " and " vicecomites ". Thus he
addressed as Earl a charter, *c.* 1117 (Lawrie, XXX), " Cospatrico . . . et
omnibus fidelibus *Tegnis* et *Drengis* de Lodeneio et de Teuegetedale " and
another, as King, *c.* 1130 (XCI), " *baronibus, vicecomitibus,* ministris et
omnibus fidelibus suis totius Laudonie ".

status was appreciably affected was perhaps small. "Barones" came in at a high level, but below that of Earls, Mormaers and greater Thanes. Knights were not set above lesser Thanes, Toisechs or Drengs. Nor were "Vicecomites", some of whom, moreover, were natives of Scotland.

On the mass of the people the change in the system of tenure can have had little practical effect. The cottars remained cottars. Serfs were still serfs. If lawyers remarked that the theory of land-ownership had undergone interesting modifications since King David came, what can it have mattered to Gillepatrick, Ragewin and Ulchil? All that is known of these three is that they were King David's personal bondsmen, his private property, and that one day towards 1126 he presented them to the church of the Holy Trinity at Dunfermline.[1] Thus was their humble, distant and, we doubt not, faithful service transferred from the throne to the altar. If in our pages little interest is shown in persons below the rank of Dreng, it is not for lack of sympathy, but because no one ever showed any interest, and their doings are unchronicled, their feelings unrecorded. The documents preserved are formal, dry, legal. What is known of David's subjects as human beings is what the writers of the time saw fit to write down—namely, a little about the family affairs of a few exalted personages, less about their private opinions, foibles, loves, hatreds, jealousies, still less about their friends or confidants, and nothing whatsoever about the feelings of Ragewin, Gillepatrick and Ulchil.

Yet, after the fullest allowance is made for changes that may have been only theoretical, the hard fact remains that Norman incomers displaced native land-holders and office-holders, and advanced at their expense. It is true that there must often have been special circumstances. A charter is only a *terminus ad quem*. Behind it there is a

[1] Lawrie, LXVIII.

story of previous ownership, lost to us, but perfectly well known to King David, and it is legitimate to assume that lands were often bestowed on a Norman for good and sufficient reason. It is certain that some were " waste ", whether in the technical sense, without a recognized landlord, or uncultivated or derelict. Some were simply purchased. Some were acquired by the peaceful process of matrimony ; at no time in the history of the British Isles were men more susceptible to the charms of heiresses, though it must be admitted that the known examples in David's Scotland are relatively few. Probably most of the lands granted were Crown property, whether held from of old or recently come into the King's power by failure of heirs or by confiscation, the regular penalty for all sorts of offences, moral as well as political. The hard fact yet remains : there were lands in the King's gift and he gave them to Normans, instead of giving them to his own fellow-countrymen. There may have been little actual expropriation, little to justify the latter-day lament :

> These fertile plains, that soften'd vale,
> Were once the birthright of the Gael ;
> The stranger came with iron hand
> And from our fathers reft the land.[1]

Yet there must have been occasional injustice. There must have been bitter remonstrance, for no man likes to have a stranger set over him, however theoretically. But complaints have not come down to us. The Sons of Margaret had a certain ruthlessness, yet could do with impunity things which if done by princes less pious and less austere might have seemed indefensible and unjust.

In the utter absence of contemporary comment we are reduced to suppositions. Perhaps a King of Scots was a law unto himself. He might be murdered—indeed he frequently was [2]—but what had been contested was rather his right to be King than his methods of exerting the Royal

[1] Scott, *Lady of the Lake*.   [2] See, for instance, above, p. 13, n. 1.

authority. So long as he reigned, perhaps he occupied a position of solitary grandeur and moved on the heights, asking advice from no one. Perhaps his people were docile. In later times Scotland was not an easy country to govern : Cromwell is said to have been the only really successful ruler. But till the end of the fifteenth century one looks in vain for any instance of collective coercion being used against the Crown by nobles or people, and then " Scotland " is post-Norman Scotland. Perhaps in David's time the leaders of the people were easily placated. Some were incomers themselves, Gospatrics and MacArkils who had received lands and titles in Scotland within recent memory. Some profited as much as any Norman by forfeiture of estates in Moray—to judge from the names of later land-holders, evidently drawn from the native aristocracy in the more southerly parts of the realm. The Normans had fellow-conquerors.

Perhaps there was an initial display of overwhelming force. A new King with a monopoly of mail-clad knights was like an upstart modern government with a monopoly of tanks and machine-guns ; even if recalcitrants could have procured the armour and the horses, they had not the technical training to make effective use of either. In mediaeval times the prayer of the people was for peace ; a strong government supported from without by a foreign power and from within by unassimilated aliens was not necessarily unpopular. There was little feeling of nationality anywhere, and perhaps there was even less in the composite Kingdom to which Earl David had succeeded. Perhaps the indifference to racial or linguistic distinctions was as profound in actual life as it is in the contemporary writers. For all that any of them tells us to the contrary, the new landowners might have been Scotsmen born and bred. A Henry of Huntingdon, an Ailred, who had been meeting them daily, does not think their French origin worth mentioning, and it has to be divined from their

French names or from common knowledge of the conditions prevailing at the time. We have to wait fifty years for a Jourdain Fantosme to express surprise at the partiality shown by a Scottish sovereign to men of alien race, and much longer for a Walter of Coventry to commiserate the Scottish people, bearing under their own Kings a foreign yoke.

Suppositions such as the above gain more probability according as more time is allowed for the operation of contributory causes. The simplest explanation—and it is consistent with what little evidence there is—is that Scotland's "Norman Conquest" or Tenurial Revolution was, like most conquests and most revolutions, less sudden than it seems. As the Norman Conquest of England proceeded from events, usually of a dynastic or family character, which had been taking place one after another since 1002, so the Normanization of Scotland was brought about by a long series of happenings which were connected with those events and which had the effect of laying the country open to Norman influence, infiltration and settlement. Possibly relations with the Normans during the reign of Malcolm Canmore were closer, and the changes made at the accession of Edgar and on Earl David's assumption of rule in Cumbria were more violent, than the surviving records can prove. After more than fifty years of Norman government in England and twenty-five of sub-Norman or semi-Norman government in Scotland, King David's changes may have seemed to his subjects who thought about these things natural enough and likely to mean little more than a reorganization of existing usage. Much of what he made explicit was implicit before. He had a gift for organization. He *organized*.

§ 19

Ailred at David's Court

As for the feelings of the Normans thus settled in their new home, we must turn to Ailred, to his life as well as to his writings. Here, as so often, Scottish history reduces itself to biography and hero-worship, and we must make what we can of Master Daniel's glowing account of St. Ailred, and the Saint's no less glowing account of David and his Norman friends. Ailred tells us little, but tells us more than anyone else, and if he is disappointingly uninformative it is not because he was uninformed. He knew David's Normans from his boyhood. He was brought up at the Scottish Court, held a post in the Household, saw the coming of the new French religious orders and joined one of them himself. He became the historian of the battle fought on Cowton Moor between Normans and Scots on the one side and Normans and English on the other, and he played a chief part in the movement for the peaceful union of the Norman and English peoples through St. Edward and his kindred in Scotland.

Ailred was born about 1110 at Hexham, where his father Eilaf was the parish priest. Situated near the point where the North Tyne and the South Tyne become one river and commanding the routes along their valleys into the hills, Hexham stands close to the Roman road that runs from York to Corbridge on Tyne and thence to Newstead on Tweed—which helps to account for its ancient ecclesiastical importance and for the fact that it was to Roxburgh, near the junction of Teviot and Tweed, that, after a brief schooling, young Ailred was sent for his further instruction.[1]   At Roxburgh he was brought up with David's stepsons, Simon and Waldef, and Henry, his son.[2] The four boys were at different stages in their education—Henry was the youngest, Ailred probably the next youngest. Three were typical Norman boys, interested in churches and castles. Simon, who took after his father the Crusader, played at castles; when he grew up, he built more, "dang doun" some that other men had built, and becoming, in his step-father's despite, Earl of Northampton, regained his esteem as a builder of convents and at length died "like a Chris-tian" (*more Christiano*).[3] Waldef, the mother's favourite, played at churches;[4] he became an Austin Canon at Nostell, an Austin Prior at Kirkham, a Cistercian at another of Walter Espec's foundations (Wardon in Bedfordshire), an Abbot of Melrose and afterwards, like Ailred, a Saint.[5] Henry led Norman cavalry into action on Cowton Moor and nearly met his end at the siege of Ludlow Castle, but lived to be the very model of the perfect Prince—one who had all the virtues of a monarch and a monk.[6] Ailred was his inseparable companion. Education at Roxburgh must have been sound. Ailred's favourite reading was the *De Amicitia*, and he made it the philosophic basis for his life-

[1] " Post scholas praepropere relictas a juventute in curia regis . . . nutritus et educatus "—Jocelin, *Vita S. Waldeui*, p. 258, col. 1.

[2] " Cum quo [Henrico] *et ipsis cunabulis* vixi et puer cum puero crevi . . . cujus adolescentiam adolescens cognovi."—Ailred, *G.R.A.* p. 756. But " from the very cradle " seems a rhetorical exaggeration : it finds no support in Jocelin.

[3] Simon, who must have been seven or eight years older than Ailred, founded the Cistercian Abbey of Sawtrey, Huntingdonshire, in 1147, and the nunnery of St. Mary at Northampton.

[4] *Vita S. Waldeui*, p. 251, col. 1.   The effect of Jocelin's story is some-what spoiled when we know that Giraud de Barri [Giraldus Cambrensis], born *c*. 1147 at Manorbier in the county of Pembroke, prefaces his work by telling the same story of himself.   When he and his brothers used to play on the sands of Manorbier—" the sweetest spot in Wales "—his brothers built castles, but he built churches.

[5] Ailred was canonized in 1191.   Waldef's grave was opened in 1170, the twelfth year after his death, by Bishop Enguerrand of Glasgow and four Abbots, who found his body incorrupt.   *Chron. Melrose, s.a.* 1170.

[6] " Ut in rege monachum, et in monacho regem praetendere videretur " —Ailred, *D.B.S.*

long cult of friendship. His cult of beauty in Latin prose, the one luxury Cistercian scholars would permit themselves, reposed on firm foundations.

He was sent to Roxburgh to acquire French culture, and he may have been something of a Norman, though at first sight no one could be more " Saxon ". His name is a contracted, Normanized form of Æthelred, and he is stated by Jocelin to have come of fine old English stock.[1] He was not merely " a son of the Manse "; he was a great-grandson. His great-grandfather was Priest of the old Saxon Church of St. Andrew at Hexham and sacrist of Durham—Alfred Westou, a man famous in his day as a zealous and privileged custodian of the chief treasure, the body of the Saint to whom Durham and Hexham belonged.[2] Alfred's son and successor, Eilaf Laureu, led the opposition party at Durham when *monachi* were introduced in 1083. He was expelled with all the other *clerici* save one, but permitted to remain Priest of Hexham,[3] in which office he was followed by his son Eilaf II, Ailred's father. But while Thomas II was Archbishop, Hexham was annexed to a prebend at York, and Eilaf II retained only the cure of souls and so inadequate a share in the endowments that he had to take to hunting and with the proceeds of the chase keep the wolf from the door. When the Austin Canons came, he was left a life-interest as parish priest. Ailred himself, had there been no Norman onslaught on married clergy, might have carried on the hereditary calling and been fourth in descent as Priest of Hexham.

Closer inspection, however, reveals flaws in the Saxon façade. Eilaf is a Danish name and Ailred had two apparently Norman kinsmen, " Willelmus filius Thole "

---

[1] " Ex veterum Anglorum illustri stirpe procreatus "—*Vita S. Waldeui*, p. 258, col. 1.

[2] Reg. Durh. *Cuthb.* IX, pp. 32 and 57. Alfred Westou was " probably a member of a younger branch of the house of Hunred ". Hamilton Thompson, *Bede*, p. 96. Alfred in his zeal was apt to go too far : see *The Contents of St. Cuthbert's Shrine*, *V.C.H. Durham*, I, p. 245.

[3] *Priory Hex.* I, p. 111.

and " Laurentius ". The first, an Archdeacon, was in the way of visiting Ailred's parents and had come to see him in his cradle. The second, who was in secular orders at Durham, afterwards became a monk at St. Albans and, *c.* 1158, Abbot of Westminster; it was at his request that Ailred wrote his " Life of Edward ".[1] French family sympathies may be reflected in the fact that a wealthy Norman landowner in Lothian, one Robert, son of Philip, married Ailred's niece.[2] Priest Eilaf's interest with the Scottish Royal House is unknown—conceivably the Augustinians at Hexham used their good offices[3]—but his interest in it is easily understood. A loyal son of Durham and united with Prior Turgot, the Archdeacon and the future Abbot in a common devotion to St. Cuthbert, St. Edward and St. Margaret, he was well aware that in the schools at Roxburgh and at the Scottish Court his boy would receive a Norman training, but one in which Northumbrian traditions would be respected. It was thus that Ailred's education and his knowledge of the world were acquired in French ; his companion Waldef is one of the few members of Scotland's French-speaking aristocracy on whose use of spoken French actual evidence happens to be available (in Jocelin). It was also thus that Ailred came to devote his life and writings to promoting the union of Normans and English by dynastic and by religious means.

In 1134, still in his early twenties, he was well embarked on a promising career as a courtier. He was high in the

---

[1] "Laurentius", the future Abbot, is to be distinguished from a namesake at Durham, a native of Normandy, who wrote a eulogy of King David in Latin verse. The poet came from Normandy as a young man, to enter the monastery of Waltham in Essex, founded by Harold and given by the Conqueror to Durham in 1072. He went on to Durham 1124 × 1130. He became Prior in 1143 and died in 1154. Ed. *Laurence*, p. xxxiv; Powicke, *Dispensator*, pp. 35-36.

[2] Reg. Durh. *Cuthb.* I, p. 188. On Philip or Robert see below, p. 312. On Ailred's relatives, see Appendix H.

[3] David and his wife Maud were both benefactors (see above, p. 171 n. 4), and the first Prior of Hexham, who had the Norman name of Aschetil († 1130), went there from Huntingdon. Sim. Durh. *H.R.* II, p. 247.

Royal favour and already in possession of a Household post. His biographer, Walter Daniel, magnifying the office, styles him variously " economus " and " dapifer summus " (Chief Steward),[1] but his tenure of so exalted an office at so early an age is unrecorded and unlikely.[2] He was probably an assistant Dapifer, like the official afterwards mentioned at St. Andrews,[3] and he is depicted by Master Daniel as standing by the King in the banqueting-hall and seeing to it in person that the rules of precedence were observed at the Royal table and every man received his proper share of viands at his proper place. Ailred said of himself, modestly, " I came to the convent from the kitchens ". But even if his sway was only over cooks and scullions, his office, his favour with the King and his popularity with all in the *palatium* were high enough to arouse jealousy. For this reason, so Daniel tells, a certain knight made a violent attack on Ailred before the whole Court. But he replied so meekly that his reviler was abashed and finally sought forgiveness.

On the Court of David's early reign we could have wished for fuller information. Its fixed habitation, so far as it had one, was the Castle, also called Marchmont, in the old town of Roxburgh, now no more, which occupied a site opposite Kelso on a narrow neck of land between the rivers Teviot and Tweed. There was a wooden tower, in which the captured Claimant of Moray was kept, with other prisoners of state. The *palatium*—the residential quarters of the Castle, as distinguished from the defensive works— included the *aula*, the usual large wooden hall divided into a number of bays by arched trusses, the common living-room and meeting-place of the Household, the scene of

---

[1] One of Ailred's correspondents calls him *Dispensator Domus regis.* Powicke, *Dispensator*, p. 34.

[2] So far as name and perhaps date are concerned, Ailred could be the " Edredus " who witnesses David's charter to the church of Paxton (in the Countess Judith's fee in the Survey), along with " Robertus dapifer " and others, mostly of Northamptonshire. The charter is published by Doris M. Parsons, *S.H.R.* XIV (1917), pp. 370-372.   [3] Below, p. 368.

much domestic business, imperceptibly merging into business of state. It was here that "barons"—of whom the one distinctive attribute was that they had always access to the King and his table—were entertained by David in the company of their fellows, discussed their affairs with him and, when asked for their advice, gave it, with well-weighed reasons in support. The resident knights were at table, not much further down, for David considered himself "the companion of Knights, not their lord",[1] and it was doubtless from his proper place there that the accuser stood forth to make his public denunciation. He was evidently a resident, familiar with house gossip, a scurrilous member of a large establishment of "milites domestici".

On the organization, the splendour, manners, culture and refinement of David's Household there is only indirect information. It must have resembled Henry's Household, a strange assortment of high-placed administrators and menial servants: "the chancellor and his chaplain; bakers and butlers, marshals and ushers, archers, horn-blowers and kennelmen, huntsmen of all kinds, including wolf-hunters and cat-hunters (*catatores*)".[2] Some of these would have fixed stipends and allowances, others would be paid for their services by lands held in sergeanty. That the banquets were magnificent we know from the Speech at the Standard composed by Ailred, who saw to their preparation, and attributed by him to Robert de Brus, who had fond recollections of the fare. From other sources we learn that David, "when at last he was King", lost not a moment in improving his fellow-countrymen's way of life—their housing, dress, food and table manners—and offered three years' tax relief to all who in these matters would undertake self-reform;[3] and that he considered it part of

---

[1] Ailred, quoted in Fordun, I, p. 239.

[2] A. L. Poole, p. 61—based on the *Constitutio Domus Regis* [*Henrici Primi*].

[3] "Denique regno potitus, mox omnes compatriotas triennalium tributorum pensione levavit qui vellent habitare cultius, amiciri elegantius, pasci accuratius."—Wm. Malm. II, p. 477.

his kingly duties to look after " gardens, buildings and orchards " and thus stir up the people to follow the Royal example and beautify the land.[1] We know not what standard in Norman " elegantia " was actually attained, but at Roxburgh rich furnishings and gorgeous raiment must have been yet more in evidence than at Margaret's (or at Turgot's) Dunfermline, for the luxury of Courts had grown, Scottish prosperity had increased and additional revenue was coming in from the two Midland Earldoms. The stray item of Court news so miraculously preserved by the unfortunate incident at St. Cuthbert's tomb [2] permits the conclusion that while Maud de Saint-Liz was Queen splendour reigned at Roxburgh. Decorum likewise. The Royal couple set an example of domestic unity. The upbringing of young Henry and his sisters, Clarice and Hodierne, left nothing to be desired.[3] Queen Maud of Scotland was much respected, and her death, in 1131, was widely mourned. Afterwards, as before, David was universally regarded as a model of the virtuous life— "ascetic, generous in alms-giving, assiduous at prayers ".

The moral tone could not fail to be high at the Court of a King with so many saints in the family.[4] There must, however, have been temptations, if Master Walter Daniel

---

[1] Fordun, V, xxxix, p. 240.   [2] Above, p. 141.

[3] Clarice is a favourite name in the Old French romances. The name Hodierne, found in the House of Boulogne, may have come into David's family through his sister Mary. Her husband Eustace had a niece and other relatives called Hodierne. The name Odierna occurs in the *Liber Vitae*, p. 65, where there is nothing to connect it with Scotland. David's two daughters are said by Orderic to have died in childhood. They are mentioned only by him (VIII, xxii) and by R. Tor., who may be simply repeating him. Orderic's story of " an eldest son, Malcolm ", who was murdered in infancy, must, though circumstantial, be mythical, and some scepticism on the two daughters is permissible if only because the probable age of Maud de Saint-Liz makes it unlikely that she had so large a second family. On the other hand, the three names are probable in themselves, and Orderic was a visitor at Crowland, Maud's ancestral home, not long after her marriage to David, and may be assumed to have been interested and kept well informed.

[4] At the least: Edith of Wilton, Edward the Martyr, Edward the Confessor, Waltheof, Margaret and afterwards Waldef.

speaks truly when he affirms that Ailred successfully withstood them. So did Waldef. Jocelin relates that the daughter of a certain noble once cast interested glances in young Waldef's direction and sent him a gold ring in token of her esteem. He liked the ring and wore it with much satisfaction, till his friends made remarks. Then he put it in the fire and simultaneously overcame two evils, of which much the worse is *auri sacra fames*, in the judgment of Jocelin, who is given to quoting Horace and Tully.[1] Unhappily Daniel's statement on temptation moved certain of his monastic readers to incredulous comment, whereupon he shifted his ground too nimbly, and his fine-drawn distinctions leave it to be inferred that the assistant Dapifer was rumoured to have had love-affairs which were not so much unfortunate as too successful.

What is beyond doubt is that Ailred possessed King David's full confidence. High destinies were believed to await him. Meantime he was entrusted with diplomatic missions and assuredly the world lay bright before him when, probably in 1135, he went to Archbishop Toustain [Thurstan] at York on the King's business. The business was no doubt connected with the claim to archiepiscopal jurisdiction over Glasgow which Bishop John was then rebutting with his accustomed vigour. At York Ailred heard from " a most familiar friend ", Waldef, already Prior of the Augustinians at Kirkham, that certain French religious had come to labour near at hand : " Wondrous they were ; outstanding by their rule, white in habit and in name ". To visit them required only the Archbishop's permission and his blessing. These obtained, Ailred and Waldef rode north together to Helmsley, where they were hospitably entertained by Walter Espec. Conversation continued far into the night. From their host's eloquent French [2] Ailred learned that the half had not been told

---

[1] *Vita S. Waldeui*, p. 252, col. 1.
[2] " Facundia ei facilis erat."—Ailred, *G.R.A.*

him. Next day, at Rievaulx, three miles away, he saw the rest. Offices had already begun under the first Abbot, St. Bernard's own secretary at Clairvaux,[1] and of a sudden the full beauty of the religious life was borne in on Ailred. Yet he hesitated. The King, his hero, " dulcissimus dominus et amicus ",[2] seemed still to have need of his service, and the thought of being parted from Henry the beloved Prince was more than Ailred could endure. After a second night at Helmsley he resolved to remain in the world yet awhile. He was proceeding on his homeward way along the road which still traverses the hillside above the valley of the Rye, when he paused to take one last look at the lovely scene, the busy little settlement and the fair new House of God. Then he understood—and went back, to spend his life in the cloister. How hard the decision had been can be judged by what, sixteen years after, he wrote of Prince Henry : " In the body, but never in mind or affection, in order to serve Christ, I left him in the full bloom of his prime, as also his father, now flourishing in hale old age, whom I have loved beyond all mortals ".[3]

The White Monks had come over from France some years before. " We send some of our own soldiery . . . these scouts . . . into your Fief ", St. Bernard had intimated to his devoted friend the King of England,[4] but at first they met with scant success. Yet all they asked for was a piece of waste land, with woods to clear, swamps to drain, fields to plough. One was put at their disposal by " Walter Espec, a great and mighty man in the sight of the King and all the realm ".[5] Thus to the Yorkshire dales came in 1132 an Abbot and twelve monks from

---

[1] " William an Englishman ", but, we doubt not, as French as " the Englishman by name Raoul " who was the first Abbot of Vaucelles, founded from Clairvaux in the same year as Rievaulx and, it is said, on the same day, March 5, 1132.   [2] *G.R.A.* p. 716.   [3] *G.R.A.* p. 757.
[4] " Mittere de nostra militia . . . nos exploratores . . . in feudum vestrum."—St. Bernard, *Epistola* XCII, Migne, *P.L.* clxxxii, pp. 223-224.
[5] John of Hexham, p. 285.

Clairvaux,[1] daughter - house of Cîteaux (" Cisterns ",
" Swamps "); they founded the first great [2] Cistercian
Abbey in England, near Helmsley in the valley of the Rye,
and called it Rievaulx. The example was not lost on David.
Cistercians liked to settle in deep well-watered valleys and
build on the border of a stream; Melrose (1136), daughter-
house of Rievaulx, was his response to the example set by
the Norman lord whose lands of Wark and Carham lay
over against his own, a little further down the silver Tweed.

[1] *Clara Vallis*, also *Clarae Valles* (Aube), arr. Bar-sur-Aube, commune
de Ville-sous-la-Ferté.

[2] The first Cistercian Abbey in Britain was Waverley, near Farnham,
Surrey, founded by Henry I's early supporter William Giffard, Bishop of
Winchester, October 28, 1129. W. Williams, p. 47. But Waverley was
somewhat in a backwater—" quasi in angulo ", Ailred said. Fountains,
three miles south-west of Ripon, was founded, from York, a few months
after Rievaulx.

§ 20

The Battle of the Standard

FOUGHT not many months after Ailred entered Rievaulx
and not many miles from its walls, the Battle of the Standard shows David and his Normans in tragic conflict with
old friends.

On December 1, 1135, the surfeit of lampreys had put
an end to a great reign and to thirty-five years of unbroken
peace between Scotland and England. At the root of the
troubles which followed was a hard legal problem on which
barons could honestly differ: Should the Conqueror's
Crown go to a son's daughter or to a daughter's son?
It was complicated by many further difficulties. For
instance, the son's daughter (the Empress Maud, *l'emperis
Mahaut*) had taken a second husband, an Angevin, therefore displeasing to Normans,[1] and the daughter's son
(Stephen) had sped across to England as fast as Rufus
and had been as promptly crowned. Moral issues also
were involved, and they were not neglected, but in the
feudal conditions prevailing the struggle necessarily proceeded along family lines. Policy could not be entirely
impersonal so long as every man was bound, generally
through the tenure of land, to another man above him in
the social hierarchy. Barons and lesser landholders had
their own succession problems, private interests and personal preferences. At the apex of the social structure

---

[1] In 1129 Henry, who in 1126 had not told his barons of any such
intention, married his daughter the ex-Empress to Geoffrey " Plantagenet ",
aged fifteen, son of Foulque, Count of Anjou. The son born March 25, 1133,
the future King Henry II, was variously styled Henri d'Anjou or fitz
Emperis or fitz Mahaut.

there was a family dispute—among the Conqueror's grandchildren over property left by his youngest son, Henry. David, one of the family, by marriage, was involved in the dispute through his two nieces, and had himself a prior claim on the English portion of the contested property, as only surviving male heir of Edmund Ironside, Æthelred II and predecessors. This claim he did not, however, assert, having bowed to " the judgment of God at Hastings " like everyone else, and benefited by it more than most. He had sworn to support his niece the Empress and he kept his oath, the only baron so to do. For some time he remained aloof, resembling in this Henry's other *novi homines*; their reforming methods and stern fiscal measures had alienated the members of the " Field of Hastings nobility ",[1] most of whom became adherents of Stephen. But David was a knight, a serious-minded one, and an appeal from a lady in distress could not fall on deaf ears. A moving appeal came from his niece in France : from a daughter defrauded of a kingdom bequeathed her by her father.[2] David took up her cause. Less meritoriously, though sensibly enough, he combined defence of her interests with promotion of those of the Scottish Royal House, or at least those of his son Henry. The failure to settle his late brother-in-law's succession had created a new situation. The question of homage had been reopened. To a usurper the territorial concessions extorted by Rufus from Malcolm Canmore need not be continued. There was no further necessity for diplomatic silence on the partition of Cumbria—or on the ancient Scottish claim to Northumberland. From nebulous it had become precise, for young Henry could be regarded as sole heir to the martyred Earl Waltheof.[3]

David, on behalf of the Empress, took possession of

[1] *Gesta Stephani*, p. 16.
[2] " A patrio testamento . . . zelo justitiae succensus tam pro communis sanguinis cognatione, tam pro fide mulieri repromissa . . ."—*ibid*. p. 34.
[3] See Appendix G.

Carlisle, Norham, Wark, Alnwick and Newcastle, and distributed his time between invasions of England and negotiations with Stephen, who, having conducted a brief counter-invasion of Lothian, had half-promised Northumberland for David's son Henry and meantime made handsome concessions, not directly to the father, but indirectly through the son. Thus Carlisle, ceded to the son in February 1136, became David's headquarters.

The third invasion, that of 1138, was on the grand scale. From the four quarters of the Scottish realm a vast host had gathered. The men of Moray, forgetting their ancient grudge, had flocked to David's banner. There was even a strong force from Galloway, whose mixed inhabitants had hitherto held aloof from Scottish affairs [1] and perhaps came in now because Fergus their Lord was interested in the family quarrel, as one of Henry's sons-in-law. In Richard of Hexham's enumeration of the Scottish effectives " Normanni " come first.[2] David had two hundred knights—a large number then even for a king. In military matters Scotland was evidently well Normanized. With one accord Saxons and Celts, Lowlanders and Highlanders, even Islesmen, who acknowledged Norse sovereignty, had joined in a campaign to be fought for the King of Scots, for his Imperial niece, for Henry his son and for the " lost provinces " :

> In that intent all on ane da to de,
> Or to possess with fredome but ganestand,
> All Cumbria and eik Northumberland.[3]

There was again the primeval urge to " haud south ". The ancient memories of lands once held beyond Tweed and Solway still lived. David was following a perfectly

---

[1] David, when Earl, had overlordship. As King he addressed, *c.* 1136, a charter " Francis et Anglis et Scottis et *Galwensibus* ". *Melrose*, No. I.
[2] So also Contin. Flor. Worc. II, p. 112: " Innumerabilem habuit exercitum, tam de *Francis* quam de Anglis, Scottis, et Galweiensibus et de insulis." [3] *Bk. Cron. Scot.* l. 42,279.

definite line of " foreign policy ", the only one the Scottish Kingdom had ever known, that laid down three hundred years before by Kenneth, son of Alpin. The line led south. Opportunity having arisen, David must assert the old claim and seek the arbitrament of war. His enterprise may have seemed to some of his subjects ill timed or ill conducted. But it harmonized with their deeper feelings. Men who were neither geographers nor psychologists felt instinctively that by the nature of the land and the character of the people the districts to the north of the Tyne and the Cumberland Derwent were more akin to Scotland than to England. Men who could see the saints in proper person intervening in a Border foray could discover a Divine purpose in the allocation of moorland and hill-pasture in Northumberland and they were not insensitive to

> The light and air—the thin and shining air
> Of the North land,
> The light that falls on tower and garden there,
> Close to the gold sea-sand.[1]

Now the age-old question presented itself in Norman-feudal form. The King and his relatives were understood to have possessed great fiefs which, on a favourable occasion, must be recovered by the sword. For that purpose barony and knight-service had proved efficacious and it was a formidable host that crossed the Tyne and the Tees and swung down the road to York—and on Tuesday, August 22, found the way stopped at Cowton Moor, some seven miles short of Northallerton.

The opposing force had mustered under French land-owners whom the French Archbishop had inspired to united action. On his shoulders the religious mantle of the Conquest had fallen. Norman monastic restoration in Northumbria was imperilled; he stood for protection of the churches against military destructiveness. He had seen

[1] Mary Coleridge.

to it that resistance should be preached, and organized, by his clergy. There had been a general levy. Villages had sent their contingents to the gathering-place, each headed by the priest. An *estandard* had been brought on to Cowton Moor to serve as a rallying-point. It was a ship's mast fixed on a wagon and bearing, high above the banners of St. Peter, St. John of Beverley and St. Wilfrid of Ripon, the sacred Host, that God might be with the army, as on the day of Hastings. *Estandard* is a French word, but the chroniclers think it an English one and associate it with " making a stand ".[1]

The Archbishop, labouring under the weight of years, had journeyed to Roxburgh and averted one invasion by intercession with the Scottish King. But incursions had continued. The country had been laid waste, the churches sacked. At Calder, on the river of that name, near Egremont, the Savignians had been driven out of their monastery; early in the spring the Cistercian abbey founded

---

[1] Standard = O.F. *estandard* : cp. *Chanson de Roland*, ll. 3265 ff. :
> " Li amiralz . . .
> Dedavant sei fait porter sun *dragun*
> E l'*estandart* Tervagan e Mahum ",

where we have both David's *dragon*, which was presumably *not* that of Wessex, and the *estandard* = in OF. (1) a banner, especially one set up as a rallying-point on the battlefield ; and (2) the enclosure round the banner.

H. Hunt., describing the battle at Ashingdon, where Cnut defeated Edmund Ironside, refers to the " draco " and the " insigne quod vocatur Standard " as separate emblems. But this must be an anachronism. The word is not found in English till 1138 ; it comes from OF. *estendre*, Lat. *extendere*, and has no connection with " stand ", or with Latin *stando*, despite the couplet preserved by Richard of Hexham, p. 163, and attributed by him to " Hugo Sotevagina " [Hugue Sottegaine, " Hugh the Cantor "], Archdeacon of York from 1139 :
> " Dicitur a stando Standardum, quod stetit illic
> Militiae probitas, vincere sive mori ".

The Standard of 1138 is defined by H. Hunt. and R. Tor. as *Regium insigne*.

The idea of the wagon was probably suggested by the *Carroccio* (med. Lat. *carrochium*) on which the banner of an Italian town was carried into battle. On the wagon there was an altar, served by priests. The practice is said to have been originated by the Archbishop of Milan when the city was besieged, exactly a hundred years before, in 1038.

by Earl Gospatric's daughter and her Norman husband at Newminster in Northumberland had been brought to naught before it was six weeks in being [1] Some barons had shown indifference. Others had welcomed Scottish raiders led by such kindred spirits as the semi-Norman William fitz Duncan. This time a stand must be made. Most of the Norman barons in the North and some in the South had therefore joined their forces to the Archbishop's levies.

In the dim religious Latin of the chronicles any patriotism except local is hard to discern. Lament is only for the material damage.[2] None but Norman names emerge. The Bishop of Orkney who (in Prior Richard's narrative) is sent out by the Archbishop to preach a holy war in the county was born at York, but he was no more a Yorkshireman than he was an Orcadian. " Radulfus cognomento Nouellus ", Raoul, surnamed Nouel or Le Nouveau,[3] had never even seen his distant diocese. Created by Thorfinn and claimed by Norway, it was represented by a contingent in the invading host.[4] The Bishop's exhortation on the battlefield begins, appropriately : " Proceres Angliae, clarissimi Normannigenae ", " Nobles of

[1] Newminster was founded by Raoul de Merlay and Julienne [Juliana] his wife, daughter of Gospatric II, and was colonized from Fountains in January 1138. Gospatric died in the same year and has been supposed to have fallen at the Standard, because of a reference in *Walter of Coventry*, I, p. 162 : " Percusso sagitta summo duce Loenensium ".

[2] For example, in Serlo's poem, *c.* 1144, in Laur. Durh. p. 75 : " Quod patriae fles *damna* tuae ? "

[3] Someone of the same name, " Randulfus Nuuel ", appears as witness in a (dubious) charter by David [after 1141, as Walter fitz Alan is a witness]. Lawrie, C.

[4] The bishopric of Orkney depended originally on Hamburg-Bremen, but after 1073 came under York. Raoul Nouel [† after 1143] was the third Norman Bishop. He was elected by a delegation of Orkneymen at York and consecrated by Thomas II in 1109. But, because of opposition from Lund and Trondhjem, he never went into residence and acted instead as suffragan of York and Durham. His claim to Orkney was apparently contested in 1125 from Scotland by a certain " Viljam " = Willelme = Guillaume, a clerk of Paris, connected in some way with Melrose. See Brøgger, pp. 156-157 and 164-165. Perhaps he was interim Bishop at St. Andrews : see above, p. 170, n. 3.

England, illustrious Norman-born ".[1]   The strength of the
French element in this Bataille de l'Étendard comes out
clearly in Ailred's account.   The commander of what he
is careful to call the " Southern " army was, according to
him, Walter Espec, but the Abbot magnifies the Founder's
military status.[2]   Guillaume, Comte d'Aumale [Albemarle],
was in command, an unpleasant and a vinous person, adds
the Archdeacon of Huntingdon,[3] who, however, favoured
the other side, as Aumale himself did—afterwards, when
he married William fitz Duncan's daughter.   Among the
" Northerners " were the Justiciar Eustace fitz John, lately
removed by the Usurper from control of Bamburgh, and
Alain de Percy,[4] who owned a little land in Scotland and
much in Yorkshire.

Naturally there had been waverers.   Among them were
Robert de Brus and Bernard de Bailleul.   They were caught
in the unhappy conflict of allegiances to which, as Malcolm
Canmore had pointed out, the Norman-feudal system would
inevitably lead ; they had to serve two lords, the Scottish
and the English Kings.   Their lords were at variance and
loyalty was not divisible.   Only after much searching of
heart had Robert de Brus and Bernard de Bailleul brought
themselves to consider renouncing their fealty to David.
They had been sent forward to hold parley with him on
the eve of battle.   In the moving appeal which Ailred
ascribes to Robert de Brus, the aged warrior, now near
his end, " grave in manner and scant of speech ", implores
David not to join battle with old and well-tried Norman
comrades.   He reminds " my gentlest lord, my most

----

[1] H. Hunt. p. 262.   The Speech is inserted, perhaps interpolated, in
Ailred, *D.B.S.*
[2] Wm. Newb. I, p. 34, though writing history for Rievaulx, does not
mention Walter Espec, nor does he use the word " Standard ".
[3] " Vino redolens ", H. Hunt. p. 264.   Guillaume [† Aug. 20, 1179],
known as " le Gros ", was the third Comte d'Aumale [Aumale, Latin *Alba
Marla*, Seine-Inférieure, arr. Neufchâtel].   He was a son of Étienne, son of
Eude, third husband of the Conqueror's sister Adelaide.
[4] See below, p. 291.

loving friend ", that, but for Norman force of arms, neither he nor his brothers before him would ever have reached the throne. Who but Normans secured him his Cumbrian heritage, which Alexander had tried to withhold ? And who saved him from Malcolm of Moray ? Robert de Brus then intimated that Bernard de Bailleul and he were empowered by King Stephen to offer Northumberland to Henry. David wept. In the moral and social code of an emotional age knights need not repress their tears—or their fury, and William, son of Duncan II, in a wild tirade denounced Robert de Brus as a traitor. As there were formalities and symbols in assuming the bond of fealty, so there were in laying it aside. At an investiture the vassal received from his lord a baton, symbolizing the feudal bond. There was a similar ceremony for ending the contract—the *diffidatio* ; when either lord or vassal had failed to carry out his part of the contract and, after legal complaint, had refused redress, the other had the right to defy him in ritual form, after a year and a day. But Robert de Brus could not wait. " In the ancestral Norman manner " he threw down the token of his enfeoffment,[1] and departed, sad at heart. William fitz Duncan's fierce words had made armed conflict inevitable. For this, and for sacrilege committed by his troops, Divine vengeance, it was thought, was wreaked upon him or upon his unoffending son, " the Boy of Egremont ".[2]

Just before the clash of arms the huge ungainly figure of a man, an ancient of days, but black as the raven, was seen to mount on the wagon of the Standard. It was Walter Espec, and his " trumpet voice " rang out upon the moor, assuredly not in Northumbrian English : " Quit yourselves like Normans ! " he cried. " To our race victory is given as in fee by the Most High.[3] We

---

[1] What the " patrius mos " was, Ailred leaves to his readers. Presumably Robert de Brus threw down a baton.   [2] See Appendix F.

[3] " Cum victoria generi nostro quasi in feudum data sit ab Altissimo."— Ailred, *D.B.S.*

conquered the men of Maine, Anjou and Aquitaine. Remember the deeds of our fathers—at Hastings, in Sicily, Apulia, Calabria.[1] . . . Remember how great William marched into Scotland, even unto Abernethy, where the warlike Malcolm made surrender and became our man. Scottish spears are long, but their shafts are wood. Our arms are steel and we are clad in mail." Normanism is Walter's inspiring theme. The Scots are Norman vassals. The English are not so much as mentioned. Their country is a " conquest ", on the same level as Apulia or Maine. For the Founder of Rievaulx, fighting his battles over again in his own Abbey, where he retired to end his days, or for the Abbot, interpreting the old soldier in flowing Latin periods and indulging a taste for epitome, the salient features of the Conquest are : its nearness in the past, its rapidity, its completeness, its extension to all Britain, its indebtedness to religion, to dependent tenure, to steel and to mail-armour, and, above all, its achievement in Law and Institutions : " Our fathers *and we* quickly mastered *this island*, quickly placed it under *our laws*, subjugated it to *our customs* ".

These sentiments may have been shared by the Normans in Scotland, perhaps conquerors in spirit if not in deed, and an authoritative statement on their war-aims might have been illuminating. But, though David and Henry must have addressed their corps commanders, native and Norman, if not their several hundred Norman knights, their speeches are not reported, an omission all the more regrettable as the battle was in great part one between Normans. On both sides there were barons and knights, demonstrating their fealty (for the time being), some to " l'emperis Mahaut ", most to " le rei Esteven ",

[1] Normans were not likely to forget ; " Normanni se Anglos et Apulos vicisse in suis sedibus gloriabantur "—Ord. Vit. XI, x. A local poet writing at Rouen *c.* 1148 was under the impression that Scotland had been conquered from Rouen and the " Scotus algidus " or half-frozen Scot brought into suitable subjection. His poem is to be found in Haskins, *N.I.* p. 144.

whose adherents had the advantage of fighting "*pro patria*", as the heads of the religious houses at Hexham and Rievaulx well say. In mediaeval Latin *patria* usually means the local neighbourhood, and fighting "*pro patria*" meant to some Normans little more than fighting on home ground for the protection of church property and private property in the "Terra Sancti Cuthberti" and in those parts of Yorkshire which, with great labour and pain, were being reclaimed by the worthy Walter Espec and by an Archbishop from Bayeux, White Monks from Clairvaux and many more good and wise men, mostly French. The Terra included, almost miraculously, the scene of the Saint's first intervention in Norman affairs and the battlefield itself, "a certain field of St. Cuthbert's fief" [*feudum*].[1] Everything has been reduced to Norman-feudal terms. For some Normans on the opposing side *patria* included preservation of their own rights and property, loyalty to "l'emperis", loyalty to her uncle and chivalrous defender, whether as King of Scots or as Earl of Northampton or as Earl of Huntingdon, and to his son, kinsman and namesake of their late King and rightful Earl of Northumberland. As to the Highland contingents who advanced to the war-cry of *Albani, Albani!*, for them *patria* must be given a spacious enough interpretation to admit such parts of Kenneth MacAlpin's dim patrimony as could be regained by large-scale raiding under Norman leadership and under cover of Norman dissensions.

In the rank and file on both sides there were sons of Old Northumbria, separated by the necessity of fighting for Norman overlords, but by no difference in culture, language or race. Except for the trained soldiers from the Boulonnais, Normandy and Flanders in the forefront of the "Southern" army, the only "barbarians" or "foreigners" conspicuous on the moor were the Galwegians, in reference to whom the author of the *Vita Thurstini* wrote

[1] John of Hexham, p. 293.

that " the Scots were preceded by actors, dancers and dancing-girls and we by the cross of Christ and relics of the Saints ".[1] The kilt had given rise to unfortunate misunderstandings.[2] Yet the warriors in unfamiliar garb were sent or, more probably, led by Fergus their Lord, a Norman in his way—by marriage and by religion. Fighting for the Empress, he was fighting for a Norman sister-in-law (his wife Elizabeth was *fille de rei*, being one of the late King Henry's numerous daughters[3]). Many founders of French monasteries were met on Cowton Moor and Fergus was one of them. The presence of his kilted men the " Southerners " resented and the " Northerners " had occasion to regret. The Scots were deficient in mail armour and some of them were critical of their own Norman knights: " Whence arises this mighty confidence in these Normans ? " asked the Earl of Strathearn, Malise, of King David. " I wear no armour, yet they that do will not advance beyond me this day."[4] Alain de Percy was ready with a sharp retort on behalf of the Normans in Scotland, but it was withheld and the imminent quarrel averted. The Galwegians putting forward an alleged traditional right to lead the assault, David, more a judge than a general, allowed their claim and let them try to do by native courage what might have been better done by his own Norman body-guard " which stood around in knightly array ",[5] if not by his son's Norman cavalry. Mounted knights proved ineffective that day. Since a stand must be made, those of the " Southern " army had dismounted to fight on foot with the infantry and those of David's body-guard

[1] In Raine, *York*, II, pp. 259-269.

[2] The kilt was much in evidence not only on Cowton Moor, but in scurrilous contemporary verse. The " dancers ", though not the " dancing-girls ", may represent continuance of Irish custom in the Isles and in the West and South-West of Scotland. " The Irish were accustomed to take the field in fine clothes and fringed mantles and gay tunics and to be accompanied by poets, musicians, jugglers and jesters."—Hodgkin, *A-S.* p. 489.

[3] See note by Stubbs, ed. Hoveden, II, p. 63.

[4] Ailred, *D.B.S.* Malise († 1150) was Earl of Strathearn from before 1124.

[5] John of Hexham, p. 294.

had done likewise, perhaps to show that there would be no turning back.

His order of battle was : first line, Galwegians ; second line, household cavalry (Norman) and men of " Cumbria and Teviotdale ", commanded by Henry, as Prince of Cumbria, with them being Eustace fitz John and his followers ; third line, men of Lothian and men of Lennox, brigaded with Islesmen ; fourth line, in reserve, " Scots " and men of Moray [the Highland Brigade] and the Royal body-guard of knights under the King's own command. All-steel spears and mail-armour proving superior to Galwegian wooden shaft and leathern buckler, the attack failed. There was a moment of panic. The cry arose that David was slain. Like Duke William on the field of Hastings, he threw back his helmet and showed his face, but as at Hastings Norman archery prevailed. David was " forced by the older men to call for the horses and withdraw with his own compact squadron ",[1] while the rest of the host was driven off the moor in disorder. Henry's knights, who had not dismounted, had been more spectacular than effective. They charged too well and drew rein too late, and found themselves cut off from the main body in retreat. On his orders they cast away their bannerets, mingled with the remounted and pursuing horsemen and, being indistinguishable from them by accoutrement or language or equestrian skill, caused yet further misunderstanding [2] and rode back, though with heavy losses, to the Scottish base at Carlisle. Northallerton is, like Alnwick, a gap made for the passage of armies. As Malcolm Canmore was stopped at Alnwick, so his youngest son was stopped at Northallerton. But perhaps for the

[1] John of Hexham, p. 294.
[2] At the battle of Brémule [Eure, arr. des Andelys], fought on August 20, 1119, the tactics were surprisingly similar : " Petrus de Manlia, aliique nonnulli fugientium, cognitiones suas, ne agnoscerentur, projecerunt, et insectantibus callide mixti signum triumphantium vociferati sunt."—Ord. Vit. XII, xviii. King Louis ordered his knights to dismount, so that they might fight the more desperately. Suger's *Life of Louis VI*, pp. 193-197.

" Southerners " it was no great victory. They made no attempt to follow up the advantage and recover the territory ceded to Scotland. It was only for defence they had gathered, only for making a stand.

The military reverse which David suffered for one French niece was turned into a diplomatic victory by the other. The way for peace was prepared by a Legate, the first since John of Crema. He was Aubry [Alberic], a monk of Cluny, French by birth,[1] become Bishop of Ostia. His mission extended to Scotland. From Durham, where he set free David's Chancellor, Comyn, captured on the Moor, he proceeded " through a wilderness " to Hexham and thence to Carlisle. He arrived on September 26, only a month after the battle. The relations between the See of Glasgow and the See of Carlisle carved out of it were adjusted ; the religious David was rebuked for the excesses of troops as much beyond his control on the march as on the Moor, and was adjured to enter into peace negotiations. Three days later the Legate departed.

He departed for Westminster, to hold a Synod in the Abbey. Ailred devoted a lifetime to the same journey, spiritually—from Durham and Hexham to the Scottish Court and thence to the Tomb of Edward. The Prior of Westminster, Osbert (of Clare in Suffolk), presented the Legate with a dedicated copy of a " Life of Edward " on which he had been long engaged, and asked him to support a request for canonization which he proposed making at Rome. To seek Papal authority had become necessary for two reasons : a Legate was at Westminster and the Saint already popularly canonized there was a King. " Exaltatio Sanctorum " was, as the Prior pointed out, part of a Legate's duty. And the question of sainthood had dynastic implications, for *who* was Edward's spiritual heir and rightful successor on the throne ? Was it the Empress, granddaughter of the Conqueror and daughter of " the good

[1] John of Hexham, p. 297.

Queen Maud, St. Edward's niece ", or was it Stephen, grandson of the Conqueror, but related to the Old English House only by marriage ? Osbert received some encouragement from the Legate and proceeded to Rome, carrying his work with him. The result of his pleading, and his reading, was that two letters left the Lateran on the same day (December 9, 1139). One was for the faithful in general, commending the virtues of Prior Osbert, but postponing canonization on the ground of insufficient testimony of bishops and abbots, " for since so great a festival must be for the honour and profit of the whole realm, so must it also be called for by the whole realm ". The other letter was for King David, urging him to complete arrangements for the anniversary of his sister Maud, buried beside Edward in the Abbey.[1] Thus closely in religious minds were the Scottish and the Norman reigning families linked together by the Holy King.

St. Margaret, his kinswoman, was the special veneration of Maud, her granddaughter, wife of one incensed monarch and niece of the other. War had not weakened Queen Maud's affection for her Scottish relatives and, being a woman of singular charm, ability and persistence,[2] she had contrived to obtain powers from her husband to negotiate peace on the basis of the grant of Northumberland to her cousin Henry. She had gone to meet Henry at Durham, where, on April 9, 1139, a treaty had been signed. The peace was a Norman family arrangement, intended to allay the dissensions among the Conqueror's next of kin and their feudal dependants. Henry was confirmed in the fiefs he had been granted by Stephen in 1136. He received, with the title of Earl, all Northumberland—except the fortresses of Bamburgh and Newcastle and the Priory lands at Hexham—while his father obtained some portion

---

[1] Williamson, p. 3.

[2] As Prior Richard of Hexham expresses it : " Feminei pectoris ardor vinci nescius quibuscunque potuit modis nocte ac die stimulando non destitit, donec regium animum ad suam voluntatem detorsit ".

of the Honour of Lancaster and was left in undisturbed possession of Carlisle and Southern Cumbria.[1] So through French feminine diplomacy and Scoto-Norman family sentiment was Malcolm Canmore's territorial expansion policy achieved and Kenneth MacAlpin's ancient dream made true. The frontier stood on the Derwent and the Tyne. David's Normans had done the State some service.

[1] David, debarred by his oath of allegiance to the Empress from acknowledging Stephen as King, held Southern Cumbria (Westmorland and Cumberland) in her interests, which of late he had much neglected. Earl Henry held Northumberland of Stephen.

CHAPTER VI

THE YEARS OF CONSOLIDATION
(1139–1153)

★

§ 21

The Great Norman Families

THE barons of Northumberland swore fealty to the new
Earl, on condition that he preserved " the laws and customs
of King Henry " unaltered. This Henry's kinsman
and namesake promised to do—the more easily as they
were already much in honour in the Scottish realm.
Hostages were sent to England. Their choice is illuminating. Richard of Hexham specifies not them, but their
fathers, evidently assumed to be the chief men in the
country: Hugue de Morville, Fergus of Galloway and
the Earls of Dunbar, Fife and Strathearn—one Norman,
one Norman King's son-in-law, two Norman sympathizers
in the Lowlands [1] and one critical observer in Strathearn.
Earl Henry also went to England, but to join in the activities
against the party of his cousin the Empress, and, when so
engaged, further distinguished himself as a Norman Knight,
by *largesse* and *élégance* and *prouesse*. At the siege of
Ludlow Castle, being caught by a grappling-iron and nearly
dragged off his horse, he was saved from an ignominious
end by the prompt intervention of the no less knightly
King Stephen.

At Nottingham, where the peace was formally ratified,
Earl Henry married Ada or Adeline, daughter of Guillaume
de Varenne (the rejected suitor of 1100) and, as the *Melrose
Chronicle* notes with pride, niece of a French King. What
is more important in Royal genealogy is that Adeline was
the descendant of one, and that her sons (Malcolm IV,

---

[1] To judge from the prevalence of Norman names in the family. Duncan
(† 1154), who in 1136 succeeded his father Gillemichel, son of Constantin,
as Earl of Fife, had a brother named Hugue. The Gospatrics of Dunbar
had long-standing Norman associations.

William the Lion and David of Huntingdon) were born into the House of Capet. Her kinsmen were among the greatest Normans in England.[1] " Bound by such relationship, Earl Henry adhered closely to the friendship of the Normans and the English."[2] His Household was as French as his father's. He had a Chancellor, Enguerrand, and a Constable, Gilbert, and his charters are attested by David's original Normans and only a few new-comers, of whom the most noteworthy is " Willelmus Masculus ", Guillaume le Mâle, Scotland's first Maule.[3] With him in

FRENCH ANCESTRY OF SCOTTISH KINGS

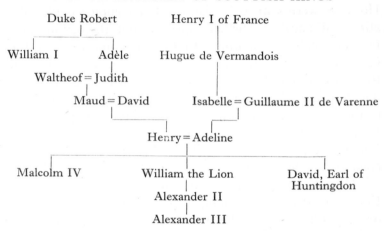

Duke Robert   Henry I of France

William I   Adèle   Hugue de Vermandois

Waltheof = Judith

Maud = David   Isabelle = Guillaume II de Varenne

Henry = Adeline

Malcolm IV   William the Lion   David, Earl of Huntingdon

Alexander II

Alexander III

[1] Adeline's mother, Isabel, was the daughter of Hugue, Comte de Vermandois, younger son of Henry I of France. Isabel was twice married. Her first husband was Robert de Beaumont († 1118), Comte de Meulan ; by him she had three sons : Robert (1104–1168), Justiciary, Earl of Leicester ; Waleran, Comte de Meulan, and Hugue. Robert and Waleran were twins. Her second husband was Guillaume de Varenne († 1138), second Earl of Surrey ; their elder daughter Gondrée or Gondrade [Gundrada] was the wife of Roger de Beaumont, Earl of Warwick ; the younger daughter was Adeline.   [2] Ord. Vit. XIII, xxxvii.

[3] " Willelmus Masculus " acquired the lands of Foulis in Perthshire. He granted, *c.* 1160, a charter of confirmation of the land of Kathelach to Alan son of Simon and, *c.* 1165, gave to the Canons of St. Andrews the chapel of Foulis, with the land which belonged to the chapel " before Foulis was given to me ", adding himself ten acres and the tithes and oblations belonging to the chapel. He witnessed a charter by Duncan, Earl of Fife, along with " Rogerus Masculus " and Osbern " Masculus " and the native bearer of an

the same charter [1] are : Robert fitz Turet, of whom nothing else is known, and Robert Foliot, who had connections with Melrose and who acted as Earl Henry's dapifer in Huntingdon.[2]

The Countess Adeline no doubt brought a numerous suite, to which Alexander de Saint-Martin may have belonged or may have afterwards been attached. After her husband's death in 1152 Alexander's name appears with hers in various charters, relating mostly to Haddington, which she held in dower, and to Fife, where she had properties.[3] He held of the Countess (" domina mea ") the land of Langelaw. During the minority of her son Malcolm IV her influence must have been considerable and perhaps it was then that Alexander and his family acquired their importance. He had a brother called Adolphe who had the misfortune to kill accidentally, while hunting, Hugue de Morville's son Malcolm. Alexander's charters are of interest, showing as they do the greater precision found at least in private charters after David's reign.[4] An

impressive name, Madecher mac Mathusalem. William's grant of the chapel of Foulis is confirmed by his grandson " Hugo de mortuo mari ", Hugue de Mortimer. *St. Andrews*, pp. 41, 242, 265, 306, 325.

[1] Round, *Cal.* I, p. 357 ; *Hist. Northd.* VIII, p. 60, n.

[2] Lawrie, CXIV and CXV, c. 1136. He witnesses Malcolm IV's Confirmation of gifts of land to Melrose. *Melrose*, No. VIII.

[3] *E.g.* in her grant, at Perth, of a toft in Haddington to Dunfermline Abbey. Lawrie, LX.

[4] For his holding at Alstaneford see above, pp. 214 and 224. He gave Langelaw to Dryburgh. His formula was : " Dedi et presentis scripti pagina munivi . . . una nocte vel una die tenendam de me et heredibus meis ". The gift was made for the soul of Malcolm de Morville " in reconciliationem et pacem " of Richard de Morville the Constable, and of all the said Malcolm's kin, and of his own kin and the kin of Adolphe [" Adulphus "] his brother, who accidentally killed Malcolm de Morville [the Constable's brother] while hunting. *Dryburgh*, p. 69. The gift was confirmed, p. 69, by the Countess Adeline and separately, p. 70, by King William. Alexander granted to Newbattle part of his peatery or peat-bog—a grant witnessed by his wife " Basilla ". *Newbattle*, p. 76, No. CI. He gave or bequeathed to his daughter " Ada " a share in the firm of the mill of Alstaneford. *Holyrood*, p. 26. Another daughter, Ela, had a life-rent of the land of Barewe from the Priory of May, " reddendo nobis inde annuatim iiij solidos . . . Et ut haec donatio et concessio rata sit et stabilis, utrique parti placuit presentis scripti interposicione et sigillorum apposicione eam roborare ". Besides

undoubted member of her suite is Guillaume Giffard who is designated " clericus Comitissae ".[1] The Hugue Giffard who is mentioned with him and who was probably a relative appears to have become the first Lord of Yester.[2] The name Giffard was widespread in England from the earliest days of the Conquest. Other Normans first mentioned in the years round 1140 are " Wilhelmus de Lamberton " [3] and Robert Frebern, who is the reputed name-father of the Fairbairns, though it seems obvious that many " fair bairns " must owe their surname to causes quite unconnected with Robert.[4] " Petrus filius Kercembaldi " had arrived in the Kingdom in time to be mentioned in the Royal charter to Newbattle, given at Edinburgh in

" domina Ela de Sancto-Martino " the witnesses include " Gilebertus de Sancto Martino " and his son " Radulphus ". *May*, No. XXXIV. But Gilbert is later styled " Gilbertus de Berewe qui dicitur de Sancto Martino ". *May*, No. XXXIII. " Radulphus " gave, after 1199, the church of Boweltun to Holyrood, saving his right to the church during his own lifetime. *Holyrood*, p. 27.

[1] " Willelmus Giffard " perambulated with King David and Herbert the Chancellor the vill of Rindalgros [in the parish of Rhynd, Perthshire] and witnessed the Countess Adeline's grants of land at Crail. *St. Andrews*, pp. 208 and 249; *Dunfermline*, p. 88. In the last of these grants he is accompanied by Hugue Giffard.

[2] " Ada comitissa mater regis scot." [Malcolm IV] gave to the church of St. Andrews and the hospital " totam terram de Pethmulin, sicut Hugo Giffard eam perambulaverat ". *St. Andrews*, p. 209. Hugue Giffard appears in Royal charters till after 1189. He was one of the hostages in 1174. *Inchaffray*, p. 304.

[3] " Willelmus de Lamberton " witnesses with Robert Frebern a grant given by David at Berwick *c*. 1136. Lawrie, CVIII. " Lambertonus " and " Lamberton Dapifer ", found in charters from *c*. 1138, may be the same person. Lamberton is no doubt the place on the high road near Berwick, which dates its wider fame only from 1753, when, because of legislation in that year, it became the goal for eloping couples in the East, as Gretna was in the West.

[4] Robert Frebern, who attests no other charter by David, is mentioned (*Newbattle*, No. III, p. 4) as having perambulated lands granted to Newbattle Abbey by Malcolm IV and, later (*Dunfermline*, p. 91), as having witnessed a grant to Dunfermline Abbey by Geoffroi de Maleville. Robert Frebern had a son Roger, and in the following century there were Freberns of Lamberton who were probably Roger's descendants. There is a charter by Malcolm IV (*Miscell. Spalding Club*, 1852, p. 241) confirming to " Radulphus Frebern " the lands of Rossive and Dunduf [near Maybole (Ayrshire)]. The signatories include the unfortunate " Willelmus de Eggremont " (see Appendix F). The name " Frebernus " appears in the *Liber Vitae*, p. 61.

1142.[1] His father has been the victim of a scribal error ; he was " Erchembaldus " and, if he came to Scotland with the son, he is her first known Archibald.[2] But among those who about this time brought a Norman name for ever to Scotland perhaps a greater merit attaches to " Galfridus de Mailvil ", *alias* " Galfridus de Malevin ", for he brought two, Melville and Melvin. Under the former name he witnessed at Forfar the grant of Alstaneford to Alexander de Saint-Martin,[3] but when he gave the church of " Maleville " to the Abbey of Dunfermline " for the souls of King David and Malcolm Junior " he gave it as " Galfridus de Maleuin ".[4] He is found with both names in the reign of " Malcolm Junior ", nearly always at a perambulation of boundaries. " Malavilla " is evidently Maleville in the Pays de Caux ; " Malevin " may be Malevigne. Melvilles long continued to call themselves Melvins and vice versa.[5] The name Avenel vanished all too soon from the records, and has now but the wistful melancholy of things past. It came with Robert Avenel, whom David settled in Eskdale, and it died out in the year 1243.[6]

[1] Lawrie, CXLVI. Cp. *c.* 1144, *Kelso*, p. 153, "Archebaldus forestarius ".

[2] The name Archibald was represented at Hastings by Erchembald, son of Erchembald the Vicomte. " Archembaldus " witnesses a charter of Bishop Ernout (1160 × 1162) with his father " Suanus de Foregrund " and his brother " Hugo ". *St. Andrews*, p. 130. In the early years of William the Lion he witnesses, as " Archibaldus de Forgrund ", a charter of " Willelmus Masculus de Foules ". *St. Andrews*, p. 265.

[3] Lawrie, CLXXXVI.

[4] *Dunfermline*, p. 91, No. CLVIII, " pro animabus D. regis et Malcolmi Junioris ". The confirmation by Bishop Hugh of St. Andrews (*Dunfermline*, p. 60) bears " ecclesia de *Maleuill* quam Galfridus de *Maleuin* dedit ". The witnesses to Geoffrey's gift were, among others, his sons Thomas, Robert, Hugh, Richard and Walter. Malcolm IV gives to Holyrood the church of Batket [Bathgate] with all the land which " Galfridus de Maleuill " and Vhtred of Linlithgow perambulated " die illa qua eos misi videre terram eandem ". *Newbattle*, p. 228. " Galfridus de Maleuill" attends the perambulation of Lethendy, with " Nessus filius Willelmi ". *Inchaffray*, No. IV. He is said to have owned Kinblethmont.

[5] See J. B. Johnston, *s.v.* MELVILLE.

[6] Avenel is a frequent name in the ducal charters in Normandy. Haskins, *N.I.* p. 139. Robert Avenel († 1185) perhaps belonged to the Northamptonshire family which was represented in 1161 by " Willelmus Avenel ". *Red Bk. Exch.* p. 31. He may be the " Robertus Avenellensis " who witnesses

When Robert de Brus dramatically threw down his baton and renounced his fealty to King David he did not throw away the family's chances in Scotland. On his death, May 5, 1141, he left his English possessions to the elder of his two sons, Adam, but he had already made over Annandale to the younger, Robert, who had fallen into his hands as a prisoner and had been placed in the custody of his mother at Annan, with the good-natured Stephen's approval. The young man having complained that Annandale did not grow wheat fit for his consumption, his father rectified this by a grant of supplementary wheat-producing ploughgates at Skelton in Yorkshire. The history of the Normans in Scotland thus continues as before, with a Robert de Brus maintained partly on Scottish land and partly on English, regulating his periods of residence according to the seasons and the state of the crops, and re-issuing at suitable intervals the paternal ukase : " omnibus hominibus suis Francis et Anglis presentibus et futuris de Valle Annant ".[1]

But three of the greatest names have still to come : Oliphant, Stewart and Comyn. Stephen having been taken prisoner at Lincoln, on February 2, 1141, and " deposed ", David's triumphant niece assumed the title " Lady of England ", and after Ascension Day he went south to arrange for her Coronation.[2] His allegiance had been fitful, he was heavily compromised by his dealings, and

the grant to Tiron, *c.* 1138 (Lawrie, CXXXVI), and, more probably, the " Robert Eunel " who witnesses the charter concerning Alexander de Saint-Martin (*ibid.* CLXXXVI). Robert Avenel received from David lands in Upper and Lower Eskdale and in the west of Fife. His wife was " Sibilla ". With the consent of his nephew and heir " Geruasius de Eincurt " he gave, 1175 × 1185, to the Abbey of Melrose " terram meam de Eschedale [Eskdale] pro anima domini mei regis David qui eandem terram dedit pro servicio meo ". *Melrose*, p. 30, No. XXXIX. Gervais d'Eincourt [? Aincourt, near Mantes] owned Basselawe. Bain, *Cal.* I, p. 7. Robert was a Justiciar in 1175. *St. Andrews*, p. 221. He afterwards became a *conversus* at Melrose. The last member of the family in the direct line seems to have been Roger Avenel († 1243). His daughter and heiress married Henry de Graham, into whose hands the Avenel estates passed. They then included Abercorn.

[1] *E. Yks. Ch.* II, p. 4.   [2] Round, *G.M.* p. 80.

his son's dealings, with the Interloper and he was not very well received. But while attending her Court in July he found solace in the company of fellow-sufferers, her chief supporters, who, like him, were kept in their proper place and had to present their petitions on bended knee, and wait long on bended knee till the stony silence was broken and the petition granted or, more often, refused.[1] They included the Lady of England's gifted half-brother Earl Robert of Gloucester, and two Shropshire friends of his, William and Walter, sons of Alain. In September her forces were defeated at Winchester and "the Scot King", having narrowly escaped being taken prisoner in the rout, hastened home, accompanied by Walter fitz Alan and by the young man who had saved him from capture, his godson and Northamptonshire vassal, David Olifart or Olifard.[2]

The signal service Olifart had rendered—perhaps not so much to "the Scot King" as to the Earl of Northampton, of whom he held Lilford on the Nen—brought him rich territorial reward in Scotland, where the family name, eventually toned down to Oliphant, was borne with distinction by numerous descendants.[3] Walter fitz Alan's

---

[1] *Gesta Stephani*, p. 76.

[2] John of Hexham, p. 311, who gives the name as Holifard, a spelling found also in thirteenth-century Scottish documents. The author of the *Gesta Stephani*, unimpressed, roundly states, p. 85, that King David was taken prisoner three times and each time obtained release by means of bribes.

[3] Lilford, the family possession, was held by the Countess Judith in Domesday. The earliest recorded member of the house is Roger Olifard, who witnessed Earl Simon's charter to the Priory of St. Andrew, Northampton, *c.* 1108. Somewhat later, Hugue Olifard of Stoke (Northants.) is a Knight of Peterborough. *Black Book of Peterborough*, p. 175. The Northampton Survey (Hen. I–Hen. II), part of which is printed by Round, *F.E.* pp. 215-219, has, p. 216: "HOKESLAWE : In Lilleford Willelmus Olyfart v. hidas de feudo Regis Scotie".

David Olifard witnesses Scottish charters from 1144. He made a grant of land in Smalham to Dryburgh, confirmed by Malcolm IV. *Dryburgh*, pp. 109-110. His name is in the *Liber Vitae*, p. 57. Osbert Olifard was Lord of Arbuthnot, in the episcopate of Richard of St. Andrews (1163–78). Skene, III, p. 260. Johan, wife of a David Olifard, received, 1214 × 1227, from the Bishop of Glasgow a grant for life of one-third of the lands of Cadder on the Kelvin. *O.P.* I, p. 50. Walter Olifard († 1242) was lord

assistance was recognized by grants of lands which he held for the service of five knights and which eventually comprised the present county of Renfrew. He rose to be David's chief " Norman ", but he was not of Norman birth. He was the second son of a Breton knight, Alain, and Ada or Adeline, daughter of Ernulf de Hesdin.[1] In the opinion of the Stewart genealogists, Alain's father Flaald was none other than Fleance, son of Banquo, Thane of Lochaber, and had escaped from Macbeth's clutches to find a home in Brittany. In reality, Flaald was the son of an Alain who had been Dapifer to the Archbishop of Dol, possibly the Dapifer and Crusader of that name and in any case an important personage, for the Archbishops had an extensive temporal lordship on the lower course of the Couesnon.[2] Dol is the nearest town to the Mont-Saint-Michel and it was no doubt thus that Flaald and his son Alain had come to the favourable notice of Henry, who soon after his accession invited Alain to England with other Breton friends, and gave him forfeited lands in Norfolk and Shropshire.[3] Probably Alain's headquarters were in the latter county and his duties included supervision of

of the manor of Bothwell. He was Justiciar of Lothian in 1229, and witnesses the Foundation Charter of Balmerino in that year. William Olifard witnesses several charters of Alexander II, 1245 × 1249. Philip, a bailie of Perth, and William Olifard were presumably his sons. Their sons were undoubtedly the two Sir William Olifards who distinguished themselves by the defence of Stirling Castle in 1304. See *Inchaffray*, p. 291.

[1] J. H. Round, *Studies in Peerage*, p. 123 ; *D.N.B. s.v.* ERNULF ; see also above, p. 98.

[2] " Alanus, dapifer sacrae ecclesiae Dolensis archiepiscopi ", accompanied Duke Robert to the Crusade—as mentioned by Baudry de Bourgueil, *H.C.* IV, p. 32, and Ord. Vit. IX, viii. It is conceivable that he was the father of Flaald. Crusaders were often elderly (*e.g.* Ernulf and Bishop Odo). The grandfather Alain may have been on Crusade before the grandson Alain left Brittany for England. According to Bower, Barbour (presumably in his lost " Stewart's Original ") maintained *inter alia* that the Stewarts took their descent from Fleance and that one of their ancestors, " Alan Stewart ", was present at the capture of Antioch [1098]. See *The Buik of Alexander*, S.T.S. (1925), I, p. ccxvii, n. 16.

[3] Alan son of Flaald († *c.* 1114) founded Sporle Priory in Norfolk. His lands were : part of those of Ernulf de Hesdin and Robert de Bellême, and a fief in Norfolk.

the Welsh border. His eldest son had been made Sheriff of Shropshire by Stephen in 1137, but soon afterwards joined the opposing party with Robert of Gloucester, whose niece he had married. The second son Walter also rallied to the support of the Empress. Her cause lost, he became, appropriately, David's Dapifer or Steward. He was the most successful of all the younger sons who founded a family in Scotland. His office of Dapifer being made in 1158 hereditary, his descendants took their name from it, and, after ruling over Renfrew and much else as fitz Alans, reigned over Scotland as Stewarts.[1]

David Olifard and Walter fitz Alan came into the Kingdom as barons with the highest status, the same status as that of the most favoured first-comers.[2] On the arrival of Richard Comyn or Comin soon after them, King David may be said to have accomplished the number of his elect. Richard might be variously classed—as Bishop's Nephew, as Refugee from the Anarchy, or as Friend of Earl Henry. Richard's uncle was David's Chancellor William Comyn, a Norman born in England and educated from boyhood by Henry's Chancellor Geoffrey le Roux [Gaufridus Rufus], Bishop of Durham from 1133. When the Bishop died, the Lady of England in her brief day of authority nominated Comyn as his successor and, had she been

---

[1] Walter son of Alan († 1177) married " Eschina ", daughter and heiress of Uchtred (" Uctredus filius Liolfi "). Lyulf appears in Earl David's Foundation Charter to Selkirk (Kelso) and, before 1136, held land near Coldingham. Uchtred granted to the Abbey of Kelso, before 1152, the church of Molle [now Mow, in the parish of Morebattle (Roxburghshire)]. Molle was part of the land which Oswy, King of Northumbria, gave to St. Cuthbert. *O.P.* I, p. 405. Walter's widow married Henry de Molle ; see *O.P.* I, p. 413. On the hereditary Stewardship see below, p. 364.

[2] They are soon to be found sitting in Edinburgh Castle, with Hugue de Morville the Constable and Guillaume de Sommerville, as a sort of Privy Council, at which " in the presence of King David and Earl Henry and their *barons* " an agreement was made between the Bishop of St. Andrews and the Abbot of Dunfermline concerning the chapel of the castle of Stirling. Lawrie, CLXXXII, 1147 × 1150. The ecclesiastical importance of the agreement is shown in *O.P.* I, p. xxix.

crowned, would have given him the ring and staff.[1] The appointment, made on David's recommendation, was unpopular at Durham and was not maintained, but it was a natural enough outcome of Comyn's career, that of an official trained in the Norman King's Chancery, an Archdeacon (of Worcester) and a Chancellor (David's). He himself has only a dubious celebrity as the intruding Bishop of Durham, but his name, carried on by his nephew Richard, became a famous one in Scotland. It was derived, Wyntoun firmly believed, from the fact that William the Lion selected a member of the family as *ostiarius*,

> Kepare of his chawmyre dure.
> Na langage couythe he spek clerly
> Bot his awyne langage of Normondy.

Nevertheless, the Door-ward learned the strict minimum of official phraseology and could exclaim on the appropriate occasions : " Cum in, cum in ! " But Wyntoun was a man without guile,[2] and it was from Earl Henry that Richard Comyn obtained his first Scottish lands. Through his marriage with Donald Bane's granddaughter, he had descendants in the line of succession to the throne. In less than a hundred years the Comyns " rose ", said George Buchanan, " to a height of power such as no other family in the land had ever reached before or obtained in any after time ".[3]

[1] Round, *G.M.* p. 86.

[2] On the origin of the name see above, p. xx, n. 1. But there is no reason to suppose any connection between the Bishop and the Conqueror's ill-fated Earl.

[3] The intruding Bishop, who had the support of neighbouring barons, Bernard de Bailleul among them, and held the temporalities of the see from 1141 to 1144, distributed land very freely. Contin. Sim. Durh. I, p. 146. In the Terra Sancti Cuthberti, at Northallerton, he built a castle which, after his expulsion in 1144, his nephew Richard was by a compromise permitted to hold under the See of Durham. Richard's wife was Hextilda, daughter of Huctred of Tynedale and Bethoc, only child of Donald Bane ; Sir Thomas Gray, in *Scalachronica* (Leland's transcription, p. 320), has an interesting but confused story about their marriage. Richard Comyn received, from Earl Henry, Linton Roderick, *i.e.* West Linton (Peebles). He gave the church to the Abbey of Kelso (as mentioned in 1159 in *Kelso*, No. I) and, 1165 × 1190,

At the age of sixty or more David had learned wisdom. After the escapade at Winchester he stayed at home and cultivated his garden, " employed his leisure in planting herbs and grafting shoots, even in the last years of his life ",[1] and only once, in 1149, made a brief departure from the ways of peace. Serene upon the heights of fame and power, renowned far beyond his realm for the most exemplary devotion to the Church, associated in men's minds with the rise and fall of princes, he ruled with acknowledged authority over dominions beyond his Celtic forefathers' fondest dreams. His Earldom of Northampton indeed was lost, but he possessed in his own name or in his son's name the Earldom of Huntingdon, Doncaster, the whole of Cumbria, and nearly all Northumberland. His Kingdom extended to the Tees ; [2] with parts of the Honour of Lancaster, his feudal authority reached to the shores of Morecambe Bay.[3] The future of his line seemed assured. Earl Henry, who held some part of South Scotland as the usual appanage [4] and who had been made to attest charters from boyhood,[5] perhaps in order that his succession might come to be regarded as a matter of course,

---

the whole land of Slipperfield to the Abbey of Holyrood, the latter grant being confirmed by his son William. *O.P.* I, p. 190. John Cumyn of Tyne-dale and Badenoch, one of the Competitors in 1291, was the great-great-grandson of Richard and Hextilda ; see Round, *The Ancestor*, X (July 1904), p. 105. The power of the Comyns was established when William Comyn, Justiciar, obtained, 1211 × 1214, the Earldom of Buchan by his marriage with the daughter of the last native Earl. Skene, III, p. 70 ; see also *Inchaffray*, p. lxxix.   [1] Fordun, V, xxix, p. 240.

[2] Wm. Newb. I, c. xxii, p. 127, says that " the Northern district which had passed into the power of David as far as the Tees remained in peace because of that King's efficiency (*industria*) ". Wyntoun's definition (VII, 1054) of what " the Kyng Davy wan till his Crown " was all the land from the Tees to the Tweed :

" And fra the wattyr of Esk the est
Till off Stanemore the Rere-Cross west ".

[3] For the Honour of Lancaster see Appendix F, p. 403, n. 1.

[4] That Henry had the same rights in South Scotland as his father had had under Alexander is obvious, *e.g.* from his own charter (Lawrie, CXCIII).

[5] *E.g. c.* 1128, in David's Charter to the Church of St. Cuthbert in Edinburgh. Lawrie, LXXII.

had been formally recognized as " rex designatus ".[1] His marriage with Adeline de Varenne was blessed with numerous offspring. He was a celebrated knight, a prince of high promise, of whom all men spoke well. St. Bernard, relating the journey of the Irish saint, Malachy, through Scotland on his way to Clairvaux, tells how he "healed King David's son, who was sick unto death. . . . This is Henry, for he still lives, a brave and prudent Knight, taking after his father, they say, in following after righteousness and the love of truth." [2]

The new Norman names appearing in David's remaining years (1145–1153) are few in number, and it may well be that their bearers when they are first mentioned had already been in Scotland for some time. Walter de Bidun, member of a Northamptonshire family, afterwards Chancellor, is likely to have come before 1145.[3] When " Ness son of William " is first mentioned—towards 1150, as cosignatory with another landowner in the district of Tranent —he was, or was about to be, a grandfather. His baptismal name is Scottish, not Norman, and the known circumstances make it probable that he was the son of an early Norman immigrant and a Scottish lady, and was born in Scotland before David came to the throne. Ness inherited lands in Fife, Perth and Lothian, probably not from the unidentified Guillaume who was his father, but from his mother, of name unknown. Lord of Leuchars, where he lived in lordly style, with as many Norman household

---

[1] Charter by Bishop Robert, dated 1144, *St. Andrews*, p. 123 : " Henricus comes et rex designatus " ; charter by David, *ibid.* p. 190 : " deo donante heres meus et rex designatus ". There is not much difference between Tanist and " rex designatus " and it seems probable, as in the case of his uncle Edmund, that Henry had been " elected " at a meeting of some such body as would choose a Tanist.

[2] St. Bernard, *Life of St. Malachy*, p. 76. At Clairvaux Malachy died, November 2, 1148, in the arms of St. Bernard, who then declared him a Saint. He was afterwards canonized.

[3] Walter de Bidun witnesses David's gift of Rhynd in Perthshire to the Abbey of Reading, 1143 × 1147. He appears several times as Chancellor, *e.g.* in the Roxburgh charter of 1159.

officers as his neighbour the Bishop of St. Andrews, Ness, Sheriff of Perth from at least 1160, was actively engaged in perambulating extensive boundaries after David and Malcolm IV had come and gone.[1] He gave his daughter and heiress the name Orable, popular in the *chansons de geste*, and afterwards in Scotland (as Arabella). Her son, Saher de Quincy, became one of the greatest magnates in England as well as in Scotland and died Earl of Winchester. Ness son of William was the founder of the very beautiful Romanesque church at Leuchars, of which the chancel and the apse still remain.[2]

His daughter Orable's matrimonial history is mysterious, the more so because she confirmed his grant of the church of Leuchars to St. Andrews as " Comitissa de Mar " [3] and the Earldom of Mar through the ages has provided the law-courts with problems for which, insoluble though they may be, some practical solution must be found. Orable was undoubtedly the wife of Robert de Quincy. Robert's

---

[1] " Nes (Neis, Ness, Nessus, Nessius) filius Willelmi " appears very frequently in Royal charters, mostly relating to Tranent, Fife and Perth. In the grant of the church of Tranent made by " Thorus son of Swain " (*Holyrood*, p. 11 ; Lawrie, CCXIV, *c.* 1150) " Neis filius Chilu' " is evidently the same person ; cp. *K*ilvert for *G*ilbert (below, p. 372). Once he appears as " Nessius filius Willelmi *Lineth* " (*Scone*, p. 5, Confirmation Charter by Malcolm IV in 1164), but " Lineth " seems odd and may be a scribal error. The name Ness is recorded in Scotland before. The Canons of St. Andrews had a *Nota* (*St. Andrews*, p. 115) saying that Ethelred, Earl of Fife and Abbot of Dunkeld, gave Admore to the Culdees " in juuenili etate " and that the gift was confirmed by his brothers Alexander [therefore before 1124] and David in the presence of Earl Constantin and Nesse and Cormac, son of Macbeath. As Ness son of William had a brother Constantin (Grant by Malcolm IV, before 1160, *Dunfermline*, p. 23) and a son Constantin, and another son " Patricius " (*St. Andrews*, p. 290), and as the succession to his estates suggests that they had come into the family through his mother, it seems likely that he had maternal connections with the native nobility. His properties included the part of Gask in Perthshire which was called by his name Nesgask or Gaskness (*Inchaffray*, p. xlix). In 1175 he was one of the sureties for the Treaty of Falaise, several of whom were elderly, as he must have been.

[2] Ness granted Leuchars to St. Andrews, 1172 × 1183. The various charters referring to the grant probably fall within these dates. The church was built 1183 × 1187.

[3] *St. Andrews*, p. 827.

father, or perhaps uncle, was Saher de Quincy, son of another Saher, and owner of Buckby in Northamptonshire in 1158; he is last mentioned in 1162.[1] Robert's mother was Matilda de Saint-Liz, whose precise relationship to David's Queen is unknown. The de Quincy family were tenants of the Honour of Huntingdon and held Eynesbury.[2] When Robert de Quincy married Orable he obtained with her considerable lands in Fife and Lothian.[3] The known facts in the life of their son Saher suggest that he was born *c.* 1153, in which case they must have married in David's reign.[4] Robert's name, however, is not found in charters till *c.* 1163, after which it occurs frequently till *c.* 1191. He was Justiciar *c.* 1175. He is supposed to have died on Crusade in 1192. But before then, in circumstances difficult to understand, though not for want of documents attested by Archdeacons, Bishops, Earls and King William, Orable married Gilchrist, Earl of Mar. She must have obtained a separation from Robert de Quincy, but no mention of this is to be found among the very plentiful contemporary references to Orable, who continues till 1191 to attest charters along with Robert and their son Saher and " G. Comes de Mar ".[5]

[1] Quincy is probably Cuinchy-lez-La Bassée, arr. Béthune, canton de Cambrin.   [2] Moore, *L.Sc.K.* p. 31.

[3] Lands in Leuchars and Lathrisk (Fife) and Tranent. *Holyrood*, p. 32.

[4] Saher de Quincy († 1219) must have been born not later than 1154. He was in 1173 a knight, a friend of Henry the Young King, and already the husband of Margaret de Beaumont, younger daughter of Robert, third Earl of Leicester. He obtained for himself, or perhaps inherited from his grandfather Saher, lands at Colum in the Honour of Eye. The name was uncommon and he may have been the Saher de Quincy who was, 1176–1178, one of the justices at the Assizes of Normandy. Haskins, *N.I.* p. 336. In 1204 Margaret de Beaumont became a very great heiress, and it was no doubt in consequence of this that in 1207 Saher was made (first) Earl of Winchester. He kept up close connections with Scotland and attested many charters. His son, the second Earl, " Rogerus de Quency, comes Wintoniae, Constabularius Scocie ", gave to Balmerino part of his *petaria* or peatery in the bog of Swanismire. *Balmerino*, No. XXXVII. On Roger's death in 1264, without male issue, the Earldom of Winchester lapsed.

[5] *E.g.* St. *Andrews*, pp. 254 and 287-291.

" Orabilis filia et heres Domini Nessi " inherited her father's estates, to the exclusion of his sons Constantin and Patrick. Presumably they were the

Towards 1150 also appear the names of " Thurstanus de crectune " [Toustain de Crichton] and " Robertus de monte acuto " [Montaigu (? Montacute) in Somerset],[1] neither of them otherwise known ; Roger, Hugue and Thomas de Ov [= d'Eu], three brothers possibly connected with the family of that name in Bedfordshire ; [2] " W. de Heriz " [3] and Alexander de Seton,[4] presumed heads of the Herries and the Seton families. By 1153 " Willelmus Finemund " (perhaps a Fleming) was lord of the manor of Cambusnethan in Lanarkshire.[5] About the same time or earlier, " Thomas de Londonia " gave to the church of St. Mary at St. Boswells tofts on the south side of the building and half of an orchard adjoining it, together with land bordering on " the great road which goes towards Eldon ". This gift was made on condition that " the parson should found an altar *in parte australi ecclesie* in honour of St. Margaret the Virgin [St. Margaret of Antioch]

issue of a second marriage, and Ness held his estates in right of his first wife. Orable, who died before 1203, gave lands in Gask to Inchaffray. *Inchaffray*, No. XXI. Saher de Quincy remained Orable's heir ; he inherited from her, *e.g.* Beith and Nesgask. The matrimonial status of Robert de Quincy, Orable and Earl Gilchrist is discussed, with varying results, by G. Burnett, *Gen.* N.S. IV, pp. 178-179 ; Joseph Bain, *Gen.* VII, p. 7 ; the editors of *Inchaffray*, Introd. p. lxxxviii ; and Dr. Alan O. Anderson, *E.S.Sc.* II, pp. 493-494.

[1] Both in the Great Charter of Dunfermline (*c.* 1150).

[2] Roger gave the church of Langetune to the Abbey of Kelso, *c.* 1150, his brothers being witnesses.

[3] Mandate by Earl Henry that the monks of Wetheral should be free of toll. Lawrie, CXXIV, before 1152. Here " Herzis " is a scribal error for Heriz. Cp. " Ivo de Heriz ". Pipe Roll of 1130 under " Nottinghamshire." " Willelmus de Heriz " held land on the Esk of Robert de Brus I or II. *St. Bees*, No. 60.

[4] David's charter, *c.* 1150, granting Lilliesleaf to Walter de Ridale. Lawrie, CCXXII. Alexander de Seton was probably the father of Philip, whose son and heir " Alexander de Setona " is frequently mentioned throughout the reign of Alexander II (1214–1249). *Inchaffray*, p. 276. The family history is related by " Schir Richat Maitland of Lethington, knycht, dochteris sonn of the said Hous " : *The History of the House of Seytoun to the year MDLIX*. Bannatyne Club, 1829.

[5] " Willelmus Finemund " is one of the witnesses to Malcolm IV's Kelso Charter, 1159. The same charter (*Kelso*, I) mentions his gift of the church of Cambusnethan to the Abbey. He appears (*Kelso*, p. 14) to have made the gift before 1153. His name and the proximity of Cambusnethan to the lands held by Flemings (see below, pp. 375-376) suggest Flemish origins.

and there sing one weekly Mass for the souls of my lord King David, of Margaret my wife and of all the faithful departed ".[1] She gave lands to the Priory of Jedburgh with the consent of Thomas and of Henry Lovel " the son of the same Margaret ".[2] This Henry Lovel was, or soon afterwards became, Lord of Castle Cary (Somerset) and Hawick. He appears to have owned land in Somerset near the Priory of Montacute.[3] Margaret's first husband was Ralph Lovel, probably a refugee from the Anarchy. There is no information at all on the Norman who in David's time owned land in Romanno (Peebles), part of which he granted to "Hugo de Paduynan [Pettinain]" and Hugo's son " Reginaldus ". His existence is known only because his son and successor in Romanno, "Philippus de Euermele" [also Evermer and Vermer: presumably his name was Philippe de Vermelles], made a gift to Holyrood[4] and one to Newbattle,[5] which gifts occasioned mention of his father's property in Romanno, though not of his father's name.

[1] *Dryburgh*, p. 44. The church of St. Boswells was given to the Abbey of Dryburgh, 1165 × 1214, by " Robertus de Londonia for the souls of King William and my father Richardus de Londonia, my mother Matilda de Ferers and Mauricius and Thomas de Londonia ". *Dryburgh*, pp. 41 and 54.

[2] *O.P.* I, p. 370.

[3] " Henr. luuel " witnesses a grant by Malcolm IV, *c.* 1163, to Glasgow. *Glasgow*, p. 16, No. XV. A Confirmation to St. Andrews by Pope Innocent III in 1183 mentions two bovates of land in Hawick " ex dono Henrici luuel ". In *St. Andrews*, p. 261, the gift, made by " Henricus Lupellus ", is exchanged for other land by his son Richard. Hugh Lovel († *c.* 1291), Lord of Castle Cary and Hawick, claimed of the Prior of Montacute a manor in Somerset held by his ancestor Ralph in the reign of Henry II. Hugh's son Richard was the last Lord of Castle Cary and Hawick. Joseph Bain, *Gen.* N.S. IV, p. 214; *Cal.* Nos. 407 and 1166; *Complete Peerage*, *s.v.* LOVEL.

[4] The gift was a carucate of land in his fief and pasture for a thousand sheep. It was confirmed, 1164 × 1165, by Malcolm IV (*Holyrood*, p. 8) and, 1189 × 1199, by Philip the son, who then increased it, and, 1223 × 1227, by the grandson, Ralph of Euermel or Vermel.

[5] *Newbattle*, p. 96, No. CXXIV. The grant was confirmed by Pope Innocent III in 1203. *O.P.* I, p. 193. A charter of Robert de Quincy, granting land in Tranent to the Cistercians of Newbattle, is witnessed by Jocelin, Bishop of Glasgow (1175–1199), and by " Philippus de Euermel " and " Philippus, filius ejus ". *Newbattle*, p. 51, No. LIV. The family was eventually succeeded in the lordship of Romanno by the Grahames of Dalkeith. *O.P.* I, p. 194.

Simon, son of Michael, witnessed King David's Commendation of the Hospice for poor pilgrims at St. Andrews, and himself gave a ploughgate of land in Kathlac.[1] He had a son Alan, of Kinnear, whose descendants took the name of Kinnear and held lands in Kathlac till the beginning of the eighteenth century.[2] But it is something of a miracle to trace back eighteenth-century Kinnears to twelfth-century Simons, and when we have safely won through to Simon, son of Michael, we cannot tell if the father, probably a Norman or a Breton Michel, came to Scotland with the son or before the son or ever came at all. In the family history of the Normans in Scotland there are three dates to be distinguished : arrival in the Kingdom, arrival in the records which happen to be extant, and arrival at the status of recognized head of a landed family or one of its main branches. In general the first date is unknown, the second only approximate, the third arbitrary and uncertain. Between these dates, could they be precisely determined, the interval might well be considerable. It is highly probable that many a later historic family took its origins from one of David's unrecorded or unidentified Normans. Thus the first known of the family which carried the name of a Scottish river to the bounds of the civilized world, William of Douglas, is absent from the surviving records till 1175, but that is no proof that in David's reign William or his unnamed father was absent from Scotland or from the banks of the Douglas Water. The proud words which Hume of Godscroft in the seventeenth century used of the Douglases apply to many more Normans in Scotland : " We do not know them in the fountain, but in the stream ;

---

[1] Confirmation by Malcolm IV. *St. Andrews*, p. 196. In the Confirmation by King William (*ibid.* p. 212) it is stated : " Simo et heredes sui terram illam adquietabunt de exercitibus et operacionibus et de omnibus secularibus exaccionibus ". " Ego Symon de Kinner, de assensu Amie uxoris meae ", grants lands to Balmerino. Confirmation by Alexander II. *Balmerino*, No. XV. In 1286 " Johannis de Kyner, miles " confirms certain donations. *Balmerino*, No. XVII.

[2] Lawrie, p. 448. Kathlac is now Kedlock.

not in the root, but in the stem ; for we know not who was the first mean man that did raise himself above the vulgar ". It is impossible to follow David's Normans in their territorial acquisitions. Perhaps it would have been possible had he contented himself with bold effects, such as his allocation of all Annandale or all Liddesdale or the whole of Renfrew to one Norman. But these were isolated efforts. Only part of Lilliesleaf went to Walter de Ridale, part having already gone to the Bishop of Glasgow. All that David could provide for Alexander de Saint-Martin was half a knight's fee, and even so Alstaneford had to be eked out with " the land which Arkil held " and " that part of Drem which I retained in my own hands when I gave Drem to Gospatric ".[1] Very little information has come down to us on the details of land-distribution. Something just happens to be known of the districts of Crailing and Ednam (Roxburghshire) because certain owners gave certain parts of their land to the monasteries of Jedburgh and Kelso, and their donations are mentioned in confirmation charters dating from near the end of David's reign.[2] The state of matters thus partially revealed as existent *before* the donations—and how long before is unknown—is not simple. In Crailing, Bérenger Engaine has two bovates of land with one *villanus* and a toft ; two bovates of land with another toft, and a toft near the church ; he also has one mark from the profits of the mill, while David Olifard has " a tithe of the mill ". Gospatric the Sheriff has a ploughgate and a half, and three acres with two *maisurae*. Orm, son of Eilaf, has the vill of " the other Crailing ". We cannot even guess how much of the remaining land in both Crailings belonged to these persons *after* their gifts or how much belonged to Normans like Olifard and how much to native owners like Orm. In Heiton, which is not in either

[1] Lawrie, CLXXXVI.
[2] Such as David's Confirmation Charter of Jedburgh. Lawrie, CCXXXIX, 1147 × 1150. See also Lawrie, p. 408.

Crailing, but near by, on the road to Roxburgh, Raoul Carpentier and Philippe de Colville hold unspecified lands;[1] 104 acres belong to Geoffrey, son of Alain de Percy, son of the Guillaume de Percy who stood by the Conqueror's side at Abernethy. Geoffrey's 104 acres are next to the land of the Hospital of Roxburgh, and he gives them to the Abbey of Kelso in agreement with his brother and heir Henry.[2]

In Oxnam, on the Cheviot Hills, Raoul Carpentier and Philippe de Colville appear again as landowners, along with Geoffrey de Percy, who has a ploughgate which he received from David and which he gives not to Kelso, but to his grandfather's Abbey at Whitby.[3] In Ednam, of which the church, with a ploughgate of land, had been given in Edgar's reign by " Thor Longus " to the monks of Durham, Pierre, son of Walter of Stirling, and Tebald [Thiébaut] of Norham (which was, and always has been, in England) hold of David, respectively, a ploughgate and half a ploughgate. The King has, however, granted to Nicholas the Clerk twenty shillings from Pierre's land and half a mark from Thiébaut's.[4] A toft with houses which was at one time held of the King by Gilbert, priest of Stitchill in the neighbourhood, had been granted in 1136 to the Priory of Coldingham, free of all service in feu and alms for a yearly payment of two shillings, but the rights of the mill belong to the Abbey of Kelso.[5] In Roxburgh an unidentified " Geroldus " and Gautier the mason [" Gauter cementarius "][6] have property. So have Raoul son of Dunegal

---

[1] In the year after David's death. Charter of Malcolm IV, 1154, in *Act. Parl. Sc.* pp. 51-53. Colville is Coleville-sur-Mer (Calvados), arr. Bayeux. Philip de Colville was a hostage under the Treaty of Falaise. There were numerous Colvilles in the North of England, but it seems likely that this is the Philip de Coleville who was a member of the Bishop of Durham's Council in 1155 (*Boldon Book*, p. 316). The Thomas de Colville († 1219), Lord of Oxnam and Ochiltree, who witnessed a charter, 1201 × 1202 (*Inchaffray*, p. 270, No. XX), was no doubt his son.

[2] Lawrie, CCLI.   [3] *Ibid.* CCLII.

[4] *Ibid.* CXCVIII, 1147 × 1153.   [5] *Ibid.* CXI.

[6] Which, or part of which, they had given to the Abbey of Kelso, as mentioned, but without detail, in *Kelso*, No. I, 1159.

and Bethoc his wife. So also has Béatrice de Beauchamp, wife of Hugue de Morville. She holds some land of King David [1] and has bought some from " Rogerus janitor ".[2] When a wife bought land it is probable that the husband bought more—and that some estates which in default of evidence are assumed to have been bestowed on Normans by King David were in fact acquired by purchase. But how little can be ascertained about even the husband's possessions is well illustrated by the case of Hugue de Morville himself. When he died in 1162 he had spent most of his long life in Scotland and had acquired vast estates, but on which of them he normally lived, or where the *caput* of his fief was, is simply not known.

If a Cadastre or Domesday Book had been compiled or had survived—and it may be remarked that Domesday has raised more problems than it has solved—it might be possible for an army of scholars to work out the family history of David's Normans, assess the extent of their grants, their holdings, their acquisitions by inheritance or by marriage, their purchases and sales of land and to mark out the stages of their territorial expansion. But all that subsists is a chance reference here and there to a few localities, mostly in Teviotdale and Fife, and the evidence can carry us no further, for the simple reason that it is derived almost wholly from the abbeys of Teviotdale and the churches of St. Andrews and Dunfermline in Fife. In any given district we cannot argue from absence of record to absence of Norman landowners ; we cannot, for instance, guess how many might be traced in Moray had the chartulary of Urquhart been preserved or had there been in 1153 a Cathedral at Elgin to receive and to record their donations.

The appearances are that David's Normans came in considerable numbers into a country which had long been divided into well-marked properties and were accommo-

---

[1] Confirmation by Earl Henry. Lawrie, CXCI, 1139 × 1152.
[2] *Ibid.* CCXXXVIII and CCL, *c.* 1152.

dated with such scattered estates or small pieces of land as happened to be anywhere available. Waves of settlement from the South would naturally expend much of their force in Lothian, Cumbria and Fife. But wherever there was a Royal castle or a burgh, a sheriff or an abbot, there were Norman landowners. By the end of David's reign it cannot have been appreciably more difficult for Normans to settle in Strathearn than in Fife, or in Moray or Mar than in Angus or the Mearns. Some are to be found in almost every region of arable land for as far inland from the East Coast as at the time, and long after, it was thought worth anyone's while to go. Freskyn had a great lordship in Moray, and it is hard to see what there was to prevent David's other friends from settling as far north had they felt so disposed. Some incomers received much land, others very little. There were Normans and Normans, some of them barons, some of them petty proprietors, " bonnet lairds " ; others, as will be clearer from the following chapter, were traders, honest artisans, unassuming masons and blacksmiths.

Descendants of the humbler immigrants could rise to fortune, rank and power, but in general the " great Norman families " in Scotland were " great " from their arrival. They obtained from the first an influence and importance which they never lost. From the Normans settled in before 1153 sprang the Bruces, the Balliols, the Stewarts, who were Kings; the Comyns, who were hardly less; the Grahams or Graemes, the Lindsays, the Melvilles, the Oliphants, the Somervilles, who are still with us; the Avenels who are no more than a name and a legend, for seven hundred years have passed since the final setting of

> The star that rose upon the house of Avenel
> When Norman Ulric first assumed the name.[1]

Whereas in England the first great Norman families

---

[1] Scott, *The Monastery.*

went not merely out of power, but out of existence, in Scotland they flourished exceedingly. Hardly one but had numerous stalwart sons. The Anglo-Norman system also flourishing as it never did in England, the owner of a wide but thinly populated domain could provide each of his sons with land, and in support of time every great family could count on the process of numerous cadets, many of them living in comparative obscurity, but maintaining the feudal tie and patriarchal bond. When surnames, long used only by the gentry, were assumed by everyone, those of the great Norman families were generally adopted.[1] To-day they still predominate. All Stewarts are not sib to the King, nor are all Bruces; all bearers of Norman surnames are not of Norman descent. But if comparatively few Scotsmen can have Norman blood in their veins, few are without one name of Norman origin. It may be a territorial designation taken by a Norman lord from a place in the Duchy (Somerville) or in England (Graham) or in Scotland (Kinnear); or a patronymic (MacWilliam, Robertson); or a surname (Oliphant); or a Christian name, whether widespread elsewhere, like Henry or Walter, or distinctively Scottish, like Archibald. To have provided so many Scotsmen with personal names is no small achievement for a small French Duchy.

[1] G. Burnett, *A Treatise on Heraldry*, 1892, II, p. 399.

§ 22

Knighthood and Chivalry

DAVID was a Knight. It is apt to be forgotten. Chivalrous feeling partly accounts for his help to the Empress and, in 1149, to her son Henry. She had gone back to Normandy, where she soon lived down her English reputation for " haughtiness " and became as popular as she had been in Germany. Perhaps she felt no need to be anything but her natural self, having handed over the Cause to her eldest son. He was a reddish-haired, ruddy-complexioned and sturdy youth of sixteen, with a disquieting temperament, half romantic, half realist. From the paternal side came perhaps his demoniacal energy, his wild, wayward fancies, his outbursts of uncontrollable fury; the Counts of Anjou were reputed to descend from the Evil One. From the maternal side came perhaps a degree of caution and hard-headedness which is deemed by the French to be characteristic of the Normans and by the English to be characteristic of the Scots. In the spring of 1149 this very remarkable young man had left Normandy on a romantic mission and, aided only by his own courage and Stephen's cheerful inefficiency, was making his way through England to be knighted at Carlisle.

A knight-errant he already was. The quest was high enough, being the Crown of England, and the way was romantic enough, by frowning hills, foaming torrents, tracts of primeval forest, moors, marshes and meres. But reasons of policy jostled in his mind with reasons of chivalry. He would unite the barons of the North against the Usurper, compose their differences, rally all well-wishers round a youthful but authentic Knight, one solemnly invested with the *cingulum militare*, the belt and sword worn as an outward sign of inward nobility. He felt, and David and his counsellors felt with him, that to be a King he must first be a Knight. Chivalry was coming into its own. However exalted a man's birth and station, something, except he were a Knight, was lacking to his stature. The word still meant a man holding by military service and also one possessing " chivalrous " qualities. These were now becoming associated with noble birth, and there were Knights *par excellence*, who were beginning to form almost an order, a close corporation from which men of low degree were excluded. For a youth of high enough degree admittance, usually at sixteen, signalized the attainment of his majority, and while co-option into this military guild, this brotherhood-in-arms, might in the opinion of some be accorded by any famous Knight upon the battlefield, in the purer faith only a King could make a Knight. Henry Plantagenet's majority was attained, and the foundation of his career was laid, at a religious and a splendid ceremony in David's " capital " at Carlisle.[1] On May 22, 1149, being Whit Sunday, the day which commemorates the descent of the Holy Spirit upon the disciples, the unseen essence which emanated from the sword of a Knight and King was by David—who received it from the first " rei Henri ", who received it from the Conqueror —imparted to him who was soon to be the second " rei Henri ".[2] Then other young men of his own age were knighted.[3] The feast which followed a knighting was

---

[1] " Excepit eum [Henricum] rex David cum reverentia magna et sumptuosa praeparatione opulentae munificentiae."—John of Hexham, p. 322.

[2] It was " in hebdomada Pentecostes " (Flor. Worc. II, p. 19) that Henry I was knighted. On a Whit Sunday, after a religious ceremony, he knighted Geoffrey of Anjou, father of the future Henry II. In the Arthurian romances Whit Sunday became the appointed day and Carlisle the appropriate place, *e.g. Fergus*, pp. 38-39. The vow which provides the beginning of Chrétien's *Yvain* is made by King Arthur on a Whit Sunday at Carlisle : " Li rois fu a Carduel en Gales. Apres mangier . . ."—Chrétien de Troyes, *Yvain*, ed. T. B. W. Reid (Manchester Univ. Press, 1942).

[3] Gervase Cant. I, p. 141.

considered an occasion for calling on God and the Saints to witness a high resolve.   Girt with the *cingulum militare*, Henry stood forth and swore that should he ever wear the Crown, he would give Newcastle to David and confirm to him and his heirs for ever possession of all the lands between Tyne and Tweed.[1]

The age of chivalry had come, or, more exactly, the age had come when the Norman ideals which prevailed when Alexander gave his Arab steed to God were blending with British or Celtic ideals and finding poetic expression in the Story of Arthur, Christian Hero and King at Carlisle. The Celts waiting through the ages for the Return of Arthur had not waited in vain.   In 1113 the monks of Laon found that people in Cornwall believed he was alive, and protected by Our Lady.[2]   In 1125, for William of Malmesbury such things were only " *Britonum nugae* ", "Celtic haverings", and yet he took care to report discovery of the tomb of Arthur's nephew Gawain, eponymous hero of *Gauvoie* (Galloway).[3]   In 1136 Geoffrey of Monmouth brought Arthur " out of faery ", back to the scenes of his glory in Strathclyde and Lothian, back to his shadowy halls at Carlisle.[4]   He set the golden mists of romance rolling over moor and fell, and spread enchantment in the

---

[1] Hoveden, I, p. 211.   Henry's promises are admitted by Wm. Newb. I, p. 106, though cautiously :   "the oath which he is said to have given to David".

[2] They visited Barnstaple and Bodmin, to collect funds for rebuilding the Cathedral of Laon, and carried with them a shrine with relics of the Virgin. A Cornishman with a withered hand offended one of the party by asserting that Arthur was still alive.   This was taken to be displeasing to Our Lady. A quarrel followed and the Cornishman was not healed.   The story is related by Herman of Tournai.

[3] The passage in Wm. Malm. may, however, be an early interpolation and Herman's testimony is not strictly contemporary.

[4] Of Arthur's Twelve Battles, enumerated in the oldest part of the ninth-century compilation known as " Nennius ", those which can be at least roughly identified are mostly in Lothian and the ancient Kingdom of Strathclyde.   See O. G. S. Crawford, *Arthur and his Battles, passim*.   In the French Romances, *e.g. Fergus*, Loenois (Lothian) is always a name to conjure with.   The post-Roman Britons took the Story of Arthur with them wherever they settled ; for " Arthurian " place-names in Scotland see Watson, *C.P-N.* p. 208.

minds of young and old—the veteran at Helmsley, the novice at Rievaulx, the boy Henry at Bristol, his illustrious grand-uncle at Carlisle.

It matters little whether the Story of Arthur came to Geoffrey on the wings of genius or only in " a very old book in the British tongue ", preserving traditions cherished among the " Welsh " of Strathclyde, Cornwall and Wales. It matters less whether his *Historia* was sound or " a pack of lies ", as the serious-minded William declared at Newburgh, when it was too late. In vain the seekers after hard fact assail the ingenious Canon of Oxford with their rude flints. He was no historian. He was an artist, and his historical importance is that from 1136 he made King Arthur reign in the minds or the hearts of men— partly by drawing on his own imagination and on a mysterious fund of Celtic myth in which memorials of time past, burial mounds, hill forts, mountain, crag and torrent, had become associated with the Bible story, the Virgin Mary, the defence of the Christian West against the Saxon pagans. The Monk of Malmesbury wrote a history of the English Kings; Henry of Huntingdon, a history of the English people;[1] Geoffrey's theme was the glory of the ancient British race. All three were writing for Normans, putting the rough island story into ordered Latin prose for men of culture with the Norman interest in history. Geoffrey alone cast a spell; he alone enthralled his readers, revealing to them Arthur, King in a mystic, unreal and therefore enchanting realm, with a " chivalrous " Court held sometimes at " Carlisle in Wales ".[2]

Walter Espec in the Speech at the Standard remarked

---

[1] Henry of Huntingdon first heard of Geoffrey's work in 1139 on a visit to Bec, where Robert of Torigny showed him a manuscript. See W. Levison, *MS. of Geoffrey of Monmouth and Henry of Huntingdon*, *E.H.R.* CVIII (1943), pp. 41-51. The fact is typical of mediaeval literary documentation. It was curiously unequal. In this matter Henry of Huntingdon may have been less well informed than Walter Espec.

[2] " A Carduel en Galles ", *Fergus*, p. 20. For the fourteenth-century Froissart Carlisle is still in " Wales ".

by way of encouragement for the younger generation that but for the call of duty he would have been at home at Helmsley " listening to histories being read or, as is my custom, lending an attentive ear to one relating the high deeds (*gesta*) of our forefathers "—a minstrel declaiming a *chanson de geste*. A great lady in Lincolnshire, Dame Custance [Constance] of Scampton, was helping her household minstrel, or perhaps chaplain, Gaimar, to collect materials for a comprehensive *Estorie des Engles* which he had undertaken to write for her edification, and she sent to Helmsley for " le livere Walter Espec ". What Dame Custance wanted was Geoffrey's *Historia Regum Britanniae*, the latest known work on the subject, not yet published, available only in advance copies, and urgently required for Gaimar's purposes of research. Contrary to expectation Walter did not possess the book : he had only heard it read. But he knew where copies were to be had and borrowed one from Geoffrey's patron, Earl Robert of Gloucester—as Gaimar explains at some length, feeling the prick of conscience, because it is one thing to borrow a book and another to return it.[1] In Earl Robert's hospitable and literary household at Bristol Henry Plantagenet, his nephew, had not spent three years of precocious boyhood with impunity ;[2] he could be at times a sombre enough realist, but he had drunk deep of romance. While he was at Bristol, one of the novices at Rievaulx whom it was Ailred's duty to interrogate and instruct confessed that religious emotion came to him less readily than when he was in the world

---

[1] Gaimar, ll. 6439-6459. He gratefully utilized the book, but when he returned it some link in the chain proved weak and the good-natured Robert of Gloucester suffered the book-lender's customary fate. Gaimar was even more indebted to Walter Espec's brother-in-law Nicole de Traylly : see above, p. 146, n. 2.

[2] Henry, at the age of nine, was brought from Normandy " litteris imbuendus " (Gervase of Cant. I, p. 125) by his uncle Earl Robert, in whose household at Bristol he lived till the age of thirteen (1142-1146). His tutor was Adelard of Bath. C. H. Haskins, *Adelard of Bath and Henry Plantagenet*, *E.H.R.* XXVIII, p. 516.

and could shed tears " even over the tales commonly told of a certain Arthur ".[1]

In the daughter-house at Melrose there must have been young men similarly affected. It was dedicated, as all Cistercian houses were, to St. Mary, but stood closer than Rievaulx to scenes associated with her and with Arthur, the Christian Knight, who, as Nennius told, bore her image on his shield in battle and routed thus the pagans. Only a few miles from Melrose and still on the abbey lands, in Wedale, " Vale of Weeping ", Vallis Doloris, the church of St. Mary at Stow preserved the fragments of a statue of the Virgin brought back from Jerusalem by King Arthur.[2] The Rock of Edinburgh was perhaps Geoffrey's " Mons Agned", his "Mons Dolorosus" perhaps Melrose.[3]

---

[1] " Et in fabulis quae vulgo de nescio quo finguntur Arcturo "—Ailred, *Speculum Charitatis*, p. 565. Ailred was appointed novice-master at Rievaulx on his return from Rome in 1141. Watkins, p. 47. His *Speculum* was written in 1142. The *fabulae* may well have been lays sung in Scotland before the publication of Geoffrey's work and heard by Ailred, who may be referring to himself.

[2] Marginal note in a thirteenth-century MS. of Nennius [Nenni, *Historia Britonum*, ed. Joseph Stevenson, E.H.S., 1838, p. 48] : " cujus fracturae apud Wedale servantur . . . Wedale est . . . vi milliaria ab occidentali ab illo quondam nobili monasterio de Meilros ". Then there is added in a later hand " Wedale, Anglice ; Vallis Doloris, Latine ". Legend says " Vale of woe " = O.E. *wá*, in reference to a great defeat of the Angles by Arthur; the name, not now in common use, is pronounced " Weedale ". The grant of lands in Wedale to Melrose Abbey is recorded in David's Foundation Charter.

[3] According to Nennius, p. 48, Arthur's Eleventh Battle was fought " in monte qui dicitur Agned ". Agned is quite unknown. It is identified with Edinburgh only by Geoffrey. His words are : " Condidit etiam Ebraucus [the mythical founder of various towns] urbem Aclud versus Albaniam, et oppidum Montis Agned quod nunc Castellum Puellarum dicitur, et Montem Dolorosum ". See Faral, III, p. 97, and R. Blenner-Hassett, *Speculum*, XVII (April 1942), pp. 250-254. Aclud is Dumbarton, the British capital on the threshold of Alban or Scotland proper. The Castellum Puellarum, first heard of in Geoffrey's *Historia*, is soon afterwards identified with Edinburgh Castle (*Newbattle*, Foundation Charter, *c.* 1142), and was from 1174 generally so understood. In 1155 Wace, translating Geoffrey, confesses himself mystified. In 1338 Wace's translator, Robert of Brunne, states that the reference is to Carlaverock Castle. In his youth at Cambridge he knew the future King Robert the Bruce and his brothers, who must have been familiar with any traditions there may have been concerning a castle so close to Annan and who were well read in French romance. Probably there was

Assuredly in the noble company gathered from the four quarters of the Scottish realm round one of the most illustrious knights in Christendom there were barons and there were churchmen who knew as well as Henry the chivalrous associations of the Cumbrian scene.

David created an aristocracy of barons and knights in the feudal sense : by 1149 both classes contained knights in the chivalrous sense.

The Earl of Chester, Renouf [Ranulf] de Gernons, was present at the Knighting, and not by chance. He had a cherished claim to the *Potestas* of Carlisle once held by his father Renouf le Meschin, and in return for the Honour of Lancaster he surrendered his claim.[1] It was resolved that a general attack should be launched from Lancaster on King Stephen, then in Yorkshire. David, conscientious to the last, kept his word and marched with the new-made Knight to Lancaster. But, the Earl of Chester failing to

more than one alleged Castellum Puellarum. Geoffrey's words seem to imply that his Mons Dolorosus is a third hill fortress, such as Stirling. The author of *Fergus, c.* 1209, who knew Scotland well, situates his own Mont Dolerous near Melrose. The *Chronicle of Holyrood, s.a.* 1171, has ". . . . Willelmus abbas de Monte doloroso . . .", where the blanks *may* suggest an obit. William, Abbot of Holyrood, is known to have died 1165 × 1174. But neither its own nor any other chronicle gives the Abbey any such name and the reference might as well be to William, Abbot of *Melrose*, who succeeded Waldef in 1159 and in 1170 *retired* to Rievaulx, where he died in 1185. (For all we know, retirement may have been as " interesting " as a death.) Geoffrey's allusion would then be to a ruined fort on one of the Eildon Hills (the ancient Trimontium) above Melrose, perhaps also to Wedale, Vallis Doloris. The remark by George Buchanan (1506–1582) that Old French tales called Edinburgh Vallis Dolorosa carries little weight. It seems unlikely that even Geoffrey's imaginary and no doubt imaginative Ebraucus in providing Caledonia with three suitable sites would have selected one at Dumbarton and two at Edinburgh, within a mile of each other.

[1] Renouf [Ranulf] de Gernons (born before 1109, † December 16, 1153) succeeded in 1129, as Earl of Chester, his father, Renouf le Meschin, who had resigned Cumbria in 1120 when he was made Earl. Renouf had withdrawn from Stephen's Court, because of indignation at the favour shown there to Earl Henry. He fought on his own account rather than for the Empress, and in 1146 joined Stephen, who in 1149 offered him Lincoln, while David offered him Lancaster. See Round, *The Earl of Chester and King Stephen, E.H.R.* X, p. 90, and *F.E.* p. 187 ; *D.N.B. s.v.* RANDULF ; Cronne, pp. 104 and 129. Renouf's sister was the wife of David's nephew William fitz Duncan.

appear, they went home without fighting, the King of Scots to Carlisle, England's future King to France, of which country he presently obtained one-half—by a marriage which was a master-stroke of realism and perhaps of romance.[1]

Four years after the Knighting, on the Sunday before the Ascension, May 24, 1153, at Carlisle, David departed in peace, Margaret's Holy Rood held before his closing eyes. Ailred of Rievaulx wrote the funeral oration: " O desolate Scotia, who shall console thee now? He is no more who made an untilled and barren land a land that is pleasant and plenteous, who adorned thee with castles and cities and lofty towers, enriched thy *ports* with foreign wares, gathered the wealth of other Kingdoms for thine enjoyment, changed thy shaggy cloaks for precious raiment, clothed thine ancient nudity with purple and fine linen, ordered thy barbarous ways with Christian religion." [2] This, for all its rhetoric, is a singularly exact epitome of David's achievement. Ailred could have said it in three words : David Normanized Scotland.

The Norman institutions by means of which he accomplished this were chiefly : the Castle, the Sheriffdom and the Burgh. These formed a compact trinity in unity, each element fostering and strengthening the other two. A further element of strength and security was provided by the Abbey,—by the French religious houses. These four elements constitute the main Norman contribution to Scottish life. They are discussed in the following chapter.

[1] Stephen, not to be outdone, knighted his eldest son, Eustace. John of Hexham, p. 323 ; *Gesta Stephani*, p. 130.

[2] Ailred wrote, and presumably delivered, a very long eulogy, quoted *in extenso* by Fordun, V, pp. 535-544. We give only part of the peroration. *Portus* may mean harbours or walled market-towns ; see *O.E.D. s.v.* PORT, *sb.*[2] and C. Stephenson, p. 11. In " barbaros mores tuos Christiana religione composuit " *religio* means " religion " in its old sense (*O.E.D.* sense 1 : a state of life bound by monastic vows).

CHAPTER VII

THE NORMAN CONTRIBUTION
TO SCOTTISH LIFE

★

§ 23

The Castle

USUALLY the lands which the Norman received had belonged to others from time immemorial and lay round a strategic strong-point and ancient centre of population. Unlike the Conquerors of England who settled grimly at some distance from the vanquished,[1] he adopted for his castle the ancient site or chose a new one as near it as possible, in accordance with fixed principles familiar to all the Norman world. The first consideration was proximity to water, the prime necessity of life, the one hope of prolonged resistance in case of siege. Height came next. A wide view was indispensable, but a low hill with one or two precipitous sides and presenting a narrow front to attack might be preferred to its higher neighbour, if beyond arrow-shot. Raoul de Soules chose such a site for the Mote of Liddel which he built on that river a little above its junction with the Hermitage Water.[2] On flat ground—and near the necessary river or burn there might be no convenient hill—the strength of the fortress was in the height of the mound and the depth of the ditch. Construction called for no great skill. A standard type was followed, the mote-and-bailey. Its essential element was an earthen mound (French *motte*), of considerable extent, surrounded by a ditch. On the summit was a palisaded bank enclosing a wooden tower. Lower down was another enclosure, the base-court (*basse cour*) or bailey, also ditched and palisaded, within which were wooden buildings: the little chapel, the smithy, the stables, quarters for the garrison. A garden was a necessary and a pleasing feature. The fields

---

[1] See Armitage, p. 96.   [2] See L. Mack, pp. 111 and 132.

around were enclosed to make the demesne or home farm.

Such was the *castellum* which Robert de Brus erected at Annan in 1124, if it was not erected already—the *Moit et Bailyie* mentioned in a sixteenth-century document [1]—and such was every Norman castle in Scotland. But of them all only the mound remains, or only the name. The " Moot Hill " or the " Castle Hill " may be the sole reminder of a Norman past. The raised earth has been reduced when it has not been swept away. The timber has perished. There is no trace of any stone building; the gaunt and battered keep is of a later day. In David's time the use of stone was an expense deemed unjustifiable except for churches; masons were scarce, trees and unskilled rustics plentiful. Moreover, it would have been unsafe to erect heavy stone buildings on made ground. The Royal castles in the South, at Roxburgh, Berwick and Edinburgh, were the more strongly built, and the more formidable.[2] But everywhere in David's Scotland the castle was only an improvised fortress, a wooden blockhouse or a hunting-lodge, set up on the edge of a cliff or on a hill, or in the loop of a river.

There is a mote-and-bailey still to be seen at Inverurie (Aberdeenshire), a work of nature which when utilized by the Norman for the purposes of a *castellum* required little adjustment with the spade. It stands on flat ground near the meeting of the Waters of Ury and Don. The mote is the mound called the Bass, a grass-covered cone truncated at the height of fifty feet. The castle was built, probably towards 1150, on the summit, sixty feet in diameter. At that time the conical outline, now artificially completed, extended round three-fourths of the circuit and from the remaining fourth a mound half the height of the Bass projected. This mound, called the Little Bass, is the bailey,

[1] W. M. Mackenzie, *Med. Cas.* p. 12.

[2] As mentioned, later, by Wm. Newb. II, xxxviii, p. 193, and as evidenced by the value which Henry II attached to the possession of castles in South Scotland.

more elevated than was necessary. The two rivers, which now meet somewhat further away, provided amenities and protection. The base was washed by " the bonny water o' Ury " which, Thomas the Rhymer erroneously prophesied, " shall bear the Bass away ". At a short distance the principal route through Mar and the Garioch crossed the Don. For a time the castle made admirable headquarters for the Earldom of the Garioch, afterwards held by King David's grandson David, Earl of Huntingdon. But nature had provided no room for expansion, administrative needs outgrew the narrow summit, and the third or fourth of the hereditary Constables moved to a more commodious site at Caskieben.[1]

A word-picture of a Norman castle in South-West Scotland is to be found in a romance written in the first years of the following century round the names of Fergus of Galloway and Somerled of Argyll, which were then passing into legend. On the confines of Galloway, " assez près de la mer d'Irlande " or Solway Firth, stands a castle belonging to " Soumilloit ", who lives in the timeless reign of Arthur, but lives in the style of a Norman baron, except that he farms his own land and tends his own cattle, though vicariously, by means of three muscular sons; whence his cognomen, " the Farmer " :

> Upon a great dark-coloured rock
> He had his house right nobly set,
> Built all about with wattle-work.
> Upon the summit was a tower
> That was not made of stone and lime.

[1] In 1849 and 1883 the mounds were reduced and trimmed and the Little Bass was separated by a cutting. The names Castle Hill and Castle Yards were in use till recent times. The Constables are on record from 1178, when David of Huntingdon granted to his Abbey of Lindores " ecclesiam de Inverurin ", one of the witnesses being " Normanus filius Malcolmi constabularius de Inuerurin ". Foundation Charter, *Lindores*, App. I. Thomas the Rhymer was unaware that the Bass is a geological survival, and stands upon a bed of boulder clay, impervious to water. See Douglas Simpson, *Mar*, pp. 127-128, and the Rev. John Davidson [Minister of Inverurie], *The Origin and Geological Associations of the Bass of Inverurie*, Trans. Aberdeen Philosophical Society, II (1892), pp. 42-56.

Of earth the wall was builded high,
And crenellated, battlemented.
The Farmer was full glad to own
So fair a home above the sea . . .
For thirty leagues he had a view
Around him if he cast his gaze.
Who is within need have no fear
Of escalade or engineer.[1]

Soumilloit's eldest son, Fergus, goes to Carlisle and offers his services to King Arthur as a " counsellor ". He is instructed how to behave, and how to dress, namely with *élégance*, and, kneeling at Arthur's feet, he asks for " clothes ". Having been knighted, he departs for " le Castel Lidel ", and, after wanderings which bring him to Roceborg [Roxburgh] and to Ayr—then, as since, unsurpassed for bonnie lasses ("les bieles femes")[2]—he proceeds to the conquest of a white shield kept under jealous guard in the Castle of Dunostre [Dunottar, in the Mearns]. On the way he visits " le Castel aux Pucelles " and " le Port la Reine " [Queensferry] :

There Lothian to its limit comes
And Scotland lies across the water ;
These countries twain the sea divides . . .

[1]
" Desus une grant roche bise
Ot sa maison molt bien asise
Faite de cloies tot entor,
En son le pui ot une tor
Qui n'ert de piere ne de caus.
De terre estoit li murs fais haus
Et crenelés et battiliés.
Li vilains ert molt aaisiés
Que si bel manoir ot sor mer.
Trente liues pooit mirer
Environ lui s'il i esgarde.
Qi ens est, ne peut avoir garde
D'engineor, de nul assaut."
                              Fergus, p. 9, ll. 18-30.

The *engineor* was one who operated " engines ", such as the stone-caster which the Scots possessed in 1173, or who constructed military works for attack or defence.

[2]
" En Aroie vint erranment,
La u les bieles femes sont,
N'a plus beles en tot le mont. . . ."

He landed on the further shore
Beneath a castle Sarasin,
And it is known as Dunfermline . . .

[At Dunottar]
He looked before him and beheld
The residence as brightly lit
As though it had been all on fire . . .
Straight through the hall he strode, and out
Into a pleasure garden came . . .[1]

The residence and the hall are the inevitable *palatium* and
aula. But the Sarasin or Saracen appearance of Dunfermline is due more to the rhyme than to the Crusade,
and some of the illumination at Dunottar comes from the
light that never was on sea or land. As a place of residence,
except in the romances, a Norman castle was extremely
primitive, with rooms few and damp and dark, windows
mere slits in massive wooden walls, stairs steep and mostly
outside. The *aula* might have but one chair, *the* Chair
for the Castellan; other people accommodated themselves on benches, sometimes covered with *pailles*, or
on folding-stools (*fauteuils*), which had the advantage
of being easily moved about. Straw or rushes covered
the floor; carpets or rugs were only beginning to come
in from the Levant. The odour of the stables, mingling
with that of wet and reeking leather, was never far away.[2]
There may be a sting of truth in the unkind definition of
mediaeval civilization : " a thousand years without a bath ".

[1]
". . . Illueques Lodien define
Et Escoche est de l'autre part ;
La mers ces deus terres depart . . .
De l'autre part est arivés
Desous un castel Sarrasin :
Si est claimés Dunfremelin . . .

Garda avant si a coisi
Le palais si enluminé
Con s'on l'eust tot embrasé . . .
Parmi la sale s'en va droit,
Si est entrés en un praiel . . .
Fergus, p. 6, 10 ff.

[2] J. W. Thompson, p. 270.

When all is said and done, Duke William's Conquest romanticized and Norman ancestry vaunted, Conquerors were only farmers. They did not set their own hands to the plough, save in romance, but they lived on farm rents and farm-produce; their fortune in the last resort was represented by their crops and the labour of their men. To hold lands meant constant attendance at different, and often very distant, places and detailed arrangements, as for produce to be ready at varying times for transport or for consumption on the spot. David's castellans were out in all weathers. The greater among them were for ever on the road, travelling with a retinue on his business or on their own from one " castel " or one monastery to another, from one " ostel " or tavern to the next, or camping in portable tents. Their womenfolk were out hunting and hawking when they were not at home directing spinsters and weavers. Our only memorial of a châtelaine is the graven image of Richard de Morville's wife Hawise [Avicia], who must have been in the bloom of her youth and beauty while her father-in-law Hugue was still Constable. She is depicted in her own seal, SIGILLUM AVICIA MORAVILLA, a full-length figure in long and flowing drapery, both arms extended, a falcon resting on the left hand.[1] Castellans were colonists or " colonials ", suffering no worse privation than many a man has voluntarily endured for sport, fresh air or Empire-building, and there was

---

[1] The seal (Laing, *Seals*, No. 482) is appended to the charter *c.* 1176, recording that Avice and her husband gave to the Abbey of Melrose the neighbouring chapel of St. Mary " de parco ", Old French *parc*, a preserve for the beasts of the chase. Richard de Morville († 1189), one of the hostages sent to England in 1139, succeeded his father as Constable in 1162. Hawise or Avice, daughter of " William of Lancaster ", brought her husband property near Furness ; he and she confirmed to the Abbey of Melrose, *c.* 1188, lands in Selside and Newby in Yorkshire. Their son William was Constable after his father. Their daughter Elena or Helena became the wife of Roland of Galloway († 1200). When her brother died, Elena inherited the Morville estates and Roland acquired the office of Constable, giving King William seven hundred marks silver for the inheritance. On the death of Roland's son Alan in 1233 the lands and lordship of Galloway were divided among his three daughters.

much comfort in furs, much in Yule logs and banquets in the *aula*. These were more copious than varied, consisting chiefly of beef or mutton in a cattle-raising or a sheep-raising region, of venison in a hunting district.[1] The Crusades were bringing in spices and condiments; pepper and cumin were in demand and when in supply were used without stint or discretion. Hector Boece maintains that there was only one meal a day in Scotland till the Normans established the deplorable practice of two. After the evening meal, when the trestles had been removed and the lord and lady and their daughters had retired to their bedroom or, in a pretentious establishment, to their two or their three bedrooms, the sons of the house, the guests and the knights slept in the warm *aula* as soundly as the dogs.

But, primitive though it was as a residence, the castle was elaborate in its organization, and only a man of some authority, a " baron " or a knight, could hope to maintain order among the miscellaneous *sergents* and men-at-arms. As an institution the Castle was an innovation, an outcome of conditions long characteristic of the French world and now spreading over Britain. In Scotland, as the abode of King, baron or sheriff, it was probably the most powerful means of Normanization. The Royal castle was an administrative centre and a military base. Justice was dispensed at the gate, later in the courtyard or " Court ", eventually under cover, when a large enough *aula* had been built. Though so often designated by the name of his estate, the Norman was apt to be an absentee landlord and he would no more have learned Gaelic in Scotland than he would have learned Welsh in Wales, but even in his absence his castle served as the social centre of the district, the rallying-point for the gentry, Norman or Scottish, resident in the neighbourhood or coming on business

---

[1] See Douglas Simpson, *Mar*, p. 137, for the conclusions to be drawn from the meat-bones found on the site of various Norman castles.

concerning their scattered lands or their rents, dues and renderings in kind. When the site was not already a centre of population a little vill grew up as the countrymen came in for sale of their surplus produce, for barter, for trade, or took up their abode, for greater security or just for the pleasure of human society.

Sometimes the vill or " ton " (the latter term reflecting the strength of the Saxon element in the local population) received its name from the Norman, as Philpstoun in West Lothian, from a Philippe, possibly the landowner whose son married Ailred's niece, and the numerous " tons " (Roberton, etc.) in Upper Clydesdale,[1] and as Melville and Mount Melville from Geoffrey de Maleville. But even in England the Normans seldom imposed their own names, except for necessary differentiation (Stoke d'Abernon, Stoke Poges, Stokesay = Stoke de Sei), and left little mark on local nomenclature. They confined their efforts to small inhabited places and their choice was singularly unimaginative; a locality is simply *beau* (*bel*), *e.g.* Beauchamp, Bewdley (in Inverness-shire, after much time for cogitation, Beauly), a " nice place " (*beau lieu*).[2] In any case they had come to Scotland too late to make a notable contribution to place-names. The Scots themselves had come too late. The Ancient British had named once for all the great natural features of the country, "the ever-flowing rivers and the ever-lasting hills".[3]

[1] Philpston is attested from 1417. Angus Macdonald, *The Place-Names of West Lothian*, Oliver and Boyd, 1941, xii + 177 pp., p. 177. " Philip " is very rare in English place-names. A certain " Levingus " gave his name to the " villa Levingi " or Livingston, West Lothian ; there seems no reason to suppose that the Latin hides a Norman name, but his son had one, Toustain. Leving granted the church of his vill to Holyrood, and the grant is confirmed by Bishop Robert. Lawrie, LXXXI (*c.* 1150). For other examples of " ton ", see below, p. 375.

[2] The Priory of Beauly (*Prioratus de bello loco juxta Beaufort*) was founded in 1230 by John Byseth (Biset, Bisset) of Lovat for the order of Vallis Caulium, founded in 1193 at Val-des-Choux in the Diocese of Langres.

[3] Sir James A. H. Murray, *The Dialect of the Southern Counties of Scotland*, Transactions of the Philological Society, 1870–1872. In Britain even the Roman has left no name on hill or river. Haverfield, p. 286.

The incomers in a district more or less dependent on a castle must often have been native Englishmen, from Northamptonshire or elsewhere, yet all were Norman colonists, inasmuch as they brought in a French civilization. To supply the needs it created, came minor officials, tradesmen, artificers, artisans, whose numbers must have been considerable, for the late-twelfth-century documents abound in bailies, falconers, fletchers (*fléchiers*, arrow-makers), foresters, lorimers, porters, sergeants, tailors, taverners.[1] These designations were soon used as proper names, and meantime represented offices, trades or callings which were requisite to a Norman society, by its nature aristocratic, baronial, knightly, and leading in however primitive a way *la vie de château* or country-house life. Many were well within native competence, but, for the time being, Normans held the field, with profitable results to themselves. At Perth, comfortably installed in a house of his own near the Royal castle, lived one Baudouin who carried on the trade ' of lorimer ' (OF. *loremier*, Mod. F. *lormier*) —made bits, spurs, stirrup-irons and metal mountings for bridles.[2] He was a burgess of Perth and his toft (building-site) was confirmed to him by King David on condition that " he should render me annually one torret and two collars ", articles of horse-harness evidently more ornamental or more pleasing to the Norman eye than those hitherto forged at Perth.[3] Perhaps Baudouin was the

[1] No writings in Scots are extant till Barbour's time (*c*. 1375). The above French words, in their Latin forms, are noted in earlier documents by Sir William Craigie, *The Earliest Records of the Scottish Tongue*, *S.H.R.* XXII (1925), pp. 61-67.

[2] Charter by David confirming to " Balduinus cliens meus " [? my officer] his toft at Perth. Lawrie, CCXLVIII. In the confirmation by Malcolm IV, *St. Andrews*, p. 204, he is " Balwinus lorimarius de Pert ".

[3] " Reddendo mihi inde per annum i turet et ii coleres." Terrets or torrets (OF. *toret* and *turet*) are metal (usually brass) rings, fixed upright on the pad or saddle, through which the driving-reins pass, or any rings attached elsewhere for a similar purpose. Cp. *Durham Account Rolls* (*O.E.D.* *s.v.* Torret), 1429–1430 : " In iiij Renes ij *coleres* de coreo novis cum *Turettes* emptis ". The reins of the early Irish charioteers passed through torrets. It was no new industry that David's " lorimer " was creating at Perth.

father, or perhaps he was only the business predecessor, of the Hugue Lorimer who had a grant of lands near Perth from William the Lion, for it is not easy to say at what point names of trades or professions become fixed surnames or what social status they previously indicated. In the Norman castle the Porter or Gatekeeper occupied (to use administrative metaphor correctly) a key position, and the residents evidently felt he should be one of themselves and a man of some standing. In accordance with the custom in England he could be provided with a piece of land, held by sergeanty; " Rogerus janitor ", from whom Hugue de Morville's wife bought land in Roxburgh, was presumably the Castle Porter or Gateward.[1] " Willelmus Cocus ", who received a toft at St. Andrews from the Bishop,[2] was probably his cook, and it is not clear whether, or for how long, his descendants used " Coquus " as a professional designation or merely as a surname (= Lequeux = Cook).[3] " Robertus Ferrarius ", probably a blacksmith but perhaps simply Robert Ferrier, owned two carucates of land near Newbattle which he had received from David " for his service ". They were, very properly, excluded by the King from the much larger gift of land which he afterwards made to the Abbey, but Robert rose to the occasion and nobly handed them over himself—nobly, we doubt not, but in what precise sense we know not.[4] If he was a smith, socially much would depend on the repute of his technical attainments; his service might be " servile " or might be " honourable ", according to the rank of his patrons or his customers or to the closeness of his connection with the nearest castle or the Abbey of Newbattle or the Royal Forest on the Pentlands.

[1] Lawrie, CCXL, *c.* 1152. Cp. " Rodbertus Janitor de Castello [de Edenesburch] ", *c.* 1166. *Holyrood*, p. 24.   [2] Lawrie, CCLXVIII.

[3] " Mauricius coquus " is a co-signatory with " Ada comitissa mater regis ". *St. Andrews*, p. 249. " Goscelinus cocus " owns the " terra de Gocelynton ". Charters by Malcolm IV. *Newbattle*, Nos. X, p. 10 and XI, p. 6.

[4] Lawrie, CXLIV, *c.* 1140 ; Perambulation, in *Newbattle*, No. III, p. 4.

The castle folk and their officials and retainers set the tone for the vill and the district. Gradually the native population, gentle and simple, began to adopt something of their way of life, their tradition of obedience to an overlord, their belief in written agreements, their feudal ideas, their manner of devotion to the Church. As the wooden castles spread over the land, Normanization, cultural, social and ecclesiastical, went with them.

§ 24

The Sheriffdom

IN Normandy the Dukes were the source of all justice.[1] In a conquered land they were not likely to tolerate a slighter jurisdiction and the Norman King was the *Fons Justitiae*. So was David, and in no mere metaphorical sense. Constantly moving about, seeing and being seen, well known personally to his people, he was no constitutional fiction. He was a man listening, weighing and bringing his practical sense to bear on difficult problems, rebuking the unruly, adjudicating on boundary disputes, hearing pleas, revising unjust sentences. He tried cases as " diligently " as he had ever done in the *curia* at Woodstock, and he freely exercised his Royal powers of summary justice. Ailred, with his own eyes, had seen him, booted and spurred for the hunt, putting his foot in the stirrup and taking it out again, at the call of a poor man seeking audience. Then David went back into his *aula* and, having heard the plea patiently and " diligently ",[2] set off for the forest, justice done, conscience free. There is no need to doubt the story, for he can be seen depicted in the miniature of the Kelso Charter, with eyes severe, beard of formal cut, every inch a mediaeval King, Lawgiver, Upright Judge.[3] But there were good deeds or good tales before David. The Conqueror, while still only Duke, " in person heard and judged the cause of

[1] Powicke, *L.N.* p. 81.
[2] Concerning David as a judge, Ailred, speaking of Scotland, uses the same word, *diligenter*, as Orderic, speaking of England : " Causas diligenter audire et singulis cum multo saepe labore satisfacere "—*G.R.A.* p. 714. Perhaps " carefully " would be a fairer translation than " diligently ".
[3] Frontispiece.

the poor, the fatherless and the widow. . . . In his days durst no man remove the landmark of his poorer neighbour." [1] Indeed Ailred seems to admit that the incident he relates was almost too edifying and that David was taking too much upon himself. David did, however, expect that recourse should be had first to a lower court, and one of the less dubious fragments of his legislation which have been preserved is a law prohibiting any of his lieges from bringing his plea before the King himself, unless he had first brought it before his lord or before the Sheriff.[2]

It is to be presumed that, as in England, some of the barons had justice of ordeal and justice of life and limb,[3] and, as in later Scottish times, presided over a court which had cognizance of disputes between the lord and his tenants, or between the tenants themselves, concerning their holdings or relating to matters necessarily arising from the occupancy and labouring of the lands. Barons sit with the King in some sort of higher tribunal, as on the matter of the chapel at Stirling,[4] or advise him on what we should now, as members of a non-rural community, scarcely consider to be matters of state, as when Earl Henry informs Earl Gospatric that he must restore certain kine to the monks of Coldingham, and that this " was decided last year in the presence of my father and Robert de Brus and his other barons ".[5] But there is no extant record of the baron's court in Scotland prior to the sixteenth century.[6] The *Vicecomes*, the Vicomte or Sheriff, is the chief legal official under the King. He had made his début at Roxburgh in the late reign and is now to be found installed at more and more places, all in the Lowlands, however, and all dominated by a Royal

[1] William of Poitiers, p. 113.   [2] J. H. Burton, II, p. 54.
[3] R. R. Reid, p. 180.   [4] Above, p. 281, n. 2.
[5] Mandate by Earl Henry not later than 1138.
[6] Dickinson, *Barony*, p. xi. The earliest extant Court-Book is that of the Barony of Alloway, 1492–1535.

castle.[1]   His origins are Anglo-Norman, though how
" Anglo- " and how " Norman " may never be known.

The Sheriff had been one of the Anglo-Saxon monarchy's few centralizing institutions.   From at least 1000,
England south of the Tees was divided into shires,
irregular in size and diverse in origin, each forming an
administrative unit.   To the shire corresponded the Shire-
reeve, chosen by the King and responsible to him alone
for the administration of local finance, the execution of
justice and the maintenance of the customs by which the
shire was governed.   By 1066 he had become the King's
chief executive agent in every branch of local government.
Coming from a land not of shires, but of cities and *châtellenies*, the Normans identified the Sheriff with their own
somewhat similar official, the Châtelain or Vicomte (in
their Latin, *Vicecomes*, in their French, *Vescunte*),—the
local representative or delegate of the central authority (the
Comes, the Count or Duke), independent of the neighbouring magnates, resident in one of the Duke's castles and
looking after his financial and other interests in the district
or *châtellenie*.   In England a Norman took over the duties
of Sheriff, and, as the English of the Chancery gave way
to Latin, *Vicecomes* became the official designation.[2]   In
contrast to his English predecessor he was, as he had been
in the Duchy, the social and territorial equal of the strongest
local magnate, and now, with all the power of a forceful
monarchy behind him and being usually a man of energy
as well as rank, he infused new life into the office.   Its
importance further increased with the introduction of new
feudal services and of ideas and methods characteristic of
the Normans, always noteworthy for their high respect for
the Royal prerogative, their fiscal efficiency, business capa-

---

[1] The earliest mentions (Dickinson, *Sheriff*, p. 349) are :   Berwick,
1124×1139 ;   Scone, 1128×1136 ;   Stirling, 1125×1147 ;   Haddington,
1131×1138 ; Crail (Fife), not before 1138 ; Edinburgh, 1141×1150 ; Clack-
mannan, 1141×1153 ;   Perth, 1147×1153.

[2] W. A. Morris, p. 426 ; Adams, *C. and C.* p. xxii.

city, knowledge of book-keeping and familiarity with hard cash.[1] During the first two Norman reigns the power of the Earl steadily diminished and in the administrative system elaborated during the third reign the Sheriff became the key-stone of the arch. He was more Norman than English when he was brought into Scotland, which, like Northumbria north of the Tees, had no shires.[2]

David introduced the Sheriff, but not the Shire. It is perhaps for that reason that, while the Sheriff is a typically Scottish figure, the Shire is still faintly exotic. " Fifeshire " is unassimilated ; " Forfarshire " has been rejected ; orthographically " Inverness-shire " is uninviting. The Sheriff or *Vicecomes* in Scotland was the counterpart not so much of the Anglo-Norman official administering a shire as of the Norman official installed in one of the Ducal castles. He obtained charge not of an old administrative unit, but of the district dependent on a Royal castle and called from the first mention, from *c.* 1125, a "castrensis provincia ". It was in fact a *châtellenie* ; it developed only gradually into a sheriffdom and, in later centuries, into a shire. In the first years of David " Sheriff " or " Vicecomes " can designate anyone holding a delegated authority—Hugue de Morville had a *Vicecomes* [3]—but the King's Sheriff quickly monopolizes the title. He is a military, administrative, judicial and financial officer. The Royal castle is his stronghold, his residence. There he discharges his military duties, chiefly local defence and recruitment, holds his Court, collects the revenue and keeps the records of the lands and owners in his district, which in process of time grows into a Sheriffdom, with the Royal castle as its head—as the *caput*

---

[1] Powicke, *L.N.* p. 65.

[2] The term " schira " occurring in early Scottish documents, *e.g.* " Coldinghamshire ", does not denote the definite administrative unit found in England south of the Tees, but a small district, such as afterwards became a parish (*e.g.* in the case of the shires of Clatt, Rayne and Daviot, mentioned in David's charter to the Bishop of Aberdeen in 1137). Lawrie, CXCVI.

[3] W. M. Mackenzie, *Med. Cas.* p. 22.

vicecomitatus. His authority increasing and his jurisdiction extending, the Sheriffdom expands and may become co-terminous with a province or Earldom. Properly the keeper of a Royal castle was the Constable, but (as in some parts of England) his office and that of Sheriff could be held together.[1]

Many, but by no means all, of David's Sheriffs were Norman. Three who successively held office at Stirling were Guillaume (*c.* 1125), Gilbert and Dufoc, the last probably the same person as "Dufoter de Calateria" [? Calatria, the Carse of Falkirk, or Calder in Midlothian].[2] Gervais Ridel, who sat at Roxburgh, was succeeded by Robert, son of Gui ; their colleague of Haddington was called Durand, the equivalent in France of Jones in Wales, and a namesake had to be distinguished from him as "Durandus miles ".[3] The Sheriff had his *curia* at Binning ; the word, now coming into use, means a residence, head-quarters, not necessarily of a *vicecomes*.[4] "Normannus Vicecomes de Berwic " leaves no doubt on his alien origins, though why he should have held land at Corstorphine is not clear.[5] They would have been strange Normans if they had had no clerk. A personal assistant was appointed, who duly rose to semi-official status, and before a century was gone there was an office, that of Sheriff-Clerk. Absence of contemporary comment makes it impossible to know if the Norman Sheriff's unpopularity, which in England dated from his first arrival in King Edward's

[1] By 1212 the castles of Crail and Kinghorn have been placed under Constables responsible to the Sheriff of Crail, thenceforth styled Sheriff of Fife. Dickinson, *Sheriff*, p. 379.

[2] Grant of Ketliston to Cambuskenneth by "Dufoc vicecomes de Striueling ", in King David's Charter, *Cambuskenneth*, p. 260.

[3] *Ibid.* CIX.

[4] *Ibid.* CXX, CXXXIV (*c.* 1141), CXXXV, CXLI (*c.* 1143). "Willelmus de Lyndeseya " granted to the Church of St. Giles of Binning half a carucate of land "quam Antecessor meus Durandus eidem ecclesiae dedit cum tofto in curia Durandi "—*St. Andrews*, p. 180.

[5] Lawrie, CLII ; *Holyrood*, p. 10, No. VIII (*c.* 1150) ; "Normannus" gave the Abbey " my chapel of Corstorphine ", near Edinburgh.

time, followed him into Scotland, but it is unlikely that he embarked on instant or revolutionary changes, whether legal or financial.   Not having at his disposal the organized local machinery of shire and hundred found south of the Tees, he had to fit himself into the existing system as best he could and observe some discretion in introducing Norman procedure.   It is far from clear what the existing system was—what, for example, were the precise duties and relative powers of the Maeor or of the *Judex*.   The Maeor, at least in later days, sat as an assessor in the Sheriff's court and long preserved his ancient dignity ; it was only by effluxion of time that he degenerated into dempster and finally into public hangman.   The Toisech, whether or not re-named the Thane, continued to have a court of his own.   He collected the Royal dues as he had always done, but now presented them to the Sheriff, who then accounted for the revenue to the Chamberlain.   As thanage lived on into the fifteenth century, the changes made under David cannot have been very drastic.   Probably the intention was not so much to create new legal machinery as to improve the fiscal system.   It was complicated and Norman experience was brought to bear on it without delay.   David had not been King a year when, advised by the Bishop of Glasgow and Raoul de Soules, he issued at Perth a mandate to the Sheriff at Stirling for the settlement of intricate problems concerning varied tithes and rents in his " castrensis provincia " due to other churches than that of Dunfermline, to which they were in future to be paid.[1]   One of the duties of a Sheriff was to see that payment of tithes was taken seriously: " If *villanus*, *rusticus*, *Thegnus* or *Dominus* has not paid tithes or dues according to the Assize of King David, my grandfather, and as was the practice in his time and is still the custom in the Diocese of St. Andrews, then shall the *Vicecomes* compel him to pay, and should the *Vicecomes*

[1] Lawrie, LXI, *c.* 1125.

neglect to carry out this my mandate then *Justicia mea* shall compel the transgressor to pay or exact the penalty, *scilicet* eight cows ".[1]

David's immediate successors established Sheriffdoms all over the country, " holding the lands in check as trees planted to hold shifting sands ".[2] Meantime the installation of the Sheriff in a district is a sign that order, financial and other, is being made to prevail, that there the King's writ runs and the rights of Church and State will be observed—at least in so far as fulminations and comminatory mandates can produce the desired effect.

[1] Mandate by King William (1187 × 1189). *Moray*, No. X, given at Elgin, witnesses the Bishops of Aberdeen and Caithness, Gilbert, Earl of Strathearn, William son of Freskyn, and others.

[2] Dickinson, *Sheriff*, p. xxxi.

§ 25

The Burgh

IN the sense of a fortress used as a base for conquest or defence or as a place of refuge the burgh had long existed in Cumbria and Lothian.[1] David's Burgh was something entirely new, an institution which was not Anglo-Saxon or even Germanic, and which was brought to England by the Normans.

In England from the days of Alfred there had been *burhs* (fortified enclosures). They became centres of administration by Earl and Sheriff, centres of trade, with a market, but their official significance came to an end in 1066, and thenceforth the administrative needs they had met were provided for by the Norman castle built at some distance from the old fortifications. Without delay the Conqueror introduced the French practice whereby selected places, not necessarily old centres, were granted privileges and trading rights, and a definite legal status as trading communities. As soon as such grant was made, a *bourg*, Latin *burgus*, was in being. In France the *bourg*[2] was essentially a trading settlement which had commonly begun as a stockaded quarter beside some older fortification and in which seigneurial obligations tended to disappear, so that personal freedom became the rule and a new status developed, that of burgess living under a special law guaranteed by the King. In England such *burgi* greatly

[1] The old place-names in -"burgh" are not found north of the Forth. Newburgh (Fife) was made a "new burgh" in 1266 ; Fraserburgh (Aberdeenshire) dates from the reign of James VI ; Colinsburgh (Fife) is modern.

[2] C. Stephenson, p. 20. His work provides an exhaustive account of the tenth/eleventh-century renaissance of town life in Western Europe and full reasons for the rise of *bourgs* and *villes neuves* in France.

increased in numbers and importance from the first years of Henry I.[1] Realizing their usefulness to the country and their advantages to the Crown, he took a personal interest in their development. He created boroughs himself, notably one at Dunstable.

David as Earl of Northampton and Huntingdon was well aware of their value. He knew how they were created and how they functioned. He derived a revenue from the borough of Cambridge,[2] he was as familiar as anyone with the workings of the Conqueror's borough at Northampton, and the rise and progress of Henry's borough at Dunstable could come under his observation from Yardley Chase. Another convenient example was the " New Castle " on the Tyne, beside which a new town arose like a *ville neuve* in France and received in due course the privileges which are on record.

That David when Earl created boroughs or, as they are called in Scotland, burghs at Berwick and Roxburgh is probable, though not proved. What is proved is that he had hardly assumed the kingly mantle when he is found referring to " *burgus meus* " of Dunfermline, of Stirling, Perth and Edinburgh. These were already prosperous places, with a Royal castle, and to confer on them the status of *burgi* in the Norman sense of the term was an appropriate Royal gesture on the part of a King used to Norman ways. David continued his creations. Fourteen of " *mei burgi* " are definitely known.[3] The four he first mentions retained their premier position. All are in situations where towns could be expected to appear earliest and develop most rapidly—near a natural stronghold, a junction of main roads, or the mouth of a river where ships

[1] For these and for their French origins see C. Stephenson, pp. 51 and 199. [2] *V.C.H. Hunts.* I, p. 334 ; Pipe Roll of 1130, p. 46.

[3] Aberdeen, Berwick, Crail, Dunfermline, Edinburgh, Elgin, Haddington, Inverkeithing, Linlithgow, Perth, Renfrew, Roxburgh, Rutherglen, Stirling. Berwick and Roxburgh may have been created by David, when Earl.

would first unload. David had initiative enough to create a burgh anywhere and, the privileges being lucrative and much coveted, he must have received applications. But a burgh was unlikely to flourish except where local conditions favoured commerce, just as the development of a port presupposes a hinterland of effective buyers, and his usual practice was to give formal recognition to an already prosperous trading-centre. In these fourteen cases there was an existent community, a vill (*villa*). David granted it exclusive rights of trading within a stated district and freedom from toll or custom; it was then *ipso facto* a burgh (*burgus*). Probably, as in England, the grant was sometimes recorded by charter, but more often left to the memory of witnesses. No charter by David has come down to us; in a few cases, however, the existence of one appears from a confirmation by William the Lion.[1] The customs adopted appear to have been similar to those of Newcastle, which were widely copied in the North of England.[2]

David's burgh generally had the outward form of a military settlement, dominated by a castle. It was a walled community, though the walls were only earthen and wooden, with defensible " ports " or gates, but essentially it was a commercial settlement made for the furtherance of trade and for the accommodation of men engaged in buying and selling and aided in their avocations by the possession of special privileges and monopolies. Business was conducted in the market-place, often a widening-out of the main street and only a few yards from the castle and the church. The burgesses (*burgenses*) held of the King, subject to the performance of certain duties, from

---

[1] *E.g.* William the Lion states (P. J. Anderson, Charter No. I): " By this my charter I have confirmed to my burgesses of Aberdeen and to all burgesses of Moray dwelling to the north of the Mounth their free hanse, to be held . . . as their antecessors in King David's time had their hanse ".

[2] They were granted by Henry I to Alnwick and by the Bishop of Durham to Durham, Wearmouth and Norham.

some of which they could, however, be exempted. At Perth the tenure of Baudouin, the " lorimer " already mentioned, was by burgage. He held of King David his toft, in North Street near the Castle, free of all service except watch and ward and his regular share in the maintenance and upkeep of the enclosing wall. Any case concerning him must be tried only in the King's Courts. Should he wish to remove from the vill he has authority to sell his house and his toft.[1]

There were other burghs than " Royal " : Walter fitz Alan speaks of " my burgh of Renfrew ". It had been created by David " on his own domain " and when he gave the district to Walter the burgh went with it, retaining its privileges as a Royal burgh.[2] The Countess Adeline refers to " my burgh of Haddington, my *Praepositus* and my *burgenses de Hadingtunes scyra* ".[3] She had received Haddington as part of her marriage portion and apparently founded the burgh herself. Bishop Robert " built ", *i.e.* created, one at St. Andrews, " by licence of David our King ".[4] Rutherglen, a Royal burgh, flourished blatantly at the expense of Glasgow, which had wide ecclesiastical fame but little worldly substance. But towards 1176 Glasgow was made an episcopal burgh and was thus enabled to struggle on till at length the tyranny of Rutherglen was overpast. The Augustinians of Holyrood obtained from David a licence to have a burgh on the land between the abbey and " my burgh " (of Edinburgh), evidently waste or unoccupied land bordering on, or part

---

[1] " In vico de north apud castellum . . . quiete ab omni seruicio burgi excepta vigilia infra burgum et claustura burgi " (OF. *closture*, Mod. F. *clôture*). He is prohibited from dealing with any plea, except " in presencia mea aut iusticie mee ". *St. Andrews*, pp. 150, 203 and 204. These provisions closely resemble those of Lorris and Verneuil. See C. Stephenson, pp. 29-30.

[2] " In fundo proprio construxisset "—*Dunfermline*, p. 93, No. CLXII ; *Glasgow*, p. 19, No. XX ; *O.P.* I, p. 74.

[3] Lawrie, CLIII, CLIX (before 1153).

[4] " licentia regis nostri David burgum . . . *aedificare* "—Lawrie, CLXIX.

of, what had been a Royal hunting-ground. The burgesses are to have the same rights " of buying and selling in my market as my own burgesses have, and all men are prohibited from taking bread, ale, cloth or anything vendible against the will of the burgesses ". The Canons are to have exemption from toll and custom " in all my burghs and throughout all my land on all things they may buy and sell ".[1] This grant of rights over the whole country and not only in a fixed local area was probably exceptional.

The marked insistence on " my " leaves no doubt that a burgh was the founder's personal creation and remained his own property. " Creation " was simple ; it need not even have taken seven days ; it was a declaration, which might or might not receive charter form. The founder set over his burgh a *praepositus* (*prévôt*, provost), sometimes two or more *praepositi*, chosen by himself and responsible to no one but himself, collecting the revenues for him and acting as an intermediary between him and the burgh. Thus, though a *praepositus* is etymologically a " provost ", he is not what is now understood by the term. It was with a provost eventually selected by the burgesses themselves that Scotland advanced along the road to municipal government, but, as everywhere else, progress was very slow.

In the end a peculiarly urban population was formed which became conscious of its own interests and powerful enough economically to make its demands heard. But even from the beginning *burgenses* were a people apart. Pedlars are attested in Scotland from the Bronze Age ; there were itinerant foreign merchants centuries before Queen Margaret gave them her patronage ; but there was no professional merchant class. Now one was coming into existence and its representatives were gathering in the burghs. There indeed a new social class was forming, of merchants, middlemen, artisans, townsfolk. In Ireland William of Malmesbury in 1125 draws a melancholy distinction

[1] *Great Charter of Holyrood.* Lawrie, CLIII.

between the uncouth and squalid multitude outside the towns, unhappy product of a barren, because incompetently tilled, soil, and the English and French within the towns, engaged in business and successfully practising " their more civilized way of life ".[1] Similarly the *burgenses* in Scotland may have felt themselves " superior ". They certainly felt themselves *different*—different from the barons and knights of the castle, the under-tenants of the countryside, the cottars and the serfs at work on the land. The *burgenses* were tenants themselves, King's tenants in a Royal burgh, where the rents of their burgages, the customs on trade and the issues of courts held in the burgh went to swell the royal revenues. But this was only a makeshift arrangement, an application of feudal theory where in reality it was inapplicable. By its nature the new institution could not be brought wholly into a lord-and-tenant relationship. In the feudal system the burgh was a foreign body.

In Scotland it was a foreign body in another sense. Its first constituents were of alien origin. They were Normans, Flemings and Englishmen attracted by the freedom from imposts in the transfer of goods and by the monopoly of local trade, but even more by the monopoly of foreign trade. A foreign merchant could buy or sell only to burgesses and they found less profit in dealing in butter and eggs than in buying cloth, wine, wax, spices and specialized articles for retail, and selling wool, hides and furs for export.[2] Local trade there had always been. Distant trade or foreign trade was the difficulty, and it was one largely due to the lack of customers collected in communities. Now town life was beginning and from the first the market was captured by aliens, whether burgesses or travellers. The Normans in the burghs were business

[1] " Angli vero et Franci, cultiori genere vitae, urbes nundinarum commercio inhabitant."—Wm. Malm. II, p. 485.

[2] Mackenzie, *Burgh*, p. 62.

men, prospectors, artificers, artisans. The Flemings were specialists in the sale of cloth and the purchase of wool; Flanders and, to a smaller extent, Picardy maintained for centuries a flourishing export trade with Scotland as with England, though it is not very clear why these countries should not have made their own cloth with their own wool. What particular trade was followed by the Englishmen is not known. Some of them presumably were worthy successors of Godric, who left a humble and Saxon home in Norfolk to engage in commerce and foreign travel ranging from St. Andrews to Jerusalem. He took cargoes to and from Scotland and Flanders, and in so doing " acquired very great riches ", notwithstanding which he withdrew from the world at an early age and spent sixty years as a solitary at Finchale near Durham.[1]

How far the Englishmen were Normanized or were of mixed descent there is nothing in William of Newburgh's much-quoted remark to show.[2] By the end of David's reign, to judge from St. Andrews, the French element in the population of the burghs was strong. The *praepositus*, who is described by Bishop Robert as a Fleming, had a French name, Mainard,[3] and before coming to St. Andrews he was the King's own burgess (*proprius burgensis*) at Berwick, where perhaps he was in the wool export trade. Confirming to the Canons the oblations and rents payable to the Church of the Holy Trinity, Malcolm IV specified that they were due " as well from Scots as from French, as well from Flemings as from English, living within or without the burgh ".[4] The first Aberdonians ever

[1] Reg. Durh. *Godr.*, *passim*. Godric died in 1170. *Chron. Melrose, s.a.* William of Newburgh (II, *c.* xx) visited him shortly before his death. Lest Godric in his solitary hermitage be suspected of magnifying his long-past business activities, it should be mentioned that the economists suspect nothing. The historians suspect piracy.

[2] " Regni Scottici oppida [fortified places] et burgi ab Anglis habitari noscuntur."—Wm. Newb. II, xxxiv. The remark is made in connection with the composition of William the Lion's army in 1174.

[3] A Robert Mainard in Fife in 1260 (*May*, No. XXVIII) was perhaps a descendant. [4] *St. Andrews*, p. 194.

mentioned by name (in his brother William's Charter [1]) are French.

The Scoto-Norman state was strengthened by the institution of the burgh. For the Crown it meant increase of indirect revenues arising from trade; greater profits of justice; higher rents and dues; support from groups of loyal subjects, grateful for the privileges and the protection they received and free from local prejudice, ancient family feuds or long-standing disaffection. The Church derived benefit directly from the episcopal and the monastic creations, indirectly from the existence of God-fearing, law-abiding citizens absorbed in peaceful pursuits. The Sheriff was aided in his introduction of business methods, his promotion of sound book-keeping and his establishment of law and order. The castellans in their colonial or pioneering enterprise gained by the collaboration of the burghers and by the assured supply of the goods and articles essential to an aristocratic society.

[1] Above, p. 325, n. 1.

§ 26

The Abbey

WYNTOUN wrote of David:

> He illumynyt in all his dayis
> His landis with kyrkis and abbayis.[1]

Wyntoun could have added that in general the " kyrkis " were served by the " abbayis " and the " abbayis " were founded for French religious communities.

In the second half of the reign reorganization on diocesan lines was completed. Seven new Bishoprics were created north of the Forth.[2] The episcopate was made as solidly French as in England. Monastic development proceeded more rapidly than before. The Church in Scotland was thus brought into general conformity with the Church in Norman England. But the monastic development was what contemporary writers took to be David's main achievement and in fact the " Abbey " (to use a generic term including the few houses which were only Priories) is the chief outward sign of his " Norman Conquest ".

The religious communities already established continued to prosper. They included the older Benedictines at Coldingham, Dunfermline and Urquhart; the Tironians at Kelso, now coming to be known simply as Benedictines, though they retained their grey habit; the Austin Canons

---

[1] Wyntoun, VII, vi, 843.

[2] Increased to nine by the addition, to St. Andrews and Glasgow, of Aberdeen, Dunblane, Brechin, Ross, Caithness and (unless they were already created by Alexander, as is often assumed on doubtful evidence) Dunkeld and Moray. Whithorn was restored by Fergus in 1133, but was under the jurisdiction of York and remained somewhat aloof. Argyll was carved out of Dunkeld, but not till 1200.

at St. Andrews and Holyrood. Aided by its close associations with the Royal family, the Abbey of Dunfermline
had acquired by 1150 much property and many varied rights.
It possessed land from Stirling to Berwick; it controlled
traffic across the Forth at Stirling;[1] it had a right to every
seventh seal taken at Kinghorn and a tithe of all the pleas
and profits of Fife and Fothrif, also of all the gold that
should accrue to David from both provinces—and by gold
was meant not what might be called mining royalties but
the precious metal itself.[2] As in the days of the " Auld
Alliance " miners brought by Marie de Guise from Lorraine extracted gold from Scottish hillsides, so perhaps
experts from beyond the Channel helped David in the
quest for gold in Fife and silver at Carlisle.

The Tironians made more progress than they ever did
in England.[3] Hugue de Morville brought not from Kelso
but from Tiron itself a colony to Kilwinning in 1140 and
another to Lesmahagow[4] in 1144; Lanarkshire was thus
well provided. The Tironians practised within the convent
whatever mechanical arts they knew, and their communities
were always strong in carpenters, smiths, masons, painters
and carvers.[5] They brought their French methods and
processes with them and the Scots who benefited by their
exertions may be supposed to have learned from their
example. Lesmahagow shows how the foundation of a
monastery could lead indirectly to the rise of a landed
family. The foundation of the Priory, the appointment of
Brice [" Bricius "] of Douglas as Prior, his promotion in
1203 to the See of Moray, his introduction into the diocese

[1] On condition that persons travelling to and from the Court of King
David or Earl Henry should be conveyed free of charge. Great Charter of
Dunfermline, *c.* 1150. Lawrie, CCIX.

[2] Granted by David. Lawrie, LXXVIII, *c.* 1128.

[3] While St. Dogmael's remained their only house in England and Wales,
the Tironians received the greatest Abbeys in Scotland, William the Lion's at
Arbroath (1178) and David of Huntingdon's at Lindores (1195).

[4] Lesmahagow = *Ecclesia Mahuti.* Mahutus was a disciple of St.
Brendan. *O.P.* I, p. 10. [5] Ord. Vit. VIII, xxvii.

of numerous brothers, at first styled simply " fratres episcopi " and soon provided with lands which, distant though they were from Douglas, provided an excellent spring-board—these were the first steps which led the Douglases to eminence.

The Black Canons at St. Andrews gained all the more importance because Bishop Robert organized his diocese on Augustinian principles. The Priory at Jedburgh was raised in 1150 to the rank of Abbey. In 1147 Augustinians, differentiated as Arrouaisians and wearing a distinctive habit, were brought from Arrouaise in Picardy [1] to Cambuskenneth. Their Abbey was known also as the Abbey of Stirling. There, under the fortress, they were as well placed as at Holyrood or at Scone to dispense the well-known hospitality of their order on the occasion of the great gatherings of notables. It was as generously given to poor travellers as to rich and was no doubt as gratefully received on the banks of the Forth as it was on the Pass of St. Bernard. Augustinians were in direct contact with the people as cloistered monks could not be, and their social influence on twelfth-century Scotland was probably wider and more profound.

The new-comers were the Cluniacs, the Cistercians, both in 1136, the Knights Templars, probably towards 1140, and the Premonstratensians in 1150.

Before 1147 Cluniac monks came from Henry I's Abbey of Reading to occupy buildings on May Island in the Forth.

The Cistercians were rapidly spreading all over Western Europe because of the energy and power of St. Bernard, and because their ideals of austerity and selflessness struck the imagination of the mediaeval world. They were intended to be voices crying in the wilderness. They sought the solitudes not as auxiliaries of baronial power but to save their own souls. They wore simple garments of undyed wool, and at first they lived by the labour of their

[1] (Somme), Diocese of Arras.

own hands. All they wanted was a sufficient area of waste, but productive, land in proximity to water and trees. A level space in the bend of a river gave them the necessary pasture, timber and fuel. They were valley-dwellers— hence Clairvaux, Rievaulx and all the other vales and fountains, and sounds of many waters. In Scotland there was no lack of waste land or sequestered valleys and they found contentment in 1136 at Melrose; in 1140 at Newbotle (since called Newbattle), where the South Esk, escaped from the green hills of Temple and the woody ravines of Dalhousie, widens out its valley into fair and level haughs;[1] in 1142 at Dundrennan, on haugh-land in a glen of Galloway; in 1151 at Kinloss in Moray near the mouth of the Findhorn.[2]

The ascetic simplicity which was their aim suited their Scottish environment. At first content with very rough buildings, they had little love of ornament. Not for them the sainted Margaret's costly vestments, gold and silver vessels, crucifix with precious gems. The good Queen Maud's gift to Cluny indisposed Abbot Bernard at Clairvaux: " instead of candlesticks we behold great trees of brass, fashioned with wondrous skill, all a-glitter with jewels as much as with candlelight ".[3] His disciple and interpreter at Rievaulx sternly denounced engraving, sculpture, wall-painting, elaborate choral services, organ-playing —" that terrible blast of bellows, simulating rather the roar of thunder than the sweetness of the human voice " (*Scotice*, a kist o' whistles). Vanity! All vanity! " Tinkling of cymbals, warblings, superfluous beauty, pleasure of the ear, lust of the eye! "[4] Thrift could be observed by Cistercian benefactors; Walter Espec's gifts to Rievaulx, and David's to Melrose, came from the heart, but they

---

[1] C. Innes, *Sketches*, p. 125; see also the Rev. J. R. Dakers, *Newbattle Abbey*, Hawick Archaeological Society, 1877 pp. 27-30.

[2] Newbattle and Kinloss were founded from Melrose; Dundrennan was a daughter-house of Rievaulx.   [3] St. Bernard, *Apologia, c.* 1129.

[4] Ailred, *Speculum Charitatis*, pp. 571-572.

were not " munificent ".[1] The Cistercians were practical
agriculturalists and knew good land when they saw it,
neglected though it might have been. In Scotland they
were quick to note that, though the soil was generally poor,
the hillsides could feed vast numbers of sheep. Much
Cistercian wool went down the Tweed for shipment at
Berwick. Prosperity came, but not at once, and not without effort. Before the Abbey of Melrose could be dedicated to the purposes for which it was founded, more than
ten years elapsed, during which time the White Monks
from Rievaulx lived in huts, like workmen on the site of
some great engineering enterprise in undeveloped country.[2]

The Templars, who probably settled on their lands at
Ballantrodach about the same time as their Cistercian
neighbours at Newbattle, towards 1140, wore white and
had customs derived from Cîteaux, but their white mantle
was worn over a suit of chain-mail and on the left breast
blazed the Red Cross.[3] They were not monks, and their
preceptories were more like manor-houses than monasteries.
David, who would himself have laid down the sceptre for
the Cross had he not been restrained " by the counsel of
priests and the weeping of the poor, kept some good
brethren, renowned in warfare for the Temple, ever beside
him and made them guardians of his conduct by day and
by night ".[4] His relatives and close friends in England

[1] The fee of Helmsley had 189 carucates, of which Rievaulx received
only nine. *Cart. Riev.* p. xlv ; *V.C.H. Yorks.* II, p. 140. Robert de Brus
was more " munificent " to his Augustinians. He gave the Priory at Guisborough 20 carucates when he founded it (1110 × 1124) and afterwards 9 more
—some 10,000 acres, of which 2000 were actually under cultivation. *Cart.
Gyseb.* p. xi.

[2] Melrose, founded March 23, 1136, was consecrated on Sunday, June 28,
1146. *Chron. Melrose, s.a.*

[3] They were authorized to bear the Red Cross in 1140 by Pope Eugenius
III, a former Cistercian Abbot.

[4] Ailred, *G.R.A.* There were two categories of militant members : the
chevaliers and the *sergents*. We take Ailred's phrase as alluding to the fact
that Templars, in accordance with the Benedictine Rule, Caput XXII, had
to sleep in a room with a light burning in it continuously till dawn. Perhaps
" some good brethren " were *chevaliers* who slept in the King's quarters.

were among the first benefactors of the Templars.[1] One of Bishop Robert's charters (interesting also for its goodly array of French witnesses) shows that in Scotland the Templars were regularly receiving donations of lands,[2] and we know that afterwards they had properties in almost every part of the country. But they have left no visible memorial. On the map of Scotland the name Temple marks here a parish and there a croft.[3] Sometimes a countryman can point to " The Templar's Grave ".[4]

In 1150, three miles below Melrose and ten miles above Kelso, at Dryburgh on the north side of the Tweed, Hugue de Morville founded an Abbey for the order of the White Canons of Prémontré, very recently come to England.[5] His Abbey was occupied from Alnwick, where a colony from Licques (Pas-de-Calais) had been established by Eustace fitz John, then living contentedly in Northumberland under Earl Henry's government and taking a very active part in the introduction of the new religious communities. The Premonstratensians who came shortly afterwards to St. Ninian's Priory, founded by Fergus of

---

[1] The earliest recorded gift of land to the Templars in England is from David's niece, Stephen's Queen Maud, *c.* 1137. Other donors were Walter Espec ; Robert de Brus († 1141) or perhaps his son, Robert II (the church of Stretton in Rutland) ; Bernard de Bailleul (15 librates near Hitchin) ; Walter fitz Alan (a virgate at Couetone, Shropshire). Lees, *Temple*, pp. xxxviii, cxii, 79, 131.

[2] Bishop Robert grants three tofts in the Burgh of St. Andrews to the Priory—the tofts of Elfgar, " Arnaldus " [Arnould] and " Willelmus cocus " —to be held on the same terms as those on which the " fratres de templo Domini in Jerusalem " hold tofts in any burgh : " Testibus Matheo archidiacono, Magistro Hereberto, Magistro Thoma, Johanne nepote episcopi, Adam capellano et Ricardo, Rogero camerario, Gamello de Findathin."— Lawrie, CCLXVIII. The church of Inchinnan in Strathgryfe and lands in the district were granted to the Templars by David. *O.P.* I, p. 78. They made few recruits in Scotland. They had a Master, " Magister Domus (vel Militiae) in Scotia ", but formed part of the English province under London. Aitken, *K.T.* p. 6.

[3] Cp. Templeton and Temple Croft, near Kildrummy in Mar.

[4] Aitken, *K.T.* p. 11.

[5] For the term " order ", cp. " fratres monasterii de Dryburgh Premonstratensis ordinis ". Privilege by Pope Alexander III, July 18, 1161, in Lawrie, *Ann. M. and W.* The order was not represented in England till 1143, at Newhouse, Lincolnshire.

Galloway at Whithorn, the old *Candida Casa*, came directly from Prémontré. Companions-in-arms at the Battle of the Standard, the founders may be presumed to have commended the virtues of the " candidus ordo " to each other.[1] It added to the new variety of the Scottish scene. The Canons wore a white cassock with a rochet and cape, a long white cloak and a square hat or bonnet of white felt. The Abbot wore red shoes.

Rapid monastic development at the time was by no means peculiar to Scotland. James I (of Scotland), standing by his great ancestor's tomb at Dunfermline, observed with a sigh that David had been " a sair sanct to the Croun ". With its air of mild reproach and its moderately grim humour the epigram is very clever and well worthy of the Poet-King, but its authenticity is uncertain and its truth only relative.[2] Put at its highest, the total number of religious houses founded in David's Kingdom during the twenty-nine years of his reign was nineteen, whereas Yorkshire had sixty-eight.[3]

The monastic foundations reinforced the French element in his Kingdom. In Scotland from the earliest times monasteries had represented the Church in the eyes of the people. In Normandy the monastic life had always been the ideal, and intending religious benefactors, ducal,

[1] Eustace fitz John died in 1157 in Wales as a very elderly warrior fighting for Henry II.

[2] The remark may be historical, but the authority for it is only Bellenden, II, p. 185, in a passage of some length interpolated in his translation of Boece.

[3] Nineteen is Ailred's number, in what corresponds to an obituary notice, and it is certainly as high as he can make it. Most of the 68 Yorkshire monasteries were founded in Stephen's reign (1135–1154, *i.e.* during the latter half of David's) and in disturbed conditions which from 1140 were not paralleled in Scotland. Comparative statistics would be hard to establish, but it may be noted that Bishop Haldon's assessment of the entire revenues of the Church in Scotland, made a century and a half after David's death, is calculated by Lord Cooper, p. 3, to be only one-fifth of the corresponding figure for England. As regards endowment, the total list of Crown lands granted by David to the Church, as recorded in the surviving charters, would certainly look impressive. But a pompous Latin phrase may designate a building-plot 20 feet by 6.

baronial or other, turned first to the monks. David's Norman beneficiaries followed this double tradition. With the exception of Hugue de Morville they were not founders, but through their connections in England they helped to introduce the religious communities, and they were the chief contributors to the necessary endowment, by donations of land or the gift of a church. They believed that a monastery promoted the general spiritual welfare, and they knew that it could not be self-supporting. It depended, as they did, on the land. Spreading fame brought an accession of new members, a need for expansion, and the original endowment became inadequate. The Norman landowners gave land, but agriculture or sheep-farming might prove a distraction, and the monks preferred a simple rent or charge on land. The regular form of benefaction was to confer on a monastery the manorial church, which thenceforth was served by a *vicar* sent by the monastery, sometimes a monk, more usually a clerk. The monastery received the revenues of the church, such as fees for baptisms and funerals. The system led to abuses, shown by a recent historian to have been less grievous in Scotland than in most countries.[1] Such grants were regularly recorded by charter and confirmed by the King; hence, incidentally, the preservation to the present day of information concerning the Norman landowners.

Castle and Abbey went closely together in partnership. Their occupants had much in common. Monks and canons had to some extent the same interests as the Norman landowners, often relatives of their own, the same faith in charters, written government, property rights, land-development, the same zest for country life. Even the Cistercians, though St. Bernard had warned them time after time against the pleasures of the chase, shared the Norman proclivities, and donors who combined piety with a due regard for the preservation of game deemed it

[1] R. A. R. Hartridge, p. 43.

advisable to insert a clause in the deed of gift expressly withholding sporting rights on the Abbey lands. Thus Robert Avenel gave to Melrose his land in Eskdale, which he had received from David, but he reserved to his family the right of game, specifying hart and hind, boar and roe, and stipulated that the monks should not hunt, or allow others to hunt, with hounds or nets, and should not set traps, save only for wolves. Taking the eyries of hawks was strictly forbidden and no damage must be done to the trees in which the hawks usually built.[1]

The dwellers in the castles and the monasteries were fellow-Frenchmen. In a religious sense the various communities were not of France or of any country. But France was their place of origin and remained their headquarters; for instance, heads of houses had to return regularly to Tiron, Cîteaux, Prémontré or Arrouaise for the general chapter. None of the orders were Norman, but all of them were French.[2] The monks, it is true, were Latin in culture and (officially) in language. They represented Latin Christendom as a whole. In the Benedictine phrase they were " in every place servants of one Lord and soldiers of one King ". But they were French-born and France gives her sons a stamp which is not easily effaced, even

---

[1] *Melrose*, No. XXXIX. Robert Avenel made his gift in 1185. *Chron. Melrose, s.a.*

[2] *Ordo* in the phrase *religiosus ordo* may mean either " ordered way of life " or " organized body ". In English " order " has been restricted to the second meaning, whereas only the first applies to the Benedictines. St. Benedict of Nursia († 543) did not found an " order " in the second sense ; one was created in the course of the eleventh century at the Abbey founded in 910 at Cluny (Saône-et-Loire). It was only to observe the Rule of St. Benedict with yet greater strictness than their fellows that some French Benedictines withdrew in 1098 from Molême (Yonne) to Cîteaux (Côte-d'Or, arr. Beaune, commune de Saint-Nicolas) and that others founded " reformed " orders at Savigny (Manche, canton Le Teilleul) as at Tiron. The Augustinian Canons had no definite place of origin, but those who came to Scotland came from France, directly or from French houses in England. The Norbertines or Premonstratensians followed the Rule of Norbert, a native of Xanten, who became Bishop of Laon. He founded in 1119 their first house in the valley of Prémontré in the Forest of Coucy, Diocese of Laon.

when they become Sons of St. Benedict. Every new religious house in Scotland was one more link with France. From France channels of information led into the Scottish monasteries and from them out into the lay world. Monasteries were not primarily intellectual agencies or educational establishments—Kelso at least had schools at Roxburgh, Dunfermline had schools at Perth and Stirling [1] —but could always disseminate knowledge as clearing-houses for the exchange of news and ideas with the clerks and laymen now passing in ever greater numbers along the roads. All led to Rome and generally through France. They also led home again, and returning natives who had lived some time in France took their part in spreading French ideas. Novices, soon no doubt of Scottish birth, often went to France for their noviciate.

The Abbey touched Scottish life at many points. Abbots were magnates of the realm, next to the Bishops in order of precedence; indeed the Abbot of Kelso claimed precedence over the Bishop of St. Andrews and the matter had to be referred to the Pope. The monasteries provided in great part the civil service of the Kingdom. The mass of varied rights which they came to possess involved much contact with the native population. Not that there was a Benedictine on the beach at Kinghorn to claim one seal out of every seven landed, but, however cloistered the monks of Dunfermline might be, they required a host of lay emissaries, agents, representatives. For equally practical purposes there was also much contact with France, directly or through the monasteries in England. David granted Tiron the right to send one ship yearly free of *can* (duty), " the men in it to enjoy his peace in buying and selling everywhere in his dominions ".[2] The shipmen who sailed

---

[1] Between 1150 and 1153 a confirmation by Bishop Robert of the lands and privileges of Dunfermline Abbey mentions the schools of Perth and Stirling. Lawrie, CCLVI. A similar document referring to the Abbey of Kelso includes " omnes ecclesias et scholas eiusdem burgi " [Roxburgh]. *Ibid*. CXCIV.   [2] Lawrie, CXXXVI, *c*. 1141.

under monastic auspices bought salted fish and sold more cheerful commodities. " Rycht crafty masons ", Bellenden informs us, were brought from France and Flanders to build Holyrood. But there is little information to be gleaned on the subject, even from the buildings themselves. They are all reconstructed or altered and only a few portions now exist : the tower at Dunblane, the nave of Dunfermline, parts of Holyrood, Dryburgh and Jedburgh. These are the only memorials left by David and his Normans that are visible to the eye. To that (limited) extent the city of God remaineth. The permanent outward Norman contribution to Scottish life was the Abbey. The wooden castles are gone. The Norman arch still stands at Dunfermline.

CHAPTER VIII

SEQUEL : THE REIGN OF MALCOLM IV
(1153–1165)

★

§ 27

Malcolm the Maiden

DAVID'S work was complete. But it was set in sudden
jeopardy by his death. Nine months before, he had lost
his only son, Earl Henry, and he was succeeded by his
eldest grandson, a delicate, girlish-looking boy of eleven,
" Malcolm to name, ane prettie plesand page ".[1] The boy
had already been taken round " ilka Sheriffdom of the land,
with honest court and company "[2] to be shown to the
people, and no untoward incident marked his accession.
Celts and Normans loved high descent and Malcolm IV
had in his favour illustrious ancestry. The splendour
of his French origins was not lost upon the King of
France[3] or upon Scotland's Norman barons, who
noted, however, one deficiency. He had no surname. In
Celtic fashion he was Malcolm MacHenry MacDavid
MacMalcolm MacDuncan and so onwards to Fergus Mór,
son of Erc.[4] In his brother William's case the deficiency
had been made good. Since Northumberland would be
held of the next King of England it had been deemed
sufficient—and prudent—that Henry should be succeeded
in his Earldom by his second son William; a surname had
then seemed desirable and the Boy-Earl was given his
mother's surname, de Varenne. His charter style was

---

[1] *Bk. Cron. Scot.* l. 42, 502. Earl Henry's sons were : Malcolm IV, b.
March 20, 1142 ; William, b. 1143 ; David, b. 1144 × 1152.

[2] Wyntoun, VII, vi, 1165.

[3] Louis VII writes in 1173 (according to Jourdain Fantosme) :

> " Al rei d'Escoce, Willame, le meilleur
> A qui nostre lignage fut jadis anceisur ".

[4] Raoul de Dicet, *s.a.* 1185, goes further—from Erc to Richaith Scot,
son of Gomer, son of Japheth, son of Noah.

" Villelmus de Gwarenne, Comes Northumbriae ".[1] Afterwards he was in the language of chivalry " Sire Willame de
Varenne, rei d'Escoce ou d'Aubanie ".[2] The Boy-King
in charter style was plain " Malcolomus Rex Scottorum " ;
unofficially to Normans he was probably " Malcolomb de
Varenne ".[3]

Hardly had the plaudits died away on the Moot Hill
of Scone when the smouldering hostility to the Sons of
Margaret flamed out again. The sons of Malcolm MacHeth
revolted and were joined by their kinsman Somerled of
Argyll, the most redoubtable of all Scotland's rebel warriors,
Celtic or Norse, and he was both. The storm subsided
when Donald MacHeth was captured at Whithorn and
sent to join his father in the tower at Roxburgh. Next
February (1154) " Arthur, who was about to betray King
Malcolm, perished in a *duellum* " [4]—thus revealing the
existence in Scotland of the special form of *judicium Dei*
known as *duellum*, or trial by combat, the Conqueror's one
and only permanent contribution to the Laws of England.[5]
In December the last of the four Norman kings quits the
English stage and the first of the Angevins comes on, the
Knight of Carlisle, Henry Plantagenet, " a boy in years, in
mind a sage ",[6] already past master in the art of making the

---

[1] *E.g.* 1152. Grant to William de Vesci ; sign. Ada (Adeline de
Varenne) ; Gilbert, Constable ; " Willelmus Masculus " = Guillaume le
Mâle. *Hist. Northd.* II, p. 469.

[2] Most of his coinage bears " WILLALMUS REX ", with the superscription
" LE REI WILLAME ".

[3] " Malcolmus de Gwarenne " appears (in error) in the Confirmation of
a grant by Earl Henry to Brinkburn. *Chartulary of Brinkburn Priory,*
Surtees Soc. (90), 1893, p. 143.

[4] *Chron. Holyrood, s.a.* 1154.

[5] The ordeal or *judicium Dei*, condemned by the Fourth Lateran Council
in 1215, was soon afterwards prohibited in England. The *duellum* was not
formally abolished till 1819. In Scotland the ordeal is supposed to have been
abandoned in 1230, and the *duellum* soon after.

[6] " Puer annis, mente senilis." H. Hunt. Henry II acceded in his
twenty-third year. After being knighted at Carlisle and returning to France
in 1149 he had continued in knightly discipline : " in patriam suam reversus,
in militaribus se exercuit disciplinis ; viribus corporis praevalidus, moribus
quiddam senile praeferens "—John of Hexham, p. 323.

best of both worlds, the English world and the French. Descendant of Alfred as of William, he can stand forth in the line of true succession, disclaim all connection with the late Interloper and rule over French and English in his island kingdom, as to the manner born.

This consummation had been seen coming, and by none more clearly than Abbot Ailred at Rievaulx. In pleasant and patriotic anticipation he had compiled a " Genealogy of the English Kings " and dedicated it to Henry, Duke of Normandy and Aquitaine, Count of Anjou. It was intended to recall the glorious past which had brought the young Angevin to the steps of the throne and to light the path of a Sovereign who in his own person would unite English traditions and French. It traces his ancestry, first to " that most saintly woman, Margaret, Queen of Scots ", granddaughter of unvanquished Edmund Ironside, next from Edmund up to Cerdic, then from Cerdic to Woden and finally to Noah and to Adam, " father of us all ".[1] The dizzy ascent accomplished, the learned Abbot comes down again, less rapidly, making brief pauses for thumb-nail sketches of the later and less nebulous kings. On both journeys some circumspection is required, because in the male line the future monarch was neither English nor Norman and could only establish a second foreign dynasty, the Angevins. Attention is prudently focused on the all-important point of junction, the marriage of his grandfather, the First Henry, with the " English " princess Maud, and on the all-important *spiritual* link, her kinsman the Holy King, on whom there is an excursus, " De Sancto Edwardo rege et virgine ". The Genealogy of which " Henricus noster " received the dedication has for exordium a lament for the death of David, " whose pure hands have girt thee with the belt of Knighthood ", and for peroration a touching appeal on behalf of David's orphaned grandsons. They are, it is

[1] *G.R.A.* p. 716.

reiterated, the descendants of Edmund the Hero and Margaret the Saint. Another descendant is Henry Plantagenet, " Head of all the House ", who is delicately left to draw the moral.

The spiritual genealogist had done his best for English, Normans and Scots. He had also done his best for Malcolm and William.[1] Meantime they stood in need of more help than genealogical. By the rules of chivalry the Coronation bells of the Sunday before Christmas 1154 should have borne glad tidings for the crowned Plantagenet's young cousins in the North.[2] But since his knighting and his promises at Carlisle in 1149 he had gone far, and they had for neighbour on the Tyne and the Derwent the ruler of an Empire stretching from there to the Pyrenees. When in 1157 Henry II demanded restoration of the ceded territory, Malcolm IV could only bow to fate—and go with Earl William to do homage at Chester and accept what terms they might be offered. He received the Honour and Earldom of Huntingdon, but relinquished Carlisle and Southern Cumbria, while William retained the Liberty of Tynedale, but lost the rest of Northumberland.[3] By such give-and-take Malcolm IV was made the King of England's vassal more definitely than David had been,[4] and the Scottish frontier was moved back again to the Solway and the Tweed.

Next June (1158) Henry made a progress through his Kingdom from Malmesbury to Carlisle. There Malcolm went to meet him, now sixteen and, like himself at the

[1] Ailred's dealings with the country of his upbringing had by no means ceased. He visited the Cistercian abbeys annually. His lifelong friend Waldef, Abbot of Melrose, was in charge of Malcolm's education. Like Malcolm, Ailred was continually travelling and no doubt made a point of meeting him wherever possible. With Malcolm's Chancellor Enguerrand, he was one of the (few) witnesses to Walter fitz Alan's Foundation Charter of Paisley Abbey. *Paisley*, No. I (1163). The others are Walter's brother Simon, Enguerrand's brother, also called Simon, and Robert de Constentin. Ailred died soon after Malcolm IV, in January 1167.

[2] Second cousins, Henry II being a great-grandson of Malcolm Canmore.

[3] The manors of Tynedale were in the Forest of Inglewood, south of Carlisle, between Greystoke and the Eden. See Moore, *L.Sc.K.* p. 21.

[4] See Appendix B.

same age, burning with ambition to be a knight. Though subject all his life to sudden and grievous illnesses, Malcolm was to achieve military renown, and already he had passed through the moral and physical discipline to which candidates for knighthood were subjected. All that was lacking was the touch of another King's sword. This was refused. The interview was stormy. Impassive demeanour was not one of Henry's characteristics. He was given to breaking off an audience and rolling in fury on the floor, biting at bits of straw or anything else within his frenzied reach.[1] His patience was soon exhausted.[2] Malcolm was mortified by the refusal of knighthood and, considering the circumstances, the time and the place, it was ungracious.

It was not, however, unstudied, and in the following spring (1159), when Henry took the new step of summoning his vassals for *foreign* service, Malcolm, who was among them, learned that he might now win knighthood, not in a better place than in the Halls of Arthur, but in a better way, by valour on a foreign field.[3] With that high hope before him, he resolved to take part in the campaign to be fought in France in support of Queen Eleanor's claim to Toulouse. Accompanied by his brother William and " numerous sons of nobles ", he sailed with a fleet of forty-five ships and, landing in Normandy on June 16, went on to join the army mustering at Poitiers.[4] There a theatrical personage was to be seen daily on the field of assembly in more than regal splendour, with seven hundred knights of his own following. This was Henry's Chancellor, Thomas Becket, still

---

[1] One of these wild scenes occurred in Normandy in 1166, when the Constable Richard du Hommet happened to make a remark about Malcolm's brother William which sounded favourable. Letter to Thomas Becket, probably by John of Salisbury, in Anderson, *E.S.Sc.* II, p. 264.

[2] To Malcolm " he took care to announce [concerning the territories ceded to Scotland by Stephen] that the King of England ought not to be defrauded of so large a portion of his dominions, nor could he *patiently* be deprived of it (nec posse patienter mutilari) "—Wm. Newb. II, iv, p. 94.

[3] Henry seems unchivalrous, but in his own knighting by David there was also a *quid pro quo*.   [4] *Continuatio Beccensis*, p. 323.

very much in the world, his imagination not yet aflame with the thought that Chancellor was less than Archbishop, Archbishop than Saint, Saint than Martyr. It was no discredit then to be theatrical and he won admiration from Malcolm and William that was deep and lasting.[1] The host was soon on the march and at Périgueux, in the Bishop's Meadow,[2] the King of England knighted the King of Scots, who then imparted the honour to his brother William [3] and thirty sons of nobles. All proceeded to the tented field at Toulouse. The siege lasted into September, when Louis VII slipped quietly into the town and, much as the Angevin coveted Toulouse, the thought of a suzerain beleaguered by a vassal offended his sense of the fitness of things. He raised the siege, dismissed his army and " with the King of Scotland, passing through Uzerche, came to Limoges about the feast of the Archangel Michael " (September 29, 1159).[4]

It is a strange reflection that none of Scotland's Normanizing Kings except the ill-fated Duncan II had ever set foot in Normandy, and now that at last one had gone there

[1] Malcolm's attachment to the cause of Becket is mentioned by Pope Alexander III in a letter to William (Ed. Reg. Durh. p. 237), who had met Becket again in London. Becket was canonized on February 21, 1173. William's capture at Alnwick, June 13, 1174, followed Henry's penance at the Tomb by a few hours (see *Vita S. Thomae*, ed. J. C. Robertson, II, p. 447) and was attributed to the intervention of the Saint by many, including William himself, whose great Abbey of Arbroath (Tironensian) was dedicated to St. Thomas of Canterbury.

[2] " In prato Episcopali." Geoffroi de Vigeois (Gaufridus Vosensis), in Bouquet, *Recueil*, XII, p. 439. According to *Chron. Holyrood* and *Chron. Melrose*, followed by Fordun and Wyntoun, the knighting took place at Tours, *after* the siege of Toulouse. But as a monk in the Abbey of Saint-Martial at Vigeois, some thirty miles north-east of Périgueux, Geoffroi († 1184) is likely to have been well informed. " The Bishop's meadow " seems an obvious place for what was partly a religious ceremony and partly a military spectacle. Moreover, the matter was fixed in the chronicler's memory. He mentions that the events of the day were for the Bishop [Giraldus] the beginning of a malady which led to total blindness.

[3] Jourdain Fantosme, l. 1259, makes William speak as if he had been at the siege of Toulouse. William was then sixteen, the regular age for knighting. He was nothing if not a knight, and there is no other reference to the time and place of the accolade. He may have been summoned as a vassal for Tynedale. [4] G. de Vigeois, *ibid.*

its glory had departed. Normandy will remain yet awhile a centre of government, the headquarters of itinerant monarchs ruling like Roman Emperors on both sides of the Channel, but as a centre for the dissemination of French ideas in Britain its importance has diminished. History has passed into Angevin times and the day is approaching when the union of Kingdom and Duchy will be dissolved for ever.

The Knight of Périgueux returned, by way of Touraine, to be next year (1160) besieged himself, " in the town of Perth, by Earl Ferteth and five other Earls who were angry because he had gone to Toulouse and who desired to seize him ". They were routed and pursued into Galloway; Malcolm " went three times there and at last subdued them ".[1] To enter into their feelings, political or other, one would have to know their names and something of their family history. Only Ferteth, Earl of Strathearn, is known and in his case there can be no question of un-friendliness towards Normans as such. His father Malise had been critical of Normans at the Battle of the Standard, but he himself was evidently less critical; he had been a hostage among them in England. He created *c.* 1150 the diocese of Dunblane or Strathearn, of which he was recognized to be patron by the Pope; he gave his son, born about that time, a French name, Gilbert, and in · due course married his daughter to a Norman, Walter Olifard. (Gilbert lived to have two Norman wives, to grant charters sealed with the device of a mounted knight in armour and to be a model Norman Earl of Strathearn, with a monastery of his own foundation, a household rich in Arthurian names and, in the place of honour, a Tristan and an Yseult.[2]) Earl Ferteth was soon reconciled with

---

[1] *Chron. Melrose, s.a.* 1160.

[2] In Bishop Ernout's list of his episcopal possessions (1161) Earl Ferteth is a co-signatory with " Magister Arturus " and " Magister Merlinus ". *St. Andrews*, p. 132. The name Arthur is common in twelfth-century Scotland. It occurs very frequently in the chartulary *Lennox*. As for

King Malcolm and till his death in 1171 was busied with all good works.

Fergus of Galloway had apparently made common cause with the six Earls. He was utterly defeated and forced to surrender his son Uchtred as a hostage and to seek sanctuary in Holyrood, where he became an Austin Canon and where he died soon afterwards. In Galloway Normanization was taken firmly in hand. Castles were built—in Galloway there are more green mounds representing Norman castles than anywhere else in Scotland. Constables or *baillis* [1] (not sheriffs) were installed in the castles. Strangers were brought in " to settle and dwell in the lands of Dunrod " which Fergus had given to Holyrood.[2] Thenceforth Galloway was definitely part of the Scottish realm, though it soon afterwards broke away

Merlin, Fordun, though not Jocelin, relates how St. Kentigern was surprised in his solitude by a wild and naked savage called Lailoken who was of old a bard in the Court of King Vortigern, where he was known by the name of Merlin. He was admitted by the Saint to the holy sacrament, but on the same day was drowned in Tweed, and buried at Drummelzier. Merlin's fame in Old French Romance is due to Geoffrey of Monmouth's *Vita Merlini* (1148 × 1149), which utilizes an early work relating to Lailoken ; see Ward, *Romania*, XXXIII (1893), pp. 504 ff.

Ferteth's son Gilbert (1150–1223), who in 1171 succeeded him as Earl of Strathearn, married Matilda, daughter of William d'Aubigny († 1215), and after her death (c. 1210), Ysende (a variant of Yseude, Yseult, Isolde, etc.), daughter of an otherwise unknown Lugan and sister of Richard, *miles*, and Geoffrey. Lugan appears as Luguen in a fourteenth-century charter. *Cambuskenneth*, p. 89. Richard held Kinbuck, a few miles N. of Dunblane, Geoffrey held part of Gask ; part had been held by Ness, son of William. In 1200 Gilbert founded the Abbey of Inchaffray (Augustinian), 6 miles E. of Crieff. One of the signatories of his Foundation Charter was " Tristrannus ", son of a Hawise [Avicia], husband of an Ela (= Adèle) and father of a Tristran and a Hawise. The name Tristan (a variant of Tristran), not hitherto attested in Scotland, is recorded in Brittany from before 1050 (R. S. Loomis, *Romania*, LIII, 1929, p. 98). It was a Breton custom to use the mother's name, and this Tristran was perhaps of Breton extraction. He held Gorthy in Strathearn and there were Tristrans of Gorthy till 1507. When Yseult gave (1221 × 1223) to Inchaffray five acres of land " in villa mea de Abercharni [Abercairney] ", she perambulated the land with Tristran, son of Tristran. *Inchaffray*, Nos. IX, XXVII and XLVI.

[1] *Baillies* (bailiwicks) first appear in Normandy under Henry's father, Geoffrey Plantagenet. *Bailli* is the generic term for the official in charge of them, but often he is simply the Constable of a castle. Valin, pp. 98-99.

[2] Charter by Malcolm IV, *Holyrood*, p. 21.

for a short time [1] and in 1305, mysterious as ever, was still living under laws and customs of its own. In the North, where there had been unrest, Normanization was intensified; in 1163 occurred the traditional " plantation of Moray " with Norman settlers.[2]

The Toulouse expedition, a purely aristocratic or knightly affair, was unpopular and expensive. Some political or financial crisis was settled at Perth, at a Convention of Prelates and Nobles. An aid, like the Norman " auxilium ad filiam maritandam ", was then given for two forthcoming Royal marriages : that of the King's second sister Margaret, in the same year (1160), to Conan, Earl of Richmond and Duke of Brittany, and that of his eldest sister Ada or Adeline, in 1162, to Florent III, Count of Holland.[3] The first marriage was of the type becoming commonplace in the upper strata of North Country society : *Le Comte de Richemont et Marguerite de Varenne*.[4]

---

[1] In 1174, after William the Lion's disaster at Alnwick, the Galwegians revolted and slew all the "strangers", English and French, they could lay hands on ; " all the strongholds and castles which the King of Scotland had built, they besieged, captured and destroyed, and all whom they seized within they slew". Ben. Abb. p. 67. In September Uchtred was slain by his brother Gilbert's son. This holocaust is sometimes taken as showing later French unpopularity in Scotland. But Galloway was a land apart ; the slaughter was indiscriminate ; one fate overwhelmed the English, the French and Uchtred. The protagonists were themselves partly French. Gilbert was baptized with a good French name and Uchtred's son Roland with a better.

[2] See Skene, III, p. 27. The words which have suggested wholesale transference of population in 1163 are vague : " Rex Malcolmus Muravienses transtulit ". *Chron. Holyrood, s.a.* But Fordun refers to the action taken as drastic, though justified by the continued unrest, and the example set in 1136 is significant.

[3] Malcolm IV had three sisters : Ada, b. before 1143 ; Margaret, b. before 1145 ; Maud, who died unmarried in 1165.

[4] Conan IV, *le Petit* († February 20, 1171), was born after September 1125. He was the son and successor of Count Alan of Brittany, Earl of Richmond, so styled from 1136. In September 1156 Conan crossed to Brittany, besieged and took Rennes, and was recognized by the Bretons as Duke. On the death, in July 1158, of Henry II's brother Geoffrey, Conan seized Nantes, but was forced to surrender the town to Henry. Conan and Margaret returned frequently to Richmond. *E. Yks. Ch.* IV, p. x ; Lawrie, *Ann. M. and W.* p. 58. Their only child Constance was the mother of the ill-fated Arthur of Brittany.

The second reflected the growing prosperity, the flourishing of the burghs, the importance of the East Coast trade and the recognition of its value in the Low Countries.

Both weddings were solemnized with much pomp. On both occasions, at the meeting of the *curia regis* after the ceremony, the Bishop of St. Andrews, Ernout [Arnold], implored King Malcolm to abandon his intention of perpetual celibacy and take a wife—as of old the " Counts and Barons " had pressed matrimony on Edward, who after much prayer had followed their advice, reluctantly and with mental reservations.[1] But on both occasions Malcolm steadfastly replied that he would never marry, " inquiens se a pueritia virginitatem suam Christo dicasse ",[2] thus saying in effect that, like King Edgar before him, he was resolved to maintain the tradition of their kinsman Edward and " live as a monk ".[3]

Other hearts than Malcolm's were inditing of the same matter, that which had been expounded in Ailred's excursus " De Sancto Edwardo rege et virgine ". At last the canonization long wished for by many was seen to be coming within the bounds of practical possibility. There was a new abbot at Westminster. The late King Stephen's illegitimate son Gervais, deposed by the Pope, had been succeeded, in 1158, by Ailred's kinsman Laurent or Laurence, formerly of Durham. The prophecy of the Green Tree still awaited fulfilment, and on its interpretation Ailred for one felt no doubt. For him the blossom of the Green Tree was " Imperatrix Matildis " and its fruit was " Henricus noster ". The political horoscope favoured this interpretation. The Angevin monarchy, as sadly as the Norman, lacked pride of ancestry. For his contempor-

---

[1] *Estoire*, l. 1058.

[2] Fordun, p. 257 ; Boece, XIII, p. 269 ; see Appendix I.

[3] In the Temptation of Malcolm, as recounted by William of Newburgh, the Countess Adeline exhorted her son " to be a King and not a monk ". Eleanor of Aquitaine, who obtained a divorce from Louis VII, said of herself " se monacho, non regi, nupsisse "—Wm. Newb. I, xxxi, p. 85.

aries Henry II was always very much his mother's son, either fitz Mahaut or else fitz Emperis. In Ireland, and no doubt in Scotland, he was Mac na-h'Imperasi.[1] In an age so addicted to pedigree-worship it was a calamity for the ruler of the world from the Cheviots to the Pyrenees to be " only the son of a Count "[2] and to require description in terms of his mother's first husband. He was in a state of manifest inferiority to his wife's previous husband, his suzerain Louis VII, in this respect, and in another: the Angevin monarchy had not the sacerdotal character which the French Kings derived from Clovis through Charlemagne. This latter disadvantage, some now thought, could be removed by the canonization of Edward.

Abbot Laurent went to Normandy to discuss the matter with King Henry. A mission was sent to Rome. The times were more propitious than when Prior Osbert went from Westminster in 1138, for there was no doubt now who was King of England. There was, however, some doubt who was Pope. The election of Alexander III was seriously contested and he was grateful for the support of temporal powers. Among the first to help was Scotland. The Chamberlain Nicholas and the Bishop of Moray, who were in Italy, on business probably connected with St. Andrews, went to Anagni to assure him of Scottish loyalty. They were received " with the highest honour " and the Bishop came home in the unsought office of Legate.[3] In the summer (1160) the King of England, speaking also

---

[1] He was so known when he landed at Waterford in 1171. Curtis, p. 25.

[2] After the Young King's Coronation, June 14, 1170, Henry II waited on his son at table " as Seneschal ". To those who spoke of the honour thus done to him, the Young King replied that it was a proper thing for one who was only the son of a Count to wait on the son of a King. Henry II was not like Henry I a Porphyrogenite (see above, p. 101, n. 2), and this was made a reproach to him in the world of flamboyant chivalry inhabited by the Young King and his friends.

[3] *Chron. Melrose* and *Chron. Holyrood, s.a.* 1159. Jocelin, *Vita S. Waldeui,* p. 270, relates that Nicholas had a dream which he described to the Pope, who thought it might portend the death of Abbot Waldef; cp. the dream of Richard the Clerk, below, p. 414.

for the King of France, acknowledged Alexander III as Pope.[1] On February 7, 1161, Alexander III issued the bull canonizing Edward and conferring the title of Confessor.[2]

The Abbot of Westminster then asked his kinsman at Rievaulx to write a Life of the Royal Saint in time for the Translation to a new tomb in the Abbey. No one could have been better qualified than Ailred. Brought up at the Court of Edward's kinsman David, he was a student of genealogy, spiritual as well as corporeal, an author of works on both branches of the subject, a celebrated religious writer, an acknowledged authority on miracles. Possessing information handed down in the family from Ælfred Westou and Eilaf I, he could tell of several, worked by St. Cuthbert, which were not generally known,[3] and in the twelfth-century view it was the bounden duty of every man who knew of such things to tell them, for they were signs sent by God to be revealed. Ailred's two chief objects of veneration were St. Cuthbert and St. Edward.[4] Next came St. Margaret and David, her departed son. The fitting sequel to the " Genealogy " was the " Life of St. Edward ", dedicated to Henry Plantagenet, "the corner-stone at which the English and the Norman peoples have met ".[5] They were united in reverence of the past. The Normans, who

[1] The power to acknowledge Alexander III was apparently delegated by Louis VII to Henry, who used it to extort from a Legate permission for the marriage of his eldest surviving son Henry, aged five (born February 26, 1155), and Louis' daughter Marguerite (born 1157). The marriage took place in November 1160. Frank Barlow, *E.H.R.* LI (1936), p. 266.

[2] The title of Confessor indicates a saint who has not suffered martyrdom, in contrast to King Edward the Martyr, murdered March 18, 978.

[3] Reg. Durh. *Cuthb.* pp. 32 and 60.

[4] Once, on a tedious journey to the General Chapter at Cîteaux, Ailred whiled away the time by writing a *prosa* in honour of St. Cuthbert. Reg. Durh. *Cuthb.* I, No. LXXXIV, pp. 175-177.

[5] " In quem velut lapidem angularem Anglici generis et Normannici gaudemus duos populos convenisse "—Ailred, *Vita S. Edw.*, *Prologus*, p. 738. His *Vita* makes no claim to originality. It claims (unsuccessfully) to be more simply written than Osbert of Clare's work, which it follows very closely, adding little more than a story of the childhood of Harold and Tostig, and a miracle which had happened to Osbert.

had adopted St. Edward, had taken their full share in providing England with a national Saint,[1] and it was appropriate that the Translation, on October 13, 1163, should be conducted by the new Archbishop, Thomas Becket, whose father was born at Rouen and whose mother was born at Caen.

It was while in England the Church, the King, Laurent of Durham and Westminster, Ailred of Durham, Hexham, Roxburgh and Rievaulx, counsellor of the Scottish Royal House, were all working together for the canonization of Edward that in Scotland the Saint's spiritual descendant twice formally reiterated his early vow to remain Malcolm the Maiden.

Among the devotees of chivalry the belief was spreading that marriage, though not a sin, was a weakness, and one into which the true Knight would not fall. Some maintained that he should take the monastic vows of chastity, obedience and poverty, like the Templar. Such views were in accordance with Cistercian thought. It was with the powerful help of St. Bernard that the Templars obtained recognition as an order; in his own words his monks were *milites*; those who prayed at Melrose were fellow-warriors with his Crusaders. Malcolm the Maiden's tutor was the Abbot of Melrose; for his self-constituted guardian, the Abbot of Rievaulx, the best Knight was one who, like Earl Henry, was " almost a monk ".

Most knights, however, preferred the more worldly, more spectacular, forms of chivalry and these were successfully practised in Scotland by William, the King's brother. While Malcolm took after his father, whom he resembled in personal appearance as closely as in way of life, William

---

[1] Edward was regarded as the Patron Saint of England till 1222. The name did not reach the Plantagenets till Henry III gave it to his son, who, inappropriately, became the " Hammer of the Scots ". In 1230 the Cistercian Abbey of Balmerino in Fife was erected " ad honorem Dei et gloriosae Virginis Mariae et sanctissimi regis Edwardi ".

took after his mother. The Countess Adeline founded a Cistercian nunnery, and for the cure of her many ailments put her trust in St. Cuthbert ;[1] but she was of the world and (if William of Newburgh speaks truly) had such small sympathy with Malcolm's ethereal aspirations that she placed temptation in his way. William was, like her, " a Norman in face and manners ".[2] He was a de Varenne, a red-faced burly figure, a Knight of the flamboyant sort.[3] He distinguished himself at tournaments, as no doubt many Normans in Scotland did, though the name of only one is recorded—Philippe de Valognes, lately arrived and soon to be King's Chamberlain and Lord of Panmure in Fife.[4] When William, immediately after succeeding Malcolm IV as King, returned to Normandy in March 1166, he won

[1] The Countess Adeline († 1178) probably spent her widowhood at Haddington. The knight whom she was in the way of sending to Durham with an offering and a note of her symptoms was one Taurin de Bailleul. Reg. Durh. *Cuthb.* p. 219.

[2] " Materni generis imaginem in vultu et moribus praetendere videbatur."—Wm. Newb. I, xxiii, p. 62.

[3] William was called " Rufus " and " Garbh " [Brawny] and a " Lion ", but " of Justice ", like Henry I. " Willelmus amicus Dei, *leo justitiae*, princeps pacis" is how Fordun describes him. Wyntoun, who (VII, 2049) calls Richard I " Lyonis Hart ", says nothing of William as a " Lion ". A poem *De Willelmo Rege Scottorum* (in Laur. Durh. pp. 82-83) refers, however, to his capture at Alnwick in 1174 in offensive terms which may possibly allude to a cognomen :

> " Fit lepus ad lites belli, qui voce *leonem*
> Expressit ; magnus murmure, Marte nihil ".

The Scottish Royal Arms, " or, a lion within a bordure flory gules ", were first used by William's son Alexander II. William joined the fleshly school early and left it late, but he rose *de profundis* to a certain dogged heroism, and at last to popular canonization. His death in 1215 was announced in different countries as that of William the Holy.

[4] " Philippus de Valoniis ", Philippe de Valognes (Manche), the fifth son of a " Roger of England ", came to Scotland in the reign of Malcolm IV. He was perhaps a descendant of Pierre de Valognes, recorded in England from 1072 and Sheriff of Essex in the reign of Rufus. Philippe († 1215) was Chancellor in or before 1166 and frequently appears again with this title, *e.g.* in 1196. Round, *Cal.* I, No. 490. He received from King William the lands of Panmure and Bervie. See J. Bain, *Notes and Queries*, series VI, vol. V (1882), p. 142. His youngest brother, Roger de Valognes, received the lands of Kilbride. See *O.P.* I, p. 98. In the early years of the thirteenth century a family of Valognes, whose principal seat was Beningham in Hertfordshire, held land in the parish of Bamburgh. *Hist. Northd.* I, p. 270.

" glorious honours of chivalry ".[1] These he won, as Wyntoun explains,

> At turnamentis and at iustingis
> And mony other knychtlike thingis.[2]

He was present with a large and well-equipped following at the tournament which laid the basis of Guillaume le Maréchal's fortunes.[3] There was a business side to chivalry. The future Maréchal, an ambitious young man, had made a careful note of the date and place of this much-heralded tournament, for he felt it might provide an opportunity for making his way in the world. On arriving he looked round the field for a suitable opponent, suitability being determined by excellence of steed and splendour of accoutrement, consequently of financial reward, to wit the discomfited opponent's horse or his armour or a " ransom ", should he prefer to pay the " penalty " in gold. To this young man's judicious eye the best-mounted and most richly armed of the knights present (whom therefore he challenged and, according to plan, overthrew) was the Scottish Chamberlain, " sire Felipe de Valoingnes ". In tournament Scotland under Malcolm IV was attaining the highest standard of the time, that set in the Duchy.

Scotland was also becoming a Land of Romance. Writers were composing chivalrous tales in " Romance ",[4] and in one of them Tristan, voyaging sadly through a Celtic world, takes service with the King of Gauvoie [Galloway],[5] on whom the Scot King is making war.[6] It is the custom of

---

[1] *Chron. Melrose, s.a.* 1166.   [2] Wyntoun, VIII, 1597.

[3] The tournament was held at Valennes (Sarthe), arr. Saint-Calais, canton de Vibraye. *Guill. le Mar.* III, p. xxvii. Son of Jean, son of Gilbert to whom Henry I as Duke of Normandy gave the office of Maréchal, " William Marshall " became in 1216 Regent of England and Guardian of Henry III.   [4] OF. *romanz* = Latin *romanice* = written in French.

[5] The land of Gawain, Arthur's nephew; *Galweia* in Malcolm IV's Roxburgh charter.

[6]   " Tristran remaigne deça mer ;
       Au riche roi aut, en Gavoie,
       A qui li roiz escoz gerroie."
                Béroul, *Tristan* (? *c.* 1165), ll. 2630-2632.

knights to swear " by St. Andrew to whom men go to pray beyond the sea, even unto Scotland ".[1] From that country Norman ladies send gifts of strange and striped material.[2] One has a fairy bower in the woods of " Calatir ", where she reposes upon a couch with a counterpane in a chequered pattern and is discovered by Désiré, son of one of the Scot King's tenants-in-chief, a young man who lives at Court, except when he goes to "Britain" for tournaments or to the paternal estate in " Calatir " for relaxation. When he is made a knight his spurs are put on by two kings—one of Moray and one of Lothian.[3] On social life in Scotland in the days when Malcolm the Maiden ruled the land Romance does not give the whole

[1]
> " Par saint André, que l'on vet querre
> Outre la mer, jusque en Escoce."
>> Béroul, *Tristan*, ll. 3132-3133.

[2] A châtelaine in Scotland had a very small cousin named Guivret. " Guivret had had two loose gowns made, one trimmed with ermine, one with vair, out of two different silken webs. One gown was of a purple silk ; the other was in striped cloth, sent him as a gift from Scotland by his cousin."

> " Ot Guivrez fet deus robes feire,
> L'une d'ermine, l'autre veire,
> De deus dras de soie divers.
> L'une fu d'un osterin pers
> E l'autre d'un bofu roiié
> Qu'a presant li ot anvoiié
> D'Escoce une soe cosine."
>> Chrétien de Troyes, *Erec* [c. ? 1165],
>> ed. W. Foerster (Halle), 1896, ll. 5233-5239.

[3] The Romance is that of *Désiré* [c. 1170], son of a great landowner in " Calatir ".

> " Tant de terre comme il avoit
> Du roi d'Escoce en chief tenoit."

The counterpane was of chequered design. The material was provided by two *pallia* of good and costly texture :

> " . . . la coute ert a eschequiers,
> De .ij. pailles bien fez et chiers ".
>> ll. 179-180.

" Calatir " in the romances is Geoffrey of Monmouth's " Calaterium Nemus " or Caledonian Forest. The Kings were of Morafe and Loonois. E. M. Grimes, *The Lays of Désiré, Graelent and Melion : Edition of the Texts with an Introduction.* Institute of French Studies, New York, 1928, v+139 pp.

truth. But neither does chronicle nor charter.

In 1164 there was one last attempt to overthrow the Scoto-Norman King. From Argyll and the Isles and from Ireland Somerled collected a great fleet and army and, sailing up the Clyde, landed at Renfrew in the domain of Walter fitz Alan, now Hereditary Steward of Scotland. The Steward, who was attending to his duties elsewhere, had not held Renfrew by knight-service all these years without training his vassals in the methods of self-defence, and, moreover, there was a French Bishop to organize local resistance, Herbert of Glasgow, as venerable now as the Archbishop who had rallied the Yorkshiremen to the Standard. Naturally, no more than Toustain did he appear on the battlefield. He prayed to his Saint, to Mungo. A spear thrown from a distance put an end to Somerled's long warfare and his head was brought to the Bishop,[1] who himself was dead before the year was out.[2]

Malcolm IV soon followed. On Thursday, December 9, 1165, he died at Jedburgh, in the twenty-fifth year of his age and the thirteenth of his reign. "His body was honourably borne by all persons to Dunfermline and buried beside Malcolm Canmore." [3] To many of the "persons" he hardly seemed to have died; the Requiem might have been only :

[1] At least so it is said in a Latin poem by a contemporary, a French clerk of Glasgow, " Willelmus " [printed, pp. 78-80, in Laur. Durh. and in Sim. Durh. (R.S.), II, pp. 385-388, and in the Book of Clanranald, quoted by Skene, III, p. 400]. The peroration of the poem, in Latin rimes, is : "Telo laesus, ense caesus, Sumerledus obiit". The defending force was small and local (" pauci comprovinciales ", *Chron. Melrose, s.a.* 1164), and hints are not wanting that it was by guile that Somerled was slain.

[2] *Chron. Holyrood, s.a.* 1164. Herbert in this respect also resembled the Archbishop, who died in the second year after the Battle of the Standard. The veneration in which the French clergy came to hold the British Saints (see above, p. 119) is illustrated by Bishop Herbert's prayer and by the fact that at his suggestion a foreign cleric had written a Life of St. Kentigern which has been partially preserved.

[3] *Chron. Melrose, s.a.* 1165 ; *personae* means persons of distinction or importance.

Sequel: The Reign of Malcolm IV

Good-night, sweet Prince,
And flights of angels sing thee to thy rest.[1]

It was told in a Latin poem that in the night after his passing he appeared to Richard the Clerk. William of Newburgh wrote that "amid a perverse and barbarous people Malcolm shone like a heavenly body", and he set him on a yet loftier pinnacle than David, praising him as a monk in all but the habit,[2] an angel upon earth, yet withal a terror to the evil-doer, a bulwark against the froward and the bold. History places him among the righteous rulers and the victorious captains. Chronicle celebrates him as Malcolm the Maiden, which gentle phrase well accords with the beardless face on the rude coinage [3] and the willowy figure drawn with fond artistry in the most beautiful of his charters. Legend cites him as an ensample of steadfast and triumphant chastity. But, with an apparently iconoclastic precision, one solitary charter records an unmarried father's tender solicitude for the proper sepulture of "my son's body, which rested for the first night after his death" in the Church of Innerleithen.

The evidence has been contested and we find it inconclusive.[4] But to what extent the Scoto-Norman King attained the nobler ideals set before him and his companions in chivalry there are no means of determining. The ideals themselves are not in doubt. They are the monastic

---

[1] "Malcolmum . . . tanquam terrenum quendam Angelum quo dignus non erat mundus caelestes Angeli rapuerunt e mundo"—Wm. Newb. II, xix, p. 138. So was the soul of Edward borne by Angels into Heaven's light :

> " Engles feredon
> soþfaeste sawle
> innan swegles lecht".
> *A-S.C.* MS. C, *s.a.* 1066.

[2] Wm. Newb. describes Malcolm IV in almost the same terms as Turgot uses of Duke Richard, and as St. Bernard and St. Ailred use of Earl Henry : " inter saeculares quibus solo habitu congruebat, monachus . . ." I, p. 76. So also Laur. Durh. p. 82 : " quamvis saeculari actui foret deditus, totus tamen fuit catholicus et erga Dei cultores benevolus ac devotus ".

[3] E. Burns, I, p. 42.
[4] See Appendix I.

and the Arthurian. They often proved to be mutually exclusive, but they meet in Malcolm the Maiden, whether he be regarded as the subject of a legend current immediately after his death or simply as the historical personage who became a King in 1153 at the age of eleven, whose ambition at sixteen was to be a Knight at Carlisle, who obtained the honour at eighteen in France and died a celibate at twenty-four. In either guise he carries on the Story of Edward, as told by Turgot and Ailred, and the Story of Arthur, as interpreted by the finer spirits of the age in whom Celtic gentleness tempered Norman strength.

He left curiously wistful memories. Perhaps he was idealized, but certainly he represented the fine flower of chivalry in the Scotland of his day. He goes down in history in many guises which are not without their paradoxical interest: the first head of a fully-established Scoto-Norman state; the first who was half-Norman by blood; the headstrong young Prince who was determined to be a Knight and won his spurs beyond the seas; the eternal invalid; the strong ruler who brought Galloway within the pale; the first King of Scots to fight upon the soil of France; the last to bear a Celtic name.

§ 28

The Last of the Normans

WHEN Malcolm IV died, a hundred years had not passed since Hastings and already the unconquered country was of the Norman world. In the Address of his charters the constituted authorities of the realm stand in their Norman array : " Malcolm, King of Scots, to Bishops, Abbots, Earls, Barons, Justiciars, Sheriffs, Provosts, Sergeants and to all other liegemen of his whole land, clerks and laics, French and English, Scots and Galwegians, greetings ". Thus on Midsummer Day 1158 he announces that Walter fitz Alan has been made the first holder of the hereditary *Senescellatus Scotiae.*[1] Malcolm's Bishops and Abbots were French clerics, the Earls were Scots, the Barons were Normans, the office-holders held Norman offices but might themselves be either Normans or Scots. Castles and Sheriffdoms were spreading over all the land. A Sheriff sat in Forfar. There was history in his name ; he was John of Hastings.[2]

In the State the only noteworthy change concerns the office of Dapifer, which had been increasing in importance and was now made hereditary. Walter fitz Alan's ancestors in Brittany were dapifers, destiny had led him to Scotland, the functions for which family history had

[1] Lawrie, *Ann. M. and W.*

[2] The Sheriffdoms created under Malcolm IV appear to have been (Dickinson, *Sheriff*, p. 352, etc.) : Lanark, 1161 × 1162, Sheriff : Baudouin [Baldwin] of Biggar ; Linlithgow, 1161 × 1162, Sheriff : Uchtred ; Forfar, 1162 × 1164, Sheriff : John of Hastings. John († after 1178) was Lord of Dun in Angus. Presumably he came from Northamptonshire ; cp. " Willelmus de Hastings ", 1161, *Red Bk. Exch.* p. 31. " Hugo de Hastings " appears in the Pipe Roll of 1130 under Rutland, p. 87, and under Leicestershire, p. 89. John's son David became Earl of Atholl in 1242. See *Inchaffray*, Introd.

marked him out had been faithfully performed, and in the announcement of Midsummer Day 1158 there was a certain fitness or even fatality.[1] In the Church the zeal of David's reign continued. New monasteries were rising in some numbers,[2] though his own buildings were unfinished. At Melrose in 1160 stonework was not even begun.[3] In 1165 when Ailred made his last annual visitation at Dundrennan he was lodged in a poor leaky hovel. We are told that a miracle took place and the rain spared his mattress, but not that a miracle hastened the completion of the conventual buildings. By 1153 the Knights Templars had been joined by the Knights Hospitallers.[4]

A cross-section of social Scotland in the reign of Malcolm the Maiden can be seen in the Confirmation Charter to the Abbey of Kelso which he gave at Roxburgh in 1159,

[1] The seal, *c.* 1170, of Walter's son Alain, who succeeded him in 1171 bears : S' ALAIN L. FI. WATIR L. F. AL. SENESCALL. RE. SCO. [Sigillum Alain le fitz Watir le fitz Alain Senescalli Regis Scotiae]. Laing, *Seals*, p. 71. Walter established the Cluniac Priory of St. James at Paisley and in 1169 brought to it monks from Much Wenlock in Shropshire, founded *c.* 1080 from La Charité. His decision to make this benefaction was announced before 1163 from Fotheringay, which in Domesday is held by the Countess Judith and which belonged to the Honour of Huntingdon. His duties as Dapifer to Malcolm, King of Scots and Earl of Huntingdon, had led him to the place where his most famous descendant suffered long imprisonment and death. Nicholas White, who in the spring of 1569 paid a visit of curiosity to the Queen of Scots during her captivity at Tutbury, wrote : " In looking upon her cloth of estate, I noticed this sentence embroidered : *En ma fin est mon commencement*, which is a riddle I understand not ". It seems understandable, historically.

[2] They included the Cistercian nunnery of Eccles, Berwickshire, 1156 ; the Augustinian Priory of Restennet, before 1159 ; Sconedale, *i.e.* Saddell, in Kintyre (Cistercian) ; the Cluniac Priory of Paisley, *c.* 1163 ; Coupar-Angus (Cistercian), founded 1164, in accordance with the dying wishes of Waldef († 1159) : the first Abbot was Foulque († 1170). At some date in the reign a Premonstratensian house was established at Tongland (Kirkcudbright). Anderson, *E.S.Sc.* II, pp. 218, 233, 251, 252, 699.

[3] *Cart. Riev.* pp. lxxiv-lxxv.

[4] A certain Bartholomew was Master of the Templars in Scotland, 1165 × 1169. Aitken, p. 6. Malcolm IV gave Merton [Oxon., 3 miles southeast of Bicester] to the Templars, " as they held it when I received the Honour of Huntingdon from King Henry ". The signatories include Walter fitz Alan and Raoul de Soules. Lees, *Temple*, p. 186. The Knights Hospitallers, first recorded in England in 1148, when they were granted land at Clerkenwell for their Priory, were in Scotland by 1153, when Malcolm IV

no doubt on the eve of his departure for Toulouse.[1] It begins: "Malcolomus Dei gratia Rex Scottorun omnibus amicis suis Francis et Anglis et Scottis cunctisque sancte Dei ecclesie filiis perpetuam salutem". To commemorate what was evidently a red-letter day, art and industry excelled as never before and as not again till long after. In the illuminated initial M of MALCOLOMUS are Scotland's first-known miniature portraits, those of her great King and his grandson, now eighteen years of age and half-way through his brief reign. The names of the witnesses are beautifully inscribed, in order of precedence: first, Bishops, Abbots, Clerks, all of Norman name; second, Earls; third, Normans; fourth and last, native landowners.[2]

confirmed by charter the foundation of their House at Torphichen; see J. Edwards, *Historical Notes on the Knights Hospitallers in Scotland*, Scottish Ecclesiological Transactions, Aberdeen, 1909, and E. J. King, *The Knights Hospitallers in the Holy Land*, Methuen, 1931, xii + 336 pp., pp. 77-78. In a General Confirmation of St. Andrews by Malcolm IV (*St. Andrews*, p. 297), one of the witnesses is "Ricardus de hospitali ierosolimitano". Another is "Robertus frater de templo". There is a "Conventio inter nos et fratres hospitaleres ierosol. de Torphichen" by Bishop Richard of St. Andrews. *St. Andrews*, p. 319. One of the witnesses, "Willelmus dolopen", acted as an emissary from William the Lion to the King of France in 1173, as related by Jourdain Fantosme. Cp. "frater Willelmus de Olepene". *Cambuskenneth*, No. 52, p. 72. The Knights Hospitallers, organized in 1114, adopted the Augustinian rule. This may account for their first connections with St. Andrews. [1] *Kelso*, No. I.

[2] Apart from the Royal family ("Willelmus et David, fratres mei, et Ada, mater mea", who come between the Bishops and the Abbots) the witnesses are: Three Bishops [Glasgow, Moray and Dunkeld]; Four Abbots [Dunfermline, Newbattle, Jedburgh and Stirling]; The Chancellor (Walter); The Prior of St. Andrews (Robert); The Archdeacon of St. Andrews (Matthew); The Archdeacon of Lothian (Turold); The Chamberlain (Herbert); [The King's] Clerk (Nicholas); [The King's] Chaplain (Richard); Two *Magistri* (Andrew and Arthur); The Chancellor's Clerk (Walter); John, Nephew of Bishop Robert; A Clerk (Serlo); The Chaplain of the Bishop of Glasgow; The Bishop's Clerk.

Then come the laity: "Godredus, Rex Insularum"; Four "Comites" (Cospatric, Ferteth, Duncan, Gillebride, "Comes de Anagus" [Angus; the others are known to have been "Comites" of Dunbar, Strathearn and Fife, respectively]); Uchtred, son of Fergus; Twelve Normans ("Gillebertus de Vmframuille", "Willelmus de Sumerville", "Ricardus de Moruille"; "Rann' de Sulas", David Olifard, "Ricardus Cumin", "Robertus Avenel", "Willelmus de Moruille", "Willelmus Finemund", "Walterus Corbet", "Asketillus de Ridala", "Henricus de Perci"). Last come "Liolphus filius Maccus" and "Orm filius Hailaph" [Eilaf].

The ecclesiastics come first, but in fact they depended on support from the other three groups. The Earls retain their exalted status, but they were beginning to have the same interests, spiritual and worldly, as the Norman clerics on the one hand and the Norman landowners on the other. Earl Ferteth, an ex-hostage, was the creator of a diocese and had a Norman son-in-law, Walter Olifard; Earl Duncan, also an ex-hostage, was the founder of a nunnery and had a Norman wife; Gillebride's territorial title may indicate that his Earldom of Angus was already considered as a feudal holding, and himself as a tenant-in-chief.[1] The Normans are classed together, without explanation or comment, as though felt to form a distinct social group. They are not described as Normans or as " barones ". Such things have to be discovered from other documents or from the French Christian names or surnames; it appears from the contents of the charter that three or four of the twelve persons thus grouped had at some date unspecified given land or a church to the Abbey. The only Normans placed outside this group are Walter de Bidun, who had an official status, as Chancellor, and John, styled " Bishop Robert's nephew ", who formed, as it were, a link between the hierarchy and the laity. Of the fourth class, the native landowners, there are only two representatives, local proprietors.

The Richard who appears in the list as " the King's chaplain " was a nephew of David's confessor Alwin, Abbot of Holyrood. Soon afterwards he succeeded at St. Andrews Bishop Ernout, who had been Abbot of Kelso till he succeeded Bishop Robert († 1159) and whose episcopate was brief, 1160 to 1162. On the manner of life led by Norman prelates in Scotland the curtain at last rolls aside and reveals Bishop Richard presiding over a house-

---

[1] Earl Duncan had already appeared as " Comes *de Fif* ". See Skene, III, p. 63. Gillebride is regularly " Comes *de Anagus* ", *e.g. Scone* (1164), No. V, p. 5.

hold of some extent and magnificence. He had with him at St. Andrews a sister, Hawise, installed in a house of her own ; [1] a brother, Robert, and two nephews, Gautier and Roland ; a dapifer, Eude, who had the services of an assistant, Geoffroi ; a chancellor, Robert de Pert ; a marshal, Guy ; a chamberlain, Guillaume ; an *ostiarius* or *huissier* or doorward, Gamel, and a *pincerna* or butler, Hugue.[2] There is something inimitably " French " about the episcopal establishment. It is so easy to see with the mind's eye Hawise, elderly and perhaps critical of the climate and the cooking ; the deserving relatives ; the less successful brother, only a chaplain ; the two young gentle-men hopefully embarking on the semi-official career of Bishop's Nephew, somewhat as their uncle Richard in his day had embarked on that of Abbot's Nephew ; the major-domo, himself a Bishop's brother,[3] well on in years, prudently provided with an assistant and successor ; [4] the episcopal *pincerna* or *bouteiller*, recalling the fact that the social conditions and conventions which produced the King's Butler, " Pincerna Regis Scotiae ",[5] and the other six Norman officers of state were those of France. Those of Scotland eventually proved too dissimilar to sustain all seven, and the King's Butler was the first to fall by the wayside. Perhaps the demand for his services was in-sufficient. Perhaps it was only on infrequent State occa-sions that the King, whether Malcolm or his less abstemious brother William, sat in Dunfermline town drinking the blood-red wine. Or perhaps it was only in the ballad.

In the Bishop's household the use of French, obviously,

---

[1] A fact mentioned by Bishop Richard in a charter (*St. Andrews*, p. 134) witnessed by " Robertus frater episcopi ".

[2] Lawrie, *Ann. M. and W.* p. 221 ; *St. Andrews*, p. 127.

[3] " Odo dapifer frater episcopi " [apparently brother of Bishop Ernout]. *St. Andrews*, p. 297.

[4] " Galfridus " appears soon after as Bishop Richard's Dapifer. *St. Andrews*, p. 135.

[5] The office was held under King William, perhaps already under Malcolm IV, by the first of the Hays ; see below, p. 371, n. 2.

was *de rigueur*. It was customary elsewhere. Latin, the
official language of the Church, was used in the religious
houses and at meetings of the clergy, but less freely than
is commonly believed.[1] Many a monk, before he took
his vows, had been long in the world or, as one might say,
in the army, and the acquisition of fluent Latin in
maturer years was not within the capabilities of all. It is
hard to imagine the knights who withdrew, war-worn or
world-weary, to a calm and cloistered life, or the high-
born *conversi* among the Cistercians, contributing much
to a discussion in Latin; or a gathering of Frenchmen,
clerical or lay, denying themselves the use of the vulgar
tongue for very long. In England the dignity of Abbot
or Prior was not attained by skill in Latin prose, nor were
the bishops always of the scholarly sort, or always of the
saintly, for practical, hard-headed organizers were needed
as much in the ecclesiastical as in the secular administration. Many were simply promoted from the Chancery.
They were ex-civil servants, worthy Frenchmen who lived
as such, used their Latin for reading or writing and their
mother-tongue for conversation, and learned little English.
They had interpreters.[2] There is no ground for supposing
that their brethren in Scotland were better linguists. They
must have learned a few current phrases of the native
tongues, but for the purposes of grave discourse such
English or such Gaelic would have been useless. On
many of the chief laymen and laywomen in the diocese
their Latin would have been lost. The people whom
bishops and abbots were in the way of meeting were
French-speakers. At meetings of the *curia regis* the business was conducted in French; barons were no Latinists.

---

[1] In the monasteries of England it was rather English and Latin that were
discouraged and French that was favoured. See V. H. Galbraith, *Anon.*
Introd. p. xviii.

[2] *E.g. Edricus interpres*, at Bury St. Edmunds, in Abbot Baldwin's time,
which lasted from King Edward's almost till the first King Henry's. D. C.
Douglas, p. 108.

If the prelates stayed behind to help the clerks in the redaction of the resolutions their efforts were not entirely successful, for the Latin wears thin in places and the French words used at the meeting shine through : *brueria*, a thicket of broom (*la bruyère*) ; *calceia*, a causeway (*la chaussée*) ; *corda*, a net used in hunting (*les cordes*) ; *logiae*, lodges (*les loges*).

The confusion of tongues mentioned by Ailred as one of the many difficulties with which the beloved David had to contend had certainly not lessened in his grandson's reign. The mass of the population naturally went on speaking their varied vernaculars while their pastors and masters, spiritual and temporal, used French for conversing among themselves and Latin for writing down their decisions, or for having their decisions written down. Malcolm the Maiden assuredly was one of the " more recent Scottish Kings " of whom Walter of Coventry wrote that " they profess themselves French in race as in manners, language and culture ". French was their language and that of their courtiers, their officials, their barons and their chief nobles in 1165, as it still was on the calamitous night of March 19, 1286, when the last of the line fell over the cliff at Kinghorn.[1]

The new Norman names recorded during the twelve

---

[1] Direct evidence during the reign of Malcolm IV is lacking. But England is a safe enough analogy, and there a distinction has evidently to be drawn not only between official circles and the rest of the country, but, in the case of individuals, between vague understanding and exact linguistic knowledge. According to Walter Map (*D.N.C.* V, c. vi, p. 237), who, being one of his courtiers, must have been well-informed, Henry II knew something of every tongue " from the Bay of Biscay to the Jordan ", but used only two, Latin and his native French. In Wales the evidence of " Giraldus Cambrensis, archidiaconus ", enlivened with wit or perhaps vitiated thereby, is that, preaching in either of these languages with equal eloquence, he could move a vast congregation to tears, and those of his hearers who knew neither wept as freely as the rest. This is testimony on his own behalf (VI, *Itin. Kambr.* p. 83), but elsewhere (I, p. 76, and II, p. 152) he recalls that in Germany St. Bernard, preaching in French, had obtained results no less remarkable. Godric, the hermit of Finchale already mentioned, to whom Malcolm IV gave two bovates of land in Lothian, had spent much

years of Malcolm's reign are few in number. Guillaume de la Haye brings to Scotland the surname Hay, to which in some parts of the country the vernacular gives a diphthongal pronunciation as in Old French. *La haye*, Modern French *la haie*, was the hedge or the barrier round a *parc* or any enclosure to be seen at any of the various places in the Duchy from which Guillaume or his forebears may have originally started for Errol in Gowrie, via England.[1] His descendants were the Earls of Errol.[2] The Frasers and the Ramsays now first appear, the Frasers perhaps a few months after Malcolm's death, for it is in 1166 that a Gillebert Frasier witnesses a charter by Waltheof, Earl

---

time in foreign travel, but learned no French, and a Norman Abbot who visited him in his hermitage required the services of an interpreter. On the other hand, we learn that Godric at times received the gift of tongues and that French was included in the gift (Reg. Durh. *Godr.* pp. 346, 353 and 434-435). But some scepticism is permissible as to the soundness of linguistic knowledge so acquired, if we bear in mind the disarming remark of a brother-hermit : " The Lord who gave me the Latin tongue gave me not grammar and declensions " (Gir. Cambr. I, p. 91).

Details on the habitual use of French by Wallace and Bruce, by Barbour's Scottish contemporaries, by Barbour himself (*c.* 1375) and by Scottish nobles till at least 1400, are given in our edition of *The Buik of Alexander*, vol. I, § 36, particularly p. clxv, n. 3. For England, see Mrs. Helen Suggett, *The Use of French in England in the later Middle Ages*, T.R.H.S. XXVIII (1946), pp. 61-84.

[1] *E.g.* " Robertus de Haie " was settled in Lincolnshire before 1130. Pipe Roll, p. 120.

[2] He is " Willelmus de Haya " in a charter, 1153 × 1157, by the Countess Adeline (*Newbattle*, p. 55, No. LIX), confirmed by Malcolm IV (*Newbattle*, p. 56), and in a precept by Malcolm IV. *Scone*, No. XV ; *Melrose*, No. VIII. He is " Willelmus de la Haye " in King William's confirmation of the Great Charter of Dunfermline, *c.* 1166. *Dunfermline*, p. 28. The family home may have been La Haie-du-Puits (Latin *Haia*), arr. Coutances ; or La Haye-de-Herce, arr. Mantes ; or La Haye-Malherbe, arr. Louviers. " Willelmus " was King's Butler in 1171 when he gave the Hospital of St. Andrews a ploughgate of land in Petmulyn " quam cepi cum uxore mea [Eua] " (*St. Andrews*, p. 313). He is said to have received from King William the lands of Errol in Gowrie. His sons were David, Robert and Malcolm. *Lindores*, No. V. David († 1237 × 1240) was Sheriff of Forfar before 1214. The seal of David's son Gilbert was *Sig. Gileberti de la Haye. Inchaffray*, p. 315. Robert the Bruce, on November 12, 1314, conferred the office of Constable on Sir Gilbert Hay of Errol and gave him the lands of Slains (Aberdeenshire). This Sir Gilbert was great-great-grandfather of Sir William Hay [† 1436], who was grandfather of the first Earl of Errol. *Complete Peerage, s.v.* ERROL.

of Dunbar, son of Earl Gospatric.[1] "Simundus de Ramesie" presumably came from Ramsey in Huntingdon. David had long-standing connections not only with the district but with the Abbey. It had four knights, and perhaps "Simundus" was one of them.[2] The names Montford, Mortimer, Vaus and Vipont come into Scotland with a "Willelmus de Munford"; a "Willelmus de Mortemer" [in one of the Countess Adeline's grants,[3] accompanied by a de Vere, "Radulfus de Ver"]; Jean de Vaus, "Johannes de Vallibus", *alias* de Wals (perhaps a descendant of Robert de Vaux, the first Norman *vicomte* at Carlisle, from 1091),[4] and "Willelmus de veteri ponte", Guillaume de Vieuxpont (near Lisieux).[5] Other apparent

[1] Raine, *North Durham*, App. p. 26, No. CXIX. In the *Liber Vitae*, p. 99, the name "Comes Patricius junior filius Waldeui comitis" is followed by "Gilebertus Fraser et Cristiana uxor ejus et Johannes filius illorum". This Gilbert is generally identified with Kylvert or Chilvert, father of Oliver Fraser, who appears 1175 × 1199 among the followers of the Earl of March and who built a castle on his domain in Tweeddale. Oliver is supposed by family tradition to have acquired his lands on the Tweed by marriage. In the thirteenth century the whole or a great part of Tweedsmuir belonged to Frasers. *O.P.* I, pp. 205-206.

[2] The Abbey's right to four knights in 1156 is mentioned in *Red Bk. Exch.* p. 74. "Simundus de Ramesie" witnesses the grant to Holyrood of the church of Leuiggestun [Livingston] by "Turstanus fil leuig" which is confirmed by Malcolm IV (*Holyrood*, pp. 15-16); also, the later deed by which Gilbert, Earl of Strathearn, gives Glendovan and Carnibo to Malcolm of Fife "cum Matilda filia mea . . . in liberum maritagium". *Inchaffray*, No. II. "Willelmus de Rameseia" witnesses King William's confirmation of the grant to Holyrood by "Gilebertus de vmphramvilla" of a ploughgate of land in Kinard (*Holyrood*, p. 34).

[3] That in which "Ada comitissa mater regis Scot." gives the land of Pethmulin to St. Andrews. *St. Andrews*, p. 209. "Willelmus de Munfort" is found again in the next reign, *e.g. St. Andrews*, p. 229, along with a "Rogerus de Mortimer", who afterwards appears in the Kinloss Charter of July 31, 1196. Round, *Cal.* I, No. 490.

[4] He witnesses Malcolm IV's Confirmation of Baldwin the Lorimer's holding at Perth as "Johannes de Vallibus" and another by Malcolm IV as "Johannis de Wals" (*St. Andrews*, p. 197). The same name appears again in 1227. *Ibid.* p. 294. Towards 1170 "Willelmus de Vallibus miles" granted to Dryburgh "the church of St. Nicholas in the island of Elbotle". The grant is confirmed by his son John. *Dryburgh*, p. 15. Vaus is supposed to be the origin of Vans.

[5] "Willelmus de veteri ponte" is a signatory to a Confirmation by Malcolm IV at Edinburgh. *Holyrood*, No. XV. His wife was "Emma de sancto hylario" = Emme de Saint-Hilaire. He gave to the Abbey of Holy-

new-comers are : " Willelmus de Audri " and " Ranulfus Mansell " [= *Mancel* = *Manceau*, inhabitant of Maine or of Le Mans] ; [1] " Radulphus Namo ", no doubt the Raoul le Naym who in a few years' time is found in possession of lands in Buchan ; [2] " Rogerus *miles* de Wiltona ",[3] and " Rodbertus filius Philippi ", who " not because of any pleasant moral qualities, but because of the abundance of his wealth obtained the name of noble ", says Reginald of Durham, who mentions him because his wife was Ailred's niece and because Ailred several times stayed with them in Lothian on his way to Dundrennan.[4] The Sheriff of Scone in 1164 is called Ewain, perhaps the Breton name Yvain. " Galfridus de Coningesburg " [Conisbrough] in the same document is otherwise unknown.[5]

Apparently it was in Malcolm's reign that Walter fitz Alan settled retainers on his lands. The most prominent among them is Robert Croc. In 1088 " Croc the hunts-man " was a member of the audience which applauded Lanfranc too vociferously and denounced Bishop " de Saint-Carilef " too rudely when Lanfranc argued with him on his duties towards Rufus—obviously in the French vernacular and not in rolling Latin periods.[6] Robert

rood the church of Boeltun (*Holyrood*, p. 28) and to the Abbey of Kelso " eschalingas " on Lammermoor (" shielings ", in its old sense of pastures). But he probably lived in the North of England. The Abbey of Kelso was under an obligation to bring his bones from England to Kelso for burial. This became the subject of a controversy between the monks and William his eldest son ; see *Melrose*, p. 60 ; *Dryburgh*, p. 11. The family held the lands of Carriden for some generations.

[1] Both witness a precept by Malcolm IV at Dunfermline. *Dunfermline*, p. 22. A " Willelmus de Alderi ", dapifer and relative of William d'Eu, was executed with him by Rufus after Robert de Montbrai's rebellion. Flor Worc. II, p. 39.

[2] Confirmation by Malcolm IV. *Melrose*, No. VIII. In the Founda-tion Charter of Arbroath (*Arbroath*, No. I) Ralf le Naym gives to the Abbey the church of Inverugie (Aberdeenshire). Besides his lands in Buchan he held Broughton (Peebles) 1175 × 1180. *O.P.* I, p. 291.

[3] Charter of Bishop Ernout. 1160 × 1162. *St. Andrews*, pp. 203, 297 and 298. [4] Reg. Durh. *Cuthb.* p. 178.

[5] Confirmation of Malcolm IV. *Scone*, No. V, p. 5.

[6] *De injusta Vexatione*, in Sim. Durh. *H.D.E.* I, p. 180.

Croc[1] thus bears a Norman name which had been long established in England. It is found in Shropshire and it may be presumed that Walter fitz Alan brought some of his vassals from his home county. Robert Croc held of him a territory near Paisley called Crocston (afterwards Crookston) and other lands in Renfrew and Ayrshire. He appears in Robert Avenel's grant of Eskdale in 1180 as " Robertus le croc miles regis ". Other vassals of Walter fitz Alan were three brothers, Robert, Walter and Nicholas " de Costentine " (also " Constentin "); " Robertus de mont'gubri " [Montgomery],[2] and " Radulfus de Kent ". All five were given lands near Inverkip, Renfrew.[3]

In Clydesdale, not far from the holdings of the Steward's vassals, several persons who form a group received lands from Malcolm IV. They have left their names in Crawford John, Lamington, Roberton, Symington, Thankerton and Wiston, places which lie close together on a principal route of which the importance is shown by the fact that it is now utilized by the railway as the main line from Carlisle to Edinburgh and Glasgow, via Carstairs.[4]

The relationship, feudal and local, between the various personages was close. Most of them were Flemings. As

---

[1] The name is also spelled Croche. Robert received from Walter fitz Alan's wife, the Lady China [Eschina] of Molle, land in the territory of Molle which he gave to his daughter Isabel on her marriage to Robert of Polloc. *O.P.* I, p. 424. Towards 1180 the monks of Paisley granted permission to the sick brethren of the Hospital built by Robert Croc on his land near Crookston to have a chapel and a chaplain. *O.P.* I, p. 68. His descendants continued for several generations in the possession of Crookston, which afterwards passed to a branch of the Stewarts.

[2] All witness a grant to Glasgow by Walter fitz Alan from his burgh of Renfrew. *Glasgow*, p. 19, No. XX. " Robertus de Mundegumeri " also witnesses the charter of Malcolm IV concerning Baldwin the Lorimer's land at Perth. *St. Andrews*, p. 203.

[3] *Paisley*, p. 5. The forebears of William Wallace, whose birth-place and inheritance was Elderslie, N.E. of Cochrane (parish of Paisley), are said to have been followers of the Steward.

[4] The distance from Crawford to Thankerton by rail is 13 miles. On the route from Carlisle the traveller, after passing through Crawford station, has on his left Crawford John and Roberton. Following stations are: Lamington (with Wiston on the left); Symington (change for Biggar, 3½ miles); Thankerton: 5 miles further on (with Pettinain on the left) is Carstairs.

certain of them were sufficiently prosperous to feel able to part with some of their land in time for it to figure in the 1159 list of possessions then belonging to the Abbey of Kelso, they may have been settled in Upper Lanarkshire before the end of David's reign. The chief personage of this group was Baldwin [Baudouin] of Biggar, first known Sheriff of Lanark.[1] His stepson, John of Crawford, held *c.* 1159 the vill since called Crawford John.[2] " Hugo de Paduinan " [Pettinain] held of Baldwin the lands of Kilpeter in Renfrew; Kilpeter thus became known as *Villa Hugonis* and as Huston, now Houston.[3] Roberton was the vill or " ton " of Robert, brother of Lambin Asa, owner of Lambiniston, now Lamington.[4] The lands on the Clyde since known as Thankerton are those given by Malcolm IV to one Thancard.[5] Symington was the " ton " of Simon

---

[1] " Baldwinus vicecomes meus de Lanark "—Charter by Malcolm IV, *Newbattle*, p. xxxvi. Baldwin granted, *c.* 1170, to Paisley the church of Inverkip beyond the moors ("ultra mores "). *O.P.* I, p. 87. He is probably the same person as " Baldewinus flam ", witness to a charter *c.* 1150 by Bishop Robert of St. Andrews (*Glasgow*, No. XI, p. 13) along with " Hugo fil. Fresechin " and " Jordane Heyrum ". The charter has been considered spurious as it contains names not commonly found *c.* 1150, but the names are very numerous and some of them may well have been added to a later copy. Baldwin was succeeded by his son Waldeve (captured at Alnwick in 1174), who transmitted his possessions to his son Robert. Robert's son " Hugh of Bygris " is mentioned in 1229. *O.P.* I, p. 134. The Inquest of 1185 (Lees, *Temple*, p. 128) has: " Apud Thimelbi, ij bouatas ex dono Iordani Hairun ", apparently a tenant of the Bishop of Durham.

[2] John of Crawford witnesses, with Baldwin his stepfather, a charter by Ernout, Abbot of Kelso till 1160, concerning lands in Lesmahagow. There is evidence *c.* 1300 that the " Villa Johannis priuigni Balduini " mentioned *c.* 1159 had by 1300 its present name, Crawford John. *O.P.* I, p. 161.

[3] *O.P.* I, pp. 83 and 138.

[4] " Robert, brother of Lambein Fleeming ", is said to have received Earnock in the district of Hamilton from Malcolm IV. *O.P.* I, p. 107. In 1160 or before, Ernout, Abbot of Kelso, gave to Lambin Asa the lands of Draffane and Dardarach in Lesmahagow. *O.P.* I, p. 113. Lambin is a French name, but several men and women called Asa whom there is no reason for supposing to have been of other than English birth appear in the *Liber Vitae*, pp. 6, 23, etc. A William, son of Lambin, witnesses with " Galfridus de Crauford " a charter by Bishop Roger of St. Andrews. *St. Andrews*, p. 153.

[5] This Thancard received also other lands in Clydesdale, part of which his son Thomas gave to the Abbey of Arbroath. *O.P.* I, pp. 107 and 143. Thomas appears in several charters by William the Lion, including that given to Aberdeen early in his reign. P. J. Anderson, No. II.

375

Loccard.[1] Wice held Wiceston, now Wiston.[2] For the weal of the souls of his lord King Malcolm and William the King's brother, Wice gave to the Abbey of Kelso the church of his manor with its two dependent chapels. They were the chapels of the vills belonging to the above-mentioned Robert and John, and became before 1300 the parish churches of Roberton and Crawford John.[3] There can be no doubt that these personages were members of a Flemish colony.[4] The properties which they held consisted largely of rich arable land along the Clyde rising into pasture ground, and there is every reason to believe that they were sheep-farmers or were otherwise connected with the wool trade.

Flemings described as such were "Jordanus le flameng" *alias* "Jordanus Flandrensis" and "Beroaldus Flandrensis". Jourdain le Flamand distinguished himself by knightly prowess in the unhappy events of 1174.[5] Beroald obtained from Malcolm IV the lands of Innes and Easter Urquhart in the Sheriffdom of Elgin; he is the first landowner in Scotland whose feudal service is ex-

---

[1] The "ecclesia de uilla Symonis Loccard", also "de Symondstone", which became the parish church of Symington, was, *c.* 1189, the subject of controversy between Simon Loccard and the monks of Kelso. See *O.P.* I, p. 144. The parochial territory was then co-extensive with his manor.

[2] "Ex donatione Withce ecclesiam villae suae"—*Kelso*, I, 1159. This gift to Kelso was confirmed, *c.* 1220, by Walter son of William, son of Wice of Wicestun. *O.P.* I, p. 146.

[3] On the ecclesiastical significance of this, see *O.P.* I, p. 148.

[4] Even if we rejected the evidence of "Baldewinus flam" on the ground that the charter is suspect, too many suggestions of Flemish origins would remain for these persons to be considered other than Flemings. Moreover, we note a striking resemblance in their names and their "tons" to those of Henry I's Flemish settlers in Pembroke, *e.g.* "Villa Lamberti", Lambston; "Villa Jordani", Jordanston in Rhos; during his reign the castle of Haverford was held by a certain Tancard, and a Fleming named "Wizo" built the castle of Wiston, known as "Castellum Wiz". J. E. Lloyd, II, pp. 424-425.

[5] "Jordanus Flandrensis."—*Kelso*, No. XXVII; "Jordanus le flamang" in Countess Adeline's charter, granting a toft in Crail to the Abbey of Dunfermline. *Dunfermline*, p. 88. His exploits in 1174 are related by Jourdain Fantosme.

plicitly defined as including castle-ward.[1] Probably these two were " castle-men ", men of the sword, as were many of the Flemings who fled from England in 1155.[2] It is to be supposed that some fled to Scotland.

No doubt before the end of Malcolm's reign some of the Normans who had lands on both sides of Tweed and Solway were, like Guillaume de Sommerville, ranging themselves more definitely on the Scottish side. It would be hard to say which of them were, or had become, subjects of which King, for some held lands in parts of England which had lately been Scottish territory and also in parts which could never have been so described. Other Normans, possibly less reputable, fled north. Sheriffs whose accounts had failed to tally continue their pathetic entries : 1163–1164, for Norfolk and Suffolk, " Richard the moneyer owes 10 *l.*, but has fled into Scotland "; 1165, for Buckinghamshire and Bedfordshire, " Thomas the moneyer owes 2 marks, but has fled into Scotland "; 1167 (though this is beyond Malcolm's reign, it is the end of the story), " Thomas the moneyer owes 2 marks. He has fled into Scotland and is dead." [3]

With but few exceptions we have now accounted for what by ancient tradition are Scotland's Norman families.[4]

[1] " In feodo et hereditate dedisse Berowaldo flandrensi in provincia de Elgin Inees et etherurecard per rectas earum divisas. Tenendum sibi et heredibus suis de me et de heredibus meis hereditarie. . . . Faciendo mihi inde seruicium vnius militis in castello meo de Elgin. Praeterea ei dono in burgo meo de Elgin vnum toftum plenarium tenendum simul cum predicto feodo suo."—Charter by Malcolm IV, *Moray*, App. p. 453. A charter was granted in 1226 by Alexander II " Waltero filio Johannis filii Berowaldi Flandrensis ". [2] Gervase of Canterbury, I, p. 161.
[3] Wyckoff, pp. 68 and 69.
[4] Ancient Scottish tradition is represented by the two subjoined lists. The names italicized are those of families which we have shown to be found in Scotland before the reign of William the Lion began, on December 9, 1165. Scotland had not to wait long for the Barclays, the Bissets, the Bois or Dubois, the Mowbrays and the St. Clairs or Sinclairs. They were established in William's reign, probably in the earlier part. Some of the remaining names are territorial designations which it is not possible to check.
Sir Thomas Gray in his *Scalachronica, c.* 1357, says that when King William returned from captivity at Falaise in 1175 he took with him to

During the forty-nine years of William's reign immigrants came in, but their connection with 1066 was becoming remote, and they can no longer be strictly called Normans. They were members of the French-descended, French-speaking aristocracy of England and they arrived in the Scoto-Norman state to find general conditions somewhat as in England—and to find the best land allocated, the best places taken, power and influence concentrated in the families of those who must be called the Last of the Normans.

In a different sense Scotland never saw and never will see the last of her Normans. Genealogically there would be much to say, but the generations of man are such that they soon pass beyond the power of record and description; it is not possible for the mind to conceive readily or the tongue to describe briefly the exact relationship between Guillaume de la Haye and his descendant the first Earl of Errol. From 1165 the genealogical tree of the Normans in Scotland branches out to infinity. Historically there is little more to say of them than that they stay where they are, acquire more lands and more power, play the chief part in the affairs of the realm, as indeed with so prodigious a start they could hardly have failed to do, and gradually become less and less Norman, more and more Scottish. Walter of Coventry, after remarking that the Scottish Kings "profess themselves French in race, as in manners,

---

Scotland several younger sons of lords in England well disposed to him and gave them the lands of other men who were disaffected. Such were [the younger sons] " des *Baillolys*, de *Brus*, de *Soulis*, et de Mowbray, et les Saynclers ; les *Hayes*, les *Giffardis*, les *Ramesayis* et Laundels ; les Bisseys, les Berkleys, les Walenges, les Boysis, lez *Mountgomeries*, lez *Vauz*, les *Colewyles*, les *Frysers*, les *Grames*, les Gourlays, et plusours autres ".

Boece supposes the following to have received lands from Malcolm Canmore and some of them to have come from Hungary with Margaret : " Hinc illa familiarum cognomina *Lindesa*, *Vaus*, *Ramsay*, *Louel*, Touris, Preston, Sandelandis, Bissart, *Soulis*, Vvardlaw, *Maxol*, aliaque complura. Aduenerant quoque nonnulli cum Margarita ex Hungaria, qui posteris quoque suis nomina reliquere ; *Crythoun*, Fothirgame, *Giffhert*, *Maul*, Brothik quae ad nos usque peruenerunt. Aliae familiae aliis aduenere temporibus ex Gallia, vt *Fraseir*, Sinclair, Bosual, Montalth, *Montgomery*, Cambel, Boas, Betuin, Taillefer et Bodenal."—Boece, XII, p. 258.

378

language and culture ", continues : " the Scots being reduced to utter servitude, their Kings take none but Frenchmen into their favour and their service ". The mediaeval
chronicler's sense of social justice is shocked, and how
much more is ours. But the Frenchmen, the professed
and the real, went the way of all Conquerors—they were
conquered in the end. By assimilation, by environment,
by intermarriage, by effluxion of time, their descendants
became Scots. One hundred and fifty years after the death
of Malcolm the Maiden their descendants, while continuing like William le Valeys and Robert de Brus to speak
French, proved themselves true Scottish patriots, and in
another hundred and fifty years, having learned English,
could have said of Scotland, with the poet :

> This is my country,
> The land that begat me.
> These windy spaces
> Are surely my own,
> And those who here toil
> In the sweat of their faces
> Are flesh of my flesh,
> And bone of my bone.[1]

[1] Sir Alexander Gray, " Scotland " in *Selected Poems of Alexander Gray*
(Maclellan), p. 19.

APPENDICES

★

A. Early Norman Connections with Scotland
B. Homage and Corrody
C. Margaret's Parentage
D. The Names of Margaret's Children
E. Turgot's *Vita Sanctae Margaritae*
F. The Claimants to the Throne of Malcolm Canmore
    (i) "The Sons of Ingibiorg"
    (ii) The Moray Claimants
G. David's Status in Cumbria, Huntingdon and Northampton
H. Norman Relatives of Ailred
I. The Maiden Tradition

A

Early Norman Connections with Scotland

THE first Duke, Rollo, arrived in Normandy, 905 × 911, with a Scottish wife whom he had married in the course of his career as a Viking and by whom he had a daughter named Kathleen; his son and successor had also been born outside Gaul, but was given a Frankish name, Wilhelm.[1] It does not, however, follow that the mother of this son, William [Longsword], was Rollo's Scottish wife or that the Norman Dukes had Scottish blood in their veins.

Wace's Continuator states that the Conqueror's wife, though born in Flanders, was known as Mahaut d'Escoce, because her mother was the daughter of a Scottish King. Mahaut, so the story runs, fell in love with an English Earl, Brictrith, and asked him to marry her. But he would not. So in anger she sped across the sea and married William Bastard instead:

> Meis Brictrith Maude refusa :
> Dont ele mult se coruça.
> Hastivement mer passa
> E a William Bastard se maria.

Becoming Lady of England, she straightway caused Brictrith to be apprehended " à Haneleye à son maner " and cast into a dungeon at Winchester, where he died in darkness, for having failed to see the light while it was yet day. Then, carrying vengeance beyond the tomb, she seized his estates.[2] It is true that we are not informed from what shores Mahaut set her cap at Brictrith or set sail to wed the Norman Duke. But if the romance soars into the realms of fantasy it starts from a broad basis of hard fact. Brictrith or Brictric, son of Algar [Alfgar], was one of Edward's greatest thegns and owned broad acres in Gloucestershire and Cornwall. He attests

[1] D. C. Douglas, *Rollo of Normandy*, E.H.R. LVII (1942), pp. 417-436.
[2] *Continuation du Brut d'Angleterre de Wace*, thirteenth-century MS., in Francisque-Michel, *Chroniques anglo-normandes*, p. 73.

William's charters in 1067, with Edric the Wild and others, but before long his lands and, with them, Hanley in Worcestershire, are found in Queen Matilda's possession.[1] We could have wished to know more of Queen Matilda's antecedents than history tells us, to learn, for instance, more precisely why her marriage languished so long under a cloud of ecclesiastical displeasure. But the little we do know makes it unlikely that Scotland can justly lay claim to Matilda.

[1] See *Regesta*, Nos. 9 and 23. " Whether there is any truth in the story . . . of Matilda's revenge, the Cornish Survey shows that Brictric was a marked man and that there was a tendency for his lands to pass to Matilda." —*V.C.H. Cornwall* (1924), p. 56. See also Freeman, *N.C.* IV, pp. 759-765, who thinks that Brictrith may have been sent on some mission to the Court of Flanders. As some connection with the Continent must be postulated, a guess might be made—that Brictrith, who owned property in Worcestershire, was the son of Ælfgeard, the " rich man of Worcester " who married Emma's Norman lady-in-waiting, Mahaut.

B

Homage and Corrody

" The Earl of York, and the Earl of the Northumbrians from the Tees to the Firth of Forth, and St. Cuthbert's Bishop Elfsi [Ælfsige, Bishop of Lindisfarne at Chester-le-Street, 968–990] conducted Kenneth, King of Scots [Kenneth II, regn. 971–995] to King Edgar [" the Peaceful ", regn. 944–975] and when he had done him homage, King Edgar gave him Lothian." [1] In addition to this early but anonymous statement, there is one by Roger of Wendover [† 1236] that Kenneth was conducted to Edgar by Bishop Ælfsige and Eadwulf, ealdorman of Bernicia, and was granted Lothian on condition that he and his successors should attend the English Court on certain festivals when the King wore his crown.   Kenneth, he adds, was given then a number of residences or stopping-places on the route (" mansiones in itinere plurimas "), for convenience in travelling to and fro, and these remained in the possession of the Scottish Kings till the time of Henry II.[2] The successors of these officials, with the Archbishop of York in addition, accompanied Malcolm Canmore on his visit to Edward in 1059.   Edgar, David and Malcolm IV made the same journey, with a " corrody "—the grant made to the Scottish Kings for travelling expenses incurred in connection with attendance at Court in England.   William the Lion refused to attend the Coronation of Richard I, on September 3, 1189, because he could not be accompanied by the Archbishop of York, Geoffrey, who was then only Archbishop-elect.   The matter was adjusted when William and Richard met at Southwell on April 7, 1194, and travelled together to the Crown-wearing at Winchester.   They agreed that henceforth the King of Scots should be met at the Tweed by the Bishop of Durham and the Sheriff and barons of Northumberland, and conducted to the Tees, where the Archbishop and the Sheriff

[1] De Primo Saxonum Adventu, in Sim. Durh. II, p. 382.
[2] Flor. Hist. ed. Coxe, I, p. 614, s.a. 975.

385

of York should be in attendance. The amount of the corrody, which William had long considered inadequate, was increased, and the details (including a daily allowance of incredible quantities of pepper and cumin) were set forth in a *carta* delivered to him at Northampton. On April 17 he bore the Sword before Richard.[1]

Malcolm Canmore's homage to Edward in 1059 was probably to a Basileus or overlord of all Britain. The nature of his homage to William I in 1072 cannot have been very clear. It was not as though fealty were being sworn by a King of Scots to an Old English King, or by a baron in Normandy to the Duke, or by the Duke to the reigning Capet. Six years after Hastings the circumstances were novel, and, whichever oath of fealty may have been selected, it cannot have fitted them very closely. There is no record of Malcolm Canmore being called on to attend the Court of William I or being supposed to hold *per servitium militare*. It must have been *simple* homage, not *liege* homage, which was based on military service. It was no doubt for that reason that in 1093 Malcolm refused to have his case put before a *curia regis* at Gloucester—which would have implied an admission of liege homage. Whether his homage applied to his Kingdom, or only to parts of Lothian or Cumbria, or to his English possessions, was a question on which doubt was evidently allowed to remain. At Abernethy William enforced a claim (though what it was is unknown, except that it included overlordship of Britain and provided rhetorical effects for Ailred or for Walter Espec in connection with the Battle of the Standard), but inevitably it would recede into the domain of theory as his forces receded into England.

Malcolm Canmore's more precise feudal relationship to William I was that of a holder of certain lands in England. These were apparently twelve vills, which are mentioned in 1091, but not specified. It was then stipulated that Malcolm should owe feudal duty to William II as to his late father William I, and that William II should restore to Malcolm " twelve vills [not *the* twelve vills, it must be noted] which he had had in England under his father ", and should give him

[1] Hoveden, III, pp. 244-248.

each year twelve marks of gold.[1] As the Conqueror's practice
was to deal with a block of lands which were scattered but had
been the property of a single owner T.R.E., it seems possible
that the twelve vills (no great acquisition for a king) which were
mentioned in 1091 were the " mansiones ", and that in 1072
they had been restored, not bestowed. It also seems possible
that one of Malcolm's twelve vills was in Northamptonshire.
In the Northamptonshire Geld Roll, compiled not later than
1078, " the Scottish King owns 3 hides in Corby Hundred ".
They were exempt from geld, as also were those owned by
" the Lady " [probably not Edward's wife Edith, but the
Conqueror's wife Matilda] in the same district. It has been
suggested [2] that the three hides had been granted to Malcolm
Canmore during his exile by his protector, Siward, who then
held the Earldom. It could be added that the collection of a
geld was generally based on an assessment which was already
ancient, and that probably the privilege of exemption was
enjoyed by David when Earl of Huntingdon and Northampton.[3]
The southern half of Rutland (a post-1066 county) was T.R.E.
an integral part of Northamptonshire. The northern half, on
which Corby borders closely, formed a great " Liberty ", de-
tached from Northamptonshire for the benefit of its Lady,
Edith.[4] If, as Sir Frank Stenton thinks, Malcolm Canmore
held the three hides in 1072, the chances are that he held them
before. For which is the more likely proposal for William I
to have made him in 1072 at Abernethy—(1) " I will give
you a small property in a distant county of mine ", or (2) " You
held some land in Northamptonshire in King Edward's time
and it will now be returned to you " ? All the evidence is
consistent with the grant to Malcolm, T.R.E., of a small estate

[1] " Ea conditione ut Willelmo, sicut patri suo obedivit, Malcolmus
obediret et Malcolmo xii villas quas in Anglia sub patre illius habuerat
Willelmus redderet et xii marcas auri singulis annis daret."—Flor. Worc.
II, p. 29.
[2] By E. W. M. Balfour-Melville, *A Northamptonshire Estate of Malcolm
Canmore*, S.H.R. XXVII (1948), pp. 101-102.
[3] Cp. Painter, *E.F.B.* p. 78 : " I suspect very strongly that the Kings
of Scotland, Earls of Huntingdon, enjoyed at least partial exemption from
danegeld ".
[4] Stenton, *A-S.E.* p. 495. As to " the Lady's " connection with Rutland,
Gaimar says that Rutland was part of Æthelred's morning-gift to Emma
in 1002.

which, whether one of the (uncorroborated) " mansiones " or not, was, after forfeiture, restored in 1072 and again in 1091, along with larger estates, more suitable objects of Royal bargaining, which also were possibly granted him T.R.E.

As the accession of Duncan II, Edgar and Alexander came about with help from the King of England, the feudal relationship to him may well have been made on each occasion somewhat stricter. Until the death of Henry I the question of David's homage as King of Scots was obscured, perhaps to the point of becoming purely academic, by the fact that before his accession, as after, he was Earl of Huntingdon and Northampton. During the Anarchy it was further obscured. But the *Melrose Chronicle, s.a.* 1156, says that Malcolm IV " became the man of Henry II in the same manner as David had been the man of Henry I, saving all his dignities ". The sense of the last phrase seems obscure. In the reign of Malcolm IV dubiety prevailed as to whether his homage concerned his Kingdom or only Huntingdon. It seems probable that the usual form by which the Scottish Kings held their English possessions was *simple* homage and that in 1157 Henry II required of Malcolm IV *liege* homage. The difficulties which would arise from this were avoided by William the Lion when he sub-enfeoffed Huntingdon to his brother David. The duty of military service was thus transferred from the tenant-in-chief to the under-tenant.

C

Margaret's Parentage

The theory has been put forward by M. Sándor Fest [1] that Margaret was St. Stephen's granddaughter. The question turns on the parentage of her mother Agatha. Agatha is variously described: by *A-S.C.* MS. D, *s.a.* 1057, as " caseres maga " = a relative of the Emperor, and, *s.a.* 1067, as descended on her mother's side from the Emperor Henry; by Flor. Worc. I, p. 181, as " filia germani imperatoris Henrici " = a daughter of the Emperor Henry's brother; by Wm. Malm. as a sister of the Queen of Hungary; by Ord. Vit. as a daughter of the King of Hungary, whom elsewhere he calls Solomon; [2] by Ailred [3] as " filia germani sui [*i.e.* Hungariorum regis] Henrici imperatoris " = a daughter of the King of Hungary's brother, the Emperor Henry. Ailred further says of Margaret: " de semine regio Anglorum et Hungariorum exstitit oriunda " = " she was of the Blood Royal of England and Hungary ", *i.e.* her mother Agatha was of the Blood Royal of Hungary.

As Stephen's wife Gisela was the sister of the Emperor Henry II, and as *germanus* may sometimes mean " brother-in-law ", M. Fest shows that the statements above are reconcilable on the assumption that Agatha was Stephen's daughter. He points out that in 1057 friendship with the Empire was an essential part of English foreign policy and that Edward the Exile's English sponsors would naturally stress his wife's relationship to the Imperial House; that she cannot well have been a sister of Queen Gisela because Gisela's father died in August 995 and consequently any other daughter he may have had—none is recorded—must have been at least twenty years

---

[1] *The Sons of Eadmund Ironside*, etc., 1938; see Bibliography, p. 419.

[2] " Edmundus clito immatura morte obiit. Eduardus vero Dei nutu filiam regis [Hunorum] in matrimonium accepit et super Hunos regnavit."— Ord. Vit. I, xxiv. " Exul conjugem accepit cum regno filiam Salomonis regis."—*Ibid.* VIII, xxii.

[3] *G.R.A.* p. 366.

older than Edward (b. *c.* 1016) ; [1] that in 1057 the King of Hungary, Andrew I, had his young son (Solomon) crowned and that this may have resulted in confusion of " Solomon " with " Stephen ".

M. Fest's theory, although it has been accepted by several scholars, seems inadmissible, for the following reasons :

(1) Although Latin is weak in terms denoting marriage-relationships and does sometimes, though rarely, express " brother-in-law " by *germanus*, the word *germanus* properly means " full brother ", in contradistinction to " half-brother ", and when used by Flor. Worc. and Ailred must be assumed to have this, its ordinary, sense.

(2) None of the authorities even mentions the name of Stephen. It was well known and much honoured in Western Europe.[2] It is all the more likely to have been known at Worcester because the Bishop conducted the negotiations for the return of Margaret's father from Hungary. Moreover, in 1058 he visited that country.[3] At Solomon's Coronation in 1057 the " ordo " was used which was composed by Dunstan for the long-deferred Coronation of Edgar the Peaceful at Bath, on Whit Sunday 973.[4] Whether the adoption of the English " ordo " was or was not due to Bishop Aldred's dealings with Hungary, he would no more have confused young Solomon with St. Stephen than he would have confused young Edgar, whom he wished to crown, with Harold or William, both of whom he did crown. MS. D of the *Chronicle* is extremely well informed on Bishop Aldred ; it, and also the work of Florence († 1118), are connected with Worcester and there, under Bishop Wulfstan († 1095), whom Margaret held in veneration, Old English memories were certainly kept green.

(3) Stephen was canonized in 1083. If Margaret had been the granddaughter of a saint, Turgot (and Ailred, whose favourite literary themes were sainthood and Royal genealogy)

---

[1] We may add that this would make Agatha over sixty at the time of her arrival in England with three children, of whom the eldest was twelve and the youngest was probably not more than six years old.

[2] A long list of eleventh-century allusions to Stephen is given, pp. 72 ff., by Albin F. Gombos, *Saint Étienne dans l'historiographie européenne du moyen-âge*, pp. 51-154, in *Archivum*, etc. (See below, Bibliography, p. 424 under FEST.)   [3] *Vita Æd.* ll. 751-760 ; Sim. Durh. *H.R.* II, p. 221.

[4] Schramm, p. 23.

could scarcely have been ignorant of the fact or have failed to record it. In the presentation of any case, whether for canonization or for dynastic succession (Margaret, Edgar Atheling, Queen Maud, Henry II), descent from a Saint *and* King was a point not to be lightly neglected.

(4) Ailred draws a sharp distinction (which M. Fest seems to overlook) between Agatha and the King of Hungary's daughter who was married to Edward's brother Edmund : " Hungariorum rex . . . eos . . . sibi in filios adoptavit. . . . Porro Edmundo filiam suam dedit uxorem ; Edwardo filiam germani sui Henrici imperatoris in matrimonium junxit." [1] This is an unequivocal statement that Edmund's wife was a daughter of the Hungarian King and that Edward's wife Agatha was not.

Ailred, continuing his narrative, says : ". . . Imperator . . . nuntios detinuit ". The " Imperator " here is the Emperor reigning in 1054 [Henry III], and it is only at this point that Ailred brings in the sentence quoted by M. Fest : " Tandem paratis navibus . . . Edwardum cum uxore sua Agatha *germani sui filia* liberisque ejus . . . ad Angliam mittit ".[2] Ailred thus says in effect that Agatha's father was a brother of the Emperor who made arrangements for Edward the Exile's journey to England, namely Henry III. Ailred, however, is in error as regards " brother ". Henry III (1017–1056, crowned in 1046), son of Conrad II (990–1039), had no brother. It should be further noted that the Emperor Henry II (973–1024, crowned in 1014) had no children.

Later writers merely darken our counsels. Thus Jocelin, who might be supposed to be writing carefully and to be correctly informed since his *Vita Sancti Waldeui* (1207 × 1214) was addressed to William the Lion, says in his Prologue : [3]

" Sanctae Margaretae mater, Agatha nomine, filia fuit germani Henrici clarissimi imperatoris Romanorum, cujus posteritas illustrat Romanum imperium. Soror ejusdem Agathae regina extitit Ungarorum, cujus uteri fructus successivos reges germinans non solum ejusdem regni possidet principatum, sed etiam aliorum regnorum plurimum nactus est sceptrum ", *i.e.* that Agatha's father was the brother of an

[1] *G.R.A.* p. 733. [2] *G.R.A.* p. 734. [3] P. 249, col. 2.

391

Emperor Henry whose descendants were Emperors in Jocelin's time; that her sister was Queen of Hungary, and that the said Queen was the ancestress of Kings reigning then (1207 × 1214). There seems to be no historical personage having such a relationship.

The new theory proving unacceptable, we are left with the old—that Agatha was a daughter of Bruno, only brother of the Emperor Henry II. It seems perfectly tenable. Their sister Gisela was Stephen's wife. Bruno, born *c.* 975, was a close friend of Stephen and lived at his Court from 1003 till 1006.[1] He had hoped to succeed Henry as Duke of Bavaria, and was in opposition to him for several years, but in 1006 found congenial compensation in the Bishopric of Augsburg, which he held till his death in 1029.[2] He played a considerable part as a statesman and it was he who was entrusted with the education of the future Emperor Henry III. There is no evidence that Bruno married or had a family. In his day there was no canonical reason for celibacy, and if he had married, even after 1006, there would have been nothing derogatory in the fact. But by the time the chroniclers concerned came to write clerical celibacy had become a more contentious subject and a daughter of the marriage would have been more impressively described as an Emperor's relative, " caseres maga ", than as a Bishop's daughter. It would also have been her correct style. Bruno's father was not an Emperor; he was a Duke of Bavaria.

[1] Gombos, p. 76.   [2] Fliche, *M.A.* p. 261.

D

The Names of Margaret's Children

The precise dates of birth of Margaret's children can only be guessed, except in the case of Edith (1080). Lord Hailes and others have noted as significant that none of Margaret's sons received the name of any Scottish king. But why should they? When they were baptized the chances of any of them ever reaching the throne were small. The eldest four, born before Edgar Atheling's renunciation in 1074, received the names of her own relatives : of her father (Edward, b. *c.* 1071), her grandfather (Edmund, b. *c.* 1072), her great-grandfather (Ethelred, b. *c.* 1073), her brother (Edgar, b. *c.* 1074). The two sons born after 1074 received names which were uncommon and might be termed uncontentious. Alexander, born *c.* 1077, may have been named from the fourth-century Saint whose Day was May 3, or from the Pope who died on April 21, 1073, or, more probably, from the hero of Romance ; the Library of Bec, in which no other poetical work, not even Virgil, found a place, possessed a *Vita Alexandri regis Macedonum* (mentioned by R. Tor.). In 1077 the name, which had a great future in Scotland, was rare. The name David (also rare among eleventh-century historical personages) was probably Biblical, but may have had some secondary reference to the sixth-century Bishop of Menevia [St. David's], who was so widely venerated that the Conqueror's Welsh expedition of 1081 was thought by many to have been for the purpose of worshipping at his shrine. David was probably the youngest child and born *c.* 1084. The elder daughter, born 1080, received the English name Edith, which was popular with Normans, even before 1066. The name of the younger daughter, Mary, born *c.* 1082, became common as a personal name only after the First Crusade.

Edith changed her name to Maud, and it has been assumed that the change took place on her marriage to Henry I in 1100. But all the chroniclers save Orderic simply state that " Henry married *Maud* ", *e.g. A-S.C.* MS. E, *s.a.* 1100 : " se Kyng genam Mahalde him to wif ". Eadmer, who was defending his dead master Anselm's treatment of the Romsey case and had every reason to be careful, never calls the betrothed anything but Matildis. Orderic states (VIII, xxii and XII, i) that Edith was her baptismal name. This is corroborated in a bare list of names in the *Liber Vitae*, p. 54, not given as having any connection with the Scottish Royal family : Eadwardus, Eadgarus, Eadmundus, Æilredus, Alexander, David, Eadgith, Maria. [It is generally held that Edgar was the fourth son, and that David was born after Edith.] Orderic does not say that her change of name took place on her marriage or had any political or other significance. These are merely assumptions by modern historians, and the reasons they adduce are mutually exclusive. The change may have taken place before the much-publicized events of 1100, perhaps at Confirmation, and it must be borne in mind that her godfather was Robert Courte-Heuse, whose own mother's name was Matilda [Mahaut, Maud]. It may be added that the Empress Maud, born in 1102, is universally described as Mahaut, *Matilda*, etc., save once as *Ædelic*, by the *Anglo-Saxon Chronicle* (MS. E, *s.a.* 1127), and twice as *Adela*, by John of Hexham. Both forms look like variations on *Ætheling* (cp. French *Adeline* and Latin *Adelina*) and there may have been some confusion with the name of Henry's second wife Adela or Aaliz. On the very slight evidence available it has been assumed that Henry's daughter was baptized Adela and adopted the name Maud on her marriage to the Emperor. But no reason has been offered and it is hard to imagine any. Adela is just as " German " as Matilda and just as " Norman "; Henry had a sister of each name. As the only son was named from the grandfather (William I), the only daughter might appropriately have been named from the grandmother, Queen Matilda.

Turgot's "*Vita Sanctae Margaritae*"

Turgot states that he was an old friend of Margaret's, a confidant and a frequent visitor, and that he had once had " for some time " [1] charge of the sacred vessels at Dunfermline. During his last visit, when he knew the Queen to be dying, she commended her sons and daughters to his care. The account of her death was supplied to him by " ejus presbytero quem ipsa propter simplicitatem, innocentiam, castitatem prae caeteris familiarius dilexerat ". After her death this beloved priest " offered himself up as a sacrifice for her at the tomb of the incorrupt body of the most holy Father Cuthbert "— which implies a solemn ceremony of dedication as well as the taking of monastic vows.

We find no cause to doubt Turgot's authorship.[2] Everything we have noted incidentally confirms it. But perhaps the priest who provided the matter of the final chapter contributed rather more. At times the tone seems less suggestive of a Lincolnshire Turgot than of a Continental cleric, come from afar and much bewildered by the " natives ". Making full allowance for mediaeval powers of self-deception, which were high, and for a free display of rhetoric, we find it difficult to believe that certain flights of fancy can have been conceived by Turgot, who knew the Scots and Scotland well. He was a successful churchman, accustomed from early days to speak with Kings—Olaf, Malcolm Canmore, Rufus, Duncan II, Edgar—and it is hard to see at what stage of his well-known career he could have discharged " for some time " the comparatively modest duties of sacrist at Dunfermline. Perhaps

[1] " *diutius*."

[2] The writer of the *Vita* describes himself as " T., servorum S. Cuthberti servus ", *i.e.* " T., Prior of Durham ". In place of " T." the text of the *Acta Sanctorum*, II, p. 328, June 10, has " Theodericus ", and in Turgot's time there was at Durham a monk of that name (perhaps a " French " Thierry or a " Lotharingian " Dietrich) who had joined the community later than himself. Fordun quotes the *Vita* as the work of Turgot.

he incorporated from the new monk's memorandum some phrases which pleased his fancy.

Turgot's *Vita* is to be read in the light of the circumstances in which it was composed—at the request of Queen Maud, two years at most after the Translation of St. Cuthbert in September 1104.[1] The dedication (to Maud), the heavy insistence on the subject of Edward, on Margaret's *spiritual* relationship to him, on his saintliness and on hers—all clearly attach a cult of Margaret to the already formed cult of Edward. Margaret was not canonized till 1249,[2] but in Turgot's mind she was already a saint.[3] The note of illustrious descent, sanctity and Divine purpose is given in the exordium. Utilizing the well-worn allusion to *Angli* and *Angeli*, Turgot, addressing Maud, writes that she was made Queen of the English by the King of the Angels, to whose Kingdom her mother had always belonged. It is next stated that Margaret's grandfather was Edmund Ironside,[4] but Edmund is dismissed in a sentence, and the subject changes to his younger half-brother Edward very abruptly. " That most pious and most gentle Edward " had to virtue almost an hereditary right, " his grandfathers being not only most noble, but most reli-

[1] Before January 8, 1107 (death of King Edgar, who is mentioned as reigning).

[2] On July 27, 1245, Pope Innocent IV caused inquiry to be made ; on June 19, 1250, the remains were transferred from the tomb opposite the high altar in Dunfermline to the new tomb created to receive them in the " Lady's Aisle ". The date of canonization is given variously as 1249 or 1251. The former date is the more probable, as preceding the Translation.

[3] Turgot expresses his opinion that a whole life spent in good works is weightier testimony than a single outstanding event and that Margaret's deeds made her a Saint, but he does quote (p. 250) one miracle : her favourite and richly ornamented Gospel-Book was inadvertently dropped by an attendant when he was crossing a ford. It was not missed at first and not recovered till it had lain for a long time in the water. But it had suffered little injury. The volume has been identified with Bodleian MS. Lat. liturg. f. 5 [" written in the first half of the eleventh century in England : $7 \times 4\frac{5}{8}$ inches, 38 leaves "]. *Summary Catalogue of Western MSS.*, Oxford, 1905, vol. v, p. 683. Folios 3 and 37 show a crinkling which might be due to the action of water. On folio 2ᵛ is written, in a twelfth-century hand, a poem in Latin hexameters, repeating Turgot's account of the incident, with textual similarities, *e.g.* " Portitor ignorat librum penetrasse profundum " and referring to Margaret as a Saint : " Saluati semper sint rex reginaque sancta ". The MS. was reproduced in facsimile with colours by W. Forbes-Leith, S.J., Edinburgh, 1896.

[4] The epithet is first applied to Edmund in MS. D of the *A-S.C.*

gious "; they were " Edgar the Peaceful, King of the English, and Richard, Count of the Normans ". Eulogy of Edgar : on the day of his birth, St. Dunstan heard the angels rejoicing in heaven.[1] Eulogy of Richard : " more fervent in his love of religion [*i.e.* of the monastic life] than any of his ancestors "; " a second David "; " a secular, to be sure, in dress, but a monk by deed ";[2] he built the illustrious monastery of Fécamp ; let those who would hear more of his munificence read the *Gesta Normannorum.*[3]

The ancestry described is Edward's, not Margaret's. She was not descended from him, or from his grandfather, Duke Richard I. This is spiritual genealogy. The link connecting Margaret and her children with Edward is of the spirit ; the doctrine is that expounded to her great-grandson William the Lion by Jocelin of Furness : " Into St. Edward flowed the holiness of all his ancestors and so from him—as flows from crystal fount a stream of religious life—into St. Margaret his grand-niece and from her into her son King David, your grandfather, and from him into King Malcolm, your brother ".[4]

Turgot's mental vagueness,[5] further dimmed by his rhetorical, perhaps sometimes meaningless, Latin, reduces Scottish historians to despair. Despair, however, takes different forms, ranging from tears to mirthless ribaldry or a dull implacable resentment against author and subject alike—a strange fate to

[1] This is related also by Adelard in his *Vita Sancti Dunstani*, ed. Stubbs (R.S.), p. 56.

[2] " Saecularis quidem habitu, sed monachus actu."

[3] *De moribus et actis primorum Normanniae ducum*, also known as *Acta Normannorum*, composed before 1026 by Dudo [Doon], a Canon of Saint-Quentin, at the request of Duke Richard II. Dudo had known the Duke's father, Richard I († 996), and had a particular affection for Fécamp. Dudo's work, the only source of early Norman history, is dismissed by Orderic, contemptuously, as " affluens multiplicibus verbis et metris panegyricum ". Modern historians are equally severe, but on the Norman mentality and *milieu* at the time it is a valuable document.

[4] Jocelin, *Vita S. Waldeui*, p. 249, col. 2.

[5] Thus Turgot seems to represent Margaret as presiding over a Church Council, which would have been unprecedented in Christendom, and must be dismissed as well-intended hyperbole. Although he must have spent much of his life attending meetings, and was writing at the request of Queen Maud, who was accustomed to sitting in the *curia regis*, he makes no comment on the constitution of the Council and expresses no surprise at the procedure. According to him, the Queen was, so to speak, in the Chair and addressed the House at the opening session, while the King

have befallen so good a man and so great a Queen. Tact was
the quality most obviously lacking in one or the other, or
perhaps in both; it is impossible to penetrate beyond the
written word and apportion the blame. Full of benevolence,
Turgot in all simplicity of heart says things that touch the
Scottish reader on the raw, things that the lamb could not
forgive nor the worm forget. His heroine is " patronizing ",
" superior ". But he is often misjudged. His description of
Malcolm Canmore kissing the Book or otherwise offering a
pathetic spectacle of illiteracy is not intended to be offensive,
and can be so only in modern eyes. It is unjust to expect
from Turgot a history of Margaret and her times. He did
write one, which has been lost. In the *Vita* he is engaged in
a literary exercise, and his approach to his subject is literary.
An author is entitled to choose his own *genre* and to lay the
emphasis where he thinks fit. Turgot chose Hagiography and
allowed himself an occasional excursus into Court Biography.
Both are recognized mediaeval *genres*. Hagiographical works
are not necessarily written for the instruction of the historically
minded, or even for the edification of the faithful, but rather
to demonstrate the sanctity of a personage, in the interests of
a cause. " T. servorum S. Cuthberti servus " is pleading the
cause of St. Cuthbert and his Church, of Queen Maud and her
family, of peace and unity under Anglo-Norman dynastic
auspices. In Court Biography his error is literary; he leaves
out nearly all the background and thus impinges on another
genre, the Character Sketch, in which his error is to leave out
the defects of his heroine's great qualities. He has the
mediaeval habit of founding his observations on what he has
read rather than on what he has seen. Instead of supplying
the detail which he must have noted and which the modern

acted as Gaelic interpreter (from what language, Latin, English or French,
is not stated) and also as executive officer. In his second capacity he
banished from Scotland all who had failed to be convinced by his wife's
arguments, as translated by himself orally—he could not read. The tone
of the proceedings is hard to discern—hence perhaps the odd discrepancies
in different translations : " Regina, praefatione praemissa . . . primum
proposuit . . . Aliud quoque proponens regina . . ." Father W. Forbes-
Leith, S.J. : " The Queen introduced the subject under discussion by
premising that . . . She then laid it down, in the first place . . ." The
Reverend Dr. Metcalfe, Minister of Paisley : " The Queen opened the proceedings by remarking that . . . The Queen raised another point . . ."

reader, and perhaps Queen Maud herself, would have found interesting, he will serve up a pleasing phrase taken, possibly, from the memorandum of Margaret's favourite priest or, un-doubtedly, from the *Ecclesiastical History* of Bede the Vener-able.[1] But this does not necessarily make his occasional contri-butions to history suspect. It merely shows him engaged, for pious and praiseworthy purposes, in essay-writing. The result of Turgot's literary labours is a touching, in some ways a beautiful, work which unhappily defeats its own purpose. Clouds of incense obscure the central figure and leave King Malcolm and all else in a perhaps unmerited shade.

Obtaining rapid celebrity, the *Vita* was freely utilized by the early chroniclers and historians. They are, like Turgot, interested not in Malcolm but in Margaret, and in her, not primarily as Queen of Scots, but as the kinswoman and the spiritual descendant of King Edward, as the mother of Maud, as the vital link between the Old English and the Norman dynasties. They minimized Malcolm's importance by magni-fying Margaret's. But it may be doubted if the Scottish people ever quite shared this marked preference for their sainted Queen. Popular feeling seems to be reflected, for instance, in the report (in Fordun) of an incident at the Translation of June 19, 1250. When the body of St. Margaret was being borne to the new Tomb, it met with an unseen obstacle above her husband's grave and could be moved no further. Then the " voice of a bystander divinely inspired " was heard claiming a like honour for Malcolm.[2] Perhaps if Ailred had carried out his intention of writing a Life of King Malcolm the bystander would have needed no Divine inspiration. Even with the scraps of informa-tion available in our own day he would have required little more than common sense.

[1] Margaret's charitable ransoming of prisoners is paralleled by St. Aidan's in Bede, III, v, and the account of Malcolm Canmore as an interpreter at Margaret's Church Council (see above, p. 12, n. 4) is taken from Bede, III, xxv: " venerabilis episcopus Cedd . . . qui et interpres in eo concilio vigilantissimus utriusque partis exstitit ".

[2] " David Camerarius ", whose work was dedicated to Charles I in 1631, counts Malcolm Canmore among the Saints. Forbes, *Kal.* p. 385.

F

The Claimants to the Throne of Malcolm Canmore

(i) "THE SONS OF INGIBIORG"

In 1097 Edgar set aside descendants of King Malcolm and Queen Ingibiorg whose title seems superior to his own, either under the old system of succession or under the new. (*a*) By primogeniture: William, son of Duncan II, eldest son of Malcolm III and Ingibiorg, was an infant; if he were set aside on that score, then the heir was Edgar's half-brother Malcolm, only surviving son of Malcolm III and Ingibiorg; if their marriage were held to be irregular (and Duncan's charter to Durham in 1094 shows it had *not* been so held), then the heir was Edgar's eldest surviving full brother, Edmund. (*b*) By Celtic custom: Donald Bane, King by election, had an only child, a daughter, Bethoc: the successor chosen for Donald in his lifetime (whether called " Tanist " or not) was Edmund; if Edmund renounced this succession, there was a surviving son of Malcolm and Ingibiorg qualified for election as King.

William fitz Duncan never asserted his claim. His wife

THE " SONS OF INGIBIORG "

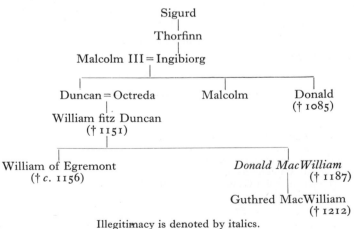

Illegitimacy is denoted by italics.

400

Alice or Adelise, daughter of Guillaume Meschin (brother of Renouf, Earl of Chester, 1120–1130) and Cécile de Rumilly, bore her mother's maiden name. Alice de Rumilly inherited her father's lands, in numerous counties, including his fee in Cumberland. Together these lands were known as the Honour of Skipton. The only son of William fitz Duncan and Alice (to whom she refers as " Willelmus filius meus de Egremont ") is " the Boy of Egremont ", whose death by drowning in the Strid at Bolton is commemorated in Wordsworth's poem *The Force of Prayer; or The Founding of Bolton Priory*.[1] The accident probably occurred *c.* 1156. In England it was taken to be a punishment for sacrilege and atrocities which William fitz Duncan († *c.* 1151) had allowed his troops to commit at Clitheroe (June 10, 1138). In Scotland it caused a profound sensation, partly because the young man was considered in some quarters the rightful heir to the throne.[2] Cécile, daughter of William fitz Duncan and Alice, became the wife of Guillaume d'Aumale.[3]

The claimant Donald MacWilliam was an illegitimate son of William fitz Duncan. In July 1187, after several years' domination of Ross and Moray, he was defeated and slain by Roland of Galloway on a moor near Inverness. Donald's son Guthred, surnamed MacWilliam, who was executed in 1212, was the last serious rival to the Canmore dynasty.

(ii) THE MORAY CLAIMANTS

When Angus of Moray, son of King Lulach's daughter, was slain in 1130, Malcolm MacHeth was hailed as his successor. He was certainly his kinsman. Ailred calls him " paterni odii et persecutionis haeredem ", which should mean the son of one who *was* hated and persecuted, therefore presumably the son of Angus. Ord. Vit. and R. Tor. make him an illegitimate son of King Alexander, but this is unlikely. Malcolm MacHeth, who had married before 1134 a sister of

---

[1] Composed 1807, published 1815. The Priory of St. Mary and St. Cuthbert was founded for Augustinians in 1120, at Embsay near Skipton, by Guillaume Meschin and his wife, Cécile de Rumilly. In 1151 it was moved to the present site by their daughter Alice.

[2] See Skene, III, p. 66.   [3] *E. Yorks. Ch.* III, p. 468.

Somerled, *regulus* or sub-King of Argyll, was released from Roxburgh, with his son Donald, by Malcolm IV and shortly afterwards made Earl of Ross.[1] He died on October 3, 1168.

Somerled joined the sons of Malcolm MacHeth, his nephews, when they revolted in 1153. Though his name is Norse and he had the blood of the Norse nobility in his veins, Somerled was Scottish on his father's side. Probably he was descended from Sigurd the Stout, father of Thorfinn and grandfather of Queen Ingibiorg. Somerled married an illegitimate daughter of Olaf I, King of Man (regn. 1102–53). Olaf's second wife was Affrica, daughter of Fergus of Galloway.[2] Godred II, the son of Olaf and Affrica, was driven out of Man by Somerled in 1158 and took refuge at the Scottish Court; he witnesses the Roxburgh Charter of Malcolm IV as " King of the Isles ". He returned to Man after the death of Somerled in 1164. The Lords of the Isles were descendants of Somerled.

The strange story of Wimund the Monk is connected with Somerled, to whom he was in some way related. Wimund claimed to be the son of Angus, Earl of Moray. He is first heard of as a monk in the Abbey of Furness. It belonged to the order of Savigny [near Mortain] which was founded *c.* 1122 by " Vitalis " [Viel], former chaplain to Robert, Count of Mortain, and which in 1127 was provided with lands in Furness by Stephen, Count of Mortain, afterwards King of England. In 1134 King Olaf, a friend and admirer of Henry I, gave the Abbey of Furness land at Rushen for the purpose of establishing a daughter-house. Among the monks who left for Rushen was Wimund. He so impressed the Manxmen by his mental and physical powers and by his torrential eloquence in some language with which they were familiar—evidently Gaelic, fortified perhaps with a little Norse—that they " asked for him as their Bishop ".[3] Their wish being granted, Wimund in the course of his visitations in Sodor [4] attained to such further popularity that at length, probably towards 1140, he could

[1] See Skene, III, p. 287.

[2] The name Affrica (Africa), found earlier in Ireland—Affrick († 739) was Abbess of Kildare—was favoured in Scotland from the twelfth century.

[3] Wm. Newb. I, xxiv, p. 62. King Olaf is said to have given the Abbey of Furness the right of choosing the Bishop. Cooke, p. 670.

[4] For the Norsemen the Hebrides were the Southern Isles, the Sudreys, *Sudreyar*. Sodor is the survival of the Latinized form *Sodorensis*.

boldly proclaim the secret of his birth. He announced that he was the son of Angus, and he put forward the ancient Moray claim to the throne. Having obtained a great following in the Isles, he descended on the Scottish mainland and with the help of Somerled set up a tyranny in the coastal districts of the West, which he held to ransom or laid under ecclesiastical contribution, as the case might be. At length " a certain Bishop " refused to pay him tribute—on the ground that " one Bishop can owe nothing to another "—and stirred up his flock to resolute and armed resistance. As Wimund led his troops into action, a small-sized battle-axe hurtled through the air, landed on his forehead and laid him low. This long-distance contribution came from his episcopal adversary. Wimund was borne off the field by his henchmen and lived to fight—so long, and with such success, that King David, making a virtue of necessity, placated him with a grant of lands.

They were lands in the district of Furness and were granted by David the less ruefully as they belonged to the Mortain fief of the Usurper and lay in a wild and dismal part of his own newly acquired possessions in what has since been known as Lancashire.[1] But Wimund, instead of settling down peaceably among his kith and kin—for, whatever his own race and language may have been, they were amply represented in polyglot Celto-Scandinavian Furness—paraded the district at the head of a band of armed ruffians and established a reign of terror. It was not brought to an end till certain of the inhabitants, with the connivance of local magnates, waylaid

[1] In Domesday, Furness and the northern part of the present Lancashire are included in the West Riding of Yorkshire. When Lancashire was carved out of Yorkshire and Cheshire, Furness remained within it. Henry I bestowed the Honour of Lancaster on Stephen 1114×1116. W. Farrer, *Notes on the Domesday Survey of the Land between Ribble and Mersey*, Trans. Lancs. & Cheshire Antiquarian Society, XVI (1899), pp. 1-38, p. 30. David must have obtained the Honour in 1139 by the Treaty of Durham ; in a charter of 1141 he confirms the monks of Shrewsbury in their possessions within the Honour. But none of his charters to Shrewsbury Abbey relate to its possessions between Ribble and Mersey and there is no evidence that he ever held any other part of the Honour than that which lay north of the Ribble. *V.C.H. Lancaster*, I, p. 294. Stephen's grant to Furness Abbey was not quite clear and conclusive ; others claimed rights in the same territory. But the monks remained paramount, though parts of Furness were in other hands. W. G. Collingwood, *The Lake Counties*, 1902, revised edition, 1932, pp. 41 and 54.

him, and " for the sake of the Scottish realm " mutilated him
and put out his eyes.[1]   The fallen tyrant was received into the
Abbey of Byland, a daughter-house of Furness,[2] where he spent
his old age, and where he had a professional audience of
soldiers and historians to hear the military and ecclesiastical
experiences which he was fond of relating.   Byland housed
" several veteran knights who had become lay brethren and
brought with them no small part of their worldly goods ".[3]
Near neighbours were Ailred, who was thus in a position to
know the facts, if not to disclose them all, and William of
Newburgh, who in his youth heard the Story of Wimund told
many a time by the hero himself with gusto and grim humour,
the peroration being that even yet his enemies would have small
cause to exult " had they left him but the eye of a sparrow ".

The credence which Wimund obtained in the West of
Scotland and the Isles, the great force he collected, the Royal
grant of land, the mutilation—all make it clear enough that he
had a case.[4]   But the significance of the story is not so much

[1] Wm. Newb. I, xxiv, p. 67 : " providing against all future excess, they
made him a eunuch for the sake of the Kingdom of Scotland, not for that
of Heaven "—in other words, because of dynastic considerations.

[2] The Abbey founded at Hood in 1138 by the youthful Roger de
Montbrai and his mother (see above, p. 65, n. 4) was occupied by monks of
Calder in Cumberland, a daughter-house of Furness, who had been driven
out by the Scottish raids of 1136.   In 1143 the Abbey was moved from Hood
to Old Byland.   It had been in uncomfortable proximity to Rievaulx—on
the opposite bank of the river Rye, which formed the division between the
lands of Walter Espec and Roger de Montbrai—and the traditional reason
for removal is that the communities were incommoded by the sound of each
other's bells.   But the jangling may have been metaphorical.   The Savignian
Order joined the Cistercian in 1147, but the Abbot of Byland had held out
as long as he could and perhaps was no great admirer of Rievaulx.   The
monastery was removed in 1147 to Stocking, and in 1177 to its present site
(New Byland).

" Bellalanda uno tantum milliario distat a Neubergensi ecclesia, quae
me in Christo a puero aluit."—Wm. Newb. I, xv, 42.   Newburgh also was
founded by Roger de Montbrai (1145).

[3] *Historia Fundationis* (Byland), quoted by Stenton, *E.F.* p. 140.

[4] Wimund might have been English, Norse or Norman, so far as his
name goes [OE. *Wigmund* or ON. *Vigmundr*].   It is common in pre-Conquest charters, English and Norman ; see Index to *Regesta* and to Round,
Cal. I.   It was the name of the Norman monk of La Croix-Saint-Lenfroy
who, according to Ord. Vit., came to England at William's bidding, but
declined preferment, reminding him that the Kingdom had come to him
by no hereditary right, and to the prejudice of Edgar Atheling.   See
Freeman, *N.C.* IV, p. 446.   Wm. Newb. says that Wimund was born " in

personal as social. Wimund was a member of one of the new French monastic orders, a Bishop, and widely believed to be the rightful King of Scots.

The relationships of the various claimants remain uncertain, mysterious, but were evidently close—and to some extent Norman. Unrest was probably chronic, though the outbreaks were only sporadic. No doubt there was " a Moray Question, a Galloway Question, an Argyll Question ",[1] though we know not what they were. But how far did an outbreak represent a rally in defence of old customs, old rights, cherished institutions, threatened by a Normanizing King, or a rally round an individual leader with a dynastic claim ? In default of information we can only note the recurrent pattern. The claimants

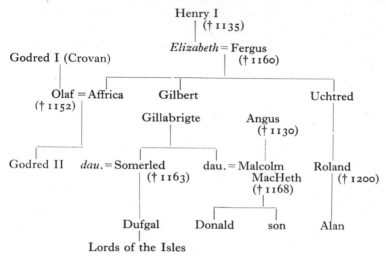

Illegitimacy is denoted by italics.

Anglia ", but obviously he belonged to the Celto-Norse community of settlers in the Isles and the West and South-West of Scotland who considered the Isle of Man as their headquarters. Ailred, naturally, is critical : " pseudo-episcopus ". There is a gap in the records of Man at the time. Matthew Paris says that in 1151 John, a monk of Séez, " became the second Bishop of Man ; the first Bishop had been Wimund, a Savignian monk, but he was blinded and expelled ". A Bishop of the Isles named Wimund, belonging to the Isle of Skye, was ordained by Thomas II, Archbishop of York from 1109 to 1114, but these dates would exclude David's Wimund.

[1] Simpson, *Mar*, p. 1.

2 E

launch the attack; the King defends himself, successfully, and in the counter-attack overruns part of their lands, which then, but only then, he proceeds to Normanize. The Sons of Margaret might well arouse resentment. They were partial to strangers, impatient of Scots, high-minded, heavy-handed. But they were not aggressive. If the last claimants gave their lives to defend the native way of life against the Norman way, there is a tragic irony in their names. The second last had as patronymic a Norman name, MacWilliam, and was brought low by a native Lord of Galloway baptized Roland. Concerning the last of them, executed in 1212 under William the Lion, Walter of Coventry wrote : " Guthred, surnamed MacWilliam, belonged to the ancient line of Scottish kings. Relying on the help of Scots and Irish, he conducted hostilities for long, now in secret and now openly, against the modern kings, as his father Donald had done before him." [1] In short, the case for the claimants was that of rightful heirs against " modern " usurpers and in the end it narrowed down to MacWilliam *versus* William. At no time was there a straight issue : Gael *versus* Norman.

[1] Walter of Coventry, II, p. 206.

G

David's Status in Cumbria, Huntingdon and Northampton

David's status in Cumbria is not determinable by documentary evidence. His extant charters before his accession in 1124 are few in number and his Foundation Charter to Selkirk (before 1120) is preserved in a late copy, which has some questionable features.[1] In these charters he describes himself as " Comes ", without designation of place. It was the highest title in use at the time and one which from 1114 may as well relate to Huntingdon or Northampton as to Cumbria.[2] In his Selkirk Charter he is " David Comes filius Malcolmi Regis Scotorum . . . Henrico regnante in Anglia et Alexandro Rege in Scocia ". Once (in the unofficial and late report of the *Inquisitio* concerning the Church of Glasgow) he is referred to as having been " Cumbrensis regionis princeps "; Fergus of Galloway, who also re-created an ancient diocese (Whithorn), is described in the *Chronicle of Melrose* as " Princeps ". The decisive part which David undoubtedly took in reconstituting the diocese of Glasgow indicates at least some independence, and possession of wide powers; in giving the Abbots of Selkirk the right to be consecrated at their own choice, by a Bishop " either in Scotland or in Cumbria ", he seems to insist on a definite administrative distinction.[3] When " Thor Longus " commended to " his dearest lord, Earl David " his grant of the church at Ednam to Durham and David confirmed it, neither made mention of King Alexander. " Alexander Dei gratia Rex Scottorum " confirmed Swinton to Durham, c. 1110, but so did " David Comes " before 1115, the witnesses being his sister Queen Maud and her son William Atheling.[4]

---

[1] Lawrie, XXXV; see his note.
[2] He is, however, " David Comes " when he attests a charter of Henry I to Anselm 1103 × 1109 (Round, *Cal.* I, 503).
[3] Lawrie, LXXXII. The right is confirmed by Malcolm IV. *Kelso*, No. I, 1159.
[4] Lawrie, XXX.

Malcolm IV in his Confirmation Charter to Kelso (1159) mentions the foundation by David " dum comes fuit " and " illam terram quam vivente rege Alexandro avus meus habuit ".[1] These indications suggest that David, while admittedly ruling under Alexander, had considerable independence.

The Earldoms of Huntingdon and Northampton David held in right of his wife Maud, daughter of Waltheof and Judith, niece of William I. Waltheof received from Edward an Earldom, comprising the shires of Huntingdon, Northampton, Bedford and Cambridge, and was made by William Earl of the Northumbrians. Both dignities were given him with some regard to hereditary right, as the son of Earl Siward. The arrangement under William was a compromise—explainable perhaps by Waltheof's previous tergiversations and his new status as a member of the Conqueror's family; he obtained with the hand of Judith the Honour of Huntingdon, but made over to her all his lands south of the Trent. After his execution in 1076 his Northumbrian Earldom was confiscated. Judith retained her title of Countess and received from William the Honour of Huntingdon, which, after her death, went to her daughter Maud, the eldest of the co-heiresses.[2]

These were : (1) Maud; (2) Adelise, m. Raoul III de Conches or de Toesny; (3) a daughter, perhaps posthumous, of unknown name, m. Robert, son of Richard de Bienfaite.[3] Raoul's family drew its style from Toesny [Tosny, just across the Seine from Les Andelys], by which name Raoul I was already known when fighting in Apulia from 1015. After the death of Raoul II, who had supported Duke Robert, Raoul III, his son, came to England in 1102, and made his peace with Henry I, who confirmed him in his English estates and gave him the hand of a ward, namely Adelise. They had two sons, Roger and Hugue, and several daughters.

[1] *Kelso*, No. I.
[2] *Vita Wald. Com.* p. 112. Cp. the account (1146 × 1153) in *Ramsey*, I, p. 60, No. C, of the foundation of Sawtrey Abbey by Earl Simon II : " Simo comes . . . filiam praedictorum Waldevi et Judetae cum toto feudo per donationem regis Willelmi qui Angliam adquisivit in matrimonium accepit ".
[3] The third daughter is mentioned by Ord. Vit. IX, x, but not by the author of *Vita Wald. Com.* Bienfaite is in Calvados, arr. Lisieux, canton d'Orbec.

David's Status as Earl

The circumstances of Maud's first marriage, to Simon de Saint-Liz, are known chiefly from the *Vita Wald. Com.*, supplemented by a MS. French version,[1] and from the pseudo-Ingulf.[2] The chronology is difficult : *c.* 1074, birth of Maud ; 1075–1076, birth of her two sisters, the younger perhaps posthumous ; May 31, 1076, execution of Waltheof ; 1086 × 1087, a settlement arranged by the Conqueror ; Maud betrothed to Simon ; 1088, Simon becomes Earl of Northampton ; *c.* 1093, marriage of Maud to Simon. He was the younger son of a certain Randel or Rondel le Riche ; the elder son Garnier went back to France. Simon is designated sometimes as *Silvanectensis* or *de Silvanecti* = of Senlis, sometimes as *de Sancto Licio* ; both forms occur at close intervals in the same document,[3] Saint-Liz being a fanciful and religious variant for the name of the town. In Suger's *Life of Louis VI*, p. 8, that monarch in his very youthful days, in 1097, fighting against Rufus, takes prisoner " comitem Symonem nobilem virum ", along with " Gillebertum de Aquila, nobilem et Anglie et Normannie ".

In accordance with Simon's last wishes, his widow and children became in 1111 the King's wards. With King Henry's consent, Maud, who must have been about forty, was married to David, 1113 × February 1114. She was a distant relative : her grandmother, wife of Earl Siward, was a sister of David's grandmother, wife of Duncan I. David obtained the Earldoms of Huntingdon and Northampton in right of his wife, to the exclusion of her elder son, Simon de Saint-Liz, at least till he came of age. When she died in 1131, Simon was already of age and David's position as Earl of Northampton was anomalous, perhaps only possible with King Henry's express permission. The Earldom of Huntingdon, however,

[1] Written in 1237 by a nun of the Cluniac Abbey of Delapré, near Northampton, founded by Earl Simon II. An account of the MS. and excerpts are given by N. Denholm-Young in the *Bodleian Quarterly Record*, VI, No. 69 (1931), pp. 225-230.

[2] The *Historia Croylandensis*, supposedly written *c.* 1095 by the first Norman Abbot " Ingulphus ", has been shown to be a forgery, dating probably from about 1360. Much of it may, however, represent true historical fact. See W. G. Searle, *Ingulf and the " Historia Croylandensis "*, Cambridge Antiquarian Society (1894), 216 pages.

[3] *E.g.* in a charter of 1136 by King Stephen, in Richard of Hexham, III, p. 148, and in the *Vita Wald. Com.* pp. 124 and 127.

was probably considered as a personal gift from the King and tenable for life.

After Henry's death in 1135 David hoped that the Empress Maud would regularize the position as soon as she was crowned. Simon, possibly in despair of obtaining satisfaction by other means, had joined Stephen and, in the opinion of David and no doubt of the Empress Maud, had put himself out of court as regards his succession to the Earldom of Northampton and also as regards any potential claim to Northumberland. Simon's only brother, Waldef, had entered religion. There thus remained, as heir to the late Queen Maud de Saint-Liz and her father Earl Waltheof, Henry, only son of her second marriage, to David. Under Stephen, Simon was recognized as the second Earl of Northampton. In 1146, or before, he obtained from Stephen the Honour of Huntingdon, which, however, in the view of the anti-Stephen party, was still held by David, whether in his own name or in the name of his son Henry. Simon II died in the same year as David (1153) and was succeeded as Earl of Northampton by his son Simon III. But the Honour of Huntingdon, whoever was deemed to have held it, reverted to the Crown, and could thus in 1157 be granted by Henry II to Malcolm IV.

H

Norman Relatives of Ailred

Walter Daniel's words, "Archidiaconus quidam nomine Willelmus filius Thole uir praeclare gratie . . . propinquus Aldredi secundum carnem et multum quoque matrem eius dilexit et patrem ",[1] may imply that Ailred's kinship with this "Willelmus" was through his mother. "Thole" is no doubt Toli (ON. Tóli), a Danish name occurring, T.R.E., in various counties.[2] "Willelmus filius Toli" was Archdeacon of York and the West Riding 1121 × 1137. Along with Walter Espec and "Turstinus archidiaconus" he witnesses a grant by Archbishop Thurstan to Beverley,[3] confirmed by Henry I, 1124 × 1133. Nothing is known of this William's age or of his ecclesiastical status, if any, at the probable date of Ailred's birth (1110), but there seems little doubt that he was the kinsman in question. "William the Archdeacon named Havegrim" is mentioned by Reginald of Durham as having been present at the Translation in 1104.[4] "Havegrim" is no doubt a misreading for Haregrim, or another of the very numerous variants of Arnegrin [ODan. Arngrim], a Danish name found T.R.E. only in North-West England, including Yorkshire.[5] Those who carried the Saint's body were : "Turgotus Prior . . . Henricus et Willelmus utrique Archidiaconi . . . ac Symeon". In the List of Monks at Durham their order according to the time of their entry into the community is Turgotus (6), Henricus (32), Willelmus (35), Simeon (38). It seems possible that the three Archdeacons William are in fact the same person.

Ailred wrote his *Vita S. Edwardi Regis* (1163) " rogatus a Laurencio abbate West-monasterii cognato suo ". His Preface is addressed " Dilecto ac diligendo *et intimis visceribus amplectendo* . . . Laurentio ", which means that Laurent or Laurence

---

[1] W. Daniel, in Powicke, *A.R.* p. 75.   [2] Feilitzen, p. 386.
[3] *E. Yorks. Ch.* I, Nos. 95 and 530.
[4] *De admirandis Beati Cuthberti uirtutibus*, Surtees Soc., 1835, p. 84.
[5] Feilitzen, p. 163.

was a near relative. The name of Ailred's father, Eilaf [ODan. Elaf], was very common T.R.E. in the North of England. Eilaf, a house-carl who had some influence with the Conqueror, was, with other important persons, in charge of the official arrangements for Bishop Walcher's ceremonial entry into Durham.[1] The sequence of names in Ailred's family would suggest that it was of Scandinavian extraction. The name William is French and the name " Laurentius " may be French ; both are consistent with some adaptation to the new order. If William, son of Tholi, was an archdeacon in 1104, the choice of his Christian name would even suggest some alacrity on the part of his parents.

[1] Sim. Durh. *H.R.* II, p. 195.

I

The Maiden Tradition

The tradition concerning Malcolm IV was in being soon after his death and remained unquestioned till 1819, when Lord Hailes drew attention to certain words in one of Malcolm's own charters.[1] The charter is later than 1159 and records, among other grants, two relating to the Church of Innerleithen in Tweeddale. The first is the grant of the church to the Abbey of Kelso; the second is the grant to the church of a special right of sanctuary. The first grant is confirmed by King William and by the Bishop of Glasgow. Of the second grant there is no confirmation and no other mention. It runs: "Precipio etiam ut predicta de Inuerlethan Ecclesia in qua prima nocte corpus filii mei post obitum suum quievit, ut tantum refugium habeat in omni territorio suo quantum habet Wedale aut Tyningham" (" I also order as aforesaid concerning the Church of Innerleithen in which the body of my son rested the first night after his death, that the Church shall have as much sanctuary in all its territory as Wedale or Tyningham ").[2] It is a Precept, a Royal order. It would follow that Malcolm had had an illegitimate son, who died very young, since he himself died at twenty-four. But it must be observed that the phrase " in qua . . . quievit " would normally imply a vigil, or a lying-in-state, or a halt for the night on the last journey of some illustrious personage,

[1] *Annals of Scotland*, I, p. 128. The charter was afterwards published as *Kelso*, No. XXI.

[2] There is no evidence of any territory attached to the Church of Innerleithen. Every church in Scotland had ordinary right of sanctuary—for thirty paces round the burial-ground and for a short prescribed time. Some had further rights, such as were confirmed to Hexham by the Kings of England and Scotland—for a mile and for however long a fugitive chose to stay. *Early Sanctuaries*, p. lxvi. Wedale is known to have claimed a special right, and one of the three judges dealing with the case of anyone who claimed the benefit of the Law of Clan Macduff was the Black Priest of Wedale. It is possible that Tyningham, one of St. Cuthbert's early churches, had special rights.

and that to specify the reasons for a grant or the circumstances in which it was made was at the time not only unnecessary but most unusual. In a Precept the mere presence of the phrase, its incidental nature and the complete absence of secrecy seem peculiar.

Sir Archibald Lawrie, in an article which was not published till after his death,[1] doubted the genuineness of this grant. If it is genuine, he thought that the transcriber in the chartulary may have written "*filii*" for "*patris*" and that Innerleithen may have been a resting-place for the body of Malcolm's father, Earl Henry, who was buried at Kelso and who probably died at Peebles. Sir Archibald pointed out that contemporary writers would hardly have alleged virginity in the case of Malcolm IV unless that was the common report and belief, and that if he made no pretence of virtue and acknowledged in a charter to a religious house that he had had an illegitimate son, the persistence of the Maiden tradition is extraordinary.

It is a curious case for the historical conscience. On the one hand there is the *litera scripta*. On the other hand there is the obvious possibility of a *lapsus calami*, the complete lack of corroboration, the early date of the tradition and its unbroken continuity for six centuries. Our faith in the *litera scripta* must be strong if it enables us, for example, to believe that because one of David's charters bears the words " dona Duncani patris mei ",[2] he was the son of his eldest brother Duncan II. This is merely a slip over a single word, a clerical error, of the sort which is easily made, and easily set right with the aid of extraneous information. In the case of Malcolm IV the extraneous information includes the following : The *Chronicle of Melrose*, though only in the marginal additions, probably written 1198 × 1214, states, *s.a.* 1165, that his life was " without a blemish (*sine labe*) " and, *s.a.* 1153,[3] that " he had continued in his virginity until his death, through inspiration of the grace of God ". The evidently contemporary *Lament*, in the form of a dialogue between Richard the Clerk and Malcolm, who appeared to him in a vision the night after

---

[1] *S.H.R.* XII (1915), pp. 437-438.
[2] King David's Confirmation of a grant to Durham, Lawrie, LXXIV.
[3] *Chron. Melrose*, inserted folio 13.

his death " in raiment of purest white (*vestibus candidissimis amictus*) ", contains such questions and answers as :

" Cur candet vestis ?—Virgo necem subii.
  Cur sic, care, taces ?—Pro me loquitur mea vita." [1]

William of Newburgh describes Malcolm as " ex corpore virgineo raptus ad Agnum virginis filium ".[2] In Fordun it is stated that the *consules* (magnates) and the whole population vainly implored Malcolm to take a wife.[3] Boece's account of the advice tendered by " Ernaldus ", Bishop of St. Andrews, and the reason for Malcolm's refusal—that he had taken a vow of perpetual virginity—is circumstantial and, as regards names and dates, correct. " Ernaldus ", Abbot of Kelso and *ex officio* the King's chaplain,[4] was elected Bishop of St. Andrews on November 13, 1160. In the *Melrose Chronicle* his death, on September 13, 1162, is mentioned *after* the marriage of Ada. A " Ricardus clericus " is mentioned in the contents of Malcolm's Kelso charter of 1159. We have already drawn attention to the dream of his Chamberlain Nicholas in 1160.[5]

If Malcolm's two alleged public declarations in the Bishop's presence took place, they took place within a period of twenty-two months. If he was then untruthful, he was daring. If he was expressing the truth then and in his charter expressing the later truth, the chronological margin is extremely small. In the following year (1163) he was for some time dangerously ill at Doncaster and had a protracted convalescence " de magna infirmitate ",[6] and on December 9, 1165, he died after a very long and painful illness. The phrase in his charter was also in its way a public declaration, and from the beginning to the end of his reign the Abbey of Kelso obtained great publicity and formed the subject of much discussion in high places.[7]

---

[1] Lawrie, *Ann. M. and W.* p. 105.   [2] Wm. Newb. II, xix, p. 138.
[3] P. 257.   [4] *O.P.* I, p. 259.   [5] Above, p. 355, n. 3.
[6] *Chron. Melrose, s.a.* 1163.
[7] In 1156 and 1157 much correspondence passed between the Pope [Adrian IV] and Bishop Robert of St. Andrews, from whose jurisdiction Abbot Ernout was endeavouring to obtain exemption. Ernout, when Bishop, was made Legate in Scotland. In 1165 " John, Abbot of Kelso, came back from Rome, mitred "—*Chron. Melrose, s.a.* 1165. John had succeeded Ernout on November 29, 1160. See R. Lane Poole, p. 273 n. Lawrie, *Ann. M. and W.* XXXV.

Monastic appropriation was for bishops and abbots a constantly burning question; sanctuary (" girth ") was for archdeacons a daily preoccupation and for fugitives of all ranks a matter of life and death. Cases of all sorts might arise in which production of the Royal charter would be called for. If circumstances in Malcolm's time were such that he could avow paternity thus openly, incidentally and, to all appearances, casually, they were circumstances singularly unpropitious for the creation of an edifying legend. Moreover it would have been one which anybody at any moment, on reading the brief charter, might inadvertently or otherwise bring to a sudden and ignominious conclusion.

The balance of probabilities seems to be in favour of a scribal error.

As for the chivalric ideal attributed to Malcolm IV, it was that of the Virgin Knight, which was in being long before it became a commonplace in extant literature some fifty years after his death. It had Cistercian associations. Towards 1220 a Cistercian monk, choosing an Arthurian setting and borrowing the names of Arthur's Knights, wrote for purposes of edification *La Queste del Saint Graal*, in which he created the figure of Galahad, Virgin Knight. This was a sublimation of Perceval in the Romance composed (? *c.* 1180) by Chrétien de Troyes and entitled *Perceval le Gallois* or *Le Conte del Graal*. Perceval departs from Carlisle on his Quest, which is for the Grail. Its significance is not explained, but was clear enough to cultivated readers knowing the small modicum of theology which Chrétien assumes them to possess. It was *Charitas*, the Grace of the Holy Spirit.[1] Chrétien's Romance is addressed to the greatest knight of his times, Philippe d'Alsace [William the Lion's ally in 1174], in the name of *charité* ; it assumes familarity with the story of Arthur and the story of Tristan and Yseult, and it is based on ideas expressed in theological treatises and in romances during Malcolm's reign.[2]

It was because Malcolm " burned with the ardour of

[1] For the full theological explanation see Gilson, *Romania*, LI (1925), p. 323.
[2] *E.g.* Robert Biquet, *Lai du cor* [ed. H. Dörner, Paris, 1907], which has been dated 1150 × 1153, tells the story of the magic chastity-testing horn sent to Arthur's Court and the failure of all save Caradoc to pass the test.

charity " that he emerged triumphant from the ordeal in William of Newburgh's narrative, an ordeal almost commonplace in the lives of early Celtic saints and later Norman saints, notably St. Thomas of Canterbury. *Charitas* was the watchword of the Cistercian order, which received its final polity when the *Charta Charitatis* was drawn up during St. Stephen Harding's Abbacy at Cîteaux (1109–1134). St. Bernard expounded the mysteries of *Charitas*, love of God, Christ-like conduct, but it was left to his interpreter Ailred to clarify Cistercian doctrine and reconcile the Christian virtue of *Charitas* with the pagan virtue of *Amicitia*, love of God with love of man, the teachings of Christ with the teachings of the *De Amicitia*, Ailred's constant guide since his early days at Roxburgh. William of Newburgh's strange use of the word *charitas*; his close connection with the three great Cistercian Abbeys of Yorkshire—" God's castles ", he says, " in which *milites* [soldiers or perhaps knights] of Christ the King keep watch and ward "; [1] the decisive part taken by the Cistercians in the institution of the military orders, particularly of the Knights Templars; King Malcolm's education under Abbot Waldef of Melrose; his lifelong association with Ailred— all help to explain how the ideal of the Virgin Knight was, rightly or wrongly, attributed to Malcolm IV.

[1] Wm. Newb. I, v, p. 44, referring to Byland, Fountains and Rievaulx. His historical work was undertaken at the request of " Ernout " [" Ernaldus "], Abbot of Rievaulx, 1189–1199.

BIBLIOGRAPHY

Works mentioned only once are described in the footnotes at the place where quoted. Full particulars are not given in the case of well-known publications, such as those in the Rolls Series.

Aberdeen = *Registrum Episcopatus Aberdonensis.* Maitland Club, 1845.

ACKERMAN, Robert W. *The Knightly Ceremonies in the ME. Romances. Speculum,* XIX (1944), pp. 285-312.

Act. Parl. Sc. = *Acts of the Parliament of Scotland, 1124–1707.* Stationery Office, 1844, vol. i, 1124–1423.

ADAMS, George Burton. *Council and Courts in Anglo-Norman England.* Yale University Press, 1926, xxv + 403 pp.
The History of England from the Norman Conquest to the Death of John, 1066–1216. Longmans, Green, 1905.

AELRED. See next.

AILRED OF RIEVAULX. *De Bello Standardi,* pp. 181-199, in *Chronicles of the Reigns of Stephen, Henry II and Richard I,* vol. iii, ed. Richard Howlett, R.S. 1886.
Genealogia Regum Anglorum, in Migne, *P.L.* t. cxcv.
Vita S. Edwardi Regis, ibid.
S.S. See under FORDUN.

AITKEN, Robert. *David, Earl of Huntingdon. The Scottish Review,* XXXI (1898, January–April).
The Knights Templars in Scotland. The Scottish Review, XXXII (July 1898).

Ancient Laws and Customs of the Burghs of Scotland. See under *Sc. Burgh L.*

ANDERSON, Alan Orr. *Early Sources of Scottish History, A.D. 500 to 1286.* Oliver and Boyd, 1922, vol. I, ci + 604 ; vol. II, 805 pp.
Scottish Annals from English Chroniclers, A.D. 500–1286. D. Nutt, 1908, xiii + 403 pp.

ANDERSON, Peter John. *Charters and other Writs illustrating the History of the Royal Burgh of Aberdeen, 1171–1804,* ed. with translations. New Spalding Club, Aberdeen, 1890.

Ann. Mon. = *Annales monastici,* ed. Luard, R.S.

Ann. Wint. = *Annales monastici de Wintonia,* in vol. ii, *Ann. Mon.*

Anonimallie = *The Anonimallie Chronicle,* ed. V. H. Galbraith, Manchester University Press, 1927.

Bibliography

A.R. = Ailred of Rievaulx.

Arbroath = Liber S. Thomae de Aberbrothoc. Bannatyne Club, 1848.

ARGYLL, The Duke of [George John Douglas Campbell, 8th Duke]. *Scotland as it was and as it is.* Edinburgh (David Douglas), 1887, 2 vols.

ARMITAGE, Mrs. E. *The Early Norman Castles of England.* *E.H.R.* XIX (1904), pp. 209 and 417.

A-S.C. = The Anglo-Saxon Chronicle, ed. Benjamin Thorpe, Longmans, Green, 1861, 2 vols. ; also, *Two of the Saxon Chronicles. Parallel* (with supplementary extracts from six others), ed. Charles Plummer. Oxford, 1892, 2 vols. Quotations are from the Thorpe edition.

Assisa Regis David, in *Act. Parl. Sc.* i, pp. 315-325.

BAIN, J. *Calendar of Documents relating to Scotland.*

BAKER, George. *History and Antiquities of the County of Northampton*, 1822, 2 vols.

BALINT, Homan. *King Stephen the Saint*, pp. 15-50, in *Archivum*, etc. ; see under FEST, Sándor.

BALLARD, Adolphus. *British Borough Charters, 1042–1216.* Cambridge University Press, 1913, cxxxvi + 266 pp.
The Domesday Inquest. Methuen, 1906, xvi + 283 pp.

Balmerino = The Chartularies of Balmerino and Lindores. Abbotsford Club, 1841. [The Abbey of Balmerino was founded in 1229, that of Lindores in 1178.]

BATESON, Mary. *Mediaeval England, 1066–1350.* T. Fisher Unwin, 1903, xxvii + 448 pp.

BELL. = BELLENDEN. *The Chronicles of Scotland, compiled by Hector Boece, translated by John Bellenden, 1531*, ed. R. W. Chambers and Edith C. Batho, S.T.S. vol. i, 1938 ; vol. ii, 1941.

BEN. ABB. *Gesta Regis Henrici Secundi* Benedicti Abbatis, R.S. 1867.

BIGELOW, Melville Madison. *Placita Anglo-Normannica* : Law Cases from William I to Richard I. Sampson Low, 1879.

Bk. Cron. Scot. = The Buik of the Cronicles of Scotland, or a metrical version of the History of Hector Boece, by William Stewart. R.S. (1858), 3 vols.

BLACK, G. F. *The Surnames of Scotland : their Origin, Meaning and History.* New York Public Library Bulletin, 1943–1946, vols. xlvii-l.

BLOCH, Marc. *La Société féodale : les classes et le gouvernement des hommes.* Paris (Albin Michel), 1940, xvii + 287 pp.
Ed. of Osbert of Clare, in *Analecta Bollandiana*, t. xli (1923), pp. 1-131.

Bibliography

BOECE = *Scotorum historiae prima gentis origine*, etc. Libri xix. Hectore Boethio Deidonano auctore. Parisii, 1574. [First published 1526.]

BOLDON *Book, The*, in *V.C.H. Durham*, vol. i, pp. 259-326. Introduction by G. T. Lapsley. [Compiled in 1183.]

BOUQUET. *Recueil des historiens des Gaules*, 24 vols. Paris, 1840-1904.

BOWER, Walter. See under FORDUN.

BRØGGER, A. W. *Ancient Emigrants: A History of the Norse Settlements in Scotland*. Clarendon Press, 1929, xi + 208 pp.

BROOKE, Z. N. *The English Church and the Papacy*. Cambridge University Press, 1931, xii + 258 pp.

BROWN, P. Hume. *History of Scotland*, 3 vols. Vol. i (*to the Accession of Mary Stewart*). Cambridge University Press, 1909, vii + 408 pp.

Scotland before 1700 from contemporary documents. Edinburgh (David Douglas), 1893.

BRUGGER, E. *The Hebrides in Arthurian Literature*, in *Arthuriana*. Blackwell, vol. ii, pp. 7-19.

BURNS, Edward. *The Coinage of Scotland*, 3 vols. A. H. Black, 1887.

BURTON, John Hill. *History of Scotland*, 7 vols. 1867-1870, vols. i and ii. Blackwood, new edition, 1897.

BUTE, John, Third Marquess of. *Scottish Coronations*. A. Gardner, 1902, 310 pp.

Cambridge Economic History, The, ed. J. H. Clapham. Vol. i, *The Agrarian Life of the Middle Ages*. Cambridge University Press, 1941.

Cambridge Medieval History, The. Vol. v, 1926, xliv + 1005 pp.

Cambuskenneth = *Registrum Monasterii S. Marie de Cambuskenneth*, A.D. *1147-1535*. Grampian Club, 1872.

CAMERON, John. *Celtic Law*. William Hodges, 1937, xvi + 272 pp.

Carlaverock. = *The Book of Carlaverock*, ed. Sir William Fraser. Edinburgh, 1873, vol. i.

Cart. Gyseburn = *Cartularium Prioratus de Gyseburn*. Surtees Society, 1880.

Cart. Riev. = *Cartularium Abbathiae de Rievalle*. Surtees Society, 1889.

CHEW, Helena M. *The English Ecclesiastical Tenants-in-Chief and Knight Service*. Oxford University Press, 1932.

CHILDE, V. Gordon. *Scotland before the Scots* (Rhind Lectures for 1944). Methuen, vii + 144 pp.

Chron. Holyrood = *The Chronicle of Holyrood*, ed. Marjorie Ogilvie Anderson, with some additional notes by Alan Orr Anderson. S.H.S. 1938.

Bibliography

Chron. Melrose = The Chronicle of Melrose. Facsimile, with an Introduction by A. O. Anderson and M. O. Anderson and an Index by W. Croft Dickinson. London, Percy Lund Humphries, 1936, lxxxii + 267 pp.

Chronicon Monasterii de Abingdon. R.S. 1858, 2 vols. [Written by a monk who entered the Abbey before 1118.]

Chronicon Petroburgense, ed. Thomas Stapleton. Camden Society, 1849, xv + 200 pp. As Appendix: *Liber Niger Monasterii S. Petri de Burgo*, pp. 157-183.

Chroniques anglo-normandes, éd. Francisque-Michel. Rouen, 1836, vol. i.

CLARE, Osbert of. See under BLOCH, Marc.

Complete Peerage, ed. G. E. C(okayne). 8 vols., 1887-1898.

Continuatio Beccensis. [Continuation (written 1157-1160) of R. Tor.] ; pp. 317-327 in R. Tor.

COOKE, Alice M. *The Settlement of the Cistercians in England. E.H.R.* VIII (1893), pp. 625-676.

COOPER, Lord [T. M. Cooper]. *The Numbers and the Distribution of the Population of Mediaeval Scotland. S.H.R.* XXVI (1947), pp. 1-9.

CORBETT, William John. *The Development of the Duchy of Normandy and the Norman Conquest of England* (chapter xv) and *England 1087-1154* (chapter xvi) = pp. 481-553, vol. v of *The Cambridge Medieval History*, 1926.

COULTON, G. G. *Scottish Abbeys and Social Life.* Cambridge University Press, 1933, viii + 293 pp.

COUTTS, James. *The Anglo-Norman Peaceful Invasion of Scotland, 1057-1200; Origin of great Scottish Families.* Illustrations by the Author, former Art Master of Edinburgh Ladies' College. Edinburgh (A. Kinross), 1922, xiv + 160 pp.

CRAWFORD, O. G. S. *Arthur and his Battles*, in *Antiquity*, IX (1935), pp. 277-291.

CRONNE, H. A. *Ranulf de Gernons, Earl of Chester.* T.R.H.S. XX (1937), pp. 103-134.

CURTIS, Edmund. *A History of Mediaeval Ireland.* Macmillan, 1923, viii + 436 pp.

DAVID, Charles Wendell. *Robert Curthose, Duke of Normandy. Harvard Historical Studies*, vol. xxv. Harvard University Press, 1920, xiv + 271 pp.

DAVIS, H. W. C. *England under the Normans and Angevins.* Methuen, xi + 577 pp.; 4th edn., 1915.

Regesta Regum Anglo-Normannorum, 1066-1154, vol. i (1066-1100), ed. H. W. C. Davis. Oxford, 1913, xliii + 159 pp.

Bibliography

D.B.S. = *De Bello Standardi.* See under AILRED.
De injusta Vexatione Willelmi Episcopi primi, in Sim. Durh. *H.D.E.* I, pp. 170-195. [Written after 1109.]
De Miraculis et Translationibus Sancti Cuthberti, in Sim. Durh. I, pp. 229-261, and II, pp. 333-364 [1100 × 1115].
DICET, RAOUL DE = RADULFI DE DICETO [† 1202]. *Opera historica.* R.S. 1876, 2 vols.
DICKINSON, William Croft. *The Court Book of the Barony of Carnwath, 1523–1542.* S.H.S. 1937, cxxiv + 235 pp.
The Sheriff Court Book of Fife, 1515–1522. S.H.S. 1928, cv + 407 pp.
DOUGLAS, David C. *Feudal Documents from the Abbey of Bury St. Edmunds.* Oxford University Press, 1932, clxxi + 247 pp.
The Development of Mediaeval Europe, in *European Civilization*, ed. Edward Eyre. Oxford University Press, vol. iii (1935), *The Middle Ages.*
The Norman Conquest. Historical Association Leaflet 73, 1928.
The Rise of Normandy. Raleigh Lecture, British Academy, 1947.
DOWDEN, John, Bishop of Edinburgh. *The Mediaeval Church in Scotland: its Constituents, Organization and Laws.* MacLehose, 1910, xliii + 352 pp.
Dryburgh = *Liber S. Marie de Dryburgh.* Bannatyne Club, 1847. [Written in a sixteenth-century hand. The first five charters are missing.]
DUKE, John A. *The Columban Church.* Oxford University Press, 1932, xii + 200 pp.
DUNBAR, Sir Archibald. *Scottish Kings: a revised Chronology of Scottish History, 1005–1625.* Edinburgh (D. Douglas), 1899, xv + 420 pp.
Dunfermline = *Registrum de Dunfermelyn.* Bannatyne Club, 1842.
EADMER, *H.N.* = Eadmeri, *Historia Novorum in Anglia*, ed. Martin Rule. R.S. 1884.
Epistola ad Glastonienses ELMERI *aliter* EDMERI, quo tempore Glastonienses asserebant se Corpus Patroni nostri Dunstani habere, in Wharton's *Anglia Sacra*, vol. ii, pp. 222-226.
Early Sanctuaries: "Cross Macduff", pp. lxvi-lxxiii in *Sculptured Stones of Scotland.* Spalding Club, 1867.
Early Yorkshire Charters. See *E. Yks. Ch.*
EDWARDS, John. *The Religious Orders in Scotland under our early Kings.* Proc. Royal Philosophical Soc. of Glasgow, XXXVIII (1906–1907), pp. 1-24.
EDWARDS, Owen M. *Wales.* T. Fisher Unwin, 1901, xxiv + 421 pp.
E.H.R. = *English Historical Review.*

423

Bibliography

E.H.S. = *English Historical Society.*

Estoire. See La Estoire.

E. Yks. Ch. = *Early Yorkshire Charters*, 4 vols. ; vols. i-iii, ed. William Farrer, Edinburgh (Ballantyne), 1914 ff. ; vol. iv (part i), *The Honour of Richmond*, ed. Charles Travis Clay, Yorkshire Archaeological Society, Record Series, vol. i, 1935.

Eyton, R. W. *Antiquities of Shropshire*, 1858, vol. vii, 397 pp.

Court, Household and Itinerary of King Henry II, 1888, xii + 344 pp.

Facsimiles of National Manuscripts of Scotland. Ordnance Survey Office, Southampton, part i, 1867.

Fantosme. See Jourdain Fantosme.

Faral, Edmond. *La Légende arthurienne.* Paris (Champion), 1929, 3 vols.

Geoffroy de Monmouth : les faits et les dates de sa biographie. Romania, LIII (1929), pp. 1-42.

Feilitzen, Olof von. *The Pre-Conquest Personal Names of Domesday Book.* Uppsala, 1937, xxxi + 429 pp.

Fergus. Roman von Guillaume le Clerc, hgg. v. Ernst Martin, Halle, 1872, xxiv + 240 pp. [Written possibly *c.* 1209 for Alan [† 1233], son of Roland of Galloway.]

Fest, Sándor. *The Sons of Eadmund Ironside at the Court of St. Stephen*, in *Archivum Europae Centro-Orientalis*. Budapest, 1938. Fasc. 1-4, vol. iv, pp. 115-146.

Fliche, Augustin. *Histoire du moyen-âge*, vol. ii, *L'Europe occidentale de 888 à 1125.* Paris (Presses Universitaires de France), 1930.

La Réforme grégorienne. Paris (Champion), 2 vols. : vol. i, 1924 ; vol. ii, 1925.

Flor. Hist. = *Flores Historiarum*, ed. H. R. Luard ; formerly called Chronicle of Matthew of Westminster. R.S. 1890, 3 vols. [Known as the Westminster version, 1265, of the *St. Albans Chronicle*, a continuation of M.P.]

Flor. Worc. = Florence of Worcester [† 1118] = Florentii Wigornensis monachi *Chronicon ex chronicis* ; continued to 1141 and to 1295 ; ed. Benjamin Thorpe, 2 vols., E.H.S. 1847. [Probably Florence was of Norman and English parentage and born *c.* 1075. He died July 7, 1118. The Continuator to 1141 was a monk of Worcester called John. But there are reasons for believing that John was in fact the author of the whole work.]

Forbes, A. P. *Kalendar of Scottish Saints.* Edinburgh, 1872.

Fordun. *Chron.* = Johannis de Fordun, *Chronica Gentis Scotorum*, ed. William F. Skene. Edinburgh, 1871, 2 vols. (*Historians of Scotland*, vols. i and ii.) [The text of Fordun, freed from accretions due to Walter Bower in his *Scotichronicon* (1447), ed. Walter Goodall, Edinburgh, 1759.]

S.S. = Extracts printed as Appendix No. IV in the Surtees Society edition of Simeon of Durham. [Some probably come ultimately from a lost work of Ailred's.]

FOREVILLE, Raymonde. *L'Église et la royauté en Angleterre sous Henri II Plantagenet (1154–1189).* Paris (Bloud et Gay), 1943, xxxv + 611 pp.

FOWLER, G. H. *Bedfordshire in 1086.* Aspley Guise, 1922.

FOX, Sir Cyril. *The Personality of Britain.* Cardiff, 3rd edn., 1938, 84 pp.

FREEMAN, E. A. *The History of the Norman Conquest of England.* Clarendon Press, 3rd edn., 1877, 5 vols.

The Reign of William Rufus. Oxford, 1882. Vol. I, xliii + 624 pp. ; vol. II, xxvii + 732 pp.

GAIMAR, Geffrei. *Estorie des Engles.* R.S. 1888, 2 vols. [1135 × 1147].

GALBRAITH, V. H. *Nationality and Language in Mediaeval England.* T.R.H.S. XXIII (1941), pp. 113-128.

The Literacy of the Medieval English Kings. Proceedings of the British Academy, vol. xxi (1935).

Gen. N.S. = The Genealogist. New Series, 1884– .

GERVASE OF CANTERBURY. *Chronicle of the Reigns of Stephen, Henry II and Richard I.* R.S. 1879–1880. 2 vols. [Written c. 1188.]

Gesta Stephani, Regis Anglorum et Ducis Normannorum, ed. R. C. Sewell, E.H.S. 1846 ; ed. R. Howlett in *Chronicles of the Reigns of Stephen, Henry II and Richard I,* R.S. 1886. (The references are to the R.S. edition.)

GIR. CAMBR. = GIRALDUS CAMBRENSIS, Works, R.S. 1861–1891. [1147 – c. 1217, youngest son of Guillaume de Barri (Barry Island, on the coast of Glamorgan) and Angharad, daughter of " Gerald of Windsor ".]

Glasgow = Registrum Episcopatus Glasguensis. Bannatyne Club, 1843.

Godr. = Godric. See under REGINALD OF DURHAM.

G.R.A. = Genealogia Regum Anglorum. See under AILRED.

GRANT, I. F. *The Social and Economic Development of Scotland before 1603.* Oliver and Boyd, 1930, ix + 594 pp.

GRAY, Sir Thomas. *Scalachronica.* Maitland Club, Edinburgh, 1836. [c. 1350–1357.]

GRIERSON, Philip. *A Visit of Earl Harold to Flanders in 1056.* E.H.R. LXI (1936), pp. 90-97.

The Relations between England and Flanders before the Norman Conquest. T.R.H.S. XXIII (1940), pp. 71-112.

Bibliography

GUILLAUME DE JUMIÈGES. *Gesta Normannorum Ducum*, éd. Jean Marx. Paris (Picard), 1914. Also in Bouquet, *Recueil*, t. xii.

Guillaume le Maréchal, L'Histoire de, éd. Paul Meyer, 1891. Vol. I, ii + 366 pp. ; vol. II, 390 pp. ; vol. III, clx + 304 pp. [Written *c.* 1225.]

GULIELMUS GEMMETICUS = GUILLAUME DE JUMIÈGES.

HADDAN, Arthur West, and STUBBS, William. *Councils and Ecclesiastical Documents relating to Great Britain and Ireland*, vol. ii, part ii. Clarendon Press, 1873.

HARTRIDGE, R. A. R. *A History of Vicarages in the Middle Ages*. Cambridge University Press, 1930, x + 273 pp.

HASKINS, Charles Homer. *Norman Institutions*. Harvard University Press, 1918, xv + 377 pp.

The Renaissance of the Twelfth Century. Harvard University Press, 1928, x + 437 pp.

HAVERFIELD, F. *The Roman Occupation of Britain*. Clarendon Press, 1924, 304 pp.

H.D.E. = *Historia Dunelmensis Ecclesiae*. See under SIM. DURH.

HENDERSON, George. *The Norse Influence on Celtic Scotland*. Glasgow (MacLehose), 1910, xii + 371 pp.

Hexham. See PRIORY OF HEXHAM.

HEXHAM, John of [(*c.* 1160 × *c.* 1209), successor of Prior Richard]. *Historia XXV annorum* in Sim. Durh. *H.R.* (R.S.), II, pp. 284-332.

HEXHAM, Richard of. *Historia de gestis regis Stephani et de bello de Standardo* in *Chron. Steph.* R.S. III, pp. 139-178. [Richard, Prior of Hexham 1141-1160 × 1178, wrote before 1154.]

H. Hunt. = Henry of Huntingdon, Henrici Archidiaconi Huntendunensis *Historia Anglorum*. R.S. 1879. [Henry d. *c.* 1155.]

Hist. Northd. See under NORTHUMBERLAND.

Histoire des ducs de Normandie et des rois d'Angleterre, éd. Francisque-Michel. Paris (Société de l'Histoire de France), 1840, li + 431 pp.

H.N. = *Historia Novorum in Anglia*. See EADMER.

Holyrood = *Liber Cartarum Sancte Crucis*. Bannatyne Club, 1840.

HOVEDEN. *Chronica* Magistri Rogeri de Houdene, ed. W. Stubbs. R.S. 1868-1871. [Hoveden d. *c.* 1201.]

H.R. = *Historia Regum*. See under SIM. DURH.

HUGH THE CANTOR. *Chronicle of the Archbishops of York, Chronica Pontificum Ecclesiae Eboracensis*, in Raine, *York*, II. [Written before 1143.]

Illustrns. Sc. Hist. = *Illustrations of Scottish History, from the Twelfth to the Sixteenth Century*, ed. Joseph Stevenson. Maitland Club, 1834.

Bibliography

Inchaffray = *The Charters of the Abbey of Inchaffray*. S.H.S. 1908.
INNES, Cosmo. *Ancient Laws and Customs of the Burghs of Scotland.* Scottish Burgh Records Society, 1868.
Lectures on Scotch Legal Antiquities. Edinburgh, 1872, xv + 326 pp.
Scotland in the Middle Ages. Edinburgh, 1860, xliii + 368 pp.
Sketches of Early Scotch History. Edinburgh, 1861, xx + 624 pp. [See also under *O.P.*]
JOCELIN, Jocelyn. *Vita Sancti Waldeni* [= Waldeui], in *Acta Sanctorum,* Augusti tomus primus quo dies primus, secundus, tertius et quartus continentur, 1867, pp. 242-278. [Walde*n*us is textual, but erroneous; the name historically is Walde*u*us = Waldef = Waltheof. The work was written 1207 × 1214.]
JOHN OF HEXHAM. See under HEXHAM.
JOHNSTON, The Rev. James B. *Place-Names of Scotland.* (John Murray) 1934, xvi + 335 pp.
JOLLIFFE, J. E. A. *The Constitutional History of Mediaeval England.* A. & C. Black, 1937, vii + 523 pp.
Northumbrian Institutions. E.H.R. XLI (1923).
JOURDAIN FANTOSME = JORDAN FANTOSME. *Chronicle of the War between the English and the Scots,* ed. Francisque-Michel. Surtees Society, 1840, xliv + 230 pp. *La Guerre d'Écosse, 1173–1174,* ed. Ph. Aug. Becker, *Zeitschrift f. rom. Philologie,* LXIV (1944), pp. 449-556. [Written *c.* 1175. Quotations are from the 1840 edition.]
Kelso = *Liber S. Marie de Calchou, 1113–1567.* Bannatyne Club, 1846.
KEMP, Rev. E. W. *Pope Alexander III and the Canonization of Saints.* T.R.H.S. XXVII (1945), pp. 23-28.
KENDRICK, T. D. *A History of the Vikings.* Methuen, 1930, vii + 412 pp.
KENNEY, James F. *The Sources for the early History of Ireland.* Columbia University Press, 1929, xvi + 807 pp.
KING, Hugh B. *A Short History of Feudalism in Scotland.* Edinburgh (Wm. Hodge and Co.), 1914, xxvii + 242 pp.
Kinloss = *Records of the Monastery of Kinloss.* Society of Antiquaries of Scotland, Edinburgh, 1872.
KINVIG, R. H. *History of the Isle of Man.* Oxford University Press, 1944, xi + 240 pp.
KNOWLES, Dom David. *The Monastic Order in England.* Cambridge University Press, 1940, xix + 764 pp.
Ben. = *The Benedictines.* Sheed and Ward, 112 pp.
R.H. = *The Religious Houses of Mediaeval England.* Sheed and Ward, 1940, 167 pp.

427

Bibliography

La Estoire de seint Aedward le Rei, in *Lives of Edward the Confessor*, ed. H. R. Luard. R.S. 1858.

Laing, Alexander. *Lindores Abbey and its Burgh of Newburgh.* Edmonston and Douglas, 1876, xx + 559 pp.

Laing, Henry. *Descriptive Catalogue of Impressions from Ancient Scottish Seals*, A.D. *1094 to the Commonwealth.* Maitland Club, 1850. Supplement A.D. 1150 to the eighteenth century, + 44 plates.

Larson, Laurence Marcellus. *The King's Household in England before the Norman Conquest.* Madison, Wisconsin, 1904. *Bulletin of the University of Wisconsin*, pp. 61-211.

Laur. Durh. = Laurence of Durham, *Dialogi* Laurentii Dunelmensis *Monachi ac Prioris.* Surtees Society, 1880, vol. lxx.

Lawrie, Sir Archibald Campbell. *Annals of the Reigns of Malcolm and William, Kings of Scotland*, A.D. *1153-1214.* MacLehose, 1910.

Early Scottish Charters prior to A.D. *1153.* MacLehose, 1905, xxix + 515 pp. [References are to the latter work except when otherwise stated.]

Lees. *Temple = Records of the Templars in England in the 12th Century; The Inquest of 1185*, ed. Beatrice A. Lees. Oxford University Press, 1935, ccxvii + 457 pp.

Lennox = Cartularium Comitatus de Levenax. Maitland Club, 1833.

Le Patourel, J. H. *Geoffrey of Montbray, Bishop of Coutances, 1049-1093.* E.H.R. LIX (1944), pp. 129-161.

Liber Vitae Ecclesie Dunelmensis, ed. J. Stevenson. Surtees Society, 1841.

Lindores. See *Balmerino.*

Little, A. G. *Mediaeval Wales*, chiefly to the twelfth and thirteenth centuries. Fisher Unwin, 1902, vii + 148 pp.

Liveing, Henry G. D. *Records of Romsey Abbey.* Winchester, 1906; also, Abridged Edition, 1912, xi + 281 pp.

Lloyd, Sir John Edward. *A History of Wales.* Longmans, Green, 1912. 2 vols.: vol. I, xxiv + 356 pp.; vol. II, vii + pp. 357-815.

Macdonald, A. J. *Lanfranc. A Study of his Life and Writing.* Oxford University Press, 1926, vii + 307 pp.

Macewen, Alex. R. *A History of the Church in Scotland.* Hodder and Stoughton, vol. i, 397-1546; xv + 487 pp.

Macgibbon, David, and Ross, Thomas. *The Ecclesiastical Architecture of Scotland.* Edinburgh, vol. i, 1896, xiii + 483 pp.

Mack, James Logan. *The Border Line.* Oliver and Boyd, 1924, xx + 316 pp.

Bibliography

MACKENZIE, William Mackay. *The Mediaeval Castle in Scotland.* (Rhind Lectures in Archaeology), 1925–1926. Methuen, 1927, vi + 249 pp.

The Scottish Burghs: an expanded version of the Rhind Lectures in Archaeology. Oliver and Boyd, 1949, 194 pp.

MACNEILL, Eoin (John). *Celtic Ireland.* Dublin, 1921, xv + 182 pp.

MAJOR, John. *History of Greater Britain.* S.H.S. 1891.

Malachy. St. Bernard of Clairvaux's Life of St. Malachy of Armagh, ed. H. J. Lawlor. S.P.C.K., 1920, lvi + 183 pp.

MALATERRA = Gaufredi Malaterrae *Historia Sicula.* Migne, *P.L.* t. cxlix, pp. 1087-1215.

MALCOLM, C. A. *The Office of Sheriff in Scotland: Its Origin and early Development. S.H.R.* XX (1923).

MAP, Walter. *De Nugis Curialium,* ed. M. R. James. Clarendon Press, 1914. Part I of *Anecdota Oxonienses.*

May = Records of the Priory of the Isle of May, ed. John Stuart. Society of Antiquaries of Scotland, 1868.

Melrose = Liber Sancte Marie de Melros. Bannatyne Club, 1837.

M.G.H. = Monumenta Germaniae Historica, ed. P. G. H. Pertz.

Migne, *P.L.* = J. P. Migne, *Patrologiae Cursus completus. Series Latina.* Paris, 1844–1864.

MOORE, Grace Edna. *The Middle English Verse Life of Edward the Confessor.* Philadelphia, 1942, xci + 142 pp.

MOORE, Margaret F. *The Lands of the Scottish Kings in England.* G. Allen, 1915, xii + 141 pp.

Moray = Registrum Episcopatus Moraviensis. Bannatyne Club, 1838.

MORGAN, Miss M. *The Organization of the Scottish Church in the Twelfth Century.* T.R.H.S. XXIX (1947), pp. 135-149.

MORRIS, W. A. *The Mediaeval English Sheriff to 1300.* Manchester, 1927, xviii + 291 pp.

MORTON, Rev. James. *The Monastic Annals of Teviotdale.* Edinburgh (Lizars), 1832, viii + 328 pp.

M.P. = Matthew Paris [+ *c.* 1259] = Matthaei Parisiensis, *Monachi Sancti Albani, Historia Anglorum.* R.S. 3 vols., 1866, vol. i, 1067-1189.

C.M. = Matthaei Parisiensis *Chronica Majora* [to 1259], ed. H. R. Luard. R.S. vol. ii, 1067–1216.

H.M. = Historia Minor [1067 to 1255]. [Much in Matthew Paris is taken from Roger of Wendover. For recent divergent views on their relationship, see Helen M. Cam, *Roger of Wendover and Matthew Paris, Medium Ævum XV* (1946), pp. 55-59.]

MURRAY, David. *Early Burgh Organization in Scotland as illustrated in the History of Glasgow.* Printed as an Appendix to

Bibliography

Proceedings of the Royal Philosophical Society of Glasgow, vol. xxxix (1907–1908).

National MSS. Sc. See under *Facsimiles.*

NEILSON, George. *The Motes in Norman Scotland. The Scottish Review*, XXXIII (October 1898), pp. 209-238.

Tenure by Knight-Service in Scotland. Juridical Review, 1899, pp. 71-86 and 173-186.

Newbattle = Registrum S. Marie de Neubotle. Bannatyne Club, 1849.

NEWBURGH, William of. See under WM. NEWB.

NORTHUMBERLAND, *History of.* Northumberland County History Committee, 1893.

O.P. = Origines Parochiales Scotiae : the Antiquities ecclesiastical and territorial of the Parishes of Scotland. Bannatyne Club, 1851, vol. i, 1851 ; vol. ii, part i, 1854; part ii, 1855. [Ed. by Cosmo Innes.]

ORD. VIT. = ORDERICUS VITALIS. *Historia Ecclesiastica*, éd. A. le Prévost (Société de l'Histoire de France), 1838–1855, 5 vols. [References are to book and chapter.] [O.V., b. 1075, ceased writing 1141.]

ORPEN, Goddard Henry. *Ireland under the Normans (1109–1216)*. Clarendon Press, 1911, 4 vols.

OSBERT OF CLARE. *The Letters of* Osbert of Clare, Prior of Westminster, ed. by E. W. Williamson. Oxford University Press, 1929. See also under BLOCH, Marc.

PAGAN, Theodora. *The Convention of the Royal Burghs of Scotland.* Glasgow University Press, 1926, xii + 268 pp.

PAINTER, Sidney. *French Chivalry : Chivalric Ideas and Practices in Mediaeval France.* Baltimore, The Johns Hopkins Press, 1940, viii + 179 pp.

Studies in the History of the English Feudal Barony. Baltimore, The Johns Hopkins Press, 1943, 211 pp.

Paisley = Registrum monasterii de Passelet : Cartas . . . complectens a domo fundata A.D. MCLXIII. Maitland Club, 1832.

PALGRAVE, Sir Francis. *The History of Normandy and of England.* 5 vols. [revised edition]. Cambridge University Press, 1919.

PATON, Lucy Allen. *Notes on Merlin in the " Historia regum Britanniae " of Geoffrey of Monmouth. Modern Philology*, XLI (November 1943), p. 88.

Peterborough, The Black Book of. See under *Chronicon Petroburgense.*

PIGGOT, Stuart. *The Sources of Geoffrey of Monmouth*, in *Antiquity*, XV (1941), pp. 269-286 and 305-319.

Pipe Roll of 31 Henry I. Michaelmas 1130. Reproduced in facsimile from the edition of 1833. Stationery Office, 1929.

Bibliography

PIRENNE, Henri. *Economic and Social History of Mediaeval Europe.* Kegan Paul, 1936, ix + 243 pp.

POOLE, Austin Lane. *Obligations of Society in the XIIth and XIIIth Centuries.* Clarendon Press, 1946, 115 pp.

POOLE, Reginald Lane. *Studies in Chronology of History,* collected and edited by Austin Lane Poole. Clarendon Press, 1934, 328 pp., pp. 115-122.

POPE, Mildred K. *The Anglo-Norman Element in our Vocabulary* (Deneke Lecture, May 1944). Manchester University Press, 1944, 14 pp.

POWICKE, F. M. *Ailred of Rievaulx and his biographer Walter Daniel.* Longmans, Green. Reprinted from the *Bulletin of the John Rylands Library,* vol. vi, Nos. 3 and 4, July 1921–January 1932, 112 pp.

The Dispensator of King David I. S.H.R. XXIII (1926).

The Loss of Normandy (1189–1204). Manchester University Press, 1913, xx + 603 pp.

PRENTOUT, Henri. *Essai sur les origines et la fondation du duché de Normandie.* Paris (Champion), 1911, 294 pp.

La Normandie, in *Revue de Synthèse historique.* Paris (Léopold Cerf), t. xix (1909); t. xx (1910).

PRIORY OF HEXHAM, THE. 2 vols., Surtees Society, 44 (1864); 46 (1865).

RADFORD, C. A. Ralegh. *The Early Christian Monuments of Scotland,* in *Antiquity,* XVI (1942), pp. 1-18.

RAINE, James. *The Historians of the Church of York.* R.S. 1879–1894, 3 vols.

RAIT, Sir Robert S. *The Making of Scotland.* A. & C. Black, 1929, viii + 326 pp.

RAMSAY, Sir James H. *The Angevin Empire, A.D. 1154–1216.* Swan Sonnenschein, 1903, xxiii + 556 pp.

The Foundations of England. Swan Sonnenschein, vol. ii, 1898.

Ramsey = *Cartularium Monasterii de Rameseia,* R.S. 1884, vol. i.

RASHDALL, Hastings. *The Universities of Europe in the Middle Ages.* Revised edition, ed. F. M. Powicke and A. B. Emden. Clarendon Press, 1936, vol. I, xliv + 593 pp.; vol. II, ix + 342 pp.; vol. III, xxvi + 558 pp.

Red Bk. Exch. = *The Red Book of the Exchequer,* Part I, R.S. 1896.

REG. DURH. = REGINALD OF DURHAM. REGINALDI monachi Dunelmensis, *Libellus de admirandis Beati Cuthberti virtutibus quae novellis patratae sunt temporibus.* Surtees Society, 1835. [Reginald had connections with Coldingham. His work on

St. Cuthbert, in which the last date given is 1172, was dedicated to Ailred († 1167) and had been submitted to him.]

Godr. = Libellus de Vita et Miraculis S. Godrici *Heremitae de Finchale*, auctore Reginaldo Monacho Dunelmensi. Surtees Society, 1847.

Regesta. See DAVIS, H. W. C.

REID, Miss R. R. *The King's Council in the North.* Longmans, Green, 1921, x + 532 pp.

Barony and Thanage, E.H.R. XXXV (1920), pp. 161-199.

R. GLOUC. = *Metrical Chronicle of Robert of Gloucester.* R.S. 1887, 2 vols.

RIDGEWAY, Sir William. *The Origin and Influence of the Thorough-bred Horse.* Cambridge University Press, 1905, xvi + 538 pp.

RIDPATH, George. *The Border-History of England and Scotland.* London (F. Cadell), 1776.

RITCHIE, James. *The Influence of Man on Animal Life in Scotland.* Cambridge University Press, 1920, xvi + 550 pp.

ROBERTSON, A. J. *The Laws of the Kings of England from Edmund to Henry I.* Cambridge University Press, 1925, xiii + 426 pp.

ROBERTSON, E. William. *Historical Essays in connection with the Land, the Church,* etc. Edinburgh (Edmonston and Douglas), 1872.

Scotland under her early Kings. Edinburgh, 1862, vol. I, x + 444 pp. ; vol. II, vi + 559 pp.

ROBINSON, J. Armitage. *Gilbert Crispin, Abbot of Westminster.* Cambridge University Press, 1911, xi + 180 pp.

ROGER OF WENDOVER [† 1236], Rogeri de Wendover *Chronica* sive *Flores Historiarum*, ed. H. O. Coxe. 4 vols., English Historical Society, 1841–1842. [Roger ceased writing in 1234. See also under M.P.]

Rou = Roman de Rou.

ROUND, J. Horace. *Calendar of Documents preserved in France, illustrative of the History of Great Britain and Ireland,* vol. i, A.D. 918–1206. R.S. 1899.

Feudal England. Swan Sonnenschein, 1909, xvi + 587 pp.

Geoffrey de Mandeville. Longmans, Green & Co., 1892, xiii + 461 pp.

Studies in Peerage and Family History. Constable, 1901.

R.S. = Rolls Series.

R. TOR. = *The Chronicle of* Robert of Torigni, Abbot of the Monastery of St. Michael-in-peril-of-the-sea, ed. Howlett, vol. iv of *Chronicles of the Reign of Stephen,* etc. R.S. 1889. [Robert of Torigni died in 1186.]

Bibliography

St. Andrews = *Liber cartarum prioratus Sancti Andree in Scotia.*
Bannatyne Club, 1841.

St. Bees Register of the Priory of St. Bees. Surtees Society, 1915,
No. CXXVI.

SALTER, H. E. *Mediaeval Oxford.* Clarendon Press, 1936, 160 pp.

Scalachronica. See under GRAY, Sir Thomas.

Sc. Burgh L. = *Scottish Burgh Laws* = *Ancient Laws and Customs of
the Burghs of Scotland,* vol. i, A.D. 1124–1424. Edinburgh,
1868, 252 pp.

SCHLAUCH, Margaret. *The Historical Background of* Fergus *and*
Galiene, P.M.L.A. XLIV (1929), pp. 360-376.

SCHRAMM, Percy Ernest. *A History of the English Coronation,* transl.
Leopold G. Wickham Legg. Clarendon Press, 1937, xv +
283 pp.

Scone = *Liber ecclesie de Scon.* Bannatyne Club, 1843.

Scotichronicon. See under FORDUN.

Scots Peerage, The, ed. Sir James Balfour Paul. Edinburgh (David
Douglas), 1911.

Scottish Abbeys and Cathedrals, article [? by Joseph Robertson] in
The Quarterly Review, LXXXV (1849), pp. 103-156.

Scottish Antiquary, The = *Northern Notes and Queries,* vols. I–IV.
Edinburgh, 1889–1890, continued as vols. V–X of *The Scottish
Antiquary,* Edinburgh, 1890–1903.

S.H.R. = *Scottish Historical Review.*

S.H.S. = Scottish History Society.

SIM. DURH. = Simeon of Durham (Symeonis Monachi *opera omnia*),
2 vols. R.S. *H.D.E.* = *Historia Dunelmensis Ecclesiae* (to 1096),
and its Continuation to 1154, are in vol. i, pp. 3-169. *H.R.*
= *Historia Regum* (to 1129) is in vol. ii, pp. 3-283. [Simeon
died after 1129, *H.D.E.* was written 1104 × 1108.]

Symeonis Dunelmensis *Opera et Collectanea,* vol. i, Surtees Society
(vol. li), 1868, lxxxi + 301 pp., ed. John Hodgson Hinde.
[Quoted generally from the R.S. edition.]

SIMPSON, W. Douglas. *The Celtic Church in Scotland.* Aberdeen
University Press, 1935.

The Province of Mar, being the Rhind Lectures in Archaeology,
1941. Aberdeen University Press, 1944, xi + 167 pp.

SKENE, William F. *Celtic Scotland.* Edinburgh, 1876–1880, 3 vols.

SMITH, R. A. L. *The Place of Gundulf in the Anglo-Norman Church.*
E.H.R. CCXXXI, July 1940, pp. 257-272.

SOUTHERN, R. W. *The First Life of Edward the Confessor.* *E.H.R.*
LVIII (1943), pp. 385-400.

S.S. = Surtees Society.

Bibliography

STENTON, F. M. *A-S.E. = Anglo-Saxon England.* Clarendon Press, 1943, vii + 748 pp.
The Danes in England. Proceedings of the British Academy, 1927.
E.F. = The First Century of English Feudalism, 1066–1166. Clarendon Press, 1932.
English Families and the Norman Conquest. T.R.H.S. 4th series, XXVI (1944), pp. 1-12.
STEPHENSON, Carl. *Borough and Town.* Cambridge, Mass., 1933, xvi + 236 pp.
STEPHENSON, J. H. *The Law of the Throne—Tanistry and the Introduction of the Law of Primogeniture.* 1900, xiv + 492 pp. *S.H.R.* XXV, 1928.
STEWART, William. See *Bk. Cron. Scot.*
STUBBS, W. *Lectures on Mediaeval and Modern History.* Clarendon Press, 1900, xiv + 492 pp.
SUGER. *Vie de Louis VI le Gros* [Latin text and French translation], éd. Henri Waquet. Champion, 1929. [Written *c.* 1145.]
SYMEON OF DURHAM. See under SIM. DURH.
Testa de Nevill: Liber Feodorum, The Book of Fees commonly called *Testa de Nevill* reformed from the earliest MSS. by the Deputy Keeper of the Records, Part I A.D. 1198–1242. 1920.
THOMPSON, Alexander Hamilton. *Monastic Orders,* in *The Cambridge Medieval History,* v, pp. 658-696.
THOMPSON, James Westfall. *Economic and Social History of the Middle Ages (300–1300).* The Century Co., New York; London, 1928, viii + 900 pp.
T.R.H.S. = Transactions of the Royal Historical Society.
TURGOT. *Vita Sanctae Margaritae.* In Symeonis Dunelmensis *Opera.* Surtees edition. See under SIM. DURH. The Life of St. Margaret, Queen of Scotland, by Turgot, Bishop of St. Andrews, ed. Wm. Forbes-Leith, S.J. Edinburgh (David Douglas), 1896.
TWYSDEN. *Historiae Anglicanae scriptores decem.* London, 1652.
VALIN, Lucien. *Le Duc de Normandie et sa cour (912–1204).* Paris (L. Larose), 1910, xvii + 292 pp.
V.C.H. = Victoria County Histories
VIGEOIS, Geoffrey, Prior of = GAUFRIDUS VOSENSIS, in *M.G.H.* t. xxvi, pp. 198-203. [Geoffrey, *c.* 1140–1184, wrote in 1183.]
Vita Æduuardi, in *Lives of Edward the Confessor.* See under LA ESTOIRE.
Vita Oswini, in *Miscellanea biographica.* Surtees Society, 1838. [The author was a monk of St. Albans who removed to Tynemouth *c.* 1111.]
Vita Sanctae Margaritae. See under TURGOT.

Bibliography

Vita S. Edw. = *Vita Sancti Edwardi.* See under AILRED.

Vita S. Waldeui. See under JOCELIN.

Vita Wald. Com. = *Vita et Passio Waldevi Comitis,* pp. 99-142 in vol. ii of *Chroniques anglo-normandes,* éd. Francisque-Michel, Rouen, 1836. [Apparently compiled from previous Lives. Parts of the documents published by Michel as the *Vita* were written after 1219 by William of Ramsey, monk of Crowland, to celebrate the Translation of the Saint.]

Vita Wulfstani. See under WM. MALM.

Vitae S. Cuthberti anonymae = *Two Lives of St. Cuthbert :* A Life by an Anonymous Monk of Lindisfarne, Bede's Pure Life. Cambridge University Press, 1940, xiii + 375 pp.

WALTER OF COVENTRY, *The Historical Collections of,* ed. W. Stubbs. R.S., 2 vols., 1872–1873. [*flor.* 1293.]

WATSON, W. J. *The History of the Celtic Place-Names of Scotland.* Blackwoods, 1926, xx + 558 pp.

Westmorland = The Westmorland volume of the Royal Commission on Historical Monuments, 1936.

WILKINSON, Bertie. *Freeman and the Crisis of 1051.* Bulletin of the John Rylands Library, 22 (1938), pp. 368-387.

WILLIAM OF JUMIÈGES = WILLELMUS GEMMETICUS. See GUILLAUME DE JUMIÈGES.

WILLIAM OF POITIERS = WILLELMUS PICTAVIENSIS [† *c.* 1090]. *Gesta Willelmi Ducis Normannorum,* in *Scriptores Rerum Gestarum Willelmi Conquestoris,* ed. J. A. Giles. Caxton Society, 1845, pp. 77-158.

WILLIAMS, Watkin. *St. Bernard of Clairvaux.* Manchester University Press, 1935, xxxviii + 423 pp.

WILLIAMSON, E. W. See under OSBERT OF CLARE.

WILMART, Dom André. *Ève et Goscelin. Revue bénédictine,* t. 46e (1934), pp. 414-430.

WM. MALM. = William of Malmesbury [† *c.* 1142]. *G.R.* = Willelmi Malmesburiensis Monachi *Gesta Regum,* Libri tres, ed. Stubbs. R.S., 3 vols., 1887–1889. [1st version *c.* 1120 ; 2nd version *c.* 1127 dedicated to Robert of Gloucester.]

Gesta P.A. = Willelmi Malmesburiensis monachi *De Gestis Pontificum Anglorum.* R.S. 1870.

H.N. = *Historia Novella* [1125–1142 ; written 1140–1142], in *Gesta P.A.* II, pp. 689-769.

Vita Wulfstani, ed. Reginald R. Darlington. Royal Historical Society, 1928, lii + 204 pp. [The references are to the *Gesta Regum* unless otherwise specified.]

WM. NEWB. = WILLIAM OF NEWBURGH. *Historia Rerum Anglicarum,*

435

Bibliography

ed. Richard Howlett in *Chronicles of the Reigns of Stephen, Henry II and Richard I*, vol. i, 1884, R.S. [" Gulielmus Parvus ", Guillaume le Petit († 1196), was born *c.* 1135 at Bridlington, Yorks., and was educated from boyhood by the Augustinians of Newburgh. He took to a secular life, and returned to Newburgh *c.* 1182. See H. E. Salter, *E.H.R.* XXII (1907), pp. 513 ff.

Worsaae, J. J. A. *An Account of the Danes and Norwegians in England, Scotland and Ireland*, translated. London (John Murray), 1852, xxiii + 359 pp.

Wyckoff, Charles Truman. *Feudal Relations between the Kings of England and Scotland under the early Plantagenets.* University of Chicago Press, 1897, xv + 159 pp.

Wyntoun, Andrew of. *The Original Chronicle.* Scottish Text Society, 1903. [Written *c.* 1425.]

INDEX

Index

438

Index

Beau-Clerc *erron.* for *le Clerc* =
Henry I, *q.v.*
Beaufort, Beauly, Inverness, 312,
312 n. 2
Beaumont (Oise)
— Marguerite de, *w.* Saher de
Quincy, 286 n. 4
— Robert de, Comte de Meulan,
274 n. 1
— Roger de, Earl of Warwick,
274 n. 1
Beauvais (Oise), 48, 149, 166
Bec, now Le Bec-Hellouin (Eure),
Abbey of, xix, 298 n. 1
Becket, Thomas, Archbishop of
Canterbury, 349-351, 357 ;
canonized, 350 n. 1, 385 n. 1,
417 ; *erron.* à Becket, 146 n. 4
Bede, 15, 43, 52
Bedford, 21, 141 n. 1, 146 n. 2
Beith, Ayr, 286 n. 5
Belief, Hill of, Scone, 129
Bellême (Orne), Robert de, 115,
115 n. 5, 116, 280 n. 3
Bellencombre (Seine-Inférieure),
99 n. 3
Bellenden, John, xlii, 162 n. 1, 218
Beningham, Herts., 358 n. 4
Benoît, 126 n. 4
Berewe, Barewe [?], 275 n. 4
Bermondsey, 134 n. 3
Bernard of Abbeville, 167, 168 n. 1
Bernard, St., 333, 334, 370 n. 1 ;
approves Templars, 202, 357,
417 ; praises Earl Henry, 284
Bernicia, 3, 4, 15, 16
Beroald, Berowald, *Beroaldus Flan-
drensis*, 224, 224 n. 3, 376,
377 n. 1
Bertram, Roger, *m.* Ada de Morville,
154 n. 2
Bervie, Kincardine, 63 n. 5, 358 n. 4
Berwick, 27, 169, 335 ; burgh, 324
n. 3, 329
Berwickshire, xxix
Bessin, Le, 150 n.
Bethoc, *d.* Donald Bane, 282 n. 2
— *d.* Malcolm II, xxx
— *w.* Raoul Dunegal, 292
Bidun, Walter de, 284, 366 n. 1, 367
Bienfaite (Calvados)
— Robert de, 408, 408 n. 3
Biggar, Lanark
— Baldwin, Baudouin of, 375 ;
Hugh of Bygris, 375 n. 1

Binning, East Lothian, 320, 375 ;
Biquet, Robert, 416 n. 2
Birsay, Orkney, 17 n.
Bishoprics created by David, 331
Bisset (Byseth, Biset), 312 n. 2
Blaye (Gironde), 155
Blois, Étienne (Estephen) de =
Stephen, King of England, *q.v.*
Blond, Le, xxi
Boar's Raik, *Cursus Apri*,
St. Andrews, 171
Bodmin, Cornwall, 297 n. 2
Boece (Bois, Boys, Boethius), Hec-
tor, xlii, 50, 162 n. 1, 311
Boelton = Bolton, *q.v.*
Boisil, 41, 117
Bolton (formerly Boeltun, Boieltun,
Boweltun), East Lothian, 275
n. 4, 372 n. 5
Bolton Priory, Yorks., 401
Boniface, St., 44
— VIII, Pope, 185 n. 1
Border, the, 26, 27
Boson, 88-90, 88 n. 3
Bosyete, Northants., 154 n. 2
Bothwell, Lanark, 279 n. 3
Bouillon, Godfrey [Godefroi] de,
107, Table 195
Boulogne (Pas-de-Calais), 26, 265
— Counts of, *see under* Eustace II
and Eustace III
— County of, 194, 252 n. 3
Bourgoin (*alias* Bourguignun, Bur-
geis, Burgonensis, Burgunnus,
Burguillun), Robert le, 203 ff.,
203 n. 3
Bourneville (Eure), 156 n. 4
— Robert de, 156, 188
Boweltun, *see* Bolton
Bower, Walter, xli
Braiosa = Briouze, *q.v.*
Brechin, Angus, 347 n. 1
Brémule (Eure), 267 n. 2
Brendan, St., 332 n. 4 ; *Navigatio
Sancti Brendani*, 126 n. 4
Bret, Hugue, *Hugo Brito*, 153, 156,
156 n. 3
Bretons, xvii, xviii, xix, xx, 55, 156 ;
at Richmond, Yorks., xx ; in
Scotland, 55, 156, 280, 280 n. 2,
351 n. 2
Brice, *Bricius*, of Douglas, Bishop of
Moray, 332
Brictric, Brictrith, *s.* Alfgar, 383-384
Bride-ale of Norwich, 137, 137 n. 4

440

Index

Index

443

Index

Index

447

Index

Index

Index

Index

Index

Index

Index

Montreuil (Pas-de-Calais), 46
Moravia, de, family, 233
Moray (Morafe, Muref), xx, xxxi,
 xxxi n. 2, 13 n. 1, 129, 258,
 331 n. 2, 332, 360 ; revolts,
 xxxvii, 131, 232, 353 ; "planta-
 tion ", 353, 353 n. 2 ; diocese,
 331 n. 2, 332
— House of, 13 n. 4, 92
— William, Bishop of, 355
Moreal, see Morel
Morebattle, Roxb., 222 n. 4
Morecambe Bay, Lancs., 283
Morel, Moreal, neph. Robert de
 Montbrai, 26, 64, 64 n. 3, 65,
 118
Moreville = Morville, q.v.
Mormaer, xxxi, xxxi n. 2, 160, 161,
 208, 238
Mortain (Manche)
— fiefs, 145 n. 1, 194
— Robert, Count of, 87, 145,
 145 n. 1
— William, Count of, 108 n. 3,
 145 n. 1, 148 n. 1
Mortimer = Mortemer
— Hugue de, "Hugo de mortuo
 mari ", grandson of " Willelmus
 Masculus ", 274 n. 3
— Willelmus de, 372
Morville, near Valognes (Manche)
— Ada (Adeline), d. Hugue de, w.
 Roger Bertram, 154 n. 2
— Elena (Helena), d. Richard, s.
 Hugue de ; w. Roland of Gallo-
 way, 154 n. 2
— Hugue de, Constable ; founder of
 Dryburgh, 150, 153 n. 1,
 154 n. 2, 188, 332
— Malcolm, s. Hugue de, 154 n. 2
— Richard, Constable, s. Hugue de,
 m. Hawise (Avicia), d. William
 of Lancaster, 154 n. 2, 310 n. 1,
 366 n. 1
Mote Hill, Scone, 129, 129 n. 1, 346
Mote of Liddel, see Liddel
Mount Melville, Fife, 312
Mow, Roxb., see Molle
Mowbray, see Montbrai
Much Wenlock, Shropshire, 365 n. 1
Muirchertach (" Murcardus "),
 King of Munster, 120 n. 3
Munford, see Montford
Mungo, St., see Kentigern, St.
Muref, see Moray

Nairn, Moray, xxxi
Namo, Radulphus = Raoul le Naym,
 373, 373 n. 2
Nennius, 297 n. 4, 300 n. 2
Neagaolt, see Caolt
Ness, Nessus, etc., name, 285 n. 1
— s. William, 284-285, 285 n. 1
New Castleton, Roxb., 187 n. 3
" new men ", novi homines, 145, 148,
 184, 257
Newbattle, formerly Newbotle,
 Midlothian, 314, 334 n. 2
Newburgh, Fife, 323 n. 1
— Yorks., William of, 262 n. 2,
 297 n. 1, 298, 329 n. 1, 354 n. 3,
 357, 362 n. 1, 416-417
Newby, Yorks., 310 n. 1
Newcastle-upon-Tyne, 51, 59, 269,
 324
Newhouse, Lincs., 336 n. 5
Newminster, Northumb., 261,
 261 n. 1
Newstead on Tweed, Roxb., 246
Newton, now Newton Don, 154 n. 2
Nicholas the Clerk, 291, 355, 362,
 366 ; his dream, 355 n. 3
Nigellus de Albineio, see d'Aubigny,
 Néel de
Ninian, St., xxxiii
Nithsdale, Dumfries, 187 n. 1,
 217 n. 1
Norbertines = Premonstratensians,
 q.v.
Norham, Northumb., 163, 258, 291
Normanni, Normannigenae, xviii,
 xxxv, 258, 261
Normannus, Sheriff of Berwick, 320,
 320 n. 5
Normans, David's, xxv, xxxv, 142 ff.;
 Edward's, xiv, xvii ; Macbeth's,
 5-6 ; Malcolm IV's, 376-377 ;
 William the Lion's, 377 n. 4,
 378
Normanus filius Malcolmi, Constable
 of Inverurie, 307 n. 1
Northallerton, formerly North Aller-
 ton, Yorks., 23, 259, 267, 282 n. 2
Northampton, 151, 324 ; Earldom,
 25, 140, 407-410 ; Nunnery of
 St. Mary, 247 n. 3 ; Priory of
 St. Andrew, 127 n. 1, 139
Northamptonshire Geld Roll, 387
Northumberland, name, 15, 31, 65 ;
 Scottish claim to, 140, 257, 269,
 348, 410

457

Index

Index

Pettinain (formerly Paduinan, Paduynan), Lanark, 154 n. 2, 375
— " Hugo de Paduinan ", his son " Reginaldus ", 288
Petty, Inverness, 233 n. 2
Pevensey, Sussex, 20, 36, 37, 128
Pezron, xxviii
Philip I, King of France, 46
— Count of Flanders (Philippe d'Alsace, Philippe de Flandre), 33, 33 n. 2, 416
Philip, f. Robert, 373
Philpstoun, West Lothian, 312
Picardy, 148, 329
Pictland, Picts, xxviii, xxviii n. 3, xxix
Pierre, s. Walter, 291
Pincerna =Butler, 160, 187 n. 2, 368, 371 n. 2
Pitmillie, formerly Pethmulin, Petmulyn, Fife, 276 n. 2, 371 n. 2
Place-names, Norman, in Scotland, 312
Poitiers, 349
Pollok, Renfrew
— Robert of, m. Isabel, d. of Robert Croc, 374 n. 1
Pont-Audemer (Eure), 156 n. 4
Pontefract, Yorks., 150, 188 n. 2
Pont-l'Évêque (Calvados)
— Roger de, Archbishop of York, xxiii
Porphyrogenite, " born in the purple ", 101 n. 2, 355, 355 n. 2
Port la Reine =Queensferry, Fife, 308
Portsmouth, 109
potestas, see Carlisle
praepositus (of a burgh), xx, 326, 327
Premonstratensians (also Norbertines), Prémontré (Aisne), 336, 336 n. 5, 339 n. 2
primogeniture, 9, 25 n. 4, 57, 60 n. 2, 61, 62, 91-92, 101, 110, 223
Prophecies, by Edward, xl, 39, 110 n. 3 ; by Margaret, xl, 112 ; by William I, 54, 54 n. 2, 54 n. 3, 128
pseudo-Ingulf Chronicle, the, 138, 409 n. 2
" purple, born in the ", see Porphyrogenite
Pytchley, Northants., 157, 157 n. 1

Queensferry (The Queen's Ferry), Fife, 72, 72 n. 4, 308
Quesnai (formerly Kesnoi-Espec), district of Auge, 147 n. 1
Quincy = Cuinchy-lez-La Bassée, 286 n. 1
— Robert de, 285, 286 ; his son, Saher de, Earl of Winchester, 285, 286, 286 n. 4

rabbit (introduced by Normans), 218, 218 n. 2
Radulphus =Raoul, name, xxv
Ragewin, 242
Raids, 26-27 ; see also under Malcolm III
Ralph, see Raoul
— Archbishop of Canterbury, see Raoul d'Escures
Ramleh, Siege of, 97 n. 4
Ramsay, name =Ramsey, Hunts, 156, 156 n. 7, 157 n. 1, 372, 372 n. 2
— " Simundus de Ramesie ", " Willelmus de Rameseia ", 372, 372 n. 2
Randolph, Sir Thomas, 72 n. 5
Ranulf, Ranulphus, Renouf, name, xxv
" Ranulphus " (Renouf), Bishop of Durham, see " Flambard "
Raoul, name, Radulfus confused with Ranulphus, xxv n. 2
Raoul d'Escures, Archbishop of Canterbury, 170, 196 n. 2
— neph. King Edward ; Earl of Hereford, 6, 6 n. 3, Table 195
— neph. Bishop Robert of St. Andrews, 196
— s. Dunegal, 291
Reading Abbey, Berks., 134 n. 2, 333
Redesdale, Northumb., Liberty of, 144
Reginald of Dunstanville, Earl of Cornwall, 135 n. 2
regular clergy, regulars, 52, 74 n. 4
Reims (Marne), xviii
— Council of, 193
Reinfrid, monk of Evesham, 42, 43, 44, 45
Remigius =Rémy, name, xxiii, xxiv
— Bishop of Lincoln, see Lincoln
Renfrew, 129, 280, 326, 361 ; burgh, 324 n. 3
Rennes (Ille-et-Vilaine), 353 n. 4

Index

Index

Ross, xxxi n. 2, 129, 131
Rossive, near Maybole, Ayr, 276 n. 4
Rosyth, Fife, 24
Rouen (Seine-Inférieure), xvi, xvii, xviii, 264 n. 1
Rougemont, Exeter, 70 n. 1
Roxburgh, 162, 162 n., 169, 291 ; meetings and councils, 196, 197, 260 ; castle (also called March-mont), 201 n. 2, 250, 346 ; church, 201 n. 2, 202 ; schools, 246-247 ; burgh, 324, 324 n. 3
— (Kelso), Charter, the, *Frontis-piece*, 366 ff.
Rumilly, Alice or Adeline de, *d.* Guillaume Meschin, *w.* William fitz Duncan, 401
— Cécile de, *w.* Guillaume Meschin, 401 ; Cécile, *d.* William fitz Duncan, *w.* Guillaume d'Au-male, 401
Rushen, Isle of Man, 402
Rutherglen, Lanark, burgh, 324 n. 3, 326
Rutland, 231, 387
Rydale, *see* Ridale
Rye, *r.*, Yorks., 254, 255, 404 n. 2

Saddell, also Sconedale, Abbey of, Kintyre, 365 n. 2
St. Albans, Herts., 249
St. Andrew, Priory of, Northamp-ton, 127 n. 1, 139
St. Andrews, Fife, xxx n. 1, xxxi, xxxiv, 45, 129, 196, 203, 205 ; burgh, 326 ; pilgrims, 72, 360
Saint-Bertin (Pas-de-Calais), 193
St. Boswells (till 17th-century Les-suden), Roxb., 41, 154 n. 2, 287
St. Botolph's Priory, Colchester, 171 n. 4
Saint-Calais, formerly Saint-Carilef (Sarthe), xxiii, xxiv, 52 n. 1 ; 359 n. 3
" Saint - Carilef, de ", Guillaume, Bishop of Durham, xxiii, xxiv, 52, 52 n. 1, 56, 58, 117, 117 n. 3, 152 n. 1, 373 ; trial, 55, 74 ; death, 90
St. Colum's Inch or Inchcolm, 172 n. 2
" St. Cuthbert's Bishop ", *see* Cuthbert, St.

St. Cuthbert's Church, Edinburgh, 200
Saint-Denis (Seine), 219
St. Dogmael's, Cardigan, 167 n. 2, 168 n. 1
Saint-Évroul, Orne, xxxviii, xxxviii n., xxxix
Saint-Hilaire, Emme (Emma) de, *w.* Guillaume de Vieuxpont [Vipont], 372 n. 5
Saint-Liz, name, xxiii, 409
— Matilda de, mother of Robert de Quincy, 286
— Maud, *w.* David I, *see* Maud, *d.* Waltheof
— Simon I, Earl of Northampton, 103, 127 n. 1, 139, 409
— Simon II, 139, 247, 247 n. 3, 409, 410
— Simon III, 410
Saint-Lô (Manche), 229 n. 2
St. Margaret's, Westminster, 11 n. 1
St. Margaret's Hope, Rosyth, Fife, 24
Saint - Martin - de - Bon - Fossé (Manche), -du Bosc, -du Bec (Seine-Inférieure), 214 n. 2
— Alexander de, 214, 224, 275, 275 n. 4, 290 ; his *bro.* Adolphe, 275 ; his *w.* Basilla ; his *ds.* Ada and Ela, 275 n. 4
Saint-Omer (Pas-de-Calais), xviii n. 1
Saint-Pierre-sur-Dives (Calvados), 63 n. 2
St. Serf's Island in Loch Leven, xlvi, 203
Saint-Valery-sur-Somme (Somme), 20
" sair sanct " (said of David I), 337, 337 n. 2
Salisbury, Wilts., 32, 33, 55
— John of, 349 n. 1
Samer (Pas-de-Calais), 98 n. 3
Sancto-Carilepho, de, see " Saint-Carilef "
Sartis = Les Essarts = Wardon, *q.v.*
Savigny (Manche), 402
— Order of, 339 n. 2, 402, 404 n. 2
Sawtrey, Sawtry, Hunts., 247 n. 3
Scampton, Lincs., 299
Scone, Perth, 13, 30, 129, 186, 346
Sconedale, also Saddell, 365 n. 2
Scotch Corner, Yorks., 70 n. 1
Scoti, Scotti, Scotia, Scotland, name, xxvii

461

Index

Index

Index